THE NEW AMERICAN COMMENTARY

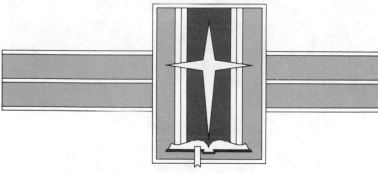

An Exegetical and Theological
Exposition of Holy Scripture

THE NEW AMERICAN COMMENTARY

Volume
19B

AMOS
OBADIAH
JONAH

Billy K. Smith
Frank S. Page

BROADMAN
& HOLMAN
PUBLISHERS

Nashville, Tennessee

© Copyright 1995 • Broadman & Holman Publishers
All rights reserved
ISBN 0-8054-0142-3
Dewey Decimal Classification: 224:20
Subject Heading: BIBLE. O.T. MINOR PROPHETS \ BIBLE. O.T. AMOS \
    BIBLE. O.T. OBADIAH \ BIBLE. O.T. JONAH
Library of Congress Catalog Card Number: 95-3034
Printed in the United States of America
1 2 3 4   01 00 99 98

Library of Congress Cataloging-in-Publication Data

Smith, Billy K.
    Amos, Obadiah, Jonah / Billy K. Smith, Frank S. Page.
      p. cm. — (The New American commentary ; v. 19B)
    Includes biographical references and indexes.
    ISBN 0-8054-0142-3
    1. Bible. O.T. Amos—Commentaries. 2. Bible. O.T.
      Obadiah—Commentaries. 3. Bible. O.T. Jonah—Commentaries.
      Page, Frank S., 1952–
II. Title.   III. Title: Amos, Obadiah, Jonah.   IV. Series.
BS1585.3.S625   1995
224'.20—dc20

To Irlene
My Wife, Companion, Associate
in Ministry

Billy K. Smith

To Willie and Nancy Page
With gratitude from a son who appreciates their
love, support, and sweet encouragement

Frank S. Page

Editors' Preface

God's Word does not change. God's world, however, changes in every generation. These changes, in addition to new findings by scholars and a new variety of challenges to the gospel message, call for the church in each generation to interpret and apply God's Word for God's people. Thus, THE NEW AMERICAN COMMENTARY is introduced to bridge the twentieth and twenty-first centuries. This new series has been designed primarily to enable pastors, teachers, and students to read the Bible with clarity and proclaim it with power.

In one sense THE NEW AMERICAN COMMENTARY is not new, for it represents the continuation of a heritage rich in biblical and theological exposition. The title of this forty-volume set points to the continuity of this series with an important commentary project published at the end of the nineteenth century called AN AMERICAN COMMENTARY, edited by Alvah Hovey. The older series included, among other significant contributions, the outstanding volume on Matthew by John A. Broadus, from whom the publisher of the new series, Broadman Press, partly derives its name. The former series was authored and edited by scholars committed to the infallibility of Scripture, making it a solid foundation for the present project. In line with this heritage, all NAC authors affirm the divine inspiration, inerrancy, complete truthfulness, and full authority of the Bible. The perspective of the NAC is unapologetically confessional and rooted in the evangelical tradition.

Since a commentary is a fundamental tool for the expositor or teacher who seeks to interpret and apply Scripture in the church or classroom, the NAC focuses on communicating the theological structure and content of each biblical book. The writers seek to illuminate both the historical meaning and contemporary significance of Holy Scripture.

In its attempt to make a unique contribution to the Christian community, the NAC focuses on two concerns. First, the commentary emphasizes how each section of a book fits together so that the reader becomes aware of the theological unity of each book and of Scripture as a whole. The writers, however, remain aware of the Bible's inherently rich variety. Second, the NAC is produced with the conviction that the Bible primarily belongs to the church. We believe that scholarship and the academy provide an indispensable foundation for biblical understanding and the service of Christ, but the editors and authors of this series have attempted to communicate the findings of their research in a manner that will build up the whole body of Christ. Thus, the commentary concentrates on theological exegesis while providing practical, applicable exposition.

THE NEW AMERICAN COMMENTARY's theological focus enables the reader to see the parts as well as the whole of Scripture. The biblical books vary in content, context, literary type, and style. In addition to this rich variety, the editors and authors recognize that the doctrinal emphasis and use of the biblical books differs in various places, contexts, and cultures among God's people. These factors, as well as other concerns, have led the editors to give freedom to the writers to wrestle with the issues raised by the scholarly community surrounding each book and to determine the appropriate shape and length of the introductory materials. Moreover, each writer has developed the structure of the commentary in a way best suited for expounding the basic structure and the meaning of the biblical books for our day. Generally, discussions relating to contemporary scholarship and technical points of grammar and syntax appear in the footnotes and not in the text of the commentary. This format allows pastors and interested laypersons, scholars and teachers, and serious college and seminary students to profit from the commentary at various levels. This approach has been employed because we believe that all Christians have the privilege and responsibility to read and seek to understand the Bible for themselves.

Consistent with the desire to produce a readable, up-to-date commentary, the editors selected the *New International Version* as the standard translation for the commentary series. The selection was made primarily because of the NIV's faithfulness to the original languages and its beautiful and readable style. The authors, however, have been given the liberty to differ at places from the NIV as they develop their own translations from the Greek and Hebrew texts.

The NAC reflects the vision and leadership of those who provide oversight for Broadman Press, who in 1987 called for a new commentary series that would evidence a commitment to the inerrancy of Scripture and a faithfulness to the classic Christian tradition. While the commentary adopts an "American" name, it should be noted some writers represent countries outside the United States, giving the commentary an international perspective. The diverse group of writers includes scholars, teachers, and administrators from almost twenty different colleges and seminaries, as well as pastors, missionaries, and a layperson.

The editors and writers hope that THE NEW AMERICAN COMMENTARY will be helpful and instructive for pastors and teachers, scholars and students, for men and women in the churches who study and teach God's Word in various settings. We trust that for editors, authors, and readers alike, the commentary will be used to build up the church, encourage obedience, and bring renewal to God's people. Above all, we pray that the NAC will bring glory and honor to our Lord who has graciously redeemed us and faithfully revealed himself to us in his Holy Word.

SOLI DEO GLORIA
The Editors

Author's Preface: Amos, Obadiah

My intense interest in Amos grew out of course assignments in the Book of Amos shortly after I began my teaching career at the New Orleans Baptist Theological Seminary on January 1, 1976. I have presented an overview of the book numerous times in the second half of Introduction to the Old Testament. Many times I taught Amos and Hosea in English in master's level work and the same two books in Hebrew in doctoral level work. Often I taught Amos as a Hebrew exegesis course. I have taught the book under the title "A Preaching Approach to Amos" as a Doctor of Ministry seminar.

Several years ago (1980) I was asked to write abbreviated commentaries on Hosea, Joel, Amos, Obadiah, and Jonah in the Layman's Bible Book Commentary series. My continuing study has resulted in some changes in my interpretation of Amos and Obadiah since that time.

Persons contributing to my understanding of the Books of Amos and Obadiah are too numerous to name. Included in the list would be my professors, my students, my colleagues on the faculty, those who have written commentaries and articles on the books, and the congregations I have served as pastor, or interim pastor, or guest teacher. The flaws in the commentaries are my own, not the fault of my teachers.

My Doctor of Ministry students helped me see the relevance of Amos for contemporary life in America. They were required to write papers on the relevance of Amos. Israel had existed for nearly two hundred years as a separate kingdom when Amos arrived with a strong message of condemnation from God. The prophet addressed the political, social, religious, moral, and ethical problems of that society. He called for repentance, justice, righteousness, and purity. My hope is that the readers will find the message of Amos and Obadiah relevant to life in their settings.

I owe three people a special debt of gratitude for assistance with manuscript production. One of these is Jane Soesbe, my former secretary. Another is Dr. Janice Meier, former secretary, former student, and current colleague, who served as proofreader at an early stage of development of the manuscript. The other person is Judy Kimmitt, who devoted hours of work putting the text into the computer, proofreading the manuscript, and inserting Hebrew words and phrases into footnotes without formal training in the Hebrew language.

Billy K. Smith

Author's Preface: Jonah

When the first word of invitation came regarding the writing of this commentary, I was deeply honored by the assignment. It was an exciting opportunity that truly changed my life. I thank the Lord for the opportunity as it strengthened me, stretched me, and deepened my appreciation of the scholars that have blessed me with their writing through the years. As a pastor I have been blessed immeasurably by those who seek to help bring light to passages that are difficult and sometimes confusing. For me to participate in bringing illumination to the minds of other believers was a profound and sacred task. At times it was even a frightening task. I have always had a very high view of Scripture. I have never taken the words of 2 Tim 2:15 lightly: "Do your best to present yourself to God as one approved, a workman who does not need to be ashamed and who correctly handles the word of truth." To "handle" the word of truth so that it provides illumination for scholars and students alike was an awesome responsibility. I give thanks to God for allowing me to be a part of the process.

When the process was initiated, I was one of three pastors involved in this great task. It is my prayer that thousands of pastors will receive solid, practical help from this volume. It also is my prayer that countless numbers of laypersons will receive needed help as they become more serious students of God's precious Word. The Bible is the Word of God, abidingly relevant to all people of all ages. I pray that all who undertake a serious study of God's Word will grow deeper in their appreciation of the depth of God's precious Word. The Book of Jonah is one of the most known of the "Minor Prophets" yet one of the most neglected. As students of God's Word in general and the Book of Jonah in particular, you will find that this little book contains far more than a story about a man and a fish. It is full of precious spiritual lessons and new insights into the character of God.

Many people have been a part of this project, and they deserve my gratitude. First I would like to thank the producers of *The New American Commentary* series, as well as the consulting editors. Specifically, I would like to thank L. Russ Bush for his constant encouragement in this process. The general editors, Mike Smith, David Dockery, and now Ray Clendenen, were also a constant source of encouragement and assistance. I could not have asked for a better team of general editors and consulting editors. While providing helpful comments, they were more than open to my contributions. I also would like to thank Russel Dilday, former president at Southwestern Seminary, for encouraging me to accept this assignment. I also want to thank the seminary students who were also my research assistants, particularly Susan Day Piggott and Jeff Cokely. At the time of the writing of this commentary I was pastor of the Gambrell Street Baptist Church near Southwestern Seminary and was blessed by the assistance from the staff of the theological library at Southwestern Seminary, where I also was an adjunct professor of evangelism. I am particularly indebted to Sueda Luttrell, my friend and editorial assistant, who has assisted me in this and other projects in a timely, competent, and supportive manner. She has always gone beyond the "second mile." I also appreciate the congregation of the Gambrell Street Baptist Church who assisted in the role of encouragers during the completing of this manuscript. I must also thank my current congregation, the Warren Baptist Church of Augusta, Georgia, for their sweet prayers and friendship during the revisions of this manuscript. It must also be noted that my current secretary and friend, Anita Mullenix, has taken care of the responsibilities for me so that I might have the time needed for this project.

Most importantly, I am indebted to my family. My wife, Dayle, and girls, Melissa, Laura, and Allison, have shown their love and patience during the time I spent on this project. While for some the writing is inimical to family life, I do not believe it was for the Pages. They have maintained a sweet and supportive stance through it all.

While I have already stated my desire for the reader of this volume, I must state my ultimate desire. I earnestly hope that through a deeper study of God's Word, believers will be so strengthened that they will feel more compelled to share the good news with a lost and dying world. It is my earnest prayer that this commentary will ultimately lead to the increased sharing of God's Word and therefore to the salvation of many souls. May it be so!

Frank S. Page

Abbreviations

Bible Books

Gen
Exod
Lev
Num
Deut
Josh
Judg
Ruth
1, 2 Sam
1, 2 Kgs
1, 2 Chr
Ezra
Neh
Esth
Job
Ps (pl. Pss)
Prov
Eccl
Song

Isa
Jer
Lam
Ezek
Dan
Hos
Joel
Amos
Obad
Jonah
Mic
Nah
Hab
Zeph
Hag
Zech
Mal
Matt
Mark

Luke
John
Acts
Rom
1, 2 Cor
Gal
Eph
Phil
Col
1, 2 Thess
1, 2 Tim
Titus
Phlm
Heb
Jas
1, 2 Pet
1, 2, 3 John
Jude
Rev

Apocrypha

Add Esth	The Additions to the Book of Esther
Bar	Baruch
Bel	Bel and the Dragon
1,2 Esdr	1, 2 Esdras
4 Ezra	4 Ezra
Jdt	Judith
Ep Jer	Epistle of Jeremiah
1,2,3,4 Mac	1, 2, 3, 4 Maccabees
Pr Azar	Prayer of Azariah and the Song of the Three Jews
Pr Man	Prayer of Manasseh
Sir	Sirach, Ecclesiasticus
Sus	Susanna
Tob	Tobit
Wis	The Wisdom of Solomon

Commonly Used Sources

AASOR	Annual of the American Schools of Oriental Research
AB	Anchor Bible
ABR	*Australian Biblical Review*
ABD	*Anchor Bible Dictionary*
ABW	*Archaeology and the Biblical World*
AC	An American Commentary, ed. A. Hovey
AcOr	*Acta orientalia*
AEL	M. Lichtheim, *Ancient Egyptian Literature*
AJSL	*American Journal of Semitic Languages and Literature*
Akk.	Akkadian
AnBib	Analecta Biblica
ANET	J. B. Pritchard, ed., *Ancient Near Eastern Texts*
Ant.	*Antiquities*
AOAT	Alter Orient und Altes Testament
AOTS	*Archaeology and Old Testament Study,* ed. D. W. Thomas
ArOr	Archiv orientální
ATD	Das Alte Testament Deutsch
ATR	*Anglican Theological Review*
AusBR	*Australian Biblical Review*
BA	*Biblical Archaeologist*
BAGD	W. Bauer, W. F. Arndt, F. W. Gingrich, and F. W. Danker, *Greek-English Lexicon of the New Testament*
BALS	Bible and Literature Series
BARev	*Biblical Archaeology Review*
BASOR	*Bulletin of the American Schools of Oriental Research*
BDB	F. Brown, S. R. Driver, and C. A. Briggs, *Hebrew and English Lexicon of the Old Testament*
BETL	Bibliotheca ephemeridum theologicarum lovaniensium
BFT	Biblical Foundations in Theology
BHS	*Biblia hebraica stuttgartensia*
Bib	*Biblica*
BibRev	*Bible Review*
BKAT	Biblischer Kommentar: Altes Testament
BO	*Bibliotheca orientalis*
BSac	*Bibliotheca Sacra*
BSC	Bible Study Commentary
BT	*Bible Translator*
BurH	*Buried History*
BZ	*Biblische Zeitschrift*

BZAW	Beihefte zur ZAW
CAD	*The Assyrian Dictionary of the Oriental Institute of the University of Chicago*
CAH	*Cambridge Ancient History*
CB	Century Bible
CBSC	Cambridge Bible for Schools and Colleges
CBC	Cambridge Bible Commentary
CBQ	*Catholic Biblical Quarterly*
CC	The Communicator's Commentary
CCK	*Chronicles of Chaldean Kings,* D. J. Wiseman
CHAL	*Concise Hebrew and Aramic Lexicon,* ed. W. L. Holladay
COT	Commentary on the Old Testament, C. F. Keil and F. Delitzsch
CTR	*Criswell Theological Review*
DOTT	*Documents from Old Testament Times,* ed. D. W. Thomas
EAEHL	*Encyclopedia of Archaeological Excavations in the Holy Land,* ed. M. Avi-Yonah
EncJud	*Encyclopaedia Judaica* (1971)
ErIsr	*Eretz Israel*
DSS	Dead Sea Scrolls
EBC	Expositor's Bible Commentary
Ebib	Etudes bibliques
EDNT	
ETL	*Ephermerides theologicae lovanienses*
EvBC	Everyman's Bible Commentary
FB	Forschung zur Bibel
FOTL	Forms of Old Testament Literature
GKC	Gesenius' Hebrew Grammar, ed. E. Kautzsch, tr. A. E. Cowley
GTJ	*Grace Theological Journal*
HAR	*Hebrew Annual Review*
HAT	Handbuch zum Alten Testament
HBT	*Horizons in Biblical Theology*
HDR	Harvard Dissertations in Religion
Her	Hermeneia
HKAT	Handkommentar zum Alten Testament
HSM	Harvard Semitic Monographs
HT	Helps for Translators
HTR	*Harvard Theological Review*
HUCA	*Hebrew Union College Annual*
IB	*Interpreter's Bible*

ICC	International Critical Commentary
IDB	*Interpreter's Dictionary of the Bible*, ed. G. A. Buttrick, et al.
IDBSup	Supplementary volume to *IDB*
IBHS	B. K. Waltke and M. O'Connor, *Introduction to Biblical Hebrew Syntax*
IEJ	*Israel Exploration Journal*
IES	Israel Exploration Society
Int	*Interpretation*
INT	Interpretation: A Bible Commentary for Teaching and Preaching
IOS	*Israel Oriental Society*
ISBE	*International Standard Bible Encyclopedia*, rev. ed. G. W. Bromiley
IJT	*Indian Journal of Theology*
ITC	International Theological Commentary
JANES	*Journal of Ancient Near Eastern Society*
JAOS	*Journal of the American Oriental Society*
JBL	*Journal of Biblical Literature*
JBR	*Journal of Bible and Religion*
JCS	*Journal of Cuneiform Studies*
JEA	*Journal of Egyptian Archaeology*
JETS	*Journal of the Evangelical Theological Society*
JJS	*Journal of Jewish Studies*
JNES	*Journal of Near Eastern Studies*
JNSL	*Journal of Northwest Semitic Languages*
JPOS	*Journal of Palestine Oriental Society*
JSJ	*Journal for the Study of Judaism in the Persian, Hellenistic, and Roman Period*
JSOR	*Journal of the Society for Oriental Research*
JSOT	*Journal for the Study of the Old Testament*
JSOTSup	JSOT—Supplement Series
JSS	*Journal of Semitic Studies*
JTS	*Journal of Theological Studies*
JTSNS	*Journal of Theological Studies, New Series*
JTT	*Journal of Translation and Textlinguistics*
KAT	Kommentar zum Alten Testament
KB	L. Koehler and W. Baumgartner, *Lexicon in Veteris Testamenti libros*

KB³	L. Koehler and W. Baumgartner, *The Hebrew and Aramaic Lexicon of the Old Testament,* trans. M. E. J. Richardson
LBBC	Layman's Bible Book Commentary
LBI	Library of Biblical Interpretation
LCC	Library of Christian Classics
LLAVT	E. Vogt, *Lexicon Linguae Aramaicae Veteris Testamenti*
LTQ	*Lexington Theological Quarterly*
MT	Masoretic Text
NAC	New American Commentary
NB	*Nebuchadrezzar and Babylon,* D. J. Wiseman
NBD	*New Bible Dictionary*
NCBC	New Century Bible Commentary
NICOT	New International Commentary on the Old Testament
NJPS	New Jewish Publication Society Version
NKZ	*Neue kirchliche Zeitschrift*
NovT	*Novum Testamentum*
NTS	*New Testament Studies*
Or	*Orientalia*
OTL	Old Testament Library
OTP	*The Old Testament Pseudepigrapha,* ed. J. H. Charlesworth
OTS	*Oudtestamentische Studiën*
OTWSA	*Ou-Testamentiese Werkgemeenskap in Suid-Afrika*
PCB	*Peake's Commentary on the Bible,* ed. M. Black and H. H. Rowley
PEQ	*Palestine Exploration Quarterly*
POTT	*Peoples of Old Testament Times,* ed. D. J. Wiseman
PTR	*Princeton Theological Review*
Pss. Sol.	*Psalms of Solomon*
RA	Revue d'assyriologie et d'archéologie orientale
RB	*Revue biblique*
ResQ	*Restoration Quarterly*
RevExp	*Review and Expositor*
RSR	Recherches de science religieuse
SANE	Sources from the Ancient Near East
SBLDS	Society of Biblical Literature Dissertation Series
SOTI	*A Survey of Old Testament Introduction,* G. L. Archer
SBT	Studies in Biblical Theology
SJT	*Scottish Journal of Theology*
SP	Samaritan Pentateuch
SR	Studies in Religion/Sciences religieuses
ST	*Studia theologica*

STJD	Studies on the Texts of the Desert of Judah
Syr	Syriac
TDOT	*Theological Dictionary of the Old Testament*, ed. G. J. Botterweck and H. Ringgren
Tg	Targum
TJNS	Trinity Journal—New Series
TLZ	*Theologische Literaturzeitung*
TOTC	Tyndale Old Testament Commentaries
TrinJ	*Trinity Journal*
TS	*Theological Studies*
TWAT	*Theologisches Wörterbuch zum Alten Testament*, ed. G. J. Botterweck and H. Ringgren
TWOT	*Theological Wordbook of the Old Testament*
TynBul	*Tyndale Bulletin*
UF	*Ugarit-Forschungen*
Vg	Vulgate
VT	*Vetus Testamentum*
VTSup	Vetus Testamentum, Supplements
WBC	Word Biblical Commentaries
WEC	Wycliffe Exegetical Commentary
WTJ	*Westminster Theological Journal*
WMANT	Wissenschaftliche Monographien zum Alten und Neuen Testament
ZAW	*Zeitschrift für die alttestamentliche Wissenschaft*
ZDMG	*Zeitschrift der deutschen morgenländischen Gesellschaft*
ZDPV	*Zeitschrift des deutschen Palätina-Vereing*
ZTK	*Zeitschrift für katholische Theologie*

Contents

Amos

    Introduction 23
      I. Title and Theme (1:1–2) 35
     II. The Words of Amos (1:3–6:14) 41
   III. The Visions of Amos (7:1–9:15). 125

Obadiah

    Introduction 171
    IV. The Lord's Pledge to Bring Edom Down (1–4) 179
     V. The Lord's Promise to Destroy Edom (5–10) 185
    VI. Edom's Wrongs against Judah (11–14) 191
   VII. The Coming Day of the Lord (15–21) 195

Jonah

    Introduction 203
  VIII. God's First Call and Jonah's Response (1:1–16) 223
    IX. God's Rescue of the Rebellious Prophet (1:17–2:10). 239
     X. God's Second Commission and Jonah's Obedience (3:1–10) 254
    XI. Jonah's Displeasure and God's Response (4:1–11) 271

Selected Bibliography 284
Selected Subject Index. 290
Person Index. 294
Selected Scripture Index 299

The Divided Monarchy

Sidon
Zarephath
Tyre

▲ MT. LEBANON
Dan
▲ MT. HERMON
Damascus

ARAM

Hazor
BASHAN

Acco

Sea of Galilee

▲ MT. CARMEL

Megiddo
Jezreel
▲ MT. TABOR
Beth-shan

Wadi Yarmuk

Jordan River

GILEAD

AMMON

Mediterranean Sea

Samaria
ISRAEL
Shechem
EPHRAIM
Shiloh
Aphek
Joppa

Bethel
Ai
Gilgal
Mizpah
Ramah
Jericho

Rabbath-Ammon
Heshbon

▲ MT. NEBO

BENJAMIN
Ekron
Gibeon
Jerusalem
Anathoth (Anata)
Beth-hakkerem
Medeba
Baal-meon

Ashdod
Beth-shemesh
Bethlehem

Ashkelon
Azekah
Tekoa
Dibon

Lachish
Hebron
Dead Sea
Wadi Arnon
Aroer

Gaza
JUDAH
Gath

MOAB

Beersheba
Kir-Hareseth

The Negev
Honoraim

Zoar
Ije-abarim
Wadi Zered

The Arabah

EDOM
Bozrah

Scale of Miles
0 5 10 20

Amos

--- *INTRODUCTION OUTLINE* ---

1. The Historical Setting
2. Amos, the Man
3. Amos, the Book
4. The Language of Amos
5. The Message of Amos
   (1) The Sovereignty of the Lord
   (2) The End for Israel
   (3) The Judgment upon Sin
   (4) The Day of the Lord
   (5) Israel's Future Restoration

--- **INTRODUCTION** ---

Amos was the first of four eighth-century B.C. writing prophets in Israel. The other three were Hosea (began ca. 750 B.C.), Isaiah (began ca. 740 B.C.), and Micah (began ca. 735 B.C.). Amos and Hosea prophesied in Israel, while Isaiah and Micah ministered in Judah. The Old Testament contains references to prophets who preceded Amos (e.g., Deborah, Samuel, Nathan, Elijah, Elisha, Micaiah, Huldah), but excerpts from their preaching have not been preserved in a separate book.

1. The Historical Setting

The title verse (1:1) contains one general clue to the date of Amos's ministry and one specific clue. Uzziah was king in Judah, and Jeroboam, the son of Jehoash, was king in Israel. Uzziah's reign in Judah was from 783 to 742 B.C.[1] with Jotham serving as coregent beginning about 759 B.C. Jeroboam's reign in Israel was from 786 B.C. to 746 B.C.[2] The broad limits of a possible time

---

[1] J. Bright, *A History of Israel*, 3d ed. (Philadelphia: Westminster, 1981), 257.

[2] Ibid.; J. M. Miller and J. H. Hayes date Jeroboam's reign 785–745 B.C. (*A History of Ancient Israel and Judah* [Philadelphia: Westminster, 1986], 286). See also E. R. Thiele, *The Mysterious Numbers of the Hebrew Kings* (Grand Rapids: Zondervan, 1983), who dates the reign 793/2–753.

frame for the ministry of Amos, when both kings were reigning, would be between 783 B.C. and 746 B.C.[3]

The specific clue about the date of the prophet's ministry is the reference to "two years before the earthquake." That reference probably pinpointed the date for the first audience, but for the modern reader it is less helpful because of the uncertainty about when "the earthquake" occurred. It was apparently a memorable event, one with which the audience would have been familiar. Some have suggested that what made it memorable was that it was accompanied by another event, perhaps an eclipse of the sun (8:7–9).[4] Such an eclipse occurred on June 15, 763 B.C. that would have been visible in Palestine. Whether for that reason or another, it probably was the same quake that was remembered near the end of the sixth century B.C. (about 520 B.C.), to which Zech 14:5 refers as "the earthquake in the days of Uzziah king of Judah." Archaeological evidence has also been found of an earthquake at Hazor dated between 765 and 760 B.C.[5] So perhaps we can narrow the time of Amos's preaching to sometime in the early 760s.[6]

At the end of the ninth century B.C., the Arameans dominated Israel, made possible by Assyrian weakness during that time. Earlier in the century (883–824) two Assyrian kings campaigned aggressively outside Assyria proper to control trade routes.[7] An anti-Assyrian coalition formed in the west to resist Assyrian aggression. Shalmaneser III fought this coalition at Qarqar in northern Aram for the first time in 853 B.C. Three principal figures in the battle were Irhuleni of Hamath, Hadadezer of Damascus, and Ahab of Israel.[8] Shalmaneser fought this anti-Assyrian coalition for the fourth and last time in 845–844 B.C. Hadadezer, king of Damascus, was the prominent leader in the coalition.[9]

Hadadezer died during or shortly after the fourth engagement with the Assyrian forces and was replaced by Hazael. For some unknown reason the anti-Assyrian coalition dissolved after Hazael became king. Following dissolution of the coalition, Hazael attacked Israel and wounded Israel's King Jeho-

---

[3] D. Stuart gave the broad limits of the period when Amos ministered as a prophet as 767–742 B.C., from the beginning of Uzziah's sole reign until two years before his death (according to his dating). See *Hosea-Jonah*, WBC (Waco: Word, 1987), 297.

[4] See R. L. Cate's treatment of this matter in his work titled *An Introduction to the Old Testament and Its Study* (Nashville: Broadman, 1987), 298.

[5] Y. Yadin, et al., *Hazor II: An Account of the Second Season of Excavations, 1956* (Jerusalem: Magnes Press, 1960), 24–37.

[6] J. Niehaus, "Amos," in *The Minor Prophets: An Exegetical and Expository Commentary*, ed. T. E. McComiskey (Grand Rapids: Baker, 1992), 1:316. He notes that the prosperity and affluence to which Amos refers would not likely have existed at the beginning of Jeroboam's reign (p. 317). J. H. Hayes dated Amos's ministry in 750–749 B.C. (*Amos* [Nashville: Abingdon, 1988], 47).

[7] Ibid., 16.

[8] *ANET*, 278–79.

[9] Ibid., 280.

ram (2 Kgs 8:25–29). Shalmaneser's campaign in the west in 841–840 B.C. was opposed by Hazael alone.[10] Jehu, who had been left in charge of Israel's army after Jehoram was wounded, paid homage to Shalmaneser before the Assyrian king departed from his engagement in the west. Under instructions from the Lord's prophet and with Shalmaneser's blessing, Jehu seized Israel's throne and killed Jehoram, king of Israel, and Ahaziah, king of Judah (9:21–10:14). Throughout the reign of the five kings in the Jehu dynasty, Israel remained pro-Assyrian. None of Israel's kings participated in the anti-Assyrian coalition generally fostered by the Aramean kingdoms of Arpad, Hamath, and Damascus.

Hazael succeeded in defending his kingdom against Assyrian campaigns in the region in 841–840 B.C. and in 838–837 B.C. He reduced Israel and the other small kingdoms in the Aram-Palestine area to vassal status. For three decades after 837 B.C. Assyria conducted no western campaigns. During this same period, Hazael dominated the region.

The Aramean domination was removed when Jehoahaz prayed (2 Kgs 13:4–5). Assyria became Israel's "savior." Adad-Nirari III crushed Damascus in 802 B.C. and placed Ben-Hadad II, Aram's ruler, under an oppressive tax.[11] For the next forty years Assyria's weak kings left Israel and Judah alone. These sister kingdoms expanded their territory, developed their economy, and entered an era of peace and prosperity.[12] Egypt's weak kings posed no threat to Israel and Judah from 850 to 750 B.C.

Jehoash, Jehu's grandson, became king of Israel (801–786 B.C.) following Assyria's defeat of Damascus in 802 B.C. He recovered all the cities lost to Aram's King Hazael (842–806 B.C.).[13] Jehoash's subsequent defeat of Amaziah king of Judah (2 Kgs 14:1–14) prepared the way for peace between his son, Jeroboam II, and Amaziah's son Azariah (Uzziah), who became king in Judah (2 Kgs 14:21–25; 2 Chr 26:1–15).

The death of Adad-Nirari III in 783 B.C. created a shift in power structures again. Urartu's ascendancy under Argisti I and Sardur III (810–743 B.C.) kept Assyria occupied from 783–763 B.C. During this time the Arameans returned to their aggressive behavior. The reference in Amos 1:3 to transgressions of Damascus in Israelite Gilead probably belongs to the decades when Urartu dominated Assyria. This long-term occupation of Assyria with Urartu probably explains why Amos did not even mention Assyria (but see 5:27).[14]

---

[10] Ibid.

[11] E. H. Merrill, *Kingdom of Priests* (Grand Rapids: Baker, 1987), 365. This Ben-Hadad is sometimes identified as Ben-Hadad III. See W. T. Pitard, *ABD* 1.663–65.

[12] H. W. Wolff, *Joel and Amos,* Her (Philadelphia: Fortress, 1977), 89.

[13] Cf. 2 Kgs 13:25.

[14] The Hebrew text in Amos 3:9 has "Ashdod." The LXX, however, followed by the RSV, has "Assyria." Wolff says that "Assyria had not yet come within Amos's political horizon" and that the text of Amos 3:9 should read "Ashdod," not "Assyria" (*Joel and Amos,* 193). See also S. D. Snyman, "A Note on Ashdod and Egypt in Amos 3:9," *VT* 44 (1994): 559–62.

The preoccupation of Assyria with Urartu, coupled with cooperation between Israel and Judah, provided the environment for these sister kingdoms to expand. Both Israel and Judah enjoyed an extended period of peace and economic prosperity. The economic boom was accompanied by an increase in religious activities. The shrines at Bethel, Dan, Gilgal, and Beer-sheba had constant streams of worshipers bringing growing numbers of sacrificial animals.[15] Amos showed God's disapproval of such religious activities by announcing God's judgment upon the religious sites, by giving counsel to stay away from the sites, and by declaring God's rejection of their religious activities (3:14; 4:4–5; 5:4–5; 5:22–24).

Paradoxically, the period was characterized by moral and spiritual decline and by social upheaval. Israel's frequent attendance at the shrines to make sacrifices did not result in moral, spiritual, and social uprightness. The rich oppressed the poor, indulged in extravagant lifestyles, denied justice to the oppressed, and engaged in immoral sexual activities (2:6–8; 4:1; 5:11–13). Israel's moral and spiritual decline, plus the social upheaval brought on by greed, contradicted their accelerated religious activities. Such were the times of Amos's arrival in Israel with a strong message of judgment from God. Israel's outward show of devotion to God, contradicted by their moral, spiritual, and social problems, called for a discerning and courageous prophet.

2. Amos, the Man

What can be known about Amos is what may be discerned only from his book. His name probably comes from a verbal root (*'ms*) meaning "load" or "lift a load." The noun may mean "burdened" or "burden bearer."[16] Names in the Old Testament often are associated with messages from God. Examples would be the names of Hosea's children (Hos 1) and of Isaiah's children (Isa 7). To suggest a connection between Amos's name and his mission would be highly speculative.[17] Even so Amos came from Tekoa loaded with a weighty word from God. The message was more important than the messenger.

Amos came from Tekoa (1:1) in Judah, a village ten or eleven miles south of Jerusalem and about eighteen miles west of the Dead Sea.[18] The title verse (1:1) identifies Amos as "one of the shepherds of Tekoa." But this may designate Amos as a sheepbreeder rather than a common shepherd employed by a

---

[15] Miller and Hayes, *A History of Ancient Israel and Judah,* 312.

[16] Cate suggests "sustained" as the meaning of עָמוֹס (*Introduction to the Old Testament,* 299–300).

[17] F. I. Andersen and D. N. Freedman, *Amos,* AB (New York: Doubleday, 1989), 185.

[18] A few interpreters have argued for a northern village named Tekoa, but the location of such a village has met with failure. S. N. Rosenbaum has presented a strong case for making Amos a native of Israel in *Amos of Israel: A New Interpretation* (Macon: Mercer University Press, 1990).

wealthy owner of the sheep (see comments at 1:1). Second Kings 3:4 is the only other place in the Bible where *noqed*, the word translated "shepherd," appears. There the term refers to Mesha, king of Moab, who supplied Joram, king of Israel, with large quantities of lambs and wool. That information about Mesha has led interpreters to consider Amos as more than a common shepherd.

In Arabic *naqad* designates a particular breed of sheep, and a *naqqad* is one who watches over this kind of sheep. The root occurs in Sumerian, Akkadian, Syriac, and Ugaritic. In Akkadian *naqidû* and *re'û* are used in parallel lines to refer to the function of the shepherd.[19] In Ugaritic usage *nqdm* were officials in charge of (royal) herds. One text refers to the chief of the priests and the chief of the shepherds as the same person. T. J. Wright has suggested that this usage reveals that in Ugarit a *nqd* had a sacral association.[20] But I tend to agree with P. Craigie and S. Paul that *nqd* does not necessarily carry any sacral or religious connotations.[21] Amos could have been a temple servant, but it is more likely that he was not.

Amos used two other terms in 7:14 to explain what he was doing when God called him to prophesy to Israel (also see comments on that verse). Those terms are translated "shepherd" (*bôqer*)[22] and one who "took care of [*bôles*] sycamore-fig trees." *Bôqer* designates a "herdsman," and *bôles* refers to one who scrapes or punctures or does something with sycamore-figs. T. J. Wright explored two possible meanings of the word *bôles*. He suggested that "one of the tasks of Amos was to nip the sycamore fruit in order to hasten ripening."[23] His other suggestion was that "the concern of Amos with the sycamore was in providing fodder for those in his charge."[24] An advantage of the latter meaning is the obvious connection between a shepherd's responsibility to feed the sheep and the possibility that the sycamore-fig provided one source of food. This latter side of his vocation would have required him to travel to lower elevations where the sycamore-fig grew.

Amos employed one other descriptive phrase in his explanation of his work. He said that when the Lord called him to prophetic ministry he was "tending the flock" (7:15). The word translated "flock" usually designates a flock of small cattle, sheep, or goats. Amos probably traveled to various places and had contacts with a variety of people in his work as a *noqed*, a *bôqer*, a *bôles*, and one who followed the "flock." Also Tekoa was a military

---

[19] T. J. Wright, "Did Amos Inspect Livers?" *ABR* 23 (1975): 3.

[20] Ibid., 4. See also J. D. W. Watts, *Vision and Prophecy in Amos* (Grand Rapids: Eerdmans, 1958), 6–7.

[21] P. C. Craigie, "Amos the *noqed* in the Light of Ugaritic," *Sciences Religieuses/Studies in Religion* 11 (1982): 33; S. Paul, *Amos,* Her (Minneapolis: Fortress, 1991), 34.

[22] בּוֹקֵר is from בָּקָר, "cattle."

[23] T. J. Wright, "Amos and the 'Sycamore Fig,'" *VT* 26 (1976): 368.

[24] Ibid.

outpost, and international news may have been available to him there (cf. 2 Chr 11:5–6). His book reveals his keen awareness of his world.

Amos also refused the term "prophet" (*nābî*) as an appropriate description of his role (see the discussion of 7:14). He claimed no special authority associated with traditional titles when Amaziah ordered him out of Bethel (7:12–13). Instead, he gave his testimony of bivocational employment as "a herdsman and a dresser of sycamore trees" (7:14) when the Lord ordered him to prophesy to Israel (7:15). He came to Bethel not as a representative of one of the prophetical guilds but as a layman under divine order to perform the function of a prophet.

Amos knew the history of Israel and the history of the nations around Israel. He knew Israelite politics, society, and religion. He had enough courage to confront those who oppressed the poor, religious leaders such as Amaziah, and greedy landgrabbers and merchants. His strong sense of the Lord's call to prophesy was the enabling force of his ministry (7:15). Such a sense of call has continued to be the authority and motivation for service to the Lord.

3. Amos, the Book

The Book of Amos has two parts: words (chaps. 1–6) and visions (chaps. 7–9).[25] "Words of Amos" and "what he saw" in the title verse (1:1) reveal these two parts. Five distinct types of material make up the book: (1) oracles (or sayings) spoken by Amos, (2) vision-reports, (3) a third-person narrative reporting Amaziah's opposition to Amos, (4) three stanzas of an old hymn, and (5) the title.

From the elements in the title verse of Amos (1:1), J. D. W. Watts has proposed an explanation for the origin of the book. He suggested that the title "the words of Amos"[26] may have been the original superscription prefixed to

---

[25] Wolff (*Joel and Amos*, 106–13) saw six parts: (1) words (chaps. 3–6); (2) vision-reports (7:1–8; 8:1–2; 9:1–4) and oracles against the nations (1:3–2:16); (3) redactional activity (7:10–17; 8:4–14; 9:7–10; 5:13–15; 6:2; 7:13); (4) pre-Deuteronomic redaction (4:13; 5:8–9; 9:5–6; 3:14b,c; 5:6; 4:6–13); (5) Deuteronomic redaction (2:10–12; 5:25; 3:1b; 8:11–12); and (6) postexilic redaction (6:5; 9:11–15). Wolff's approach is too atomized and disjointed to be helpful in handling the interpretation of the text of Amos. Andersen and Freedman (*Amos*, 16) suggest three major parts with an epilogue: The Book of Doom (chaps. 1–4), The Book of Woes (chaps. 5–6), The Book of Visions (7:1–9:6), and an Epilogue (9:7–15). While this approach to analysis of the structure of Amos is helpful, I do not see it as an improvement over my two-part analysis and following discussion. The three-part structure of G. Smith and G. Hasel is identical to my own except that they divide the "words" section to isolate the judgments on the nations. See G. Smith, *Amos: A Commentary* (Grand Rapids: Zondervan, 1989), 7–9; G. Hasel, *Understanding the Book of Amos* (Grand Rapids: Baker, 1991), 91–99. Hasel has an excellent summary of various approaches to the structure of Amos. While these various interpretations are helpful, none improves on the twofold structure, which is based on the title of the book itself and reflects the book's coherence and unity.

[26] The expression "the words of" a prophet is found elsewhere in the OT only in Jer 1:1.

what is now Amos 1–6.[27] These "words" may have been "reduced to writing by some in the prophetic circles of Bethel."[28] After the fall of Samaria in 722 B.C., these materials would have been carried to Judah.

The other clause in the title verse, "which he saw concerning Israel," Watts suggested referred to the second half of the book made up of five visions. He thought the first three visions described the prophet's ministry in Israel "from the beginning to its end in his appearance in Bethel."[29] Since the prophetic "words" of this phase of the prophet's ministry are contained in Amos 1–6, no resultant "words" are found in the section where these vision accounts are given (7:1–9). The third-person account of the prophet's encounter with the priest of Bethel (7:10–17) may recount the event that precipitated the end of the prophet's ministry in Israel.

According to Watts, Amos 8–9 may describe the continuation of the prophet's ministry in Judah, and the hopeful prophecies at the end of the book followed the fall of Samaria in 722 B.C. Watts thought the two separate parts of Amos may have been joined only at the time when the Book of the Twelve was formed (after Babylonian exile). This is an unnecessary assumption, and his whole theory of composition contains much speculation.[30] In the midst of God's judgment there is always the prophetic word of hope as evidenced by the other classical prophets. While chaps. 8 and 9 may be from late in Amos's prophetic career, they may just as well be from the same time as the other prophecies recorded in the book.

While the trend in scholarship has been to ascribe some if not much of the Book of Amos to later disciples and other prophets, "this scissors-and-paste method is to be seriously questioned."[31] As S. Paul has suggested: "When each case is examined and analyzed on its own, without preconceived conjectures and unsupported hypotheses, the book in its entirety (with one or two minor exceptions) can be reclaimed for its rightful author, the prophet Amos. The results of the investigation support the integrity of the book."[32] There is, therefore, no reason to ascribe any part of this book to anyone other than the prophet Amos. While the exact composition of the book is uncertain, its origins and author are not in question.

The title identifies Amos, his hometown, the kinds of material in the book, Israel as the addressee, and clues to the date of the prophet's ministry. A one-verse oracle follows the title, a theme verse for the entire book (1:2). The first major section of the book (1:3–6:14) begins with an extended, formulaic

---

[27] J. D. W. Watts, "The Origin of the Book of Amos," *ExpTim* 66 (1954–55): 109.

[28] Ibid.

[29] Ibid.

[30] See Smith, *Amos,* 216, 219, 244.

[31] Paul, *Amos,* 6.

[32] Ibid. See also Andersen and Freedman, *Amos,* 141–44.

oracle (1:3–2:16) addressed to Israel (2:10). Two of the three hymn stanzas are in the remaining oracles in the first section (4:13; 5:8–9). The second major section begins with three of the five vision-reports (7:1–9).

The narrative about the encounter between Amos and Amaziah (7:10–17) comes between the first three vision-reports and the fourth vision-report (8:1–3). Then a prophetic oracle (or oracles) finishes out chap. 8. Chapter 9 comprises the final vision-report (9:1–4), the third and final hymn stanza (9:5–6), a judgment oracle (9:7–10), and a restoration oracle (9:11–15).

J. Limburg's six major sections of the Book of Amos based on divine speech formulas give further helpful divisions of the text for interpreters: 1:3–2:16; 3:1–15; 4:1–13; 5:1–6:14; 7:1–8:3; and 8:4–9:15. Counting 1:1–2 as the first section of the book gives a total of seven sections.[33] This proliferation of sections in the book, however, overlooks some major divisions. The twofold structure of "words" and "visions" gives Limburg's six sections some needed unity. Our detailed outline reflects the sevenfold structure as a further subdivision of the two major sections of the book.

4. The Language of Amos

Amos employed a wealth of rhetorical forms in bringing God's message to Israel.[34] Speech forms in the book include (1) messenger formulae: "this is what the LORD says," "says the LORD"; (2) an oracle formula: "declares the LORD"; and (3) vision-reports introduced by "this is what the Sovereign LORD showed me." These speech forms cite the source of the prophet's authority and, at the same time, present his credentials as a prophet. Amos went to Israel under divine appointment to bear strong messages of judgment and hope.

Other features are (1) graded numerical sayings: "for three sins of . . ., even for four" (e.g., 1:3,6,9); (2) participial style: "you women who oppress" (4:1); (3) quotation of the audience: "and say to your husbands, 'Bring us some drinks'" (4:1); (4) climactic patterns (1:3–2:16; 4:6–12); (5) woe oracles (5:18–20; 6:1–7); and (6) wordplays: "a basket of ripe fruit" in 5:5b and "the time is ripe" in 8:1–3.[35]

Additional features of language use in Amos include (1) oath formula (4:2; 6:8; 8:7); (2) antithesis (5:4–5); (3) richness of imagery (2:13); (4) disputation (3:3–8; 9:7–10); and (5) curse formula (7:17). These features of language give convincing evidence that Amos was familiar with the best wisdom, priestly, and prophetic forms of rhetoric. Such use of rhetorical forms must have

---

[33] J. Limburg, "Sevenfold Structures in the Book of Amos," *JBL* 106 (1987): 218.

[34] Wolff has an extended discussion of language use in Amos (*Joel and Amos*, 91–100).

[35] קִיץ and קֵץ are the two words involved in the wordplay in 8:1–3.

enhanced the power and attractiveness of his verbal presentations as it does his literary work. The first audiences of the spoken and written messages of the prophet must have resonated readily with his rhetorical forms typically used by wisdom teachers, priests, and prophets. The book offers a striking display of language use.

5. The Message of Amos

Amos testified that the Lord took him from tending the flock and said to him, "Go, prophesy to my people Israel" (7:15). His oracles and vision-reports give the contents of his message, a message from God to Israel. The sovereign Lord commissioned Amos to bear his message of judgment upon Israel, a judgment so destructive the nation would not survive. Israel's sin against God caused God's judgment against Israel. The coming day of the Lord would be a day of darkness and destruction, not light and salvation for "the sinful kingdom" (9:8). Some of "the house of Jacob," however, would survive the judgment of God and form the nucleus of a restored, blessed, and secure future Israel (9:11–15).

(1) The Sovereignty of the Lord

The Lord's sovereignty extended over Amos, Judah, Israel, the nations, and all creation. So strong was the Lord's call of Amos that Amos felt he had no option but to go to Israel with the message of God (3:8b). As sovereign over his own people (Judah and Israel), the Lord called them to account for their rebellion (2:4–16). His sovereignty extended over foreign nations, even though they expressed allegiance to other gods (1:3–2:3). They had to answer to the Lord for their inhumanity. The hymns in Amos picture the Lord as creator and controller of the universe (4:13; 5:8–9; 9:5–6). His sovereignty was and is all-encompassing. God has not relinquished his control over the universe to any other entity, authority, or power. He is sovereign over all people.

(2) The End for Israel

The prophet's message of the imminent destruction of Israel was based on Israel's sin. Amos indicted various segments of the population: greedy land-grabbers (2:6); the rich (3:10,15; 6:4–6); the women of Samaria (4:1); religious frauds (4:4–5; 5:4–7,21–23); the merchants (8:4–6); and those responsible for injustice in the courts (2:7; 5:7,10,12; 6:12). The message of Amos was that Israel would not survive the judgment of God (2:13–16; 3:11–12; 5:2,18–20; 6:7,14; 7:8; 8:2; 9:1–4,8a). Israel, the Northern Kingdom, did not survive the assault of the Assyrians in 725–722 B.C. (2 Kgs 17). That attack was the judgment of God upon his people Israel.

(3) The Judgment upon Sin

The end of Israel as a nation may be traced backwards through God's judgment to the root cause in the nation's sin against God. Israel's privileged relationship as people of God did not shield them from the judgment of God. From the vivid imagery of a bloodcurdling roar of the Lord (1:2) to the word of Israel's destruction "from the face of the earth" (9:8), the prophet's message of judgment upon sin is persistent. Amos proclaimed God's judgment upon the nations because of their sins. He singled out groups of people within Israel, as well as one individual (Amaziah), who would suffer the judgment of God because of their sins.

God's people face a day of judgment for their sin. Paul wrote to the Corinthians: "We must all appear before the judgment seat of Christ, that each one may receive what is due him for the things done while in the body, whether good or bad" (2 Cor 5:10). All nations and all people face a day of accounting to God for their sin, and "the wages of sin is death" (Rom 6:23).

(4) The Day of the Lord

The Book of Amos has the earliest reference to the day of the Lord in the Old Testament (assuming the Book of Joel was not written in the ninth century). Amos may not have been the original source of the concept, but he offered a corrective to Israel's current misconception of it (5:18–20). The popular opinion among the people was that the day of the Lord would be a day of "light," or salvation. Amos said it would be a day of "darkness," or defeat. Ironically, the people longed for the day to come. Amos said that day of darkness was coming indeed and that it would be inescapable. The final picture in the book is of a day in the future when the Lord's intervention would bring restoration, plenty, and peace to his people (9:11–15).

(5) Israel's Future Restoration

Many of Amos's interpreters have tended to characterize him as a prophet of doom. Any hint of the possibility of hope for a future for Israel has been explained by them as the work of a later editor/redactor.[36] That is not the position of a growing number of Old Testament scholars. G. F. Hasel notes many interpreters who have supported the authenticity of the final hope passage in Amos (9:11–15).[37] In the larger context the hope extended by Amos

---

[36] E.g., Wolff (*Joel and Amos*) and J. Mays (*Amos: A Commentary*, OTL [Philadelphia: Westminster, 1969]) assign passages expressing future hope for Israel to later editors.

[37] G. F. Hasel, *Understanding the Book of Amos: Basic Issues in Current Interpretations* (Grand Rapids: Baker, 1991), 118. The list contains forty-six names of recognized OT scholars (see n. 58).

for Israel's future restoration is only for a remnant of the nation. The end of Israel came at the hands of the Assyrians (722 B.C.). The end of Judah came at the hands of the Babylonians (586 B.C.). But survival of remnants of both nations, reunion of the people, and restoration to the land also occurred near the end of the sixth century and into the fifth century B.C. Later, James asserted that God was still fulfilling the prophecy of Amos 9:11–15, accounting for the success of the early church in reaching Gentiles for the kingdom of God (Acts 15:12–21).

Complete fulfillment of Amos 9:11–15 may be reserved for some "day" in the distant future. Interpreters differ on what exactly the prophecy projects with the expressions related to restoration, plenty, and security and when exactly that might occur. Stuart questions whether the prophecy has been fulfilled in the distant past (Ezra 1:1–11)[38] and whether the modern state of Israel or the Christian church might constitute some aspect of fulfillment.[39] Andersen and Freedman think the restoration described in Amos 9:11–15 "requires a united Israel under the rule of its long-standing dynasty (that of David)."[40] Hubbard identified the restoration as "a more distant (than the imminent judgment) undefined future" for Israel.[41] He thinks "the messianic age" was the distant future toward which the words of Amos pointed.[42] While the words may be variously interpreted, one thing is certain: restoration comes only from God, not from any human endeavor (Amos 9:14–15).

--------------------- OUTLINE OF THE BOOK ---------------------

  I. Title and Theme (1:1–2)
     1. Title (1:1)
     2. Theme (1:2)
 II. The Words of Amos (1:3–6:14)
     1. Words of Judgment upon the Nations (1:3–2:16)
        (1) Oracle against Aram (1:3–5)
        (2) Oracle against Philistia (1:6–8)
        (3) Oracle against Phoenicia (1:9–10)

---

[38] On this idea see the significant article by J. G. McConville, "Ezra-Nehemiah and the Fulfillment of Prophecy, *VT* 36 (1986): 205–24. While McConville focuses on Jeremiah and Isaiah 40, the principles could be adapted in Amos studies (pp. 213–23).

[39] Stuart, *Hosea-Jonah*, 399–400.

[40] Andersen and Freedman, *Amos*, 893.

[41] D. Hubbard, *Joel and Amos: An Introduction and Commentary* (Leicester: InterVarsity, 1989), 239.

[42] Ibid., 240.

(4) Oracle against Edom (1:11–12)
(5) Oracle against Ammon (1:13–15)
(6) Oracle against Moab (2:1–3)
(7) Oracle against Judah (2:4–5)
(8) Oracle against Israel (2:6–16)
2. Words of Punishment for Israel's Sins (3:1–15)
(1) Punishment for the Whole Family of Rebels (3:1–2)
(2) Justification for the Prophet's Ministry (3:3–8)
(3) Lessons in Violence and Oppression (3:9–11)
(4) Prophecy of Belated Rescue (3:12)
(5) Judgment against Every Aspect of Israel's Life (3:13–15)
3. Words of Condemnation of Israel's Women, Worship, and Stubbornness (4:1–13)
(1) Condemnation of Samaria's Wealthy Women (4:1–3)
(2) Condemnation of Israel's Worship (4:4–5)
(3) Condemnation of Israel's Stubbornness (4:6–13)
4. Words of Doom for Israel (5:1–6:14)
(1) Funeral Song for Fallen Israel (5:1–17)
(2) Darkness of the Day of the Lord (5:18–20)
(3) Rejection of Israel's Worship (5:21–27)
(4) A Preeminent Nation (6:1–7)
(5) A Doomed Nation (6:8–14)
III. The Visions of Amos (7:1–9:15)
1. Visions of Israel's Imminent Destruction (7:1–8:3)
(1) First Vision: The Locusts (7:1–3)
(2) Second Vision: The Fire (7:4–6)
(3) Third Vision: The Plumb Line (7:7–9)
(4) Who Is in Charge? (7:10–17)
(5) Fourth Vision: A Basket of Summer Fruit (8:1–3)
2. Oracles and a Vision of Israel's Future Destruction and Ultimate Restoration (8:4–9:15)
(1) Indictment of Greedy Merchants (8:4–6)
(2) The Lord's Oath against Greedy Merchants (8:7–10)
(3) The Lord's Threat of Famine (8:11–14)
(4) Fifth Vision: The Lord Standing by the Altar (9:1–4)
(5) The Lord Almighty (9:5–6)
(6) Destruction of the Sinful Kingdom (9:7–10)
(7) Future Restoration of Israel (9:11–15)

I. TITLE AND THEME (1:1–2)
   1. Title (1:1)
   2. Theme (1:2)

I. TITLE AND THEME (1:1–2)

Verse 1 is the title of the book, similar to the titles of other prophetic books.[1] While it is possible that it was provided by a disciple who edited the prophecies of Amos,[2] v. 2 serves as the theme of the entire book and is from Amos.[3] The original audience of Amos's spoken messages was the Northern Kingdom of Israel. Judah may have been an early reading audience of Amos's written messages.

Some interpreters see signs of repeated editorial work on the title verse,[4] which supplies the reader with "the most complete superscription to be found in all of prophetic literature."[5] T. J. Finley notes, however, that while "the unusual grammar Wolff notices would be irregular for ordinary narrative," it is "not without precedent for biblical titles or headings." He goes on to suggest that Isa 1:1 is structurally parallel to Amos 1:1, "even though a relative clause is not used to qualify the prophet."[6]

G. Smith goes further and agrees with W. Rudolph that "the reference to the prophet's previous occupation, the absence of an initial allusion to the word of the Lord, and the clumsy syntax of 1:1" are arguments for the verse's early origin. They suggest that "the introduction must have been written before any standard style was established. A later redaction of the verse would have smoothed out the rough syntax and reconstructed the introduction on the basis of more traditional patterns."[7] Regarding v. 2, G. Smith believes

---

[1] See Isa 1:1; Hos 1:1; Mic 1:1; Jer 1:1–3.

[2] J. Niehaus believes that the third person used in 1:1 is the result of the covenant lawsuit genre of Amos rather than a separate author ("Amos," in *The Minor Prophets: An Exegetical and Expository Commentary* (Grand Rapids: Baker, 1992), 1:320–22.

[3] D. Stuart (*Hosea-Jonah,* WBC [Waco: Word, 1987], 300–302) sees v. 2 as an independent unit functioning as a "thematic prelude to the whole message of Amos."

[4] See J. L. Mays, *Amos,* OTL (Philadelphia: Westminster, 1969), 18; H. Wolff, *Joel and Amos,* Her (Philadelphia: Fortress, 1977), 117–18.

[5] S. Paul, *Amos,* Her (Minneapolis: Fortress, 1991), 33.

[6] T. J. Finley, *Joel, Amos, Obadiah* (Chicago: Moody, 1990), 129.

[7] G. Smith, *Amos: A Commentary* (Grand Rapids: Zondervan, 1989), 20.

that the reference to Zion shows that it "was added to his [Amos's] oral message when he left Israel and went home to Judah." It was there that he edited the book. "Neither verse contains material which must be dated to a period later than Amos."[8]

1. Title (1:1)

[1]The words of Amos, one of the shepherds of Tekoa—what he saw concerning Israel two years before the earthquake, when Uzziah was king of Judah and Jeroboam son of Jehoash was king of Israel.

1:1 The task of collecting, arranging, and affixing a title verse may have been done by the prophet himself, by his disciples, or by some representative from the community of faith. Third-person reference to the prophet would not necessarily rule out Amos as editor. Listing Uzziah the Judahite king before Jeroboam the Israelite king suggests an original Judahite reading audience, although the original audience to the spoken oracles was no doubt Israel.

"The words of Amos" designates the contents of the entire book. "Word" (*dābār*) in its technical usage means "a saying," or spoken message from God. The plural "words" (*dĕbārîm*) can be a title in Scripture for a collection of sayings (Neh 1:1; Eccl 1:1; Prov 30:1; Jer 1:1). The typical usage in prophetic literature is the singular form ("word") in relationship with "the LORD" (Hos 1:1; Mic 1:1; Ezek 1:3; Joel 1:1; Jonah 1:1; Zeph 1:1; Hag 1:1; Zech 1:1). "Words of Amos" does not imply that his messages were not the "word of the LORD."

The qualifying phrase "what he saw" makes clear that what follows are divinely revealed messages delivered by the prophet Amos. Everything is the "word of the LORD": sayings, vision-reports, doxologies, and even the account of conflict between the prophet and the priest (7:10–17). Thus, Amos had the credentials of a true prophet; he had the "word of the LORD" for Israel.

Proper credentials for God's spokespersons have always been more than formal training, formal ordination, and an official title. These things do not qualify one to speak for God. Biblically speaking, only one who has a word (revelation) from God has proper credentials to speak for God (cf. Jer 23:9–40).

This collection of material was God's solemn message for Israel, not merely the somber words of a Judahite shepherd. As such they merited Israel's careful attention. The title served notice to all readers of the Amos materials that they were venturing into the word of the Lord.

The next phrase in the verse locates Amos vocationally and geographically (cf. 7:15). He was one among the "shepherds" (*nōqdîm*) from Tekoa. *Nōqēd*

---

[8] Ibid., 21.

is not the word for "shepherd" but designates Amos as a breeder/tender of livestock (sheep and goats; cf. "sheep-breeder," REB). This assessment is based on 2 Kgs 3:4, the only other text in the Old Testament where the term is used. Reference there is to Mesha, king of Moab, who was a *nōqēd*. The fact that he supplied the king of Israel with a hundred thousand lambs and with the wool of a hundred thousand rams implies considerably more than a man who worked as a shepherd.

Tekoa probably is the Judahite village about ten miles south of Jerusalem, not the Galilean Tekoa mentioned in the Talmud.[9] Joab brought a wise woman from Tekoa to convince David to allow his son Absalom to return to the court (2 Sam 14:1–24). The village supplied one of David's mighty men (2 Sam 23:26). Rehoboam fortified it to defend his kingdom (2 Chr 11:5–12). Tekoa must have been a suitable site for breeding and tending sheep.

"What he saw" was a conventional expression for the prophet's method of receiving revelation from God. *Ḥāzâ* means "see," or "understand." The noun *ḥāzôn* may designate both the experience of perception and the message received (Isa 1:1). The verb describes both the act of reception and the act of proclamation of the message (Isa 2:1; Mic 1:1). A major component of the Book of Amos is his vision reports (7:1–9; 8:1–3; 9:1–4). "What he saw" in the title verse designates the message (or revelation) Amos had received and proclaimed to Israel (cf. 7:12; 1 Sam 9:9).

"Concerning Israel" refers to the subject matter and original audience of Amos's spoken messages. The prophet's words and visions were about Israel. They were also against Israel in an adversative sense. Amos addressed Israel as the covenant people, not as the breakaway Northern Kingdom.[10] The people of Israel, especially the king and official leadership, had seen themselves as a separate kingdom from Judah since their radical break with the Southern Kingdom in the days of Rehoboam of Judah and Jeroboam I of Israel (1 Kgs 12:16–17). That break occurred either in 930 or 922 B.C.[11] Almost two hundred years later, Amos came to them as the people of God. Their recent history of rebellion had not canceled their covenant with God. Amos called them to account as responsible covenant partners.

The reference in "two years before the earthquake" assumes such a notable disaster that no one needed more information. S. Paul described the quake as

---

[9] J. H. Hayes, *Amos* (Nashville: Abingdon, 1988), 43.

[10] See M. Polley, *Amos and the Davidic Empire* (New York: Oxford University Press, 1989).

[11] J. Bright followed W. F. Albright in dating the demise of Solomon in 922 B.C. and, thus, setting the split in the kingdom at that time (*A History of Israel*, 3d ed. [Philadelphia: Westminster, 1981], 229). J. Miller and J. Hayes gave support to Bright's position by suggesting approximately 925 B.C. as the separation date (*A History of Ancient Israel and Judah* [Philadelphia: Westminster, 1986], 220). Many, however, follow E. R. Thiele in dating it in 930. See Thiele, *Mysterious Numbers of the Hebrew Kings* (Grand Rapids: Zondervan, 1983), 67–78.

"extremely violent and unparalleled."[12] The earthquake is mentioned again in Zech 14:5. Archaeologists have dated traces of an earthquake at Hazor to 765 to 760 B.C.[13] This dating accords with the reference to Uzziah's reign in the Zechariah passage.

Amos ministered as a prophet during the reigns of Uzziah (783–742 B.C.) in Judah and Jeroboam II (786–746 B.C.) in Israel. Dating a prophet's ministry in this manner is common but imprecise. "Two years before the earthquake" is a more specific framework for the prophet's activity. The latter reference may imply a brief ministry of a few months. Since precision could have been attained in the more customary manner of giving the year of the king's reign, it may be that reference to the earthquake is to set an ominous tone for the predominant words of judgment that follow (cf. 2:13; 4:11; 6:11; 8:8; 9:1,5).

2. Theme (1:2)

²He said:
"The LORD roars from Zion
  and thunders from Jerusalem;
the pastures of the shepherds dry up,
  and the top of Carmel withers."

1:2 Translators have struggled with verb tense in the verse, that is, whether it is to be translated as present or future. The solution to the verb tense problem waits on the decision about the function of the verse. If the verse summarizes the message of Amos, present tense is appropriate.[14] If the verse introduces the extended oracle that follows, future tense is in order.[15] Most modern translations use present tense or a combination of present and future tenses.[16] As to function, the better option is to treat the verse as a summary of the Amos material and as the theme of his preaching.[17]

Poetic style with graphic imagery characterizes v. 2. The first line of the double couplet describes the awesome noise of the Lord's message through Amos. The second line reveals the devastating effect of that message. In Hebrew clauses the verb usually comes first. But here both "the LORD" and "from Zion" precede the verb in the Hebrew text. Similarly, "from Jerusalem" shares emphatic status. This grammatical arrangement calls attention to the speaker and the speaker's presence in Zion, where the covenant people encoun-

---

[12] Paul, *Amos,* 35.

[13] Y. Yadin, et al., *Hazor II: An Account of the Second Season of Excavations, 1956* (Jerusalem: Magnes Press, 1960), 24–37.

[14] Mays, *Amos,* 20.

[15] Hayes, *Amos,* 55–56, 62–63.

[16] NRSV, GNB, NIV, NASB.

[17] Stuart, *Hosea-Jonah,* 330.

tered the covenant God (cf. 2 Sam 5:7). They are to hear that message as people in covenant relationship with God (cf. Joel 3:16 [Heb. 4:16]; Jer 25:30).

The enduring principle here is that every message based on the Bible has its origin with the covenant God and has as its intended audience the people of God. Only people in covenant with God are attuned to hear the message of God. Ideally, when God speaks, covenant people listen. They pay attention because the message has the ring of authority and authenticity and because they want to know and do the will of God.

But if this message were delivered in the Northern Kingdom orally by Amos, it would have had a striking effect in view of the apostate worship that Jeroboam I had set up there following Solomon's death (1 Kgs 12–13).[18] To insist there that God spoke not from Bethel but from Jerusalem would have had the arresting effect of a lion's roar or a clap of thunder.

"Roars" (*yiš'āg*) is either the roar of a lion (3:4–5,8; Judg 14:5; Ps 104:21) or the roar of an approaching storm (Job 37:4). "Thunders" is literally "he gives his voice," which often is described as thunder (Ps 29:3–9). Such imagery suggests awesome force, like the roar of a predatory lion and the thunder of a gathering storm. The genre of this verse is that of a theophany, "a manifestation of the Deity and the resultant catastrophic effects upon the cosmos and nature."[19] This description of theophany originated in the image of God as a warrior. Accounts of theophanies in Mesopotamian, Canaanite, Egyptian, and Greek literature have similar wording to this account in Amos 1:2. This imagery depicts the Lord's enforcement of a Mosaic curse (Lev 26:22; Deut 32:24) against Israel for violation of the covenant.

The message of Amos must have sounded like the roar of a lion capable of freezing its prey in its tracks (cf. Isa 5:25–30). As loud claps of thunder rattle buildings, so the word of the Lord through Amos startled and shook his audiences with its power. God's message delivered by his authorized messengers will always have an authentic ring and a startling effect.

The effect of the Lord's thunderous voice would be devastation. Older English translations have the homonym "mourn" instead of "dry up" as their rendering of the verb *'ābĕlû*. In the context "dry up" is correct.[20] It is parallel to "withers" in the second half of the line. Usually thunder accompanies rain. Instead, the "thunder" of the Lord would produce a general and devastating

---

[18] Polley, *Amos and the Davidic Empire,* 109–11.

[19] Paul, *Amos,* 38.

[20] J. De Waard and W. A. Smalley, *A Translator's Handbook on the Book of Amos* (New York: UBS, 1979), 27. "The pastures" is the translation of a term נְאוֹת with a general meaning of "abode" or "residence." Reference may be to the abode of animals, men, or God. "Of the shepherds" narrows the meaning to the usual habitat of shepherds with their flocks. "Pastures" is the obvious intent of the term in the context. For that reason "dry up" is the proper translation of אָבַל. This rendering matches the parallel thought in the second half of the line.

drought, from the "pastures of the shepherds" to the "top of Carmel." This is a figure of speech known as merismus, which uses opposites to convey the idea of the whole. That is, the Lord will bring about devastation throughout the land.

The message of Amos was primarily an announcement of the Lord's judgment upon his disobedient people. Verse 2 is a terse summary of that message. It is the theme to which the prophet turned again and again.

II. THE WORDS OF AMOS (1:3–6:14)
  1. Words of Judgment upon the Nations (1:3–2:16)
    (1) Oracle against Aram (1:3–5)
    (2) Oracle against Philistia (1:6–8)
    (3) Oracle against Phoenicia (1:9–10)
    (4) Oracle against Edom (1:11–12)
    (5) Oracle against Ammon (1:13–15)
    (6) Oracle against Moab (2:1–3)
    (7) Oracle against Judah (2:4–5)
    (8) Oracle against Israel (2:6–16)
        What Israel Had Done to Deserve Judgment (2:6–8)
        What God Had Done to Establish the Nation (2:9–11)
        How Israel Responded to God's Provision (2:12)
        How God Would Respond to Israel's Rebellion (2:13–16)
  2. Words of Punishment for Israel's Sins (3:1–15)
    (1) Punishment for the Whole Family of Rebels (3:1–2)
        Divine Deliverance from Bondage in Egypt (3:1)
        Divine Punishment for His Covenant People (3:2)
    (2) Justification for the Prophet's Ministry (3:3–8)
        Natural Cause and Effect (3:3–6)
        Spiritual Cause and Effect (3:7–8)
    (3) The Downfall and Devouring of Israel (3:9–12)
        Lessons in Violence and Oppression (3:9–10)
        The Lord's Judgment upon Practitioners of Violence and Oppression (3:11)
        Prophecy of Israel's Devouring (3:12)
    (4) Judgment against Every Aspect of Israel's Life (3:13–15)
        Israel: The house of Jacob (3:13)
        Bethel: The House of God (3:14)
        Residences: Houses of Luxury (3:15)
  3. Words Condemning Israel's Women, Worship, and Stubbornness (4:1–13)
    (1) Condemnation of Samaria's Self-serving Women (4:1–3)
        The Cows of Bashan (4:1)
        The Undignified Departure (4:2–3)
    (2) Condemnation of Israel's Worship (4:4–5)
        Parody of a Priestly Call to Worship (4:4a)
        Proliferation of Sacrifices (4:4b–5)
    (3) Condemnation of Israel's Stubbornness (4:6–13)

Famine (4:6)
Drought (4:7–8)
Plant Disease and Locusts (4:9)
Plague and War (4:10)
Overthrow (4:11)
Final Encounter (4:12)
The Awesome God (4:13)
4. Words of Woe for Israel (5:1–6:14)
(1) Funeral Song for Fallen Israel (5:1–17)
Lament over Fallen Israel (5:1–3)
Appeal to Repentance (5:4–6)
Condemnation of Injustice (5:7)
The Creator's Sovereign Control (5:8–9)
Silent in an Evil Time (5:10–13)
Hope for God's Gracious Response (5:14–15)
Wailing When God Passes Through (5:16–17)
(2) Darkness of the Day of the Lord (5:18–20)
Desiring the Day (5:18)
No Escape from the Day (5:19)
No Brightness in the Day (5:20)
(3) Rejection of Israel's Worship (5:21–27)
Feasts (5:21)
Offerings (5:22)
Music (5:23)
Lack of Justice and Righteousness (5:24)
No Sacrifices or Offerings in the Wilderness (5:25)
Idolatry (5:26)
Exile (5:27)
(4) A Preeminent Nation (6:1–7)
Preeminent in Leadership (6:1–3)
Preeminent in Luxury (6:4–6)
Preeminent in Leaving (6:7)
(5) A Doomed Nation (6:8–14)
The Lord's Oath (6:8)
Death for Survivors (6:9–10)
Total Destruction (6:11)
An Absurd Happening (6:12)
Oppression for a Proud People (6:13–14)

──────────**II. THE WORDS OF AMOS (1:3–6:14)**──────────

The two major sections of Amos are characterized by words (1:3–6:14) and visions (7:1–9:15), although each of these sections contains other kinds of material. Hymnic pieces are evident in both divisions (4:13; 5:8–9; 8:8; 9:5–6). Some sayings follow the fourth (8:1–3) and fifth (9:1–4) visions. Even so the general categories of words and visions suggest a helpful arrangement of the material.

1. Words of Judgment upon the Nations (1:3–2:16)

The oracles against Israel's neighbors formed the introduction to the oracle against Israel. Amos did not travel to the nations surrounding Israel to proclaim the oracles to them. He used the report of God's threatened judgment upon sinful neighboring nations to shock his audience with the following message of God's threatened judgment upon sinful Israel. As J. Barton explains:

> Having won the people's sympathy and agreement, he rounds on them by proclaiming judgment on Israel, too. This technique has two obvious advantages. First, it ensures that the prophet's word of doom will be heard, since he has gained his audience's attention by flattering their feelings of superiority and their natural xenophobia. Secondly, it makes it much harder for them to exculpate themselves or dismiss the prophet's message as mere raving, since they have implicitly conceded that sin and judgment are rightly linked, by their approval of what has gone before.[1]

That some assembly of Israelites was the audience Amos addressed with this extended numerical saying is demonstrated by the second-person language in 2:10.

J. L. Mays questioned the originality of the oracles against the nations. He concluded that "the sayings against Judah and Edom, and probably Tyre," were later additions to the series.[2] However, K. N. Schoville argued convincingly for acceptance of all the oracles as "authentic expressions of the prophet."[3] He based his conclusion on S. Paul's argument of bonding based

---

[1] J. Barton, *Amos's Oracles against the Nations: A Study of Amos 1:3–2:5* (Cambridge: Cambridge University Press, 1980), 3–4.

[2] J. Mays, *Amos*, OTL (Philadelphia: Westminster, 1969), 25.

[3] K. N. Schoville, "A Note on the Oracles of Amos against Gaza, Tyre, and Edom," in *Studies on Prophecy, Supplements to Vetus Testamentum* (Leiden: Brill, 1974), 56. See also J. H. Hayes, *Amos* (Nashville: Abingdon, 1988), 52–55; F. Andersen and D. Freedman, *Amos,* AB (New York: Doubleday, 1989), 213–14; G. F. Hasel, *Understanding the Book of Amos: Basic Issues in Current Interpretations* (Grand Rapids: Baker, 1991), 57–69.

on catchwords and other literary devices.[4] The oracles against Gaza, Tyre, and Edom appear to be linked by such literary devices. Gaza and Tyre were charged with the crime of taking captive "whole communities" (1:6,9) and delivering them to Edom.

The seven judgment speeches against Israel's neighbors show movement toward a climax. Part of the movement is from foreigners (Aram, Philistia, Phoenicia) to blood relatives (Edom, Ammon, Moab) to sister kingdom (Judah). R. Alter called the prophet's pattern in these oracles "a rhetoric of entrapment."[5] The audience would have been delighted with the seven speeches, including Judah as the subject of the seventh oracle, since seven would have suggested completeness and finality (note the judgment formula in 1:3 and elsewhere adds up to seven). Until Amos began the eighth oracle against Israel, his audience did not realize they were the subject of the prophet's climactic oracle, although the order of the first four oracles in geographically encircling Israel (Damascus in the northeast, Gaza in the southwest, Tyre in the northwest, and Edom in the southeast) also suggests the focus was on Israel. When the Israelite audience began to celebrate the judgment about to fall on their enemies, Amos sprang the trap. He made clear with the eighth oracle that Israel was the primary target of the Lord's judgment because their guilt exceeded that of their neighbors.[6]

The general form of 1:3–2:16 is that of messenger speech. (1) It begins with the introductory messenger formula, "This is what the LORD says." (2) Next comes a statement of the certainty of judgment, "For three sins of . . . even for four, I will not turn back my wrath." (3) Then follows the specific charge of guilt. (4) The succeeding item is the announcement of punishment, "I will send fire." (5) The closing element is the concluding messenger formula, "says the LORD."

Variations are found, however, in the general pattern.[7] The fifth element is absent from the Tyre, Edom, and Judah oracles. That element is altered in the Gaza oracle to "says the Sovereign [ʾădōnāy] LORD" instead of simply "says the LORD." The closing oracle formula in the message to Israel is "declares [nĕʾum] the LORD." What is the meaning of these variations?

Interpreters explain the variations in the fifth element in different ways.

---

[4] S. M. Paul, "Amos 1:3–2:3: A Concatenous Literary Pattern," *JBL* 90 (1971): 399.

[5] R. Alter, *The Art of Biblical Poetry* (New York: Basic, 1985), 144. In modern slang Amos, once he observed the shocked expressions on the listeners' faces, might have exclaimed, "Gotcha!"

[6] R. B. Chisholm, Jr., "'For Three Sins . . . Even for Four': The Numerical Sayings in Amos," *BSac* 147 (1990): 190.

[7] Andersen and Freedman have an excellent and thorough treatment of what they call "The Great Set Speech" in Amos 1:3–2:16 (*Amos*, AB [New York: Doubleday, 1989], 341–69). They argue forcefully for the integrity of all of the oracles as the work of Amos.

Some take the position that variations reflect later editorial work on an earlier, limited number of oracles against the nations.[8] This assessment is applied especially to the shortened oracles against Tyre, Edom, and Judah. Other interpreters see in the variation evidence of creativity.[9] This is the more reasonable view since a later editor adding oracles would likely have followed the pattern set by the original composition. Amos altered the form for the sake of variety and to stimulate interest.

J. Limburg has stated that "the number seven appears to play a significant role both in the structure of the book of Amos and in the makeup of certain of the sayings."[10] He concluded from his study that Amos used divine speech formulas as a structuring device to introduce or conclude prophetic sayings as well as to identify them as coming from the Lord. The book contains forty-nine divine speech formulas arranged in such a way that each major section has seven (in one case fourteen, 1:3–2:16) of them. Since seven is a symbol of completeness, this divine speech formula usage is a way of certifying the book as a whole and each section of the book as the word of the Lord.[11]

The placement of the oracles against foreign nations at the beginning of the book is unique to Amos in prophetic literature. Perhaps the reason was to get Israel's attention and to gain their agreement that the threatened judgment against the nations was justified. One can imagine how pleased Amos's audience must have been to hear threats of judgment against many of their most hated enemies. Perhaps an escalating round of amens accompanied the criss-cross pattern of the prophet's message. At least that may have been the case until Israel's sister kingdom, Judah, was named. Perhaps some recognized in the mention of Judah a clue that Israel would be next.

These chapters assume the Lord's sovereign authority over all peoples and nations by virtue of his role as Creator and King of all the earth.[12] This assumption of God's universal kingship formed the basis of Israelite faith, particularly in how they related to the rest of the world and in their expectations about the eschatological future.[13] It pervades Scripture from the beginning of biblical revelation in Genesis 1 to the subjection of all things to his lordship in the Book of Revelation (cf. also 1 Cor 15:24–28). God's entering a special relationship with a select group such as Israel did not mean his relin-

---

[8] Mays, *Amos*, 25; Wolff, *Joel and Amos*, 140.

[9] Hayes, *Amos*, 55; Stuart, *Hosea–Jonah*, 309.

[10] J. Limburg, "Sevenfold Structures in the Book of Amos," *JBL* 106 (1987): 217.

[11] Ibid., 222–23.

[12] Barton's objection that this would mean the nations were "condemned for breaking an edict they were unaware of" (*Amos's Oracles against the Nations*, 43) is countered by the apostle Paul in Rom 1:18–32; 2:14–15. T. J. Finley observes that "Barton fails to consider the creation theology of Amos" and cites Amos 4:13 (*Joel, Amos, Obadiah* [Chicago: Moody, 1990], 138).

[13] W. J. Dumbrell, *Covenant and Creation: A Theology of the Old Testament Covenants* (Grand Rapids: Baker, 1984), 34.

quishing his role as Governor of the world he had created. It was this role that had led to his judgment of the first human family in Genesis 3, of the world of Noah's day in Genesis 6–9, and of the Canaanites in the Book of Joshua. It will also be in this role that God will judge the earth in the last days (cf. Isa 24:1–23; Jer 25:15–38; Joel 3:1–16; Zech 14:1–15). Each foreign nation is accountable directly to God for its actions. Even though no formal covenant agreement binds them to God, the nations are subject to God's standards of conduct, the breach of which can lead to indictment and appropriate punishment (cf. Rom 1:18–32; 2:14–15). In the words of W. Eichrodt, there is "a universal ethical will of God, which gives the moral norms established within his covenant people validity for the whole world."[14] The view that the cosmic Lord will judge the earth, he says, "drives prophetic thinking on to the unity and universality of the morality required by God, which is binding on all who bear the face of Man."[15] All the more could Judah and Israel be indicted and punished for breach of God's standards. Their covenant with God did not give them immunity.

(1) Oracle against Aram (1:3–5)

> ³This is what the LORD says:
> "For three sins of Damascus,
>   even for four, I will not turn back [my wrath].
> Because she threshed Gilead
>   with sledges having iron teeth,
> ⁴I will send fire upon the house of Hazael
>   that will consume the fortresses of Ben-Hadad.
> ⁵I will break down the gate of Damascus;
>   I will destroy the king who is in the Valley of Aven
> and the one who holds the scepter in Beth Eden.
>   The people of Aram will go into exile to Kir,"
>   says the LORD.

1:3 "Damascus" was the capital of Aram, located to the northeast of Israel. The Arameans were Israel's most frequent and most powerful enemy. Gilead, the Transjordan Israelite region south of Damascus, was attractive territory for Aramean expansion. Territorial disputes between Israel and Aram often erupted into border wars characterized by terrorist atrocities. Such wars were common during the ninth and eighth centuries B.C., not only between Israel and Aram but among the other small nations of the region as well.

The oracle against Damascus has all the elements of messenger speech mentioned earlier. It begins with the messenger formula, "This is what the

---

[14] W. Eichrodt, *Theology of the Old Testament* (Philadelphia: Westminster, 1967), 2:332.
[15] Ibid., 2:334.

LORD says."[16] With it the prophet claimed authoritative status for himself and for his message. The switch from third person in the introduction to first person in the message is noteworthy. With the introductory third-person phrase, Amos pointed to the source and authority for his message. Then he cast the message in the first-person divine speech in order to confront his audience directly and to call for their response.

What this messenger formula means for any messenger who would speak for God is that the messenger's authority is in God, the sender, not in the one who delivers the message. Messengers must live in such intimate relationship with God as to know his mind and heart, and they must be faithful to deliver God's message clearly regardless of how it is received. The concern must be to be true to God rather than to be popular with the people (see 7:10–17 and comments there).

The second element in the Damascus oracle is the general declaration of certain judgment, "For three sins of Damascus, even for four, I will not turn back [my wrath]." Graduated numerical sayings are common in the Old Testament.[17] Sometimes the elements in the numbered saying are listed, the last serving as the climax of the series.[18] Here only one element is listed, as with the oracle against Israel. The one listed may be the fourth and climactic "sin" or simply representative of all.[19]

How Amos's audience understood his use of the graduated numerical sayings is not clear. Did the prophet intend the numbers "three" and "four" to be taken literally or symbolically?[20] Did his audience know the three sins not listed? "Three" probably represented fullness; and "four," an overflow. The one sin named is the one that pushed God's patience to the breaking point.[21] God's judgment had to fall.

"Sins" (pĕšaʿîm) is one of the three major words for sin in the Old Testament. The term may be translated "transgressions," "rebellions," "crimes," or "sins." The wrongdoing named in each oracle represented rebellion against God's standard of conduct, not simply rebellion against Judah or Israel based on prior treaty agreements. With the sin named, Damascus had exceeded the limit of God's tolerance.

---

[16] Hayes prefers "attribution formula" to "messenger formula" as a description of this introductory phrase (Amos, 69).

[17] Prov 6:16–19; 30:15–16,18–19,21–31; Ps 62:11; Job 5:19; 33:14–15; Hos 6:2; Mic 5:5; and Eccl 11:2.

[18] Prov 6:16–19.

[19] Mays, Amos, 23–24; R. L. Smith, "Amos," BBC 7 (Nashville: Broadman, 1972), 91.

[20] Limburg ("Sevenfold Structures in the Book of Amos," 222) cited M. Weiss's suggestion that what is meant by "three transgressions and for four" is three plus four, or seven ("The Pattern of Number Sequence in Amos 1–2," JBL 86 [1967]: 419). As attractive as that suggestion is, nothing in the text implies that the reader/listener should add the two numbers.

[21] Mays, Amos, 24; R. Smith, "Amos," 7:91; Hayes, Amos, 69–70.

"I will not turn back my wrath" is literally "I will not cause it to turn/ return." The pronoun is masculine and can be either "it" or "him." If the pronoun "it" refers to the Lord's awesome voice in v. 2, that would be a normal grammatical connection. "It" may point forward to the announced judgment by fire, in spite of Wolff's reservation that a feminine pronoun would be expected.[22] The reference may be to the people indicated by the place named (Damascus). If so, God would be stating his unwillingness to take back in a treaty relationship the people of Damascus. The reason for God's decision was their repeated rebellious acts.[23]

The third element in the Damascus oracle is the identification of one specific sin. That sin was brutal treatment of some Gileadites conquered by the Arameans. Both the Septuagint and a Qumran fragment of Amos have "the pregnant women of Gilead" as the recipients of Aramean cruelty. This reading is obviously connected to 1:13b. Regardless, the cruel and inhuman treatment of the Gileadites is the concern here.

"Threshed" refers to the process of separating seed from the stalk. The process could involve animals walking back and forth over the harvested grain piled on a flat rock (Deut 25:4). Use of sledges with iron spikes driven through them increased the efficiency of threshing. Such an implement drawn over helpless captives, if taken literally, brings to mind shamelessly brutal conduct. But taking the description metaphorically does not lessen the image of extreme cruelty.[24]

Was a recent event of threshing Gilead in the memory of Amos's audience? Subsequent reference to Hazael and Ben-Hadad is inconclusive evidence, since these dynastic names were used for generations to designate Aramean rulers.[25] The brutality pictured in the imagery probably summarized all sorts

---

[22] Paul, *Amos,* 46–47; Wolff, *Joel and Amos,* 128, n. b.

[23] M. L. Barre', "The Meaning of *l' sybnw* in Amos 1:3–2:6," *JBL* 105 (1986): 611–31. Barre' takes the expression לֹא אֲשִׁיבֶנּוּ in Amos 1:3–2:16 to be a description of Yahweh's decision not to take back into treaty relationship the people named because of their rebellious actions. The people named in each case were vassals to Yahweh, the divine suzerain. Barre' based his interpretation on other biblical texts (Jer 15:19; Lam 5:21; Ps 80:4,8,20) and on similar Hittite and Babylonian usage. This line of interpretation fits the general impression that God is sovereign over the nations named and that all are accountable to God for their rebellious acts. Wolff (*Joel and Amos,* 153–54) translated the suffix on the verb שׁוּב as "it" and interpreted the "it" as the judgment of God about to be spoken. The NIV adds "my wrath" to the text to reflect the translator's interpretation of the suffix on the verb שׁוּב. R. P. Knierim has argued similarly that the suffix refers to God's "anger," אַף ("'I Will Not Cause It to Return' in Amos 1 and 2," in *Canon and Authority,* ed. G. W. Coats and B. O. Long [Philadelphia: Fortress, 1977], 163–75). Against this interpretation is the fact that nowhere in Amos 1–2 is the Lord's anger mentioned explicitly.

[24] D. A. Hubbard takes the term "sledges having iron teeth" to be "a figure of speech implying extreme cruelty and utter thoroughness in the treatment of those who opposed the Damascan invasion" (*Joel and Amos,* TOTC [Downers Grove: InterVarsity, 1989], 131).

[25] Wolff, *Joel and Amos,* 156.

of horrible treatment experienced by previous generations of Gileadites. Because Aramean aggression frequently focused on Gilead, some in Amos's audience likely would have had knowledge of such brutal conduct.

1:4 The fourth element in the Damascus oracle is the announcement of God's judgment. Three first-person verbs in vv. 4–5 outline God's actions: "I will send," "I will break down," and "I will destroy."[26] The Lord himself will be the agent of judgment, though such language would not rule out his use of an intermediate agent. The Assyrians actually carried out the threatened punishment of Aram.[27]

"Fire" was an occasional tool of warfare in Old Testament times (2 Kgs 8:12). Destruction by fire was a type of covenant curse (Deut 32:21–22) and an expression of divine wrath (Gen 19:24; Num 11:1–3). The image of God sending fire suggests the concept of Holy War. The Lord was portrayed as the military leader of Israel's army. Whatever was devoted to destruction (*ḥerem*) was "either killed, if alive, or burned, if flammable (Deut 7:25–26; 12:3; Num 31:10; Judg 1:8)."[28] The particular property of fire that made it suitable as a method of warfare was its power to consume (*ʾākal*, "eat," "devour").

The targets of the Lord's judgment by fire would be "the house of Hazael" and "the fortresses of Ben-Hadad." Two or possibly three Ben-Hadads appear in the Old Testament (1 Kgs 15:18,20; 20:1ff.; 2 Kgs 6:24; 8:7,9; 13:3). The one Hazael mentioned became king of Aram by murdering the reigning king Ben-Hadad (2 Kgs 8:14–15). Assyrian documents refer to the new dynasty he founded as "the house of Hazael,"[29] the same expression used here in Amos. His son Ben-Hadad succeeded him (2 Kgs 13:3). Rezin, who may have been king in Damascus when God sent Amos to Israel as his prophet, was the last king of Aram-Damascus before the Assyrians annexed it in 732 B.C. He probably was not a descendant of Hazael.[30]

"House" may denote the reigning house, the reigning king, or the royal palace. "Fortresses" (*ʾarmĕnôt*) probably designate fortified towns, distinct from fortified city walls and the royal palace. Neither would be a match for the Lord's consuming fire.

1:5 Other places and rulers than the Damascus king would fall under the Lord's judgment. To break the "gate" (or bar that secured the gate) of Damascus would allow an attacking enemy to destroy that city, its king (perhaps Rezin), and its people. The Lord himself was the one who threatened to shatter the gate-bar of Damascus. He would also "destroy" (*kārat*, "cut off") two

---

[26] Use of first-person singular verbs is reminiscent of the style found in Mesopotamian war annals. See Paul, *Amos,* 50.

[27] 2 Kgs 16:9.

[28] Stuart, *Hosea-Jonah,* 311.

[29] Mays, *Amos,* 29.

[30] See W. T. Pitard, "Rezin," *ABD* 5.708–9; Hayes, *Amos,* 73.

other rulers. The first of these sat as ruler (*yôšēb,* "one sitting")[31] in the Valley of Aven (meaning "wickedness"). The second held the "scepter" (an insignia of rulership) in Beth Eden (meaning "house of pleasure"). Who were these rulers, and to what geographical areas did these epithets refer? Current available evidence leaves the answers to these questions uncertain.[32]

What seems clear is that the Lord's judgment would affect three different rulers in as many geographical locations. Only Damascus was named in the indictment. But all the areas would suffer the punishment. This same pattern of indictment and punishment holds for the Philistine oracle that follows.

The final element of the Lord's judgment against the Arameans is their removal to Kir, the place of their origin (Amos 9:7). "People of Aram" is an inclusive expression, referring to Arameans living in the region between the Euphrates and northern Transjordan. The location of Kir is uncertain, even though it is mentioned in Isaiah (22:6), Amos (1:5; 9:7), and 2 Kings (16:9). Deportation of the Arameans to Kir would put an end to their proud history.

The closing messenger formula is a claim of authority for the messenger and his message. God was the source and the enforcer of the message Amos declared. Ultimately, the judgment of God will fall on the nation or individual guilty of brutal and inhumane treatment of fellow human beings.

(2) Oracle against Philistia (1:6–8)

> **[6]This is what the LORD says:**
> **"For three sins of Gaza,**
> **even for four, I will not turn back [my wrath].**
> **Because she took captive whole communities**
> **[7] and sold them to Edom,**
> **I will send fire upon the walls of Gaza**
> **that will consume her fortresses.**
> **[8]I will destroy the king of Ashdod**
> **and the one who holds the scepter in Ashkelon.**
> **I will turn my hand against Ekron,**
> **till the last of the Philistines is dead,"**
> **says the Sovereign LORD.**

The similarity of this and subsequent oracles against the nations to the first one in the series makes detailed analysis unnecessary. Amos established the formula in the first oracle. All that changes from oracle to oracle is both the name of the foreign nation and the nature of the sin committed. Gaza is the

---

[31] Not "one inhabiting" as a collective for "inhabitants," since it is matched in the next line by *tômēk,* "one wielding" a scepter. Each participle appears to refer to a ruler.

[32] Hayes's identification of Pekah as the one ruling in the valley of Aven and Shamshi-ilu as the one holding the scepter in Beth Eden seems worthy of consideration (*Amos,* 76–78).

only Philistine city-state named initially in the oracle against Philistia. However, three other Philistine city-states were threatened with God's judgment: Ashdod, Ashkelon, and Ekron (v. 8). Only Gath of the Philistine pentapolis is missing. Similarly, in the judgment against Aram-Damascus only the city of Damascus is mentioned in the opening, but then three locations are mentioned at the end, followed by a reference to "the people of Aram" (1:5). Here following the mention of three cities is a reference to "the Philistines." The first oracle, then, is against Aram under the name of its chief city, Damascus, and the second is against the Philistines under the name of its chief city, Gaza. Likewise, the third oracle is against Phoenicia under the name of its chief city, Tyre.[33]

1:6 The commercial and political importance of Gaza may account for the prominence of that city-state in the Philistine oracle. Gaza was a port city, located just inland from the Mediterranean coast and on the main north-south trade route.

The sin of Gaza was the capture and sale of either "whole communities" of people, including women and children, or people at peace with Gaza. The word *šĕlēmâ* may be translated either "whole" or "peaceful." Deportation of an entire community (or a community keeping a covenant of peace with Gaza) was only one aspect of Gaza's double-edged sin. Sale of captives to Edom was the other side of it.

Who the captives were and what Edom did with them are left unexpressed. One clue may be found in the oracles against Tyre (1:9–10) and Edom (1:11–12). Amos accused Tyre of "disregarding a treaty of brotherhood" and Edom of pursuing "his brother" with a sword. These statements hint at a breach of covenant. Such a treaty was established by David with Hiram, king of Tyre (2 Sam 5:11; cf. 1 Kgs 5:1ff.). David's friendliness with Achish of Gath suggests the possibility that such a treaty existed with the Philistines (1 Sam 27:1–7). The "whole communities" may have been Israelite.[34]

Philistine border raids on Israel and Judah often resulted in the deportation of captives. Probably the exiles referred to here were Judean, or Israelite, or both. Edom may have used the captives for their own labor needs or sold them to yet other parties.

The concern of Amos seems to have been the freedom and dignity of persons regardless of their national origin. Sale of such captives for use as slave laborers was to treat precious humans made in the image of God (Gen 1:26–27) as mere commodities. The driving force behind these atrocities was nothing higher than the profit of the mighty.

---

[33] Cf. Finley, *Joel, Amos, Obadiah,* 142, 148.

[34] Hubbard confidently asserts that "the Philistines raided the neighbour towns of Judah and Israel and sold their prisoners to Edom" (*Joel and Amos,* 133).

1:7 First-person verbs (cf. 1:5) describe the direct action of God against Gaza, Ashdod, Ashkelon, and Ekron (vv. 7–8). "Fire upon the walls of Gaza" suggests a military attack under the Lord's direction. The "fortresses" of Gaza would succumb to the consuming (*ʾakelâ*, "devour," "eat") fire of God. The fire would gobble up Gaza's defenses.

1:8 The Lord threatened to destroy the rulers of Ashdod and Ashkelon. The participle translated "king" is literally "one sitting," a reference to the ruler of Ashdod. Another participle, "one who holds" (*tômek*), apparently refers to the ruler in Ashkelon. The one holding the scepter is a figurative description of the one wielding royal authority. Wording here is almost identical to the structure found in v. 5. The main difference is the place names. Like Gaza, Ashdod was a coastal city located about twenty miles north of Gaza. Ashkelon was about halfway between the two.

Ekron is identified with Khirbet el-Muqanna (Tel Miqne) about twelve miles inland and northeast of Ashdod.[35] God's threat of judgment upon Ekron is clear. "I will turn my hand" is a Hebraism for "I will turn my power." The preposition attached to Ekron means "against." Ekron would feel the full strength of God against its inhabitants.

"Till the last of the Philistines is dead" is literally "and the remnant of the Philistines will perish." "Remnant" has a military ring to it, since it usually designated those who survived a battle. No Philistine could hope for survival. That was the solemn declaration of "the Sovereign LORD," as the closing messenger formula indicates. Though the practice of taking, deporting, and selling captives was common, Philistine involvement in it had not gone unnoticed and would not go unpunished. "The Sovereign LORD"[36] would see to that.

The God of Amos was no national deity limited in power to particular geographical boundaries or to a special nation. He ruled and rules over all nations including Judah and Israel, Aram and Philistia, Tyre and Edom, Ammon and Moab, the United States of America and the United Kingdom. The theology of Amos allowed room "only for one God supreme over life and history."[37]

(3) Oracle against Phoenicia (1:9–10)

> **⁹This is what the LORD says:**
> **"For three sins of Tyre,**
>   **even for four, I will not turn back [my wrath].**

---

[35] Hayes, *Amos,* 85; Wolff, *Joel and Amos,* 138.

[36] "Sovereign LORD" is literally "Lord Yahweh." Yahweh is the name of Israel's covenant God. The preceding oracle is the settled decision of Israel's God. אֲדֹנָי, "lord" ("Sovereign"), is not found in 1:5,15 or 2:3. It is missing in the LXX, though it is attested in many versions and in the Amos manuscript from Murabbaʿat.

[37] C. G. Howie, "Expressly for Our Time: The Theology of Amos," *Int* 13 (1959): 276.

> Because she sold whole communities of captives to Edom,
> 10 disregarding a treaty of brotherhood,
> I will send fire upon the walls of Tyre
> that will consume her fortresses."

Most interpreters acknowledge what appears to be a deliberate crisscross pattern in the oracles against the nations. Damascus was in the northeast. Gaza was in the southwest. Tyre was in the northwest. Edom, Ammon, and Moab were all in the southeast. Judah was in the south. Amos's Israelite audience must have grown less and less enthusiastic and more and more apprehensive as the prophet honed in on Israel, the final target.

1:9 Tyre was the strongest of the Phoenician cities in the mid-eighth century B.C. Its wealth and influence derived from its strategic position as the hub of a vast trading empire (Ezek 26–28). One of Tyre's commercial activities was slave trading.[38] This activity links the oracle against Tyre with the preceding oracle against Gaza. The indictment against Tyre is a similar, though shortened, version of the indictment against Gaza. They "sold whole communities of captives to Edom." Unlike the oracle against Gaza, this oracle elaborates on the act's treacherous nature.

The phrase translated "disregarding a treaty of brotherhood" is literally "and they did not remember a covenant [*berît*] of brothers." "Did not remember" does not mean they forgot in some kind of mental lapse. To remember a covenant meant to fulfill its obligations, and not to remember it meant to break the covenant (cf. Gen 9:16; Ps 105:8; Jer 14:21).[39] What kind of covenant and between what partners are questions left unanswered. "A covenant of brothers" is a unique expression in the Bible. Treaties between states were common in the time of Amos. Solomon of Israel entered a covenant with Hiram of Tyre (1 Kgs 5:12). With Ahab's marriage to the Sidonian Jezebel, Israel must have entered into a treaty with the Phoenicians (1 Kgs 16:31). Such covenants made the partners "brothers" (1 Kgs 9:13), a term describing a close tie characterized by loyalty and love. Breach of covenant (probably between Israel and Tyre) made the sinful act of selling slaves (probably Israelite) to Edom far worse.[40]

Broken treaties have marred the pages of history from ancient to modern times. God has a low tolerance level for those who break treaties, who take away human freedom and dignity, and whose motive is material profit. Such people should brace themselves for the destructive judgment of God.

---

[38] Paul, *Amos*, 59.

[39] A. Bowling, זָכַר (*zakar*), *TWOT*, 241

[40] S. Paul may be right in his conclusion that "there is no need, however, to identify the 'exiled population' as consisting of Israelites" (*Amos*, 59). At the same time nothing in the text argues against that identification.

1:10   The Lord's judgment by fire would fall on Tyre with destructive force. "Fire," a common method of warfare (see comment on 1:4), suggests the way Tyre would experience God's judgment.

The Assyrians subdued Tyre several times and forced them to pay tribute. Then Alexander the Great conquered the island fortress after a seven-month siege and sold thirty thousand into slavery. The Saracens finally destroyed it in A.D. 1291.[41]

The oracle was not expanded to include other Phoenician cities in the Lord's judgment, as the two previous oracles were. Neither is it rounded out with a closing messenger formula. The absence of the closing messenger formula brings the oracle to an abrupt and startling halt. Perhaps there is some significance in the pattern (or oral rhythm) of the formula's use in oracles one and two, its absence in three and four, its use in five and six, its absence in seven, and its alteration ("declares the LORD") in eight.

(4) Oracle against Edom (1:11–12)

> [11]This is what the LORD says:
> "For three sins of Edom,
>   even for four, I will not turn back [my wrath].
> Because he pursued his brother with a sword,
>   stifling all compassion,
> because his anger raged continually
>   and his fury flamed unchecked,
> [12]I will send fire upon Teman
>   that will consume the fortresses of Bozrah."

Edom was an enemy of Israel throughout most of Israel's history.[42] The Edom oracle completed the crisscross pattern of movement from nation to nation on the compass points surrounding Israel. It also begins the group of oracles against nations that had ethnic connections with Israel.

1:11   Edom's relationship to Israel in the time of Amos is not clear. From the days of King David (2 Sam 8:13–14; 1 Kgs 11:15–16) Edom at times had been subject to and at other times independent of Israel. Always the mood was hostile, stemming back to the prenatal struggle between the twins, Jacob (Israel) and Esau (Edom; cf. Gen 25:22–23). Most of the time Edom was subject to Israel.

The specific sin of Edom was hostile action against his brother. Most interpreters identify the "brother" as Israel.[43] Some see the most likely setting for

---

[41] Cf. J. Niehaus, "Amos," in *The Minor Prophets,* ed. T. E. McComiskey (Grand Rapids: Baker, 1992), 1:349; H. J. Katzenstein and D. R. Edwards, "Tyre," *ABD* 6.686–92.

[42] For more on Edom see Obadiah and the commentary later in this volume.

[43] Hayes, Honeycutt, Mays, Stuart, Wolff.

the action of Edom against Israel as the aftermath of the destruction of Jerusalem by the Babylonians.[44] The language is similar to the other Old Testament materials associated with that fateful event.[45] Since the hostility between Edom and Israel was the norm, however, the attitudes and actions described in v. 11 fit any number of settings. The adverbs "continually" and "unchecked" suggest that "the contemporary incident is an outburst of the age-old feuding between the brothers that Amos is condemning."[46] After their rebellion from Jehoram (2 Chr 21:8–10) they may have joined an alliance with the Philistines and Arabs to attack Jerusalem (2 Chr 21:16–17).

The object of Edom's pursuit was not the nation's enemy but "his brother," possibly suggesting a treaty partner. The verbs "pursued" (*rādap*) and "stifling" (*šiḥēt,* "destroy" or "annihilate") are terms associated with warfare. Pursuit with intent to kill was Edom's singular purpose. Any natural inclination to show "compassion"[47] to a brother was suppressed sharply. They would not let brotherly love deter them from their murderous intent.

With Edom's pursuit of his brother unchecked by "compassion," his anger "raged" (*tārap,* "tear" like an animal; cf. Job 16:9; 18:4; Ps 7:2 [Eng., v. 3]) on and on, and his fury blazed perpetually.[48] The prophet viewed Edom's treatment of his brother as "hideously extravagant."[49] Anger, like a bonfire, will die down in time. Adding fuel to the fire keeps it going. That is what Edom did. Relationships in many families are constantly stirred up by family members whose anger rages on and on, unchecked by brotherly love.

1:12 God's threatened judgment on Edom would be "fire," or warfare, affecting the whole country. At least the two place names, Teman in the south and Bozrah in the north, apparently refer to districts. By reference to these extreme regions, the implication is that the judgment would encompass the entire land. One of the terrifying features of God's judgment (especially when warfare is the instrument) is that the innocent often suffer alongside the guilty.

---

[44] Mays, Wolff.

[45] Ezek 35:5–6; Obad 9–14; Ps 137:7; Isa 34:5ff; Jer 49:7ff; Joel 3:19.

[46] Andersen and Freedman, *Amos,* 266.

[47] רַחֲמָיו is a plural of intensity meaning "his compassions." The term has tender, emotional, familial associations in its usage. Edom deliberately ignored the natural loving feeling between family members. Andersen and Freedman, however, because of the parallelism with the first line, prefer to translate "his allies," yielding "and he destroyed his allies" (*Amos,* 266–67).

[48] The verb translated "flamed" is שְׁמָרָה from שָׁמַר, "watch, guard," although there is an Akk. cognate *šamāru,* "to rage." While the final ה makes it appear to be third feminine singular, it is vocalized as a masculine, whereas "fury" is feminine. It probably is better to translate the line "he retained his fury endlessly," assuming the final ה is a resumptive feminine suffix without *mappiq* (GKC § 58g). Edom nursed his hostility, tending it like a shepherd (cf. Jer 3:5). Cf. Niehaus, "Amos," 2:351.

[49] Hayes, *Amos,* 93.

(5) Oracle against Ammon (1:13–15)

¹³This is what the LORD says:
"For three sins of Ammon,
  even for four, I will not turn back [my wrath].
Because he ripped open the pregnant women of Gilead
  in order to extend his borders,
¹⁴I will set fire to the walls of Rabbah
  that will consume her fortresses
amid war cries on the day of battle,
  amid violent winds on a stormy day.
¹⁵Her king will go into exile,
  he and his officials together,"

says the LORD.

Ammon was located on the east side of the Jordan between Gilead on the north and Moab in the south. Rabbah, called Philadelphia in Greco-Roman times and Amman since the Muslim conquest of the region, was located on the King's Highway about twenty-five miles northeast of the Dead Sea.[50] Like many of the nations in these oracles Ammon had a long-standing relationship with Israel (Gen 19:30–38).

1:13 The sin of Ammon was that "he ripped open the pregnant women of Gilead." In the "three sins . . . even for four" formula, this atrocity was the nation's overflowing sin. What circumstances caused the Ammonites to resort to such brutal treatment of the pregnant women of Gilead? Were the perpetrators at war with the region? This act was a common feature of border wars to terrorize and to decimate the population (2 Kgs 8:12; 15:16; Hos 13:16 [14:1]). In all four references to this heinous crime in the Old Testament, the same verb, "ripped open" (*bāqaʿ*), is used. The stated reason for the atrocity against the pregnant women of Gilead was to extend the nation's borders. Their purely materialistic motive added to the wrongness of the act.[51]

1:14 Amos announced the judgment of God upon Ammon for their brutal treatment of the pregnant women. God's involvement in the judgment would be direct, "I will set fire," and destructive, "that will consume her fortresses." The method of judgment would be warfare. God's judgment often comes in the form of natural forces, such as fire (warfare) and storm.[52]

---

[50] Paul, *Amos,* 69.

[51] S. Paul cited a Middle-Assyrian hymn composed to extol the conquests of the king who slit the wombs of pregnant women, gouged out the eyes of infants, and cut the throats of their strong men. Comparing that account with Ammon's brutal atrocity, he wrote: "For Tiglathpileser I, such behavior was worthy of heroic adulation; for Amos, it was an example of a brutal act of savage and unforgivable cruelty committed against defenseless human beings" (*Amos,* 68).

[52] Paul concluded that "on the day of battle" and "violent winds on a stormy day" are "variant expressions for the 'Day of the LORD'" (ibid.).

1:15 The result of God's judgment on Ammon would be exile for the king and his court. "Officials" could designate representatives of a foreign king (Gen 12:15). Exile was a usual method of handling conquered people. "Says the LORD" (cf. 1:5; 2:3; 4:18) cites the prophet's authority for his message.

(6) Oracle against Moab (2:1–3)

¹ This is what the LORD says:
"For three sins of Moab,
  even for four, I will not turn back [my wrath].
Because he burned, as if to lime,
₂ the bones of Edom's king,
 I will send fire upon Moab
  that will consume the fortresses of Kerioth.
Moab will go down in great tumult
  amid war cries and the blast of the trumpet.
³I will destroy her ruler
  and kill all her officials with him,"
                                  says the LORD.

Moab was a brother nation to Ammon (Gen 19:30–38), located east of the Dead Sea with Edom to the south and Ammon to the north. Israel and Judah had varied relationships with Moab across an extended time period. King David treated Moab harshly, even though he had Moabite ancestors (Ruth 4:17–22; 1 Sam 22:3–4). Israel controlled Moab while Omri was king of Israel. Moab's King Mesha rebelled against Israelite control after the death of King Ahab, Omri's son and successor (2 Kgs 1:1; 3:5).

2:1 Moab's representative crime neither harmed Israel nor concerned them in any way. Desecration of an Edomite king's remains was Moab's sin. Border fortifications between Moab and Edom suggest the probability that the two nations engaged in armed conflict from time to time. Warfare may have been the setting for the Moabite atrocity against the king of Edom.[53] Either Edom's king was burned to death, or his corpse was burned, or his skeletal remains were exhumed and burned to lime. The last suggestion best fits the wording, since the specific reference is to "the bones of Edom's king."

Burning the bones to lime suggests total destruction.[54] The Targum interpreted the term rendered "as if to lime" to mean that the Moabites used the ashes of the king's bones in a substance to whitewash houses. The treatment of a human being as mere material was reason enough for Amos's indictment.

---

[53] A possible occasion may have been the war between Moab and an alliance of Israel, Judah, and Edom (2 Kgs 3:5–10,26–27).

[54] Andersen and Freedman interpreted the meaning of this act as "a violation of the sanctity of a tomb" (*Amos,* 288). Hubbard explains the point of this act as "degradation of personhood" (*Joel and Amos,* 137).

Moab's atrocious act disturbed the Edomite king's resting place and in Moabite and Edomite thought prevented peace in the afterlife and perhaps even immortality.[55] As J. Niehaus explains: "Crimes against humanity bring God's punishment. This observation is a powerful motivation for God's people to oppose the mistreatment and neglect of their fellow human beings."[56]

2:2–3　For God to send fire on Moab was for him to bring an enemy nation against them. That interpretation is strengthened by the military language in the rest of the oracle. "Consume the fortresses," "great tumult," "war cries," and "blast of the trumpet" represent the sights and sounds of battle.

"Consume" describes a characteristic of fire. The power of fire to consume fortresses, buildings, and walls made it an effective method of warfare. "Go down" means "die." The nation would die as a result of God's judgment by fire. Two targets of Moab's punishment would be the fortresses of Kerioth and the nation's ruler (lit., "judge," i.e., the ruler as responsible for justice) and officials (as in 1:15). The fortresses would be consumed by the fire, the ruler cut off, and the officials slain. Indeed Moab would die.

(7) Oracle against Judah (2:4–5)

[4]This is what the LORD says:
"For three sins of Judah,
　even for four, I will not turn back [my wrath].
Because they have rejected the law of the LORD
　and have not kept his decrees,
because they have been led astray by false gods,
　the gods their ancestors followed,
[5]I will send fire upon Judah
　that will consume the fortresses of Jerusalem."

The geographical swings of the oracles against the nations have moved full circle around Israel. With the Judah oracle the swing is toward the center, since Judah, a sister kingdom, was in the same geographical area as Israel. The Judah oracle is different from the preceding oracles in the number and kind of items in the indictment. The most significant difference is that whereas previous oracles cited various forms of inhumanity perpetrated on others as the repeated indictment, the wrongs cited in the Judah oracle are covenant related. Breach of covenant was Judah's intolerable rebellion against God.

Many scholars have been convinced that the Judah oracle is not an Amos original.[57] The basis for that conclusion is that this oracle, along with the ones

---

[55] Stuart, *Hosea-Jonah,* 315.
[56] Niehaus, *Amos,* 2:358.
[57] Wolff, *Joel and Amos,* 112; Mays, *Amos,* 34.

against Tyre and Edom, is unlike the others in structure and components. Missing from the three oracles, for example, is the concluding messenger formula (but see comment at 1:10). It is like the others in general outline.[58] But Andersen and Freedman cogently argue that discarding the Tyre, Edom, and Judah oracles on the basis of their differences when compared to the others "is heavy-handed, and the hypothesis is a weak one when every oracle in the series has to be touched up or else crossed out to make the theory work."[59]

2:4 The specific sins of Judah calling down divine judgment were (1) rejection of "the law [tôrâ] of the LORD" as evidenced by (2) failure to keep the Lord's decrees (i.e., his specific instructions) and resulting in (3) being led astray by the lies their ancestors followed. All these involve rebellion against the Lord and breach of covenant.[60]

Tôrâ ("law") may refer to the Ten Words (i.e., Ten Commandments) and more broadly to the Pentateuch. Here the term is defined by association with the name of Israel's covenant God, Yahweh. Tôrâ of the Lord means his teaching or instruction, not general instruction. It is the embodiment of justice and righteousness and may be equated with the knowledge of God, the rejection of which results and consists in all manner of religious and social wickedness and amounts to breaking the covenant (cf. Isa 5:7,18–24; Hos 4:1–13). For Judah to reject the Lord's instruction was comparable to the atrocities committed by foreign nations (cf. Ezek 5:6).

The term rendered "false gods" (v. 4) is literally "their lies," and the phrase "the gods" in the last line is not in the Hebrew but has been added by the NIV for clarification. Andersen and Freedman make a good case that while idolatry is the common interpretation of "their lies" and may be included, the reference is more directly to false prophecy.[61] Rather than following the Lord's instructions as conveyed by his prophets (cf. 2 Kgs 17:23), they followed the lies of prophets who led them astray like shepherds leading their sheep into the jaws of ravenous wolves (Jer 23:30–32; Ezek 13). To follow any path other than the one illuminated by the Lord's Word is to follow lies that lead to destruction.

The final line of v. 4 is literally "after which their fathers followed." The comparison may be positive, referring to the statutes their ancestors followed, or negative, referring to the lies they followed. The latter is more likely.[62]

---

[58] Andersen and Freedman, *Amos,* 294.

[59] Ibid., 295. For an excellent summary of the case against the oracle's originality as well as a convincing counterargument, see Paul, *Amos,* 20–27.

[60] Andersen and Freedman, *Amos,* 299.

[61] Ibid., 301–5.

[62] Ibid., 306. Hayes considers the term "lies" to be more political than religious, referring to the counsel of a pro-Egyptian party in Judah to revolt against Assyria (cf. Isa 28.15–17). Various groups in Judah's past history had resorted to such "lies" in order to steer the nation through troubled political waters. See Hayes, *Amos,* 103.

2:5 The threatened judgment on Judah was "fire" of the sort with which Tyre and Edom were threatened (1:10,12). Destruction in warfare does not seem to be too harsh a judgment for the atrocities committed by Tyre and Edom. But what about Judah's judgment? Were Judah's sins comparable to the atrocities of these nations? God's assignment of identical judgment would seem to answer in the affirmative. Furthermore, being "God's people" does not create immunity to the judgment of God but in fact increases accountability. Their guilt placed them alongside those foreign nations who perpetrated atrocities on fellow human beings.

(8) Oracle against Israel (2:6–16)

6This is what the LORD says:
"For three sins of Israel,
  even for four, I will not turn back [my wrath].
They sell the righteous for silver,
  and the needy for a pair of sandals.
7They trample on the heads of the poor
  as upon the dust of the ground
  and deny justice to the oppressed.
Father and son use the same girl
  and so profane my holy name.
8They lie down beside every altar
  on garments taken in pledge.
In the house of their god
  they drink wine taken as fines.
9"I destroyed the Amorite before them,
  though he was tall as the cedars
  and strong as the oaks.
I destroyed his fruit above
  and his roots below.
10"I brought you up out of Egypt,
  and I led you forty years in the desert
  to give you the land of the Amorites.
11I also raised up prophets from among your sons
  and Nazirites from among your young men.
Is this not true, people of Israel?"
                           declares the LORD.
12"But you made the Nazirites drink wine
  and commanded the prophets not to prophesy.
13"Now then, I will crush you
  as a cart crushes when loaded with grain.
14The swift will not escape,
  the strong will not muster their strength,
  and the warrior will not save his life.

¹⁵The archer will not stand his ground,
  the fleet-footed soldier will not get away,
  and the horseman will not save his life.
¹⁶Even the bravest warriors
  will flee naked on that day,"
                        declares the LORD.

The direct address of Amos 2:10 identifies the prophet's audience for all the oracles against the nations.[63] That audience was an assembly of Israelites at some location in Israel, possibly Bethel (cf. 7:10). The report of God's treatment of the other nations was meant to instruct Israel. Israel is the eighth nation addressed but is the primary audience of all of these oracles. While the other oracles were valid concerning God's word for the other nations, Israel was meant to hear God's word therein for them as well. Rhetorically, waiting until the end to pronounce judgment on Israel heightened the tension and anxiety of Amos's original audience. He does not conclude this oracle as he did the others because to do so would have diminished its importance. By changing the conclusion from the expected to the unexpected, Amos's words were heard more clearly than otherwise.

What lessons should the Israelites and modern readers glean from the previous oracles? The first lesson is the sovereignty of God. God's sovereign rule means that every nation is accountable to him. Foreign nations were not immune to God's judgment because of their allegiance to other gods. Israel and Judah did not enjoy immunity because they were in covenant with God.

The second lesson is the tolerance of God. "For three sins . . . even for four" describes God's tolerance of sin to a point. His tolerance is impartial, for all nations alike, and limited, for "four" but no more. Ultimately a nation's sin reaches a point when God's tolerance ends and judgment is the only outcome (cf. 8:1–3).

The third lesson concerns the judgment of God. His judgment is impartial for any nation regardless of relationship to him. It matches in severity the sins judged. Inhumanity to humans in the case of foreign nations is comparable to rejection of the Lord's instruction in the case of Judah. Judah's covenant relationship with God did not immunize the nation from judgment.

The oracles against the foreign nations and the oracle against Judah prepared Amos's audience to hear the oracle against Israel. Likely, the enthusiasm of that audience diminished as the focus of the oracles fell on Judah their sister kingdom. What remained for Amos to do was to fill in the blank with his target audience.

---

[63] Mays, *Amos,* 23. Andersen and Freedman suggest that the switch to second person "may be due to the use by Amos at this point of traditional material already familiar in the second person, which he incorporates into his oracle without altering that feature" (*Amos,* 330).

WHAT ISRAEL HAD DONE TO DESERVE JUDGMENT (2:6–8).   The oracle
against Israel begins like all the others, using the established numerical formula. Two areas of the formula are expanded greatly: the indictment of
wrongs committed and the details of the coming judgment. Even the recita-
tion of Israel's history (vv. 9–12) functions as an extension of the indictment
(vv. 6–8). The number of sins for which Israel was indicted is in question. The
oracles previous to the Judah oracle mention only one sin for which each
nation must suffer judgment. Supposedly the sin listed is the last one, the one
beyond God's tolerance level. Each sin mentioned was some act of inhumanity to man. The sins Judah had committed were covenant related. Israel's sins
were social in nature.[64] How should they be counted?

One way of assessing Israel's indictment is to consider the four elements as
components of one sin, oppression. Another way is to count each of the four
elements a sin. Yet another method of counting results in a total of seven, or
possibly eight, sins.[65] The last method could have figurative reference to the
completeness of Israel's sinfulness (represented by seven sins). Taken as an
eighth sin, v. 12 would give the sense of overflow beyond all limits.

2:6   The first "sin" named in Israel's indictment involved selling human
beings for a price. Who did the selling or buying is left unanswered. More
than one practice may be in view: (1) corrupt judges/jurors who accepted
bribes to decide cases against the righteous or (2) the righteous who were sold
into slavery for failure to pay a debt.[66]

"The righteous" may be a legal term designating the innocent. These persons should have been declared not guilty, or innocent of the charge(s)
brought against them. For such people to be counted guilty would be sinful
indeed.

Interpreters differ on how to understand the phrase "a pair of sandals." The
point may be the insignificance of the bribe for which judges/jurors were willing to pervert legal cases or the very small debt (equivalent to the price of a
pair of sandals) for which the debtor was sold into slavery. "A pair of sandals"
may be an idiom for the legal transfer of land (cf. Ruth 4:7). In the parallel
lines "a pair of sandals" matches "silver." Thus the expression implies the
ridiculously low payment required (a pair of sandals) to purchase the poor.
Amos was emphasizing the low value being placed on human life. Throughout
the history of humankind evil people have found ways to devalue human life.

2:7   The first part of v. 7 presents problems for translators. The first problem is the translation of the participle *haššoʾapîm,* which may be from the
verb *šaʾap,* "pant" (see KJV), a homonym meaning "trample, crush," or a

---

[64] Paul, *Amos,* 76.

[65] Hayes, *Amos,* 107.

[66] Paul, *Amos,* 77.

similar verb *šûp,* "bruise, crush" (used in Gen 3:15). The second possibility is the most likely.[67] A second problem is that two prepositional phrases seem to serve as objects (literally), "who trample upon the dust of the earth on the head of the poor." The two phrases can be taken as equivalent and thus in apposition, except that two different prepositions are used. The NIV translates the first phrase as a simile, which would seem more likely if the phrases were reversed. Perhaps the best explanation takes the first preposition (*ʿal*) with the common meaning "against" and the second preposition as introducing the object. Thus it could be translated "who trample/crush the head of the poor against the dust of the earth" (see RSV).[68]

However it is translated, the expression is clearly figurative. The powerful, rich landowners stepped on the poor by using the courts to pervert justice. Thus they revealed their contempt for those less fortunate, treating the poor like dirt.[69] A literal rendering of the third line of v. 7 reveals the emphasis of the speaker: "And the way of the afflicted they turn aside." Needy ones were pushed off the road, "bullied and oppressed by the wealthy,"[70] pushed aside as they sought justice at the gate (cf. 5:12; Exod 23:6; Prov 17:23). The specific charge is unclear; however, some circumvention of justice is the obvious reference.

The third accusation against Israel concerns sexual relations with the same female by a man and his father (Amos 2:7b). The girl may have been a female slave purchased by the father either for himself or for his son. For both to have sexual relations with her in either case would represent a breach of covenant (cf. Exod 21:7–11; Lev 18:7–8; 19:20–22; 20:17–21; 22:32).[71] Such an infringement on a divinely sanctioned relationship profaned the name of the Lord.[72]

2:8 The number of indictments issued in v. 8 is difficult to determine. The NIV has reversed the order of the first two lines and shifted the verb from the line where the MT places it, resulting in a greater emphasis on Israel's lying "beside every altar." The order of the last two lines has also been reversed. The Hebrew reads more literally:

---

[67] T. E. McComiskey, however, argues for the meaning "pant" here ("Amos," EBC 7:294, 296).

[68] See the discussion in Andersen and Freedman, *Amos,* 313–16. Some would also eliminate the first phrase (as in BHS), but this is unnecessary.

[69] Hubbard, *Joel and Amos,* 142.

[70] Paul, *Amos,* 81. Andersen and Freedman (*Amos,* 316) offered an excellent summary interpretation of v. 7a as not only denial of justice but physical abuse and bodily harm.

[71] Paul (*Amos,* 81) noted that the female is not referred to as a קְדֵשָׁה ("cult prostitute") but a נַעֲרָה ("young woman").

[72] Hayes, *Amos,* 112. Andersen and Freedman (*Amos,* 318) interpreted וְאִישׁ וְאָבִיו (lit., "and a man and his father") as a distributive use of אִישׁ (usually rendered "each" when used distributively). The NIV has "Father and son" as the translation of the terms.

> And on[73] garments taken in pledge they lie down
>   beside every altar.
> And the wine of those being fined they drink
>   in the house of their God/gods.

The verb translated "lie down" (*yaṭṭû*) also occurs in v. 7 with the meaning "turn aside" ("deny"), suggesting a continuation of the theme of perverting justice. The law required creditors to return pledged garments to the owner by sunset (Exod 22:26–27; Deut 24:12–13), and a widow's garment was not to be taken in pledge at all (Deut 24:17). A poor man's cloak was the only covering he had against the cold of the night.

S. Paul concludes that "garments taken in pledge" did not constitute "security or pawn when a loan is granted by a creditor"; instead, such garments were seized by the creditor "only when the loan falls due and the debt is defaulted."[74] "They lie down" is a reference to either bedding down for the night or stretching out to eat.

While the consumption of wine was a common practice, the source of the wine was the problem. It may have been directly or indirectly a fine for misconduct, a tax on the people, or a payment on a debt. The point may be that the fines were unjust.[75] Whatever the nature of the payment, Amos considered the exaction of it an oppressive act. Drinking such wine instead of that produced by the worshiper was especially odious to the oppressed. Fines for misconduct (cf. Exod 21:22; Deut 22:19) were aimed at compensation for damages, not promotion of drunkenness.

The parallels in the verse suggest that the sins involving the garments and the wine were concurrent and both part of the oppression of the poor seen in v. 7. The powerful and wealthy in Israel were enjoying themselves at the expense of the powerless and destitute. The nature of their enjoyment, however, is not so clear. Legitimate religious festivals may be in view, leaving the only indictment in the verse a social one.[76] The lying down, however, seems to have involved sexual immorality fueled by drunkenness.[77] While the multiplication of altars in Israel was clearly contrary to God's will (1 Kgs 12–13; Deut 12:5–11), those engaging in such activities may have thought that they

---

[73] The preposition עַל may be causal here, yielding "and because garments taken in pledge they lay down" (so Anderson and Freedman, *Amos,* 319).

[74] Paul, *Amos,* 83.

[75] Andersen and Freedman suggest the verse may be figurative: "In the shrines they are using fabrics and wine, both symbols of indulgence, acquired by fraudulent loans and unjust fines" (*Amos,* 320). Self-indulgent priests, then, were in collusion with unscrupulous merchants and magistrates.

[76] Keil, *Twelve Minor Prophets,* 254; H. Mowvley, *The Books of Amos and Hosea* (London: Epworth, 1991), 34–35.

[77] Niehaus, "Amos," 1:367.

were worshiping the Lord, hence the translation "the house of their God." But since the Lord rejected such "worship" as well as the altars at which it was practiced, the nature of such activity was essentially pagan (cf. 8:14; Hos 8:11; 10:1–2), making appropriate a rendering "the house of their god(s)."

WHAT GOD HAD DONE TO ESTABLISH THE NATION (2:9–11). The shift from third to first person in v. 9 marks a new paragraph. God's gracious actions in behalf of Israel were in sharp contrast to Israel's oppression of the poor.[78] Israel's treatment of the poor was destructive. God's works on Israel's behalf were constructive. The result of God's actions had been the establishment of Israel as a nation. The pronoun "I" is added emphatically to the verbs "I destroyed" and "I brought you up" in vv. 9–10 to mark the contrast: "I on the other hand."

2:9 The first action of God Amos mentioned was the destruction of the Amorite. Why that action was given priority over the chronologically preceding exodus from Egypt (v. 10) is a puzzle. Could it be that Amos gave priority to the destruction of the Amorite because that action alone allowed Israel to possess the promised land?[79] Or was it because Israel's continued possession of the land was at stake, since they were engaging in the kinds of behavior for which God had judged the Amorites?[80] Deterioration of their moral and spiritual condition would surely result in their being driven off the land just as the Amorites had been (9:7–8). Another possibility is that following the rhetorical pattern of 1:3–2:16, that is, announcing this message to Israel last, he reversed the chronology to make the historical and theological point all the more significant. This prophetic word is not just about the Amorites; it is about Israel's covenant with God dating back to the exodus, the act of God par excellence.

"Amorite" refers to the population of Palestine before Israel occupied the land. Their reputation for abnormal size and strength preceded Israel's encounter with them (Num 13:28,31–33). Perhaps Amos intended reference to God's complete annihilation of the Amorite as an implicit warning to Israel, the present occupant of the land. "Before them" may have the double meaning of geographical displacement of the Amorites and causative action on account of the Israelites.[81]

Amos employed two metaphors to describe the abnormal size and strength of the Amorite: "tall as the cedars" and "strong as the oaks." Cedars and oaks were the most massive of native trees in Israel. The prophet also used a common idiom regarding the "fruit" and the "roots" to express total extermination of the Amorite.[82] Destruction of "his fruit" left no possibility of future life

---

[78] Paul, *Amos,* 87.

[79] Hayes, *Amos,* 114; Mays, *Amos,* 50; Hubbard, *Joel and Amos,* 143.

[80] R. Smith, "Amos," 7:98.

[81] Paul, *Amos,* 87.

[82] Ibid., 89.

from seed. Destruction of "roots" left no possibility of future life for the tree. God is able to deal decisively with the enemies of his people.

2:10 The second divine act Amos referred to was the exodus of Israel from Egypt. Typical references to the exodus make use of one or the other of two verbs, to focus either on God's redemptive act of liberating his people from slavery (*yāṣāʾ*, "to deliver") or on possession of the land (*ʿālâ*, "to bring up"). The latter term is the one Amos used. "I," referring to God, is emphatic: "It was I who caused you to go up from the land of Egypt" (author's translation). God's goal was more than their liberation from slavery. He brought them up in order to put them in the land of promise. God's action of abundant provision is the basis for his judgment against them (2:10; 3:1; 9:7).[83] The act of deliverance from Egypt was the single most important event of Israel's history. It was the foundation of the covenant between God and the nation Israel (Exod 19–24) and fully revealed God's providential care of his chosen people (Josh 2:10; Judg 2:1; 6:8; 1 Sam 8:8; 2 Sam 7:6; Isa 11:16; Jer 2:6; 7:22; 11:4; 23:7; Ezek 20:10; Dan 9:15; Hos 2:15; 11:1; 13:4; Mic 6:4).

The third divine act aimed at establishing Israel as a nation was to lead them in the desert forty years (v. 10b). But the last line of v. 10 gives the aim of the exodus, the wilderness experience, and the conquest. Attention is on possession of the land.

Israel's possession of the land resulted from divine actions. The implication of that fact, though not stated by Amos, was that the nation was not free to deal with the land as they chose. Yet their actions for which Amos indicted them presumed such freedom (2:6–8).

The shift in v. 10 to the second person in referring to the prophet's audience heightens the direct and personal nature of the appeal. The use of the third person in vv. 6–9, as in the preceding oracles, serves to place Israel in the same category as the rest of the foreign nations. God's intolerance of rebellion among his own people was no different from intolerance of rebellion among foreign nations. God's judgment falls on his own people just as it does on foreign people.

2:11 The fourth action of God was the gift of spiritual leaders. God raised up prophets to proclaim his message to Israel and Nazirites to serve as models of dedication to God. With prophets and Nazirites, God provided guidance to Israel for their life in the land. Nazirites vowed abstinence from alcoholic beverages, from cutting their hair, and from contact with corpses (Num 6:1–21). Samson, the best known Nazirite in the Old Testament (Judg 13:5,7; 16:17), was to be a Nazirite from birth to death. Samuel is the other identifiable Nazirite in the Old Testament (1 Sam 1:11). God's care and provision for the welfare of Israel had been constant throughout their history. Call-

---

[83] Andersen and Freedman, *Amos*, 330.

ing attention to the prophets and Nazirites served as part of the indictment against Israel because of Israel's response to these gracious provisions (v. 12).

The raising up of prophets and Nazirites was a divine act comparable to the destruction of the Amorite, the exodus from Egypt, guidance in the desert, and placement in the land. The function of prophets and Nazirites was to promote the well-being of Israelite society by promoting their righteousness according to God's purpose for the nation.

With his question, "Is this not true, people of Israel?" the prophet called on his audience to acknowledge the truth of his indictment. The rhetorical question demanded the answer, "Yes, of course it is true." But God's gracious acts toward Israel aimed at their redemption had been matched throughout their history by acts of rebellion.[84]

"Declares the LORD" also occurs at the end of the Israel oracle in 2:16. Besides being an expression used often by the prophets to cite the source and authority of their messages, it also serves to mark the end of a paragraph (or subparagraph) and the midpoint of the Israel oracle. As the indictment against Israel in vv. 6–8 is balanced by the announcement of judgment in vv. 13–16, so the description of the Lord's faithful provision in vv. 9–11 is balanced by v. 12, which declares Israel's faithless rejection of the Lord.[85]

HOW ISRAEL RESPONDED TO GOD'S PROVISION (2:12). **2:12** Israel's response to God's gracious provision of spiritual leaders was a deliberate effort to prevent them from functioning. They forced the Nazirites to break their vows of dedication to God, and they commanded the prophets not to function as messengers of God. Israel thus manifested rebellion against the Lord (cf. Amos 7:12–13).[86]

Worldly minded people are uncomfortable around those who have a message from God and who model their lives after his character. They have only two options: (1) bring life into line with God's message and God's model or (2) bring the messengers and models into line with their twisted lives (Rom 12:1–2). Israel chose the latter option.

HOW GOD WOULD RESPOND TO ISRAEL'S REBELLION (2:13–16). God's judgment against the other nations has been described under the figure of "fire" (cf. 1:4,7,10,12,14; 2:2,5). Ancient nations used fire as a method of warfare. They destroyed buildings and terrorized entire populations with fire. In the judgment announcement against Israel, however, the figure of fire is replaced by detailed description of a devastating military encounter. For the third time the emphatic pronoun "I" spotlights the actions of God in contrast to the actions of sinful Israel. The one who destroyed the Amorites (v. 9), who brought Israel

---

[84] Hubbard, *Joel and Amos*, 145.

[85] Cf. E. R. Wendland, "The 'Word of the Lord' and the Organization of Amos," in *Occasional Papers in Translation and Textlinguistics* 2.4 (1988): 10–11.

[86] Paul, *Amos*, 93.

up from Egypt (v. 10), will be the one who will judge his people (v. 13).[87]

2:13 Amos used a metaphor from farm life to describe the method of God's judgment against Israel. As a cart overloaded with grain crushes[88] the earth (a possible allusion to an earthquake), so God would crush his people with the same force he used to demolish the Amorites. The verb translated "crush" (*meîq*) occurs only here, and so its meaning is uncertain. The root may occur in Ps 55:3 (Heb., v. 4) as a noun (*ʿaqâ*) meaning "pressure"[89] and in Ps 66:11 as another noun (*mûʿaqâ*) meaning "burden." Thus a meaning for the verb such as "press down" or "crush" is reasonable. The following word in the first line, however, literally means "under you," suggesting to Andersen and Freedman that in the image it is not Israel under the cart but the Lord and that the verb means "creak, groan, totter, tremble." The sense, then, would be that "Yahweh groans under the burden of Israel just as a cart groans under the burden of the sheaves that fill it."[90] The context, however, seems to require an act of destruction on God's part from which "the swift will not escape" (v. 14). Therefore the NIV translation is preferred.

"Now then" (*hinneh,* "behold"), together with the following participle, alerts the reader (listener) to an upcoming, startling event with significant results. God himself was the active agent of judgment. The verb is a causative participle, indicating that God is now crushing (or pressing down) his people.

2:14–16 Amos described the panic that would prevail among Israel's military forces when God approached in judgment. The sevenfold scheme of Amos's portrait suggests total chaos and overwhelming defeat for Israel.[91] The "swift" would not be swift enough to escape (v. 14a), the "strong" would not be able to muster enough strength to stand (v. 14b), and the "warrior" would not be able to escape with his life (v. 14c). The "archer" would not be able to stand (v. 15a), the "fleet-footed soldier" would not be able to escape (v. 15b), and the "horseman" (charioteer) would not be able to escape with his life (v. 15c). The "bravest warriors"[92] would flee away naked in the day of God's judgment (v. 16). Israel's best soldiers would drop their weapons and run.

Israel expected the day of the Lord to come for them as a positive benefit

---

[87] Ibid., 94.

[88] This is the only place in the OT where the verb עוּק is found. The form is that of a causative participle, suggesting God ("I") as acting agent in a continuous movement.

[89] So KB, but the NIV translates as "stares."

[90] Andersen and Freedman (*Amos,* 334). Paul (*Amos,* 94–95) favors "hamper" or "hinder" as the basic idea in the term מֵעִיק and interprets the meaning to be the complete "immobility and helplessness of the entire Israelite army."

[91] Andersen and Freedman (*Amos,* 335) interpret vv. 14–16 as "a crushing military defeat and the demolition of the entire army." The details of the day of defeat for Israel are scattered throughout the remainder of the book.

[92] אַמִּיץ לִבּוֹ means "stout of his heart." S. Paul (*Amos,* 98) suggested that לֵב, usually translated "heart," probably means "courage" here.

(5:18–20; cf. Zeph 1:14–18). Amos announced the opposite result of that day. It would be a day of God's judgment against his rebellious people. The day would bring defeat, not deliverance. "Declares the LORD" (v. 16) is the prophet's way of punctuating his announcement as well as pointing his audience to the source and authority for his message.

The entire oracle (1:3–2:16), preached to some assembly of Israelites, is as relevant to Christians today as it was to its original audience. All nations are accountable to God when they oppress, dehumanize, and take away the rights of people, especially helpless people. God's judgment is severe against those who exploit, abuse, and oppress fellow human beings. God judges indiscriminately. Claims of a special relationship to God does not immunize such people from his judgment. Military prowess and preparedness are no match for the mighty God when his judgment comes.

2. Words of Punishment for Israel's Sins (3:1–15)

Form-critical analysis has tended to isolate five units in the chapter: vv. 1–2,3–8,9–11,12,13–15. Wolff, Mays, and other scholars suggest that chap. 3 is made up of various speeches from different settings.[93] But these units do not make complete statements. Only in the larger context of the entire chapter does the meaning of individual units become clear. For example, the "two" who "walk together" (v. 3) are God and his "chosen" people Israel (v. 2). The reader would not know that from a study of vv. 3–8 in isolation. Whereas the authenticity of some verses in Amos 3 has been questioned (e.g., vv. 3–8,12–15), Y. Gitay has argued convincingly that Amos 3:1–15, from a rhetorical perspective, "constitutes a complete discourse."[94]

Gitay describes the chapter's structure rhetorically. After the introductory call in v. 1 the thesis is introduced in v. 2. Then the prophet refutes his opponents in vv. 3–6 and establishes his credibility in vv. 7–8. The audience having been sufficiently prepared, Amos then describes in detail in vv. 9–12 the people's sins and God's punishment. Finally there is an epilogue in vv. 13–15 that "refreshes the audience's memory by repeating the main theme of the introduction (cp. v. 2 with v. 14a) in similar language."[95]

---

[93] Ibid., 294–97.

[94] Y. Gitay, "A Study of Amos's Art of Speech: A Rhetorical Analysis of Amos 3:1–15," *CBQ* 42 (1980): 293.

[95] Ibid., 300–301.

(1) Punishment for the Whole Family of Rebels (3:1–2)

¹Hear this word the LORD has spoken against you, O people of Israel—
against the whole family I brought up out of Egypt:
  ²"You only have I chosen
    of all the families of the earth;
  therefore I will punish you
    for all your sins."

The introductory formula "hear this word" is similar to the language employed by a wisdom teacher (Prov 8:32). Amos used the formula to call for attention and to introduce three oracles of judgment against Israel (3:1; 4:1; 5:1). It alerts the audience to the announcement of an important message.[96]

What follows here in Amos is a benchmark oracle that explains the basis for subsequent announcements of judgment. That basis was the Lord's relationship to Israel. Yahweh was Israel's God, and Israel was Yahweh's people, a relationship he shared with no other people. The Lord had moved other people from one country to another, just as he had brought Israel from Egypt (9:7). However, he selected only Israel to be his chosen people (Exod 19:3–6).[97]

DIVINE DELIVERANCE FROM BONDAGE IN EGYPT (3:1).   **3:1**   The "word" or revelation to which Israel must pay attention was a word the Lord had spoken. It was "against" or better "concerning" (^cal) the "people of Israel."

"The whole family" refers to more than the ten northern tribes called Israel. The phrase designates all of the people God delivered out of Egypt into the promised land (cf. 2:10). God's work to place them in the promised land is the emphasis of the verb rendered "I brought up" (see comments at 2:10). While some ponder whether or not 3:1b was included by a later editor,[98] the connection to 2:10 would suggest that it is original to Amos. The importance of the phrase is that it serves as a rhetorical device that reminds the people of their origins, of God's past activity on their behalf, and of their relationship of dependence on God.

DIVINE PUNISHMENT FOR HIS COVENANT PEOPLE (3:2).   **3:2**   "You only" is in the emphatic position ahead of the verb, contrary to normal word order. "You only" means "you alone, you and no one else." The verb translated "chosen" ($y\bar{a}da^ct\hat{\imath}$) is "know" and suggests an intimate relationship between God and his people. As such the phrase implies the "elect" nature of Israel.

---

[96] Stuart, *Hosea-Jonah,* 321.

[97] Paul, *Amos,* 101.

[98] Hayes, *Amos,* 123; Paul, *Amos,* 100.

God selected one family (Israel) from among all the families of the earth to be in a special relationship to him. The verse may be a reference to Gen 12:3 (cf. also Gen 28:14) with the phrase "all the families of the earth." If so, Amos traces the relationship between God and his people prior to Mount Sinai all the way back to Abraham and Sarah.

Gitay observes that to this point Amos's audience had heard nothing new or surprising. He had only affirmed them in their relationship with their God. The connection of cause and effect, however, that Amos proceeds to make between relationship and punishment, introduced by the word "therefore," may have sounded "contradictory if not absurd."[99] Such an unexpected turn would have grabbed their attention and called for an explanation. Israel was about to learn that their special relationship carried with it special responsibility and accountability.[100]

"Therefore" reaches back to God's having "chosen" Israel for the explanation of his forthcoming judgment upon them. What God vowed to do was "punish you [Israel] for all your sins." The term translated "punish" (*pāqad*) has a neutral meaning of "visit." Visit to inspect is the essential idea in the verb. Context alone determines what kind of response the visitation calls for. Punishment may be the result if the inspection reveals a flaw, a fault, some disobedience, or a sin. The idiom here and elsewhere (cf. 3:14) is literally, "I will visit upon you all your sins." The word "visit" in this case means "inflict" and the word "sins" is figurative, representing the effect (punishment) by means of the cause (sin). The word rendered "sins" is often translated "iniquities." Activity that is crooked or wrong is the essential idea in the term. Depending on the context the word may refer to "iniquity," "guilt" over the iniquity, or "punishment" due the iniquity. When read in connection with 3:14, the phrase "I will punish . . . for sins" forms an inclusio (envelope structure) to the chapter as a whole.

Israel's privileged relationship to God carried with it heavy responsibility to God. As seen in the Book of Deuteronomy, living in relationship with God demanded loyalty and faithfulness.[101] If the people failed, judgment and punishment would come. God holds his people accountable for their sins.

(2) Justification for the Prophet's Ministry (3:3–8)

³Do two walk together
unless they have agreed to do so?

---

[99] Gitay, "A Study of Amos's Art of Speech," 300.

[100] Andersen and Freedman concluded their discussion of יָדַע with the strong assertion that "the intimacy of the covenant relationship of Yahweh and Israel was no guarantee of the latter's continued prosperity and security" (*Amos,* 381).

[101] See E. Merrill, *Deuteronomy,* NAC (Nashville: Broadman & Holman, 1994), 31, 55.

⁴**Does a lion roar in the thicket**
   when he has no prey?
 Does he growl in his den
   when he has caught nothing?
⁵**Does a bird fall into a trap on the ground**
   where no snare has been set?
 Does a trap spring up from the earth
   when there is nothing to catch?
⁶**When a trumpet sounds in a city,**
   do not the people tremble?
 When disaster comes to a city,
   has not the LORD caused it?
⁷**Surely the Sovereign LORD does nothing**
   without revealing his plan
   to his servants the prophets.
⁸**The lion has roared—**
   who will not fear?
 The Sovereign LORD has spoken—
   who can but prophesy?

Amos 3:3–8 is a dispute-saying consisting of a "chain of rhetorical questions"[102] in vv. 3–6. Some people in Amos's audience must have protested his radical message of judgment.[103] Perhaps they questioned why Amos spoke such a harsh message against Israel. The cause-and-effect questions in 3:3–6 prepared for the climax in vv. 7–8. Amos spoke because God had called him. The prophet had heard the lion's roar of the Lord's judgment against Israel, and he faithfully relayed that message to Israel (1:2; 3:8). Amos spoke here as the defender of his office as messenger as well as the messenger of his God.

NATURAL CAUSE AND EFFECT (3:3–6). All seven questions in this section illustrate the interrelationship of cause and effect. The questions in vv. 3–5 expect the answer no. The questions in v. 6 still concern cause and effect, but both questions imply the answer yes. The questions and implied answers of 3:3–6 prepare for the prophet's conclusion in vv. 7–8.

3:3 Only v. 3 has one question. The remainder of the verses (vv. 4–6,8) contain two questions each, which are structurally parallel. Various translations of v. 3 reflect the difficulty of the text. "Can two walk together, except they be agreed?" is the KJV rendering. The NRSV has, "Do two walk together unless they have made an appointment?" A number of recent commentaries render the final verb "met,"[104] as in Exod 25:22 and 30:6,36. God's meeting with Moses is the reference of the term there. That simple meaning

---

[102] Gitay, "A Study of Amos's Art of Speech."

[103] Paul, *Amos,* 105.

[104] Hayes, *Amos,* 121; Stuart, *Hosea-Jonah,* 323; Paul, *Amos,* 109.

makes sense in Amos 3:3. The condition for two people traveling together, as stated in the rhetorical question of v. 3, is that "they have agreed to do so." They must have met, worked out travel plans, and agreed on time to depart, destination, and the route to take. His use of an everyday "life situation in the first question lured his listeners into his train of thought."[105]

Amos's initial question may have been only proverbial. But could the Lord and Israel be the "two" in the prophet's mind? Certainly they had met (3:2). Their walking together was a grave concern of the prophet. Their failure to do so was the result of their sin (vv. 9–10) and would surely bring down the judgment of God upon them (vv. 11–15). As Micah would urge, all people are to walk with God (Mic 6:8). As Gitay observes, this connection between vv. 2 and 3 is suggested by the fact that only in v. 3 does he have a rhetorical question in this paragraph that is not paired with another. Also, v. 3 (like v. 6) has nothing to do with animals hunting or being hunted as do vv. 4–5.[106] The relationship between God and Israel is the result of a covenant.[107]

3:4 Both questions in v. 4 concern the typical behavior of a lion when stalking and capturing prey (cf. 1:2). Amos and his audience knew that a lion hunted quietly and let out a roar just before capturing the prey.[108] The roar comes just before the catch in order to freeze the prey in its tracks, making it easier to seize the prize. The Lord's roar from Zion in 1:2, therefore, indicated that he was in process of attack. The two phases of a lion's kill are (1) the stalking, roaring, and downing of the prey in the thicket and (2) the dragging of the victim to the den to feed the young, followed by a growl of victory.

The verbs translated "roar" (yiš°ag) and "growl" (yittēn qôlô) are the same verbs rendered "roars" and "thunders" in 1:2, where the terms refer to the Lord. Here they refer to a lion. Amos compared the lion's roar to the Lord's speaking in 3:8. That is the point of the whole series of rhetorical questions. As the lion's roar was to frighten and unsettle the prey, so was the Lord's speaking to frighten and unsettle Israel. The expected answer to the questions in v. 4 is no. The lion does not roar unless he has prey to attack, and he does not growl unless he has captured something. The Lord's roar from Zion (1:2) precedes his judgment on his people. As such, the rhetoric of judgment serves to prepare the prey for the "kill."

3:5 The two questions in v. 5 concern the trapping of birds. Amos mentioned two implements used in hunting birds: the "trap" (paḥ) and the "snare" (môqēš).[109] Perhaps originally the môqēš designated the triggering device,

---

[105] Paul, *Amos,* 109.

[106] Gitay, "A Study of Amos's Art of Speech," 295.

[107] This idea may be suggested as well by the similarities between יָדַעְתִּי in v. 2 and יֵהָדְוּ and נוֹעָדוּ in v. 3, the latter being translated in the LXX by γνωρίσωσιν ἑαυτούς.

[108] Paul, *Amos,* 110.

[109] פַּח is not reflected in the LXX in the first question.

the sling, or the bait of the *pah*.[110] Later it designated the trap itself. One interpreter suggests that the *môqēš* was a wooden missile, a boomerang or throwing stick, since it causes a bird to fall to the earth; but this understanding is based on removing *pah* from the text, for which there is no sound reason.[111] The two questions illustrate clearly the prophet's principle that an action must have an adequate cause.

3:6 The heightened significance of this verse is marked in four ways. First, while vv. 3–5 have demanded the answer no, the questions in v. 6 demand the answer yes. Second, the order of effect explained by cause is reversed in the first question of v. 6. Third, the questions are introduced by the conditional particle *ʾim*, "when," rather than the interrogative particle of vv. 3–5. And finally, the audience is brought closer to the point of the interrogation with the climactic reference to "the LORD" in the last line of v. 6.

From experience Amos and his audience knew the significance of blowing a trumpet (*šôpār*) in a city. The trumpet blast signaled the approach of an enemy, causing residents in a city to tremble with fear. Observable phenomena do not just happen. Some cause lies behind each effect.

No one in Amos's audience would have objected to his argument up to this point. All would have answered no to each rhetorical question in vv. 3–5 and yes to the question in v. 6a. The answer to the next question was not as clear-cut. Some people may not have been willing to answer yes to the idea that "disaster" (*rāʿâ*)[112] in a city could be traced to the Lord as causative agent. The popular belief was that the Lord would not bring any misfortune upon his chosen people. A yes answer to the rhetorical question would undercut popular sentiment.[113] But the dilemma created by the answer no would mean that some other deity had caused the disaster, a claim they would have been unwilling to make.

Apparently Amos sought agreement from his audience on the implications of the first six questions (vv. 3–6a). Then, based on that agreement, the prophet hoped his audience would assent to the final proposition.[114] Agreement with the general proposition that disaster in a city should be attributed to the Lord would lend support to the prophet's contention that Israel's oppression by surrounding nations was the work of the Lord. The emphasis of the sentence structure is that the Lord and no other "caused" (*ʿāśâ*, "worked" or

---

[110] S. Paul argues convincingly that מוֹקֵשׁ referred to "none other than the 'bait' or 'decoy' that is attached to the trap" (*Amos*, 111). His argument is based on his understanding of the correct nuance of the phrase נפל על, which is "swoop down."

[111] Wolff, *Joel and Amos*, 185.

[112] Usually רָעָה is translated "evil." Here it refers to a calamity created by the attack of a vicious enemy (cf. Jonah 1:7).

[113] Paul, *Amos*, 112.

[114] Hayes, *Amos*, 125.

"performed") the disaster. As Gitay expresses it, "Amos's main concern is the recognition that God reveals himself not only in matters of success but also in terms of sins and punishment" and "to convince his audience that an unbroken relationship exists between their sins and a divinely inspired catastrophe."[115] The implication of this line of argument is that God, the Sovereign Lord, controls everything that happens.

SPIRITUAL CAUSE AND EFFECT (3:7–8). **3:7** The declarative sentence in v. 7 links the questions in vv. 3–6 with the declaration-question pattern in v. 8.[116] Again Amos used a series of seven, which his audience would have expected to be complete, to prepare for his main point, which comes in an eighth member of the series. S. Paul wrote: "The first seven oracles (1:3–2:16) as well as the seven rhetorical questions (3:3–8) serve as an effective decoy for his ultimate trap."[117] The audience must have been caught off guard, thinking the seventh item was the final one. Instead, the prophet added an eighth oracle and an eighth question as the surprise finale.

With v. 7 Amos elaborated on the point of his cause-and-effect questions (vv. 3–6). The Lord can be the cause of disaster in a city (v. 6b); when he is, he reveals his plan to his servants the prophets (v. 7). This argument would be designed to support Amos's credibility as he delivered such an unpopular message.[118] Proclamation of the message the Lord has revealed is the legitimate activity of prophets. The basis for a prophet's authority is that he has stood in the council of the Lord (Jer 23:18,22). That was true for Amos in the distant past. He had been with the Lord. His proclamation had the stamp of God's authority upon it. Modern preachers also must receive their message from God to have the stamp of God's authority upon their proclamation.

The harsh message of judgment upon Israel (2:6–16) was the message Amos received in the council (*sôd*) of God. Consistent with the general principle that the Lord "does nothing" (*lōʾ yaʿăśeh . . . dābār,* "performs nothing") "without revealing his plan to his servants the prophets," God gave Amos a strong message to preach.

3:8 The style shift in v. 8 alerted Amos's audience (reader) that he had reached the climax. He turned from hypothetical situations (vv. 3–6) to statements of fact. "The lion has roared," the first statement of fact, is the cause of

---

[115] Gitay, "A Study of Amos's Art of Speech," 296.

[116] Gitay argues that v. 7 was original to Amos, not a later prose insertion. He bases that argument on the significant rhetorical function of the verse in the context. Those commentators who take the verse to be a later insertion use as evidence the fact that the verse is prose in the midst of poetry, that it is the only statement in the pericope that does not refer to a causal relation. Gitay has correctly explained the switch in style and structure to enable the prophet to get the attention of his audience, to reveal the source of his harsh message, and to add important details ("A Study of Amos's Art of Speech, 304–5). See also Paul, *Amos,* 113.

[117] Paul, *Amos,* 105.

[118] Gitay, "A Study of Amos's Art of Speech," 299.

"fear." Here the lion's roar strikes fear in humans, *"who* will not fear?" The effect of the lion's roar in v. 4 was on other animals. Since "the lion has roared" is parallel to "the Sovereign LORD has spoken,"[119] both expressions refer to God. This usage accords with the parallel statements in 1:2, "The LORD from Zion will roar, and from Jerusalem he will give his voice" (author's translation).

Amos had heard the lion's roar of the Lord's judgment upon Israel. That roar struck "fear" in Amos. He knew the lion's roar signaled a kill. Amos spoke God's message in Israel because he had heard the Lord speak. The prophet's message was not his own. He only spoke what he heard the Lord speak. With this rhetorical unit Amos would justify his appearance in Israel as spokesman for God. S. Paul captures Amos's point: "The prophet speaks when commanded but, once commanded, must speak."[120] Gitay explains the significance of this point as adding to Amos's credibility. Amos did not enjoy his task of conveying unpleasant words. He was simply "one of the audience, one who [had] no choice but to prophesy."[121] D. Hubbard's concluding paragraph on the unit contains a striking statement about how Amos "won his points": "He has done so by leading his hearers through a catechism of common-sense questions to his double conclusion that reinforces all that he said in the beginning verses of this chapter: Yahweh will bring disaster on his people (v. 6b), and Amos has no choice but to announce it" (v. 8b).[122]

(3) The Downfall and Devouring of Israel (3:9–12)

[9]**Proclaim to the fortresses of Ashdod**
   and to the fortresses of Egypt:
"Assemble yourselves on the mountains of Samaria;
   see the great unrest within her
   and the oppression among her people."

[10]**"They do not know how to do right," declares the LORD,**
   "who hoard plunder and loot in their fortresses."

[11]**Therefore this is what the Sovereign LORD says:**

"An enemy will overrun the land;
   he will pull down your strongholds
   and plunder your fortresses."

[12]**This is what the LORD says:**

---

[119] אֲדֹנָי יְהוִה דִּבֶּר stresses that "the Sovereign LORD" is the one Amos heard speaking. The same grammatical structure is used in the first line.

[120] Paul, *Amos,* 114.

[121] Gitay, "A Study of Amos's Art of Speech," 299.

[122] Hubbard, *Joel and Amos,* 150.

"As a shepherd saves from the lion's mouth
   only two leg bones or a piece of an ear,
   so will the Israelites be saved,
   those who sit in Samaria
   on the edge of their beds
   and in Damascus on their couches."

Having prepared his audience for the message and justified his ministry of judgment in Israel, Amos then spelled out the crimes the Lord would punish. This oracle has a mixture of forms. The call for witnesses suggests the covenant lawsuit[123] form (v. 9) and serves as an introduction to the second half of the message in this chapter (cf. v. 1). Emphasis on the word of the Lord is a feature of the messenger form (vv. 10–11). Samaria was the likely location of the prophet's proclamation, and Samaria's leading citizens probably were the prophet's target audience.

LESSONS IN VIOLENCE AND OPPRESSION (3:9–10). Amos rhetorically ordered that messengers be sent to two pagan nations with an invitation to come as witnesses to the violence and oppression in Samaria (cf. "city" in 3:6). Israel's law required at least two witnesses in cases where the death penalty was imposed (Deut 17:6).

3:9 The prophet probably did not intend messengers actually to go to these foreign nations. His call for witnesses from these nations was meant for Israel's ears. These nations were experts at violence and oppression. The implication is that Israel could give these experts a few lessons. "The hypothetical coming of immoral barbarians from neighboring states to judge the morality of Samaria is used because of the dramatic effect it will have on the listeners."[124]

We do not know why Amos selected Ashdod and Egypt. The Septuagint has Assyria instead of Ashdod (v. 9). Hosea's usage (7:11; 9:3, etc.) may have exerted influence on the Septuagint translators.[125] A few interpreters think Assyria and Egypt (both major powers) would be a more natural pair,[126] but since Assyria would be the instrument of punishment it is unlikely they would also be called as witness to the crime. Also, although Amos never referred to Assyria, he did mention Ashdod (1:8). Perhaps Amos chose the Philistines and the Egyptians here because they were especially remembered for their cruel oppression of Israel.

---

[123] G. V. Smith, however, thinks the similarity is insufficient and prefers to call it "prophetic judgment speech" (*Amos: A Commentary* [Grand Rapids: Zondervan, 1989], 114).

[124] G. Smith, *Amos,* 119.

[125] Similarity in appearance of the two Hebrew terms, בְּאַשּׁוּר ("in Assyria") and בְּאַשְׁדּוֹד ("in Ashdod"), probably accounts for the LXX reading.

[126] Stuart is one example (*Hosea-Jonah,* 328). The overwhelming evidence of the versions is against Assyria as the original reading.

The dominant word in the pericope (vv. 9–11), occurring four times, is "fortresses." That is where witnesses to Israel's violence and oppression were to be enlisted (v. 9), that is where Samaria hoarded plunder and loot (v. 10), and that is where an enemy would plunder what Samaria had hoarded (v. 11). "Fortresses" (ʾarmĕnôt) were multistoried structures that often formed part of a city's defense system (Pss 48:13; 122:7). The palace of a king could contain such a structure (1 Kgs 16:18). They often served as storehouses for loot taken in military raids, and God's judgment on Israel would mean that the plunderer would be plundered. The repetition of the term with both the witnesses and Israel enhances the subtle comparison being made between Israel and their pagan neighbors.

From "the mountains of Samaria" those who did not know God or follow his laws would be able to recognize the "great unrest" and "oppression" in Israel's capital city. The term "unrest" is literally "panic," except that it is plural (mĕhûmōt), which together with the adjective points to a scene of unchecked social chaos. Such "panic" usually is the result of divine judgment (cf. 1 Sam 5:9,11; Zech 14:13), so here we may assume that it has resulted from the "oppression" in Israel. The term "oppression" (ʿăšûqîm) also is plural. It refers to extortion, robbery, bribery, and other acts of greed (cf. Lev 6:2,4; Deut 28:29; 1 Sam 12:3; Jer 21:12; Ezek 18:18; Mal 3:5). Order and justice should have prevailed in the city. Instead, chaos and oppression reigned.

3:10 The ones "who hoard plunder" are those who had lost the ability to do right. Ḥāmās ("plunder") usually denotes violence to persons, while sôd ("loot") typically describes destruction of material goods.[127] "Plunder" and "loot" were the gain generated by Samaria's acts of violence and destruction. Samaria's leaders had been warped by their practice of violence and destruction. They were so twisted in their thinking they did not know how "to do right." The expression "declares the LORD" (nĕʾum YHWH; cf. 2:16) points to the prophet's source of authority for his indictment and punctuates this brief look at Israel's sins.

THE LORD'S JUDGMENT UPON PRACTITIONERS OF VIOLENCE AND OPPRESSION (3:11). **3:11** "Therefore" refers back to the indictment in vv. 9–10 as the basis for judgment. The prophet's audience must have grown afraid when they heard "therefore." With that word Amos regularly introduced God's devastating judgment upon Israel. His use of the messenger formula "this is what the Sovereign LORD says" trumpeted the message as well as reminded his audience of its source. The strong words of judgment were

---

[127] S. Paul describes the two terms as "well-known substantives, often occurring together . . ., representing the lawlessness and corruption of the society" (*Amos,* 117). Andersen and Freedman (*Amos,* 407) identify the two terms as an example of hendiadys, meaning "the spoil of violent action."

not his own. They came from Israel's God.

The second line is difficult. It consists of only three words. The first word is the subject (*ṣar*), which may mean either "enemy" or "distress." It is also the antecedent subject of the last two lines. The second word, associated with the first by the conjunction "and," is either a preposition, "around," or a noun "surrounding," which paired with the last word would mean "the surrounding of the land." The line is perhaps best taken as a cry of alarm: "An enemy! And the surrounding of the land!"[128] Israel's defenses would fail to secure their "plunder" and "loot" from the unnamed enemy. The "enemy" would serve as God's instrument of judgment. Stashing loot in their fortresses would not protect Israel from the enemy God would send to "plunder" their fortresses.

PROPHECY OF ISRAEL'S DEVOURING (3:12). **3:12** Like the wisdom teachers of Israel, Amos liked to employ metaphors, illuminating or dramatizing his message with scenes from everyday life.[129]

3:12 "As" and "so" set up the comparison. The audience Amos addressed could identify with the predicament of the shepherd in the prophet's comparison. A shepherd who attended sheep for other owners had to give an account for missing animals. Such a shepherd would count himself fortunate if he could find evidence sufficient to convince the owners that a lion had ravaged the flock. In that case he would not have to pay for the loss of the animal (Gen 31:39; Exod 22:10–13).

"Two leg bones or a piece of an ear" might get a hired shepherd off the hook, but only bits and pieces of an animal ravaged by a lion meant the lion's attack was successful. That aspect of the comparison implied that Israel would not survive the attack of the enemy (v. 11). Only fragments of their former luxurious lifestyle would be found after the enemy overran the land. Finding bits and pieces of the animal only indicated its destruction. If Israelites were to "be saved" like that (apparent irony), all hope of survival would be shattered. "Only enough will survive to prove who the victim was."[130]

The target of the prophet's message was Samaria's wealthy rulers, who were living in luxury (cf. 6:4).[131] Translators disagree over the correct way to render the last four words in the Hebrew text. Compare the NIV with the following: "with the corner of a couch and part of a bed" (NRSV); "like a corner of a couch or a chip from the leg of a bed" (NEB); "with the corner of a bed and the cover of a couch" (NASB).

What is clear from the translations is the reference to sleep furniture, couch and bed (*mittâ* and *ʿāreś*), on which "they were accustomed to while away

---

[128] T. J. Finley, *Joel, Amos, Obadiah* (Chicago: Moody, 1990), 190.

[129] Other places in Amos where the style may be observed include 2:13; 5:24; and 6:12.

[130] Andersen and Freedman, *Amos,* 408.

[131] Paul rendered יֹשְׁבֵ ב־ "dwell with," not "sit on" (*Amos,* 120). The expression points forward to "the paltry pieces of property that the wealthy Israelites will barely manage to save."

their time in feasting and carousing."[132] The reading "Damascus" as in the NIV would require *dammeśeq,* where the MT has *děmešeq,* a word occurring only here and meaning something like "corner."[133] Reading "Damascus" produces an elliptical last line (literally), "and in Damascus, a couch." Making sense of a reference to Damascus here also is difficult. Hayes suggests that Samaria's rulers were exiled to Damascus[134] or that an Israelite merchant colony there was "delivered" when Jeroboam II conquered it (2 Kgs 14:28).[135] The term more likely refers to a part of a couch. The sense is either that they would perish "suddenly while living lavishly, sprawled on beds and couches"[136] or that the "number of Israelites who survive the disaster will be like the few bits of a mutilated sheep left by the lion, or like a few scraps of furniture salvaged from a looted city."[137] Clearly the message of the verse is pessimistic as regards the future for Samaria.

(4) Judgment against Every Aspect of Israel's Life (3:13–15)

13"Hear this and testify against the house of Jacob," declares the Lord, the LORD God Almighty.
14"On the day I punish Israel for her sins,
 I will destroy the altars of Bethel;
 the horns of the altar will be cut off
 and fall to the ground.
15I will tear down the winter house
 along with the summer house;
 the houses adorned with ivory will be destroyed
 and the mansions will be demolished,"
 declares the LORD.

Samaria was the likely location of the prophet when he preached the message, though the name of the city is not used. The royal palace, ivory houses, winter and summer houses, and mansions were more likely to be found in Samaria than in any other location.

The persons summoned to "hear" and "testify"[138] are left unidentified. Perhaps they are the people from Ashdod and Egypt called to assemble in the mountains of Samaria to observe Israel's unrest and oppression (v. 9). More

---

[132] Ibid.
[133] See the note in Wolff, *Joel and Amos,* 196–97.
[134] Hayes, *Amos,* 135.
[135] Niehaus, "Amos," 1:386.
[136] Finley, *Joel, Amos, Obadiah,* 192.
[137] Andersen and Freedman, *Amos,* 410; G. Smith, *Amos,* 122.
[138] Paul translated הָעִידוּ as "warn" rather than "testify" and identified "court heralds" as those who might serve the warning (*Amos,* 123). That is a possible alternative, but the larger context calls for "witness" as the meaning of the term (3:9).

important than the identity of the prophet's audience was the covenant lawsuit motif the summons introduced. The fact that only a hint of indictment is visible ("on the day I punish Israel for her sins," v. 14) indicates the close connection with the previous sections in chap. 3.[139] The indictment is stated plainly: the practice of violence and destruction (3:10) and an opulent lifestyle (3:12).

ISRAEL: THE HOUSE OF JACOB (3:13).   The integrating word in this section is "house" (bêt). With this term reference is made to (1) Israel as the covenant people of God; (2) Bethel ("house of God"), the primary royal shrine in the Northern Kingdom; and (3) winter and summer houses, houses of ivory, and the mansions, indicators of the wealth and extravagance of Israel's leaders.

3:13 A double imperative opens this message. Unnamed witnesses are ordered to "hear" in order that they may testify to the verdict. They needed to hear God's threat of punishment for sins associated with Israel's worship at Bethel and with their lifestyle ("winter house" and "summer house"). The preposition bĕ ("in" or "against") designates "house of Jacob" as the entity against whom the witnesses were to testify.

"House of Jacob" as a title for Israel marks the nation as a people in covenant with the Lord.[140] They were not simply Jeroboam's people. They were God's people. In that relationship they were to hear the message Amos brought. In that relationship they were to be judged. Amos alerted his audience that his message was from God, their covenant partner. Only here does Amos employ the expanded title for God, "the LORD, the LORD God Almighty."[141] That title pictures Israel's God in his role as leader of Israel's armies (or the heavenly host) on occasions of holy war, but here holy war would be conducted by God against Israel.

BETHEL: THE HOUSE OF GOD (3:14).   The foci of divine judgment were Israel's worship and Israel's lifestyle, symbolized by Bethel and Samaria. Their "sins" (pĕšāʿîm) in both realms were rebellion against God. Pĕšāʿîm designated covenant violations of various sorts. At the top of the list were worship violations at the Bethel sanctuary.

3:14 The "day" referred to points to an unspecified future intervention of Israel's God, "the day of the LORD." The term translated "punish" (pāqdî) has a broad range of meanings (see comments on 3:2), but in the prophets it usually means "punish."[142] In a sense the nation's rebellious acts carried in

---

[139] Stuart (Hosea-Jonah, 329) sees 3:9–11,12,13–15; and 4:1–3 as subsections of one message.

[140] It was at Bethel that the Lord appeared to Jacob in a dream confirming the Abrahamic covenant with him and his descendants, and Jacob vowed that "this stone that I have set up as a pillar will be God's house [בֵּית אֱלֹהִים]" in Gen 28:22.

[141] אֲדֹנָי יְהוִה אֱלֹהֵי הַצְּבָאוֹת, "Lord Yahweh God of the hosts."

[142] Stuart, Hosea-Jonah, 331.

themselves the judgment of God. This is not to suggest that the divine visitation would be impersonal and mechanical. To the contrary, this oracle portrays God acting directly and without an intermediate agent to judge Israel.

First the Lord stated his general program of judgment. Then he specified the particular targets of it. At the top of the list were Bethel's altars. The plural may designate multiple worship sites dedicated to various pagan deities or multiple altars at one site.[143] Reference may be to the two altars of the Bethel sanctuary dedicated to the worship of the Lord. If the Bethel sanctuary was patterned after the Jerusalem temple, an altar for burning sacrifices was in the outer court, and an incense altar was inside the structure.

Condemnation of the altars could have been because of their use in worshiping foreign deities. But worship at Bethel was syncretistic in that while they thought they worshiped the Lord, they did so through pagan practices using golden calves as the images to which they paid homage. Over a century earlier Jeroboam I had set up golden calves for worship, one at Bethel and one at Dan (1 Kgs 12:28). Not long thereafter the Omride dynasty, led by Ahab and Jezebel, instituted pagan deity worship. Despite the prophetic protest by Elijah and Elisha and the massacre by Jehu (note Jehu's decision not to destroy the calves in 2 Kgs 10:28), the north always participated in the worship of other gods (2 Kgs 17:16), even though they thought their worship was right. As such, they broke the first and most important commandment. Despite their infidelity, God continued to send prophets, most notably Amos and Hosea, to persuade them to change their hearts and their ways. Worship carried on at the Bethel sanctuary was contradictory (practice and proclamation did not match) and contrary to God's will (Deut 12; Hos 4:15). Basically, it was wrong because it ignored the true God (Deut 6:4–5).

The second use of the word "altar" in v. 14 is singular. Only the altar for burning sacrifices had "horns" or projections at the corners. These horns functioned to hold the wood and the victims in place on top of the altar. The implication of the horns being "cut off" is that no longer would guilty Israel have a place of asylum (1 Kgs 1:50; 2:28). So guilty was Israel that God would destroy the nation's refuge.

RESIDENCES: HOUSES OF LUXURY (3:15). "House of Jacob" designated the family of Israel as a covenant partner with God. "Bethel" ("house of God") stood for the place where Jacob had first encountered God above the stairway to heaven (Gen 28:11–17; cf. 35:1–7) and where Israel engaged in counterfeit worship. "Winter house," "summer house," "houses adorned with ivory," and "the mansions" signaled the opulent lifestyle of Samaria's leading citizens.

3:15 The first-person style clearly indicates that Israel's God was to be

---

[143] Andersen and Freedman, *Amos*, 411.

their judge. He threatened to judge their worship (v. 14) and their luxurious lifestyle (v. 15). Sometimes winter houses and summer houses were in different geographical locations (1 Kgs 21:1,18). Winter quarters and summer quarters could be separate parts of one building complex.[144] The latter interpretation would require translation of the preposition ʿal in an adversative manner: "I will smite the winter house *against* the summer house." The preposition rendered "along with" (ʿal) may mean "upon" or "above." Wolff proposed the meaning "together with," arguing that in a two-story structure the upper airy one would be the summer quarters, not the winter space. Wolff was correct in his assessment that the context calls for total destruction, not the destruction of the upper story only.[145] More important than the location of these houses was the announcement of their destruction.

"Houses adorned with ivory" describes an extravagant use of ivory inlay as a decorative procedure. Only the very wealthy could have afforded use of ivory in this way. Such houses were destined to perish in the coming judgment. "The mansions" (*bāttîm rabbîm*, either "many houses" or "great houses") designates either sprawling structures that previously only kings could afford to build or the proliferation of houses as an indication of the nation's wealth. In any case God's judgment would put an end to them. Josiah, king of Judah (639–609 B.C.), destroyed the altar at Bethel as a part of his radical reform movement. Residents of the area identified a tomb there as that of "the man of God who came from Judah and pronounced against the altar of Bethel" (2 Kgs 23:15–17). They understood that the prophecy of Amos found fulfillment in Josiah's destruction of the altar of Bethel. The enduring principle here is that God will destroy elaborate altars, expensive houses, and other accoutrements of an extravagant lifestyle when these items are acquired through oppression, fraud, and strong-arm tactics. The idolatry of the people led to their opulent lifestyles. Life apart from God may yield temporary material gain, but it will surely result in eternal loss.

3. Words Condemning Israel's Women, Worship, and Stubbornness (4:1–13)

(1) Condemnation of Samaria's Self-serving Women (4:1–3)

[1]Hear this word, you cows of Bashan on Mount Samaria,
    you women who oppress the poor and crush the needy

---

[144] S. Paul concludes that "wealthy residents of Samaria followed the example of royalty and built for themselves separate pleasure estates in accordance with the climatic conditions of their country" (Paul, "Amos III 15—Winter and Summer Mansions," *VT* 28 [1978]: 359). See also Wolff, *Joel and Amos,* 201. Separate geographical locations is probably the best understanding of what is meant by winter and summer houses.

[145] Wolff, *Joel and Amos,* 202.

> and say to your husbands, "Bring us some drinks!"
> ²The Sovereign LORD has sworn by his holiness:
> "The time will surely come
> when you will be taken away with hooks,
> the last of you with fishhooks.
> ³You will each go straight out
> through breaks in the wall,
> and you will be cast out toward Harmon,"
>   declares the LORD.

The call for attention ("hear this word") ties the oracle to the previous ones beginning at 3:1 and to the subsequent ones beginning at 5:1. Wendland analyzes the chapter as a series of seven judgment oracles (vv. 1–3,4–5,6,7–8,9,10,11), all ending with "declares the LORD," followed by a conclusion (v. 12) and final doxology (v. 13). This first oracle, he notes, has links in both directions.[146] The first oracle in chap. 4 contains an accusation (v. 1) and an announcement of the Lord's punishment (vv. 2–3). Commentators generally agree that the addressees were the elite women of Samaria's indulgent, wealthy upper class, while the occurrence of masculine pronouns (e.g., the first "you" in v. 2) may suggest that the male population was not excluded.[147] Some have argued that these women considered themselves to be the "worshipers of the mighty bull of Samaria (Hos 8:5–6), a north Israelite manifestation of Yahweh."[148] "Cows of Bashan" could have been a name these particular women called themselves as disciples of the cult that was a conflation of Yahweh and Baal.[149] Their idolatry was their sin, and thus they were not followers of the Shema (Deut 6:4–5), which proclaimed Yahweh as the one true God. There is little evidence, however, to support this view.[150]

THE COWS OF BASHAN (4:1). **4:1** Bashan was a fertile plain and mountain range on both sides of the middle and upper Yarmuk River. The region was noted for its lush pasturage and fine cattle (cf. Deut 32:14; Ps 22:12; Isa 33:9; Jer 50:19; Ezek 39:18; Mic 7:14; Nah 1:4).

The basic charge against the "cows of Bashan" was exploitation of the poor. Three plural participles describe their indirect methods of getting what

---

[146] Wendland, "The 'Word of the Lord' and the Organization of Amos," 12.

[147] Andersen and Freedman weigh the arguments that men are here figuratively portrayed as women and opt for "the lordly women of Samaria" as the primary reference (*Amos,* 415–17, 420–21).

[148] K. Koch, *The Prophets* (Philadelphia: Fortress, 1983), 46.

[149] Ibid. H. M. Barstad, *The Religious Polemics of Amos,* VTSup 34 (Leiden: Brill, 1984), 37–44; Paul, *Amos,* 128; P. Jacobs, "'Cows of Bashan'—A Note on the Interpretation of Amos 4:1," *JBL* 104 (1985): 109–10; A. J. Williams, "A Further Suggestion about Amos IV 1–3," *VT* (1979): 206–12.

[150] There is no biblical evidence of a Baal cult in Bashan in spite of efforts to find it in Ps 68:15–16. See G. Smith, *Amos,* 127–28.

they wanted: "the ones oppressing the poor"; "the ones striking the needy"; "the ones saying to their husbands." The imperative "bring" addressed to the husbands reveals the indirect methods employed by the women. They nagged[151] their husbands to "bring" more and more to satisfy their thirst. Thus, while pagan worship may be in the background, it is more likely the term "cows of Bashan" was simply a figure for women whose every desire was being abundantly met. In turn the lords exploited the poor, taking their meager material wealth to satisfy the insatiable desire of their women. While the term ʾādôn is rare for "husband" (see Gen 18:12; Judg 19:26; Ps 45:12), it probably is best understood as being used in contrast to ʾādonāy in the next verse.[152]

The term translated "poor" (dallîm)[153] means "scanty," "helpless," "powerless," or "insignificant." Samaria's pampered darlings oppressed the poor indirectly by nagging their husbands to extort the scanty fare on which the poor subsisted. The verb translated "crush" means "smash up," "ill-treat," or "abuse." "Needy" ones were those lacking the basic necessities of life. Through their lords Samaria's women abused this segment of society.

Use of the imperative "bring" indicates the strong will and determination of Samaria's court women to satisfy their indulgent appetites. Their demand for an indulgent lifestyle led to oppression of the poor to support that lifestyle.

THE UNDIGNIFIED DEPARTURE (4:2–3).   God put himself under oath to announce his verdict on "the cows of Bashan." That fact indicates the strength of his reaction to the women.

4:2   "Has sworn" (v. 2) is an oath formula and is more forceful than the messenger formula ("thus says the LORD") as the procedure for announcing judgment.[154] "His holiness" refers to God's essential being and to a quality of his character. As surely as God is separate from humankind, his verdict on the court women of Samaria was to be executed (cf. Ps 89:35).

The future condition of Samaria's court women would be far worse than the condition their self-indulgence had created for the poor. A language signal that something startling was about to be announced is the term beginning Yahweh's message in Hebrew, usually translated "behold" (hinnēh). Unfortunately, the NIV regularly leaves it out. "For behold days are coming" is a literal rendering of the first part of the verdict (v. 2b). What it does functionally is designate some indefinite future time for the fulfillment of the announced judgment.

---

[151] "Saying" is an active participle implying repetitious saying.

[152] Paul, *Amos,* 129. The normal word for husband in the OT is בַּעַל.

[153] The feminine plural form of the term translated "poor" (דַּלִּים) refers in Gen 41:19 to scrawny cows.

[154] According to Wolff, "When the oath formula replaces the messenger formula, the irrevocable nature of that which is proclaimed is set forth in the strongest terms" (*Joel and Amos,* 206).

The remainder of v. 2 poses many problems for translators and interpreters. Rough and radical removal of the offending women is the sense, but how they would be removed, in what condition, and to what location are not clear.

The terms frequently translated "hooks" (*ṣinnôt* and *sîrôt*) do not appear anywhere else in the Old Testament with this meaning. *Ṣinnôt* usually means "shields" (1 Kgs 10:16). *Sîrôt* means "pots" for cooking meat (2 Kgs 4:38). A masculine form of each word means "thorn" (Job 5:5; Isa 34:13). By extension from this meaning, many translators render the terms as hooks for dragging away corpses or to fasten captives together.[155] God's verdict envisions a major effort to dispose of the corpses followed by a mop-up exercise to dispose of the remainder (v. 2c).

Hayes has a convincing argument against deportation of exiles as the meaning of 4:2b–3.[156] The essence of his argument is that Amos utilized normal exile vocabulary elsewhere in the book (1:5–6,9; 5:27; 6:7) but avoided that vocabulary here. He suggests the disposal of human corpses following a violent battle as the meaning of the language.

4:3 The purpose of the wall would have been to protect the livestock. "Breaks in the wall" would mean that the "cows" were no longer protected. The dead bodies of Samaria's once-pampered darlings would be picked up like so much meat. Breaches in the wall around Samaria would be so numerous that each corpse could be lifted up and carried away in any direction, "each opposite her,"[157] through the nearest gap. Final disposition of the dead bodies is unclear. "Toward the Harmon" is the reading of the Hebrew text. The problem is that no such place is known. Alternative readings in the earlier versions, such as Remman, Mount Hermon, and Armenia, appear to be guesses. Hayes assumes the original reading was a rare word meaning "the dung-pit," or "the garbage heap" (the word appears in Isa 25:10).[158] With all the uncertainties of the text, undignified departure of Samaria's court women from their former life of luxury seems plain enough. The closing messenger formula again punctuates the Lord's verdict on them. Those who oppress the poor and crush the needy in order to support an extravagant lifestyle can expect God's harsh judgment to fall upon them.

---

[155] S. Paul, after consideration of all the possibilities, concluded that "the least amount of difficulties are attached to the interpretation of צִנּוֹת and סִירוֹת as 'baskets' and 'pots' respectively," used for packing and transporting fish ("Fishing Imagery in Amos 4:2," *JBL* 97/2 [1978]: 188). Contrary to A. J. Williams's suggestion that Amos may have been dealing with mythological concepts and fertility cults, the prophet seems to be concerned with God's judgment upon and radical ejection of Israel's wealthy court women ("A Further Suggestion about Amos IV 1–3," *VT* 19 [1979]: 209).

[156] Hayes, *Amos*, 140–41.

[157] אִשָּׁה נֶגְדָּהּ means "a woman [or each] opposite her" (4:3).

[158] Hayes, *Amos*, 142.

(2) Condemnation of Israel's Worship (4:4–5)

> ⁴"Go to Bethel and sin;
>   go to Gilgal and sin yet more.
> Bring your sacrifices every morning,
>   your tithes every three years.
> ⁵Burn leavened bread as a thank offering
>   and brag about your freewill offerings—
> boast about them, you Israelites,
>   for this is what you love to do,"
>   declares the Sovereign LORD.

The form of these two verses is that of a priestly call to worship. A typical priestly call would have directed the worshiper to come to the shrine to seek God and to find life (5:4,6). The audience must have been shocked when Amos invited them to come to the worship site to sin. They would immediately recognize the sarcasm in this parody as an accusation for doing not what the Lord requires but rather the very things that are detestable.

PARODY OF A PRIESTLY CALL TO WORSHIP (4:4a).   **4:4a**   The imperative "go" (*bōʾû*) also means "come" or "enter." Normally pilgrims gathered at a worship site expected to hear a priest invite them to enter the sanctuary to worship. Since Bethel had been a revered worship center from patriarchal times (Gen 12:8; 28:19), the command to enter Bethel implied a religious pilgrimage. "Sin" (*pišʿû*, "rebel") is the direct opposite of the purpose of entering a sacred shrine. To find restored relationship with God and thus to find life is the usual direction issued by a priest. Ordering pilgrims to enter the sanctuary to break with the Lord is the point of the prophet's command.

Jeroboam I (son of Nebat) erected calves at Bethel and Dan as alternate worship sites to the temple at Jerusalem (1 Kgs 12:26–30a). By the time of Jeroboam II (son of Joash), Bethel and Gilgal were Israel's popular shrines. Gilgal had been the first camp for Israel after they entered the promised land. There they arranged stones taken from the Jordan River as a memorial of their miraculous crossing of the Jordan (Josh 4:20–24). That site became a popular place for Israel to worship God. In Josh 5:9 the name Gilgal is associated with the verb *gālal*, "to roll," when the Lord explains after the circumcision of Israel's new generation that "Today I have rolled away the reproach of Egypt from you." Now because of Israel's behavior at Gilgal they would bring reproach upon themselves again (cf. Pss 44:13; 79:4; Jer 24:9; 29:18; Ezek 5:14–15).

Amos ironically invited Israel to go to Bethel and "sin" (*pišʿû*) and go to Gilgal and "sin yet more." He was not calling them to do something new but ironically to continue their sinful worship. The following verses show that the ritual itself was not at fault. They were bringing the prescribed sacrifices, even freewill offerings and tithes. Where they were at fault was in making their rituals an end in themselves when they were meant to be a means toward and an expression of fellowship with God.[159]

PROLIFERATION OF SACRIFICES (4:4b–5).   **4:4b–5**   Was the reason for condemnation of Israel's worship at Bethel and Gilgal the proliferation of sacrifices? But "every morning" may be rendered "in the morning," with no suggestion of extravagance or proliferation. The pilgrim would present his sacrifice (*zebaḥ*) on the morning of his first day at the sanctuary. However, the dissonant note sounded in v. 4a ("sin yet more") may control v. 4b. If so, the time references are distributives, "every morning" and "every third year [lit., "day"]."[160]

The law prescribed daily offerings (Lev 6:8–13) and a special tithe every three years for the benefit of the Levites (Deut 14:28–29). Leavened bread as well as unleavened was to be brought with the thank offering (Lev 7:11–13), which along with the freewill offering was voluntary. The thank offering was brought either in anticipation of or gratitude for a deliverance of some kind. The freewill offering was to be an expression of gratitude for God's goodness more generally. These were both types of peace offerings, unique in that the worshiper was to share in the sacred meal.[161]

The terms translated "brag" (*qirĕʾû*) and "boast" (*hašmîʿû*) could also be rendered "proclaim" and "make known." Together the terms suggest a prideful and boastful attitude toward their generous sacrifices and offerings. Their motive was to magnify their generosity toward God, not to praise God's gracious provisions for them.

An expected report from the priest under normal circumstances was a statement of God's acceptance of the offering and his pleasure in the worshiper. In the place of that kind of response, Amos accused the worshipers of loving to brag about their generosity. Israel loved religious activities. That is not the same thing as loving God. Worshipers must practice a constant vigil as regards motive in performing religious rituals. Is the motive to show love for God or only to show love for the practice of religion? The problem in Israel, of course, was even greater in that while on the one hand they were pretending piety at the illegitimate altars, on the other hand they were pursuing an ostentatious lifestyle by trampling on the heads of the poor (cf. 2:6–8; 3:9–10; 4:1).

---

[159] Hayes argues that the reason for calling Israel's worship activities "sin" was associated with political factions identified with the two sites. He supposes that all worship activities at the sites promoted strife between those loyal to Jeroboam II at Bethel and those loyal to Pekah at Gilgal (Hayes, *Amos*, 143). But as Finley notes, this involves a number of unlikely assumptions (Finley, *Joel, Amos, Obadiah*, 205).

[160] Finley points out that the use of יָמִים for "years" has parallels and perhaps "stresses the completion of a particular period of time as measured in so many days" (*Joel, Amos, Obadiah*, 207). He agrees with Driver that a literal translation would involve a rather extreme exaggeration.

[161] G. J. Wenham, *The Book of Leviticus*, NICOT (Grand Rapids: Eerdmans, 1979), 76–81, 123–25.

(3) Condemnation of Israel's Stubbornness (4:6–13)

⁶"I gave you empty stomachs in every city
   and lack of bread in every town,
   yet you have not returned to me,"
                                            declares the LORD.
⁷"I also withheld rain from you
   when the harvest was still three months away.
 I sent rain on one town,
   but withheld it from another.
 One field had rain;
   another had none and dried up.
⁸People staggered from town to town for water
   but did not get enough to drink,
   yet you have not returned to me,"
                                            declares the LORD.
⁹"Many times I struck your gardens and vineyards,
   I struck them with blight and mildew.
 Locusts devoured your fig and olive trees,
   yet you have not returned to me,"
                                            declares the LORD.
¹⁰"I sent plagues among you
   as I did to Egypt.
 I killed your young men with the sword,
   along with your captured horses.
 I filled your nostrils with the stench of your camps,
   yet you have not returned to me,"
                                            declares the LORD.
¹¹"I overthrew some of you
   as I overthrew Sodom and Gomorrah.
 You were like a burning stick snatched from the fire,
   yet you have not returned to me,"
                                            declares the LORD.
¹²"Therefore this is what I will do to you, Israel,
   and because I will do this to you,
   prepare to meet your God, O Israel."
¹³He who forms the mountains,
   creates the wind,
   and reveals his thoughts to man,
 he who turns dawn to darkness,
   and treads the high places of the earth—
   the LORD God Almighty is his name.

The oracle formula "declares the LORD" (*nĕʾum YHWH*) separates 4:6–11 into five sections.[162] Preceding that formula is the repeated refrain "yet you

---

[162] The expression appears after vv. 6,8,9,10,11.

have not returned to me." The refrain strengthens the fivefold division of the material. Just as there are seven items in vv. 4–5 delineating Israel's sin, these five sections contain seven divinely controlled calamities (cf. Lev 26:24, "I myself will be hostile toward you and will afflict you for your sins seven times over"). The calamities are past actions of the Lord aimed at securing Israel's return to God by bringing upon them the curses for covenant disobedience set forth in Leviticus and Deuteronomy (cf. Deut 4:29–31; 30:1–10; Isa 9:11–13; Jer 32:33–42; Hos 2:5–13: (1) famine (v. 6; cf. Lev 26:26), (2) drought (vv. 7–8; cf. Lev 26:19; Deut 28:22–24), (3) blight and mildew (v. 9a; cf. Deut 28:22), (4) locusts (v. 9b; cf. Deut 28:38,42), (5) plagues (v. 10a; cf. Lev 26:14; Deut 28:21–22,27,35,59–61), (6) the sword (v. 10b; cf. Lev 26:25,33; Deut 32:23–24,41–42), and (7) complete overthrow (v. 11; cf. Deut 29:23). The number seven carries the symbolic meaning of completion, or fullness. God had done all he could do to gain Israel's repentance.[163] But they failed to connect the calamities with God's purpose. With his "therefore" in v. 12 Amos shifted the focus to Israel's future encounter with God. The doxology or hymn fragment in v. 13 reveals the kind of God Israel must meet.

FAMINE (4:6). **4:6** Famine was a common event in the ancient Near East. Here the famine is brought by God as a warning to the people, but they did not heed the warning. "Empty stomachs" is literally "cleanness of teeth." "Lack of bread" is the reason. Taken together the two expressions experientially describe a famine. A literal translation reveals the emphasis on God as the causative agent in the calamity: "And also I, even I, gave to you cleanness of teeth." Both phrases affirm the reality of a famine. The verb translated "returned" (sŭb)[164] is the primary word for repentance in the Old Testament. Famine should have driven Israel to repentance and return to God, but it failed to elicit that response.

DROUGHT (4:7–8). Drought was a chief cause of famine in Israel and a major concern for the economy. Thus two verses are used to describe its effect on crops (v. 7) and on people (v. 8). Sparse rain during the rainy season from October to April would result in a sharply limited harvest of grain in May and June.[165] The drought described here was no natural calamity from the prophet's perspective. God caused it.

4:7 Again the language is emphatic in the declaration that God caused the drought. For God to withhold the rain "when the harvest was still three months away" was certain to have an adverse effect on the grain harvest. Perhaps to dramatize God's control of the rain, he sent rain on one town but withheld it from another. He caused rain on one field, but not on another. The

---

[163] Wendland, "The 'Word of the Lord' and the Organization of Amos," 13; Paul, *Amos*, 144.

[164] The basic meaning of שׁוּב is "turn" or "return," but when God is the object toward which the action of turning is aimed, repentance is the technical meaning of the term.

[165] Hayes, *Amos*, 146.

result was a controlled drought. One area was affected; another area was untouched by the drought.

4:8 The most obvious result of drought is thirst for water. People from towns where rain fell preserved water in cisterns. People from drought-stricken towns had to go to adjacent towns in search of water. The NRSV provides a more literal rendering of the first line, "So two or three towns wandered to our town to drink water." Amos painted a verbal picture of people staggering from town to town hoping in vain to slake their thirst. The verb translated "staggered" ($nā^c\hat{u}$)[166] captures the weakness and panic of people frantically searching for relief.

God's purpose in the drought was to reveal that only he is God, not some image in a shrine. While the Israelites probably were involved in some form of Canaanite worship, the Lord revealed that their prayers to calves did not yield a full harvest. But again Israel failed to return to God and live (5:6).

PLANT DISEASE AND LOCUSTS (4:9). **4:9** Two additional categories of calamities affecting food production in Israel were plant diseases and insects. Blight and mildew represent crop diseases in general (cf. Deut 28:22; 1 Kgs 8:37; Hag 2:17), and locusts represent pests (cf. 7:1–3; Joel 1:4). While Israel prayed to golden calves for a plentiful harvest, God smote Israel with blight, mildew, and locusts.[167] But Israel failed to recognize God as Lord and did not return to him.

PLAGUE AND WAR (4:10). **4:10** The reason for treating plague with war ("sword") probably stemmed from the link of the two items in Lev 26:25 and in Deut 28:49–59. Plagues of various sorts often accompanied war.

"Plague" is a general term referring to any lethal epidemic,[168] but Amos's words would have reminded the people of the plagues God sent on Egypt to redeem Israel from bondage, to punish the Egyptians for opposing him, and to manifest his holy name (cf. Exod 9:16; Deut 7:8–20). Now they had placed themselves in the position of Egypt, opposing God's will, and they were being punished as Egypt had been (cf. Deut 28:27,60). But war and plague did not persuade Israel to return to God.

OVERTHROW (4:11). The final calamity Amos described may have been like an earthquake in the days of Sodom and Gomorrah. At least that is the usual interpretation of how God overthrew the sinful cities of Sodom and Gomorrah (Gen 19).

4:11 The fact and extent of Israel's overthrow, not the method, were primary concerns of the prophet. Total destruction was conveyed by the refer-

---

[166] The root נוע means "stagger," "quiver," "waver," "totter," or "tremble."

[167] The translation "many times" is uncertain. It translates an infinitive construct (הַרְבּוֹת) that occurs later in the clause. It may also refer to the produce of the gardens and vineyards or to their number. Cf. Finley, *Joel, Amos, Obadiah,* 214.

[168] Wolff, *Joel and Amos,* 221.

ence to the overthrow of Sodom and Gomorrah (cf. Deut 29:22–24; Jer 20:16). Israel, like Lot and his family, was like a brand snatched from the fire, fortunate to be alive. But even Israel's narrow escape did not turn them toward God. Secular society sees only natural phenomena when various calamities adversely affect people. God's people correctly inquire about the possible purpose of God in such calamities. Always the right question to ask when people are hit by destructive calamities is, "What does God want to see happen as a result of the calamity?" Is repentance the appropriate response?

FINAL ENCOUNTER (4:12). The litany of past calamities God had brought upon Israel had failed to gain Israel's return to God. Amos urged Israel to prepare to meet their God. Enigmatic language veils the nature of the encounter Amos announced. As we have grown accustomed, Amos "heightens the suspense of his audience by alluding to some enigmatic horror yet to come,"[169] thus filling them with "dread uncertainty."[170]

4:12 "Therefore" (*lākēn*) in Amos usually introduces a message of judgment from God. "Prepare" and "meet" describe an awesome theophanic encounter with God in Exod 19:10–19. The circumstance here, however, is one of covenant breaking rather than covenant making. Amos alludes here to that terrifying experience when Israel first encountered their God, "who is a consuming fire, a jealous God" (Deut 4:24). But the theophany of judgment Amos was announcing would be not to discipline Israel (Deut 4:36) but to destroy them because of their stubborn refusal to return to the Lord.

The duplication of "I will do to you" (*ʾeʿĕśeh-lāk*) is difficult to understand, and so is the reference to "this" (*kōh* in the first line and *zōʾt* in the second). While redaction and form critics see this verse as conflated and edited, S. Paul and others see the repetition as perhaps involving some sort of hand gesture, the original proclamation meaning undetectable in written form.[171] The phrase is reminiscent of an oath formula (e.g., 1 Kgs 2:23) in the context of blessings and curses.[172] The repetition, if spoken aloud slowly, heightens the anticipation of the ultimate declaration of the prophet: "Prepare to meet your God, O Israel." G. Smith translates, "Therefore, thus I will do to you, Israel, // and because I will do this to you / prepare."[173]

In the exodus setting "prepare" involved the people in purification rites, among other things. The term conveys the idea of qualification for cultic par-

---

[169] Paul, *Amos,* 150.

[170] Niehaus, "Amos," 1:405.

[171] Ibid.; Wolff, *Joel and Amos,* 217.

[172] Paul, *Amos,* 150–51.

[173] G. Smith, *Amos,* 137. Cf. Mays, *Amos,* 82. Finley, however, thinks that כֹּה, which usually points ahead, points back here (as in Ezek 23:39; Neh 13:18; 2 Chr 19:9–10; 24:11) to the overthrow of "some" in v. 11. The point is that God is about to overthrow "all of Israel, not merely part of her, just as He overthrew Sodom and Gomorrah" (*Joel, Amos, Obadiah,* 215).

ticipation in covenant making. That would not seem to be the meaning in Amos 4:12, based on the prophet's strong denunciation of Israel's sanctuaries and their cultic activities. They are to prepare for the ultimate confrontation.

"Meet" in the exodus setting of covenant making involved getting the people in a proper location for the encounter with God (Exod 19:17). Moses led the people out of the camp to the foot of Mount Sinai. Then God appeared on the mountain. The text magnifies the awesome holiness of God. Perhaps Amos wanted his audience to reflect upon the implications of encounter with God, especially in light of their steadfast refusal to return to God. The calamities God had brought upon them in the past (4:6–11) would appear as mere warm-up drills when compared to the catastrophic encounter with God they faced now. The prophet's exhortation, "Prepare to meet your God, O Israel," was neither a call to repentance nor an invitation to covenant renewal;[174] rather, it was a summons to judgment.

"Your God" implies the relationship God held to Israel in his role as Lord of the covenant and thus points to their accountability to him. His people failed to return to him in faith, subjection, and obedience. He would come to them in devastating judgment.

THE AWESOME GOD (4:13).   The reason Israel should be shaken to their senses by this summons to judgment is offered in v. 13, which is introduced in Hebrew by *kî hinnēh*, "for behold." The verse usually is identified as a hymn fragment by its use of participles to describe God as creator, revealer, and performer of awesome acts. Participial construction characterizes hymnic passages throughout the Old Testament. Two similar hymnic sections in Amos are 5:8–9 and 9:5–6.[175] That each of these contains the refrain "the LORD is his name" may suggest that they were all from a hymn known in Amos's time.[176] He quoted from it to reveal the nature of the God who would judge Israel, although like the theophany motif the hymn would not originally have had this purpose. "Amos transforms the good news of God's glorious might into a fearful warning of judgment because his power will be used against rather than for Israel."[177]

4:13 Five assertions in this hymn fragment portray the nature of God. Two phrases describe God's creative activity: "forms the mountains" (*yôṣēr hārîm*) and "creates the wind" (*bōrēʾ rûaḥ*). Both verbs are also found in Genesis 1–2. The one whose power could form the majestic greatness of the mountains and control the fierceness of the storm is one before whom the

---

[174] Paul, *Amos*, 151.

[175] See Paul's excursus on the doxologies (*Amos*, 152–53).

[176] Andersen and Freedman, however, argue that the formal similarity of the hymns and the woes throughout the book "points to Amos as their presumptive author or at least adapter. They were deliberately composed, and both series were composed to go together" (*Amos*, 463).

[177] G. Smith, *Amos*, 148.

wise should tremble. One phrase notes God's act of revealing his plan to humankind. While God certainly knows our thoughts and motives (Jer 11:20; Ps 94:11) and can recognize false worship, the verb "reveals" (*maggîd*) suggests *revelation,* not *declaration.*[178]

The two final phrases concern God's awesome acts of judgment. The word for "darkness" (*ʿêpâ*) occurs elsewhere only in Job 11:22 in a context of death. G. Smith explains that "the turning of dawn into darkness describes how God can turn the positive potential of dawn into a dark and dismal night (4:6–11)."[179] In the context of a hymn of praise the "high places" would refer to mountains (cf. Deut 32:13; 2 Sam 1:19; Ezek 36:2), but it also can suggest the places of Israel's idolatry (cf. Hos 10:8; Amos 7:9). "Treading" (*dōrēk*) can symbolize ownership (cf. Deut 11:24; Job 9:8, where "waves" also is the term for "high places"), the subjugation of enemies (Deut 33:29, where it occurs with "high places," Ps 91:13), or the Lord's judgment like one treading grapes in the winepress (Isa 63:3; Lam 1:15). Perhaps the closest parallel occurs in Mic 1:3–4 in a context of judgment against Israel:

> Look! The LORD is coming from his dwelling place;
>> he comes down and treads the high places of the earth.
> The mountains melt beneath him
>> and the valleys split apart,
> like wax before the fire,
>> like water rushing down a slope.

4. Words of Woe for Israel (5:1–6:14)

(1) Funeral Song for Fallen Israel (5:1–17)

> [1]Hear this word, O house of Israel, this lament I take up concerning you:
> [2]"Fallen is Virgin Israel,
>   never to rise again,
> deserted in her own land,
>   with no one to lift her up."
> [3]This is what the Sovereign LORD says:
> "The city that marches out a thousand strong for Israel
>   will have only a hundred left;
> the town that marches out a hundred strong
>   will have only ten left."
>
> [4]This is what the LORD says to the house of Israel:
> "Seek me and live;
> [5]do not seek Bethel,

---

[178] Finley, *Joel, Amos, Obadiah,* 217–18, contra G. Smith, *Amos,* 148, and others.
[179] G. Smith, *Amos,* 148.

do not go to Gilgal,
  do not journey to Beersheba.
For Gilgal will surely go into exile,
  and Bethel will be reduced to nothing."
[6]Seek the LORD and live,
  or he will sweep through the house of Joseph like a fire;
it will devour,
  and Bethel will have no one to quench it.

[7]You who turn justice into bitterness
  and cast righteousness to the ground
[8](he who made the Pleiades and Orion,
  who turns blackness into dawn
  and darkens day into night,
who calls for the waters of the sea
  and pours them out over the face of the land—
  the LORD is his name—
[9]he flashes destruction on the stronghold
  and brings the fortified city to ruin),
[10]you hate the one who reproves in court
  and despise him who tells the truth.

[11]You trample on the poor
  and force him to give you grain.
Therefore, though you have built stone mansions,
  you will not live in them;
though you have planted lush vineyards,
  you will not drink their wine.
[12]For I know how many are your offenses
  and how great your sins.
You oppress the righteous and take bribes
  and you deprive the poor of justice in the courts.

[13]Therefore the prudent man keeps quiet in such times,
  for the times are evil.

[14]Seek good, not evil,
  that you may live.
Then the LORD God Almighty will be with you,
  just as you say he is.
[15]Hate evil, love good;
  maintain justice in the courts.
Perhaps the LORD God Almighty will have mercy
  on the remnant of Joseph.

[16]Therefore this is what the Lord, the LORD God Almighty, says:

"There will be wailing in all the streets
  and cries of anguish in every public square.
The farmers will be summoned to weep

and the mourners to wail.
[17]There will be wailing in all the vineyards,
for I will pass through your midst,"
                              says the LORD.

Andersen and Freedman analyze chaps. 5–6 as a unity entitled "The Book of Woes" following "The Book of Doom" in chaps. 1–4. Whereas in the first four chapters the verdict has been announced and the punishment is forthcoming and inevitable, in chaps. 5–6 "the prophet still has hope that repentance might avert the final catastrophe."[180] Herein are the calls to repentance assumed in 4:6–11 and constituting "the first and primary message of the prophet."[181] Introduced by the third call to "hear this word" (cf. 3:1; 4:1), these chapters are unified by the themes of lament for Israel's fall and Israel's perversion of justice (5:7,14–15,24; 6:12).

Andersen and Freedman understand the two chapters as comprising the two main parts of the unit, sharing similar conclusions in judgment oracles employing the same divine name (5:27; 6:14).[182] But most scholars see a major break at the end of 5:17. For Wendland there are five sets of oracles against the house of Israel: 3:1–15; 4:1–13; 5:1–17,18–27; and 6:1–14. He analyzes 5:1–17 as "the structural-thematic center of Amos."[183]

The chiastic features of this rhetorical unit have been set forth forcefully by a number of interpreters.[184] The overarching structure of the unit may be observed in the following arrangement:

5:1–2   Introduction to Lament
  5:3   Lamentation/Decimation
    5:4–6   Exhortation
      5:7   Accusation
      5:8–9   Hymn
      5:10–13   Accusation and Judgment
    5:14–15   Exhortation
  5:16–17   Lamentation

The centerpiece of this unit is the hymn stanza in 5:8–9 (cf. 4:13), which sets forth the nature of Israel's God. Another feature of this unit is the interweaving of the words of Amos (vv. 1–2,6–9,14–15) with the words of God (vv. 3–5,10–13,16–17).

The chiastic arrangement of Amos 5:1–17 is a strong argument against Wolff's suggestion that 5:8–9,13,14–15 are later additions.[185] Movement

---

[180] Andersen and Freedman, *Amos*, 461.

[181] Ibid., 471, 469.

[182] Ibid., 461, 469–70.

[183] Wendland, "The 'Word of the Lord' and the Organization of Amos," 14.

[184] Stuart, *Hosea-Jonah*, 344; Hayes, *Amos*, 153; Wolff, *Joel and Amos*, 231–35; J. De Waard, "The Chiastic Structure of Amos V 1–17," *VT* 27 (1977): 170–77; N. J. Tromp, "Amos V 1–17: Towards a Stylistic and Rhetorical Analysis," *OTS* 23 (1984): 56–84.

between second- and third-person references appears to be a rhetorical device to "urge the audience to action."[186] Denial of parts of the chiasm to Amos is indefensible in that it is "very unlikely that Amos would write an unfinished chiasmus that later was completed by one of the wisdom writers."[187]

LAMENT OVER FALLEN ISRAEL (5:1–3). A common element in several oracles in Amos is the call to attention. Three consecutive chapters open with the call, "Hear this word" (3:1; 4:1; 5:1). The audience addressed in Amos 3 is "people of Israel"; in Amos 4, "cows of Bashan"; and in Amos 5, "house of Israel." Where Amos delivered the oracles contained in chaps. 3–5 is uncertain. Variations in the prophet's messages suggest various audiences and locations for delivery of his messages.

5:1 Amos identified his revelatory "word" here as a "lament" (*qînâ*). A *qinah* was a funeral song, a dirge sung over the deceased (cf. 2 Sam 1:17–27; 3:31–34). It usually consisted of lines set in a three-beat/two-beat pattern. The result was a halting or limping rhythm. Singing a funeral song about Israel implied that the nation was dead. That understanding must have stunned the audience, since the nation then was strong and prosperous. What that use of language suggests is that the future death of the nation was so certain Amos saw it as an accomplished fact, and it made him grieve. Once God declares war on a people, they are as good as defeated. Having just declared the destruction of Israel, it was appropriate that Amos should lament (cf. 3:11–12; 4:2–3,12).

"O house of Israel" may designate only the ruling house, not the entire nation. In that case the end of the Jehu dynasty would be the focus of the dirge. His house fell when Shallum assassinated Jeroboam II's son, Zechariah (2 Kgs 15:10). But its occurrence in v. 25 would indicate the term designated the entire nation.

5:2 "Fallen" usually refers in the Old Testament to a person who died tragically or unnecessarily, not to someone who died from disease or old age (cf. 2 Sam 1:12,19,25,27; Lam 2:21). The verse has an alternating *A B A′ B′* structure. In the first and third lines is the parallel idea that Israel is fallen and deserted in their own land. In lines two and four is the idea of their inability to rise. They are like an army of corpses abandoned on the field of battle.

"Virgin" connotes both youthfulness and purity. Israel's demise was the more lamentable because the nation thought "herself to be in the full flush of youthful vigor."[188] Even if "Virgin Israel" should be translated "Virgin of

---

[185] Wolff, *Joel and Amos,* 231–33; 241–49.

[186] G. V. Smith, "Critical Notes: Amos 5:13, the Deadly Silence of the Prosperous," *JBL* 107 (1988): 290.

[187] D. A. Garrett, "The Structure of Amos as a Testimony to Its Integrity," *JETS* 27 (1984): 276.

[188] Wolff, *Joel and Amos,* 236.

Israel" and refer to Samaria as suggested by Hayes (cf. Isa 47:1; Jer 31:21; Ezek 23:4–8),[189] the ultimate outcome of Samaria's fall would be the fall of the whole nation. Israel could not endure long if Samaria fell. The prophet's proclamation of the catastrophe about to break upon Israel must have had a terrifying effect.

5:3 The lament is substantiated in v. 3, which begins with a particle often translated "because" (*kî*). Following the particle is an expanded messenger formula pointing to the source of the message (*ʾadōnāy YHWH*) and the certainty of its fulfillment.[190] "The city going out a thousand / will have left a hundred" is a literal rendering of the first couplet. In a military context the verb translated "going out" means "marching out." The verse has a descending numerical pattern that emphasizes the decimation (cf. Deut 28:62). The numbers themselves reflect the size of military units: a thousand, a hundred, and ten, which Stuart reflects by translating "company," "platoon," and "squad."[191]

APPEAL TO REPENTANCE (5:4–6). These verses are marked as a unit by the opening and closing commands to seek the Lord and by the threefold reference to Bethel, the cult center of the Northern Kingdom. Especially marked is its occurrence at the beginning and end of the unit.

Seeking the Lord and finding life is in stark contrast to the lamenting over the finality of Israel's death (5:2). Wolff calls the contrast a contradiction.[192] Others understand the lament as hyperbolic[193] or the call to repent as ironic.[194] This is unnecessary. According to Jer 18:1–10, the Book of Jonah, and countless other places in Scripture, until judgment comes individuals still have the opportunity to repent by the grace of God (cf. v. 15). Amos's words in chap. 5 were his last effort to persuade them to repent and return (*šûb*) to God.

5:4 The particle *kî* (often translated "for," or "because"), which begins the Hebrew text of this verse, may be taken emphatically to mean "yes," or "indeed." Handled in this way the messenger formula may convey what the Lord had said to Israel before the sentence of judgment was finally passed. But Amos and his audience understood that the absolute language of pro-

---

[189] Hayes, *Amos,* 155. Cities are referred to as "virgins." Against Hayes see Finley, *Joel, Amos, Obadiah,* 225.

[190] At the end of the verse in Hebrew is the phrase לְבֵית יִשְׂרָאֵל, which could be understood as dittography (cf. v. 4) and deleted (NIV), taken as the completion of the messenger formula like v. 4, "to the house of Israel," as a vocative, "O house of Israel," or as completing the last line and so disrupting the poetic pattern. See Andersen and Freedman, *Amos,* 476; Finley, *Joel, Amos, Obadiah,* 226.

[191] Stuart, *Hosea-Jonah,* 341.

[192] Wolff, *Joel and Amos,* 231–34.

[193] Tromp, "Amos V 1–17," 72–73.

[194] A. Weiser, *Die Profetie des Amos,* BZAW 53 (Giessen: Töpelmann, 1929), 190–222.

phetic speech (5:2) always left open an avenue of hope should the audience repent. In this light the Lord's earlier exhortation, "seek me and live," was still a viable option for Israel.[195]

Seeking the Lord may involve a prophetic consultation with the Lord (cf. 1 Chr 10:13–14), a turning to the Lord in repentance and faith (Deut 4:29; 1 Chr 16:10–11; 2 Chr 15:12–13), or a visit to the temple (Deut 12:5; 2 Chr 11:16).[196] The context of v. 5 suggests that a seeking of God in the central sanctuary in Jerusalem may be involved, but the parallel in v. 14, "Seek good, not evil, / that you may live," indicates that the passage's emphasis is not on a mere geographical change but rather on justice (vv. 7,15,24; 6:12). The concept of seeking the Lord is a major theme in Chronicles, where it describes "how one was to respond to God and thus defined one who was a member of the believing community."[197] More than looking for God's help and guidance, it "stood for one's whole duty toward God"[198] and entailed keeping God's laws. Every search for God through a prophet or in a house of worship should result in doing right, for seeking God ultimately means living under his authority and in dependence upon his power.

5:5 Over against the exhortation for Israel to seek the Lord and live, Amos set the admonition not to seek God at Bethel, or Gilgal, or even Beersheba (at the southern edge of Judah). Then he gave a reason for not going to Gilgal or to Bethel. These centers were doomed, under a sentence of divine judgment. All three cities were ancient worship sites. Jeroboam I turned Bethel into a royal sanctuary (1 Kgs 12:26–33). Gilgal had become a popular worship center since its establishment as a memorial to the God who led Israel into the promised land. Though Beersheba was located in southern Judah, it became a favorite center of worship for pilgrims from Israel, perhaps because Jacob had worshiped there (cf. Gen 26:23–25).

The admonitions of 5:5 need to be read in light of the oracle against Bethel in 3:14 and the sarcastic oracle in 4:4–5. If rebellion was what Israel did at Bethel and Gilgal, the prophet's admonition to stay away from those sites is understandable. Amos used a play on words to make memorable his directives for Israel to avoid pilgrimages to these popular sites. Gilgal (*haggilgāl*) would go into exile (*gālōh yigleh*), and Bethel would become nothing (or empty). The term translated "nothing" (*ʾāwen*) may mean "evil," "trouble," "harm," or "false." Hosea joined the term to the first part of Bethel and coined a word, Beth Aven (Hos 4:15; 5:8; 10:5), to condemn Bethel (the house of God), which had become Beth Aven (the house of evil or trouble). But Israel's problem was not just that they had been worshiping in the wrong place.

---

[195] Paul, *Amos*, 162.
[196] J. Lust, "Remarks on the Redaction of Amos V 4–6, 14–15," *OTS* 21 (1981): 138–39.
[197] J. A. Thompson, *1, 2 Chronicles*, NAC (Nashville: Broadman & Holman, 1994), 266.
[198] Ibid.

"Amos was condemning attendance at the shrines because they had become a substitute for 'seeking' YHWH himself."[199]

5:6 Here Amos adds a prophetic exhortation (third person) to the divine oracle (first person) of vv. 4–5. But the admonition not to go to the sanctuaries at Bethel, Gilgal, and Beersheba and the pronouncement of certain judgment on these sites is not repeated. Rather a conditional threat of judgment by fire follows the exhortation to seek the Lord and live in v. 6. "House of Joseph" may designate the tribes of Ephraim and Manasseh only, but here it refers to the entire Northern Kingdom (Ezek 37:16,19). The judgment is broadened from the destruction of sanctuaries to include the whole family of Joseph. No one would be able to quench the fire and prevent the destruction of Bethel. But it is even clearer here than in v. 4 that life is a real alternative for any who will seek the Lord.

CONDEMNATION OF INJUSTICE (5:7)   **5:7** While the word "woe" (*hôy*) does not occur here, Andersen and Freedman consider this the first of a series of woes. Their reason is that it begins with a participle (lit., "those who turn") that describes the wrongdoing in Israel.[200] G. Smith, however, probably is right that the participle in v. 7 is used to contrast with the participle in vv. 8–9 that describe the actions of God.[201]

The characterization of the audience Amos addressed functions as an indictment. They were changing sweet justice into bitter injustice. The same verb for "turn" (*hāpak*) is used in 4:11 of God's "overthrow" of Sodom and Gomorrah, thus of their obliteration. In 8:10 God declares that he will "turn" Israel's feasts into mourning, their singing into weeping. In the following hymn of 5:8 God is the one "who *turns* blackness into dawn" (italics added). But here and in 6:12 Israel is the subject, and the object of their transforming work is "justice." Andersen and Freedman speak of 5:7 and 6:12 as providing "the twin pillars that support the entire structure of the Book of Woes."[202] "Justice" refers to legal matters such as fairness in the courts and more broadly to the divinely given moral principles by which society was to be ordered. "Righteousness," which is not transformed but thrown away, connotes fulfillment of the responsibilities in a relationship. Its focus is on rightness, doing what is right. The two terms together designate a right and just order in society. When justice is overthrown and righteousness is cast to the ground, the result is chaos (3:9), and the judgment of God must follow to set things right again. That principle remains operative in society in every generation.

---

[199] H. Mowvley, *The Books of Amos and Hosea* (London: Epworth, 1991), 54.

[200] Andersen and Freedman, *Amos,* 462.

[201] Smith, *Amos,* 154. Andersen and Freedman recognize that the juxtaposition of woes and hymns draws a sharp contrast "between the majesty of the divine activity and the misery of human behavior" (*Amos,* 464).

[202] Andersen and Freedman, *Amos,* 464.

The people exhorted to seek the Lord instead of the shrines were those in Israel who turned justice upside down and who caused righteousness to lie prostrate on the ground. Life would be the reward of those who would turn to the Lord. By implication death would be the result of pilgrimages to the shrines.

THE CREATOR'S SOVEREIGN CONTROL (5:8–9).   This second of three hymn fragments (see 4:13; 9:5–6) is recognizable by its participles and by its refrain, "the LORD is his name" (cp. with 4:13, "the LORD God Almighty is his name"). The theme of the hymn is praise to God the Creator who exercises sovereign control over creation. Since the refrain comes at the end of v. 8, v. 9 may represent the prophet's own composition in an effort to apply the principle of God's sovereign control to Israel. Alternatively, Amos may have placed the refrain to serve as the center of the chiasm of vv. 1–17. Furthermore, if the chiasm is the "structural-thematic center of Amos," as Wendland argues, then this hymn, and especially its refrain, is at the center of the book.

The assumption here is that Amos selected for use a hymn familiar to his audience. A common verb, *hāpak* ("turn/turns"), in vv. 7–8 connects the characterization of the audience (v. 7) with the characterization of God (v. 9). Just as Israel had the power to change (or overturn) some things in their society, so God had the power to change (overturn) things in his universe. To that powerful God Israel was accountable.

5:8   "He who made" (*ʿōsēh*) is the translation of a verb often used of God's creative activity, occurring with "create" (*bārāʾ*) in Gen 1–2. The God who created the mountains and the wind (4:13) also created the constellations. "Pleiades" ("cluster," or "heap") and "Orion" ("fool," or "brash one"), two well-known constellations in the mind of the ancient world, stand as representatives of the heavenly bodies created by God and subject to his sovereign control.

God's control also stands behind the rhythmical rotation of night to day[203] and day to night and behind the provision of rain. In light of 4:7–8 (see the comments there) Amos reaffirmed that famine, rainfall, and flood are in God's control. The Canaanites thought their god Baal was the one who controlled rainfall. According to the hymn, Israel's God, Yahweh, had the power to call for "the waters of the sea" and to pour them out "over the face of the land." The Hebrew word for "land" (*ʾ ereṣ*) also occurs in v. 7, translated "ground." While the land was where Israel perverted justice, for the Lord it was a recipient of the blessing of rain or the judgment of flood.[204] The shortened refrain (cf. 4:13 for the expanded version) closes v. 8. It is two words in Hebrew

---

[203] The word for "blackness" is צַלְמָוֶת, usually understood as a compound, "shadow of death" (cf. Ps 23:4). It refers to the deepest darkness. See J. E. Hartley, "צַלְמָוֶת," *TWOT*, 767.

[204] Cf. Andersen and Freedman, *Amos*, 489, 491; Finley, *Joel, Amos, Obadiah*, 233–34.

(*YHWH šĕmô*), which without a verb serves as a clause of identification, "the LORD is his name."

5:9 The participles continue in v. 9, but the theme changes. Still the emphasis is on God's control. He is the one who causes destruction to flare up (or burst forth) against a "stronghold" (or fortress). He brings destruction upon a fortified place. "The fortified city" is literally "a fortified place," a synonym of "the stronghold" (or "fortress") in the first part of the verse.[205] God might use some foreign army to bring destruction in Israel, but Israel needed to understand that God was in control of that army. Israel's God—who created the constellations, controls day and night, and is in charge of rainfall—also brings destruction on his people in the very fortresses where they thought they were secure. Israel had perverted and discarded the principle of justice by which God had structured society. But the divine order was not so easily cast aside. God was also the one who had established the eternal laws of nature. He is able to turn the deepest darkness of human depravity and destruction into light again, as he can also bring to an end the day of prosperity and power. What Israel needed to understand and what God's people always need to remember is that no man-made security system protects them against God's judgment.

SILENT IN AN EVIL TIME (5:10–13). The condemnation of injustice begun in v. 7 is resumed in v. 10. These verses identify and characterize those whom Amos addressed with his exhortation to seek God and live (vv. 4–6). The special concern of Amos in these verses was the corruption of the judicial process in Israel.

5:10 Those seeking justice ran up against a system corrupted by the wealthy. "Hate" and "despise" describe their passionate rejection of justice. "In court" is literally "at the gate," which is where cases were argued (Deut 21:10; Ruth 4:1–12). "One who reproves" translates a participle that can refer to a judge who decides the case, but the context here suggests that it is either a plaintiff who has been wronged or an advocate of right (cf. Isa 11:3; 29:21; Job 13:3; 32:12).

The word for "truth" (*tāmîm*) refers to something complete, blameless, and honest (Ps 18:30; Ezek 15:5). Witnesses with integrity were available who could provide necessary information to see that justice was done, but their testimony was squelched. The system was anything but impartial. It was manipulated by wealthy landowners through bribes and intimidation.[206]

5:11 This passage is framed by third-person verbs in Hebrew in vv.

---

[205] On the translation problems in this verse see Andersen and Freedman, *Amos,* 492–94. They translate, "The one who makes destruction burst upon the stronghold, / and destruction upon the fortress when he comes." The NIV translation "brings" is based upon an emendation. The second line in the MT as it stands could be translated "and destruction comes upon the fortress."

[206] Cf. Wolff, *Joel and Amos,* 246; Stuart, *Hosea-Jonah,* 348; Mays, *Amos,* 93.

10,12d–13. But at the heart in vv. 11–12 it uses second-person verbs and pronoun. The switch to direct address (second person) does not require a change of audience. Such switches are common (5:1; 6:1–2). Here it marks the primary message of vv. 10–13, which is one of judgment. Introducing v. 11 in Hebrew is the climactic particle *laken*, "therefore," followed immediately by *ya'an*, "because" (a juxtaposition unique in the OT). Surrounding the pronouncement of judgment in the second half of v. 11 with dependent clauses adding accusations ("because" in v. 11 and "for" in v. 12) heightens its climactic effect. The fruit of their corrupt business and legal practices would be snatched from them before they really had opportunity to enjoy them.

The two parts of the accusation, "trample on the poor" and "force him to give you grain," may describe only one charge. One way to handle the term translated "you trample" (*bôšaskem*) is to relate it to an Akkadian term (*šabašu*) meaning "to levy taxes."[207] That makes the expression parallel to the next part of the verse where exaction of grain is condemned. Another way to handle the term is to relate it to a Hebrew verb meaning "tread" (*bûs*). The way some people in Israel trampled on the poor was by taking from them the fruit of their labor. As Mays explains: "The small farmer no longer owns his own land; he is a tenant of an urban class to whom he must pay a rental for the use of the land, a rental that was often a lion's share of the grain which the land had produced."[208]

The greed of those condemned would be matched in God's judgment by taking away the material advantages gained from trampling the poor. The statements here are similar to futility curses found in ancient Near Eastern texts. They will build houses, but not dwell in them; they will plant vineyards, but not drink their wine (cf. Deut 28:30–44; Mic 6:15; Zeph 1:13). The oppressors had taken from the poor to build their fine houses and to plant their lush vineyards. But others would dwell in their houses and drink their wine. The future reversal of this curse is announced in 9:14.

5:12 Both God and the prophet knew how many were the "offenses" (*piš'êkem*, the same word rendered "sins" in 1:3 and elsewhere) and how great were the "sins" (*hatto'têkem*) of Samaria and of Israel. Using first-person speech, Amos spoke for God. The particular culprits Amos accused may have been the leading citizens of Samaria.

The first sin enumerated was oppression of the righteous. "Oppress" (*sorerê*) carries the idea of constricting or impeding, that is, of causing distress. It is a participle indicating its continuous occurrence. The same is true of the second sin, bribery. The "righteous" (*saddîq*) were the ones in the right. They

---

[207] Wolff, *Joel and Amos*, 230; H. R. Cohen, *Biblical Hapax Legomena in the Light of Akkadian and Ugaritic*, SBLDS (Missoula, Mont.: Scholars Press, 1978), 49.

[208] Mays, *Amos*, 94.

were innocent. Bribery implies either taking money for declaring cases the poor brought against the rich to be without merit or by favoring the rich in cases against the poor.[209] *Kōper* usually means "ransom" (Exod 21:30). Here it may refer to bribes (cf. 1 Sam 12:3) to set free the guilty who have been accused of defrauding the poor. In that case the juxtaposition of oppressing the righteous and (no conjunction in Heb.) taking bribes expresses opposite sides of the system of injustice. The final sin listed was that of depriving the poor of justice in the court. "And poor ones in the gate they turn aside" is a literal rendering of the text. For the poor to be turned aside in the gate meant to be denied their only source of help (cf. 2:7). The protection they sought in the legal assembly was not available to them because of corruption there. God knows intimately the corruption rampant in every arena of life, in politics, family, religion, industry, and business. Claims of innocence are useless. God knows the facts.

5:13 A somewhat literal translation of vv. 10–13 shows their chiastic structure and how v. 13 is set off from the rest of the paragraph as a prominent conclusion:

> *They* hate *at the gate* one who reproves,
> and one who tells the truth *they* despise. (v. 10)

>> Therefore, because *you* trample the poor and *take* part of their grain,

>>> stone houses *you* build,
>>>> but *you* will not live in them;
>>> lush vineyards *you* plant,
>>>> but *you* will not drink their wine. (v. 11)

>> For I know *your* offenses are many and *your* sins are great—
>> oppressing the poor, *taking* bribes,

>> And the poor *at the gate they* turn aside. (v. 12)

> Therefore, the prudent keeps silent at such a time,
> for it is an evil time. (v. 13)

Interpreting v. 13 presents several difficulties. The semantic range of the three key words the NIV translates "prudent," "keeps quiet," and "evil" allows for several interpretations. The word "therefore" (*lākēn*) usually introduces a judgment message in the prophets and elsewhere in Amos (3:11; 4:12; 5:11,16; 6:7; 7:17). Yet the word *maśkîl* ("prudent"), except when it designates a type of psalm (Ps 32:1, etc.), refers to a person with insight or understanding (cf. Prov 10:5,19; 14:35). Therefore many interpreters consider the verse a wisdom saying rather than an expression of judgment.[210] Silence, however, is not recommended in the verse. Certainly Amos was not silent in

---

[209] On bribes in the OT see Exod 23:8; Deut 16:19; 27:25; 1 Sam 12:3; Job 36:18; Ps 15:5; Eccl 7:7; Prov 17:23; 21:14; Isa 1:23; 5:23.

[210] Mays, *Amos,* 98; Wolff, *Joel and Amos,* 250.

his time, nor were those referred to in v. 10, though silence would have been the safest and easiest course. Although speaking out might be a waste of effort, the righteous could not keep silent. The point could be that the times were such that wise men, who in better times would be consulted for their wisdom, were silent because no one would listen. Or the term *maśkîl* could be a morally neutral reference to one who knew how to avoid trouble, in which case silence would be the best policy in such evil times.[211]

The word translated "evil" (*rāʿâ*) likely means here "disaster, calamity," as in 3:6; Ps 37:19; Jer 15:11; and especially the end of Mic 2:3, which is identical to the last line here. "In such times" is literally "at that time," and "the times are evil" is "it is/will be a time of evil/disaster." The time referred to, then, is perhaps the future divine judgment when the prudent or thoughtful person will be stunned to silence by such disaster (cf. Lam 2:10; 3:28).[212] The verb translated "keeps silent," *yiddōm,* may even refer to the silence of death and be translated "will perish" (cf. 1 Sam 2:9; Ps 31:17; Jer 8:14; 25:37; 48:9; 49:26; 50:30; Zeph 1:11). Perhaps the prudent will perish "because the times will be so bad that goodness will not be tolerated."[213]

G. Smith has argued cogently that since the root of *hammaśkîl* (*śākal*) can mean "to be clever" or "to prosper," the meaning of the noun here that best fits the context is "the prosperous." This would make the word refer to the very people Amos had been describing who used their position, power, and wealth to oppress the poor (v. 11). Smith translates the sentence: "Therefore, the prosperous will be silent at that time, for it will be a disastrous time." This silence he takes either as the silence of grief or of death.[214] Whatever details of interpretation are adopted, it seems clear that the verse is a prediction of judgment.

HOPE FOR GOD'S GRACIOUS RESPONSE (5:14–15). These verses resume and parallel the exhortation of vv. 4–6 in keeping with the chiastic form of vv. 1–17. The Lord's exhortation earlier to "seek me" (5:4), echoed by the prophet's "seek the LORD" (5:6), held out life for those who responded. But the offer of hope here following the parallel exhortation to "seek good" is stronger than the clause in v. 6 (lit.), "lest he sweep through the house of Joseph like fire."

5:14 While the first exhortation to "seek" was set in contrast to seeking

---

[211] Finley, *Joel, Amos, Obadiah,* 239.

[212] Stuart, *Hosea-Jonah,* 349. S. Paul may be right in his suggestion that יִדֹּם ("quiet") may mean "wail" or "moan" (*Amos,* 175–76). Andersen and Freedman grant this as "a slender possibility" (*Amos,* 504).

[213] Niehaus, "Amos," 1:421.

[214] Smith, *Amos,* 156, 160, 170; id., "Amos 5:13: The Deadly Silence of the Prosperous," 289–91. J. J. Jackson came essentially to the same conclusion as Smith about how to handle the verse. He translated the terms הַמַּשְׂכִּיל and יִדֹּם "prosperous" and "lament" respectively. His translation is, "Therefore the successful/prosperous person will wail/lament at that time for it will be a time of disaster" ("Amos 5,13 Contextually Understood," *ZAW* 98 [1986]: 434–35).

corrupt sanctuaries (5:4) and the second with receiving the fiery blast of God's judgment (5:6), here it is in contrast to seeking evil. Seeking what is good is not the same as seeking God, but it is a corollary. Seeking God and seeking good represent the two dimensions of true religion, not rituals and forms but relationships with God and other persons. "Good" (*tôb*) refers to that which pleases God, here especially justice for the poor. To "seek" it in this context means not only to live in such a way oneself but also actively to endeavor to see good prevail over evil (*rāʾ*), the denial of justice for the poor. The implication of the larger message in this passage is that one who truly seeks the Lord also seeks the welfare of the poor.

Twice in vv. 14–15 Amos formulated highly conditional promises. One promise is that God will really be with his audience as they claimed he was (v. 14b). The phrase that begins the promise (*wîhî kēn*) is the command form (called *jussive*) of the phrase in Genesis 1, "And it was so." After the imperative "seek" it expresses purpose and could be translated, "That it may be so, [that] Yahweh God of hosts will be with you, just as you have said."[215] Followed by the term translated "just as," Amos's words also are similar to those of the divine messengers who accepted Abraham's offer of hospitality with the response, "Do as you say" (Gen 18:5). The language refers to the relationship between speech and reality. While the relationship in the case of God's words is direct and immediate, this is not so with human speech. In spite of their practice of injustice and corrupt worship, the people in Israel continued to claim that God was with them and to encourage one another with these words. But as long as they continued seeking evil rather than good, it was not so. Israel had only been lying to themselves.

The title for God here is literally "Yahweh God of hosts." While the title "Yahweh of hosts" ("LORD Almighty") occurs many times in Scripture, the longer designation used here is found only in Amos (4:13; 5:14–15,27). It stresses that the God of Israel has sovereign power over the affairs of earth and heaven. If such a God were with them, at their side and on their behalf, they could be assured not only of military victory (cf. Josh 1:9; Judg 1:22) but also of true success and security (cf. Hag 2:4). But to offend such a God meant certain disaster. Just as seeking him and his ways meant life, failing to do so meant death.

5:15 If Israel were to seek good, they must love good, almost an equivalent expression. To love (*ʾāhab*) something means to choose it and to delight in it. And to delight in seeing good prevail, one must hate (*śānēʾ*) evil. That is, one must abhor behavior that displeases God, as the wicked hate and despise righteousness (v. 10). Amos was exhorting his audience to pursue and embrace justice passionately and to hound and crush injustice just as passionately.

---

[215] See *IBHS* § 34.6.

The third exhortation in the verse would be the outcome of carrying out the first two. "Maintain" is the translation of a verb that means to "set in place" or "establish" (Judg 6:37; 8:27; 1 Sam 6:17). "In the courts" is again the term found in vv. 10,12 that is literally "at the gate." At the time there was no justice at the gate for the poor. Amos was ordering his audience to reestablish it.

Following the commands in v. 15 is another highly conditional promise introduced by the conditional particle *ʾûlay*, "perhaps." It expresses humility before a sovereign God who is not under compulsion to be gracious. "His presence was an act of grace. It could not be bought by magic or bribery, and it was not an eternal possession that could be manipulated to advantage."[216] The hope was that repentance might move God to spare some, "the remnant of Joseph,"[217] when the inevitable destruction came upon the Northern Kingdom, as it did in 722 B.C. The concept of a remnant may be said to run through the Book of Amos, since the term (*šěʾērît*) also occurs in 1:8 and 9:12, where it refers to a remnant that will not be left to the nations. But the necessity of repentance and of seeking God and the resulting presence of God indicate that the promise of "life" meant more than the physical survival of a portion of Israel. Life in relationship with God is always life in its fullness. "Purity in moral behavior and complete devotion to Yahweh in worship were synonymous with life in the presence of Yahweh."[218]

Andersen and Freedman believe that 5:14–15, with its focus on justice, is the physical and thematic center of the book.[219] But one does not have to accept fully their structural analysis to recognize that these verses are crucial, bringing together faith and practice, devotion and duty.

> It is their total lifestyle—the combination of ruthlessness with religiosity, their values, attitudes, and actions in court and cult—that makes the religion they profess and practice in their rites abhorrent and abominable to God. . . . It is the smugness and self-satisfaction of those who presume to violate the covenant and at the same time act as though nothing were amiss. They revel in sacrilege and injustice yet believe that they are welcome in the Lord's house, at the altar of sacrifice and the communal table. It is the gap between unrighteous doing and living and the profession and practice of official and formal piety which disturbs the prophet or, more properly, the God who sent him.[220]

WAILING WHEN GOD PASSES THROUGH (5:16–17).   The closing lament matches the opening lament (5:1–3). Amos began the first lament with a call for attention, "Hear this word." He began the closing lament with an

---

[216] Smith, *Amos*, 174.

[217] Note the other references to "Joseph" in Amos surround this one: "the house of Joseph" in 5:6 and "the ruin of Joseph" in 6:6.

[218] Smith, *Amos*, 174.

[219] Andersen and Freedman, *Amos*, 465.

[220] Ibid., 470–71.

expanded and solemn messenger formula, "Therefore this is what the Lord, the LORD God Almighty, says." He punctuated this lament with an abbreviated messenger formula, "says the LORD" (ʾāmar yhwh).[221] The source of the prophet's message and his authority for delivering it rested in God, who sent him. As usual "therefore" precedes an announcement of judgment, but here it does not logically connect to the immediately preceding paragraph of exhortation. Rather it resumes the "therefore" of v. 13. After the messenger formula these verses describe a future scene of lament throughout Israel, ending with the cause—"for I will pass through your midst."

5:16–17 "Wailing" (mispēd) is the translation of a term that connotes rites of mourning (v. 16). The mourning would be widespread: "in all the streets," "in every public square" (v. 16), and "in all the vineyards" (v. 17). "Cries of anguish" (v. 16) represents an interpretation of yōʾmĕrû hô hô,[222] literally "they will say woe, woe." The prophet did not say what calamity in Israel would produce such widespread lamentation. He dealt only with the consequences of the calamity. Everyone from farmers to professional mourners would be needed to express Israel's grief over the unnamed calamity that would come upon them.

The background for the image Amos used of the Lord passing through the midst of his people has been interpreted regularly as an allusion to the Lord's passing through Egypt (Exod 12:12). M. Hauan argued for a covenant ritual theophany as the background for Amos's image, citing Genesis15, Exodus 34, and Joshua 3–4. But what Amos did here, as frequently elsewhere (cf. 5:18–20), was to reverse completely the usual use of theophany. Instead of covenant renewal and confirmation of the Lord's promises, the appearance of the Lord was to judge disobedient Israel.[223] The Lord himself was the one who stood behind the massive loss of life implied by the widespread mourning.

(2) Darkness of the Day of the Lord (5:18–20)

> [18]Woe to you who long
>   for the day of the LORD!
> Why do you long for the day of the LORD?
>   That day will be darkness, not light.
> [19]It will be as though a man fled from a lion
>   only to meet a bear,
> as though he entered his house
>   and rested his hand on the wall

---

[221] The expression has not been used in this way since the oracles against the nations (1:5,15; 2:3). After this it occurs only in 5:27 and 9:15, where it concludes the book with the expanded form אָמַר יהוה אֱלֹהֶיךָ.

[222] A double interjection shortened from the usual הוֹי.

[223] M. J. Hauan, "The Background and Meaning of Amos 5:17b," HTR 79 (1986): 337–48.

only to have a snake bite him.
20Will not the day of the LORD be darkness, not light—
pitch-dark, without a ray of brightness?

Some interpreters treat 5:18–27 as a rhetorical unit.[224] Others propose three divisions of the material: vv. 18–20, vv. 21–24, and vv. 25–27.[225] Wolff and S. Paul divide it into two parts: vv. 18–20 and vv. 21–27.[226] The last method will be followed here. Verses 18–20 constitute a woe oracle announcing judgment. Verses 21–27 contain an indictment furnishing additional reasons for judgment. The background for the woe oracle introduced with the term *hôy,* "woe" or "alas," was the funeral lament (cf. 1 Kgs 13:30; Jer 22:18; 34:5).[227]

The woe oracle is addressed surprisingly to those "who long for the day of the LORD" (cf. Mal 3:1). Apparently the concept of the day of the Lord was well known to Amos's audience, though this is the earliest reference to it in the Old Testament.[228] It is generally recognized that it would involve an appearance of the Lord (theophany) and sometimes was associated with covenant curses and holy war.[229] The prophet was concerned to correct theological error that gave Israel false hopes and contributed to their sinful behavior.[230] He challenged the popular understanding that (1) Israel's covenant assured them of God's presence, (2) their prosperity confirmed it, and (3) the day of the Lord would be solely a day of salvation for Israel.

DESIRING THE DAY (5:18). **5:18**   The prophet's announcement of woe for those desiring the day of the Lord must have shocked his audience. They expected the day of the Lord to bring victory, blessing, and brightness. They considered themselves to be God's people and worthy of God's rescue. But Amos rebuked and warned them that it would be rather a day of "darkness not light." "Darkness" implies defeat, calamity, and evil. Contrary to their expectation for the day, no victory, no blessing, and no brightness would come for them.

NO ESCAPE FROM THE DAY (5:19). **5:19**   To illustrate how dark the day would be for Israel, the prophet used two comparisons, both showing the inescapability of disaster. The first comparison is with one who flees from a lion

---

[224] Stuart, *Hosea-Jonah,* 351–56; Hayes, *Amos,* 169–79.

[225] Mays, *Amos,* 102–13; R. Smith, "Amos," 115–18.

[226] Wolff, *Joel and Amos,* 253–68; Paul, *Amos,* 182–98.

[227] Cf. R. J. Clifford, "The Use of *HÔY* in the Prophets," *CBQ* 28 (1966): 458–64.

[228] Paul, *Amos,* 182.

[229] Cf. C. van Leeuwen, "The Prophecy of the *YÔM YHWH* in Amos 5:18–20," *OTS* 19 (1974): 113–34; Y. Hoffman, "The Day of the Lord as a Concept and a Term in the Prophetic Literature," *ZAW* 93 (1981): 37–50.

[230] Andersen and Freedman point out that there is no reason to think that those addressed are different from those referred to in 5:7,10–12; 6:1–7,13. "They came from different walks of life—merchants, magistrates, soldiers—but their general outlook was the same" (*Amos,* 465).

only to run headlong into a bear. Whichever direction he goes, he is doomed. The second comparison is with the one who enters a house, thinking he is safe, only to be bitten by a snake. The day of the Lord in all its darkness will be that inescapable for Israel.

NO BRIGHTNESS IN THE DAY (5:20). **5:20** Amos concluded with a final rhetorical question aimed at challenging the popular understanding of what the day of the Lord would mean to them. This reversal of popular sentiment is a repeated pattern in the Book of Amos. Only a dismal future awaited those whose false sense of security was encouraging them in sinful behavior. "Pitch-dark, without a ray of brightness" describes a gloomy, hopeless future.

In a sense the error of the prophet's audience was not so much in their understanding of the general characteristics of the day of the Lord. Defeat of God's enemies and blessing for God's people were the two cardinal elements of the day. But God's people failed to understand the nature of their relationship with the Lord. By their corrupt lives they had become God's enemy, and as such they would experience defeat and destruction.

A constant danger for God's people is false presumption of how God's revelation relates to them. Often they see themselves as God's friends when in reality they are God's enemies (cf. v. 14). Enthusiastic proclaimers of the Lord's return must be careful to identify correctly their relationship to God.

(3) Rejection of Israel's Worship (5:21–27)

> [21]"I hate, I despise your religious feasts;
>   I cannot stand your assemblies.
> [22]Even though you bring me burnt offerings and grain offerings,
>   I will not accept them.
> Though you bring choice fellowship offerings,
>   I will have no regard for them.
> [23]Away with the noise of your songs!
>   I will not listen to the music of your harps.
> [24]But let justice roll on like a river,
>   righteousness like a never-failing stream!
> [25]"Did you bring me sacrifices and offerings
>   forty years in the desert, O house of Israel?
> [26]You have lifted up the shrine of your king,
>   the pedestal of your idols,
>   the star of your god—
>   which you made for yourselves.
> [27]Therefore I will send you into exile beyond Damascus,"
>   says the LORD, whose name is God Almighty.

A style shift to first-person divine speech beginning at 5:21 sets off this passage (5:21–27) from the previous one (5:18–20). The entire passage reflects the messenger speech style, containing the messenger formula at the end (v. 27).[231] Nevertheless, a connection between vv. 18–20 and vv. 21–27 is that both deal with Israel's false hopes—first through the day of the Lord and then through the sacrificial system.[232]

The setting for 5:21–27 probably was Bethel at the royal sanctuary. Amos may have interrupted a cultic festival there. This could explain the abrupt divine first-person address without the usual introductory messenger formula. These verses demonstrate clearly that Israel was not judged for lack of religion. They were celebrating religious holidays with "feasts" and "assemblies" (v. 21); they were bringing "burnt offerings," "grain offerings," and "choice fellowship offerings" (v. 22); and they were filling the air with "songs" of worship and with instrumental "music" (v. 23). But the Lord's rejection of this religious activity could not have been expressed more strongly: "I hate, I despise," "I cannot stand," "I will not accept," "I will have no regard," and "I will not listen." God rejected every aspect of Israel's worship. They were inundating him with rivers of religiosity when he wanted rivers of righteousness and justice (v. 24).

FEASTS (5:21). **5:21** Amos, acting as God's representative, methodically considered each element in Israel's worship and rejected each one. One function of a cultic priest was to announce to the worshiper God's acceptance of and delight in the sacrifices (cf. Lev 1:3–4; 22:18–19). To be greeted by a barrage of words of rejection from God's prophet must have been shocking to the prophet's audience.

"Hate" and "despise" are strong words. The term for "hate" (sane') is used three times in Amos, all in this chapter. Rather than hating evil (v. 15), Israel hated advocates of righteousness. Therefore God hated their presumptuous worship (v. 21).[233] The term for "despise" (ma'as) is a synonym of the one in v. 10. It also means "reject" (cf. Jer 2:37; Ezek 20:13,16,24; Hos 4:6) and so is not only the opposite of "love" but also of "choose."[234] Those events the Old Testament designates as "feasts" (hag) were the annual pilgrimage festivals of Unleavened Bread or Passover, Weeks or Harvest, and Tabernacles or Ingathering (Exod 23:14–17; 34:22–25; Lev 23:34). Whether the Northern Kingdom followed this calendar is uncertain, but their festivals would have been similar.

The negated verb translated "I cannot stand" (lo' 'arîah) means literally to "smell" or "enjoy the smell" of something. It usually refers to God's evaluation of sacrifices (cf. Gen 8:21; Lev 26:31; 1 Sam 26:19). The related noun (rîah) occurs in the phrases "a pleasing aroma" and "an aroma pleasing to the LORD" (Exod 29:18; Lev 1:9). It pictures God receiving with delight the

---

[231] Paul, *Amos,* 188.

[232] Smith, *Amos,* 184–85.

[233] For other examples of things God hates, cf. Deut 12:31; 16:22; Isa 1:14; 61:8; Jer 44:4.

[234] Andersen and Freedman, *Amos,* 526–27.

rising odor of the offering, so its negation here means he rejects it. But rather than an individual sacrifice Amos applied the term to Israel's whole festive "assemblies," which were like a foul odor to God. False worship arising from sinful lives is worse than unacceptable to him.

OFFERINGS (5:22).   **5:22**   The next element of Israel's worship that God rejected was the presentation of sacrifices. The three sacrifices mentioned here are the first three of the five main Levitical offerings presented in Leviticus 1–7. These are the "pleasing-aroma offerings" because of the phrase occurring with them (Lev 1:9,13,17; 2:2,9,12; 3:5,16) and because they are the ones that in particular represent consecration and worship as opposed to the other two offerings used solely for atonement.[235] Clearly they represent here the false worship in Israel that the Lord despised.

"Burnt offerings" (*ʿōlôt*) were sacrifices in which the entire animal was consumed on the altar and arose to God in smoke. "Grain offerings" (*minḥōt*) could also be used of various sacrifices brought as a gift. "Fellowship offerings" (*šelem*) were those in which part of the animal was consumed on the altar and part of it was eaten by the worshiper, thus symbolizing communion between the worshiper and God. The negated verb translated "I will have no regard" means literally to "look at." Here the idea is that God is not pleased to see them.

MUSIC (5:23).   **5:23**   Singing and playing the "harp" (*nebel*, perhaps "lute") were forms of rendering cultic praise. God evaluated the sound of their songs as "noise" and ordered that it be taken elsewhere. He refused to listen to their instruments. The passage pictures God's rejection of Israel's worship in terms of body language: shut nostrils, closed eyes, and stopped up ears.[236] The Lord's attitude was similar to that expressed in Mal 1:10: "'Oh, that one of you would shut the temple doors, so that you would not light useless fires on my altar! I am not pleased with you,' says the LORD Almighty, 'and I will accept no offering from your hands.'" While Israel's worship was required to be in accordance with divine regulations (cf. Lev 7:18; 19:7), that was not the problem that faced Amos. Then as now, God's acceptance or rejection of human expressions of worship is based on his assessment of the motives of the heart.

LACK OF JUSTICE AND RIGHTEOUSNESS (5:24).   **5:24**   Only words of rejection greeted the prophet's audience as he spoke of element after element of their worship. The missing ingredient in their worship was authenticity manifested in a lifestyle of obedience. Israel's rejection of justice and righteousness in the social order made inevitable God's rejection of their worship activities.

---

[235] The occurrence of these offerings in Lev 1–3 in the same order as they are found here might suggest Amos's familiarity with the Leviticus pericope, usually dated by critical scholars to the postexilic period.

[236] Paul, *Amos,* 192.

Verse 24 begins with a third-person command form (jussive) that expresses the will of the speaker (Amos speaking for God) and expects response from the audience.[237] God's will was for justice and righteousness to prevail in Israel's social order as an outward sign of their religious devotion. Here justice would mean "reparation for the defrauded, fairness for the less fortunate, and dignity and compassion for the needy"; righteousness would entail "attitudes of mercy and generosity, and honest dealings that imitate the character of God" as revealed in the law of Moses.[238] Finley makes an important point, however, that while these are always a part of God's demands for an obedient lifestyle, they are not his only requirements. If Amos were evaluating worship activities today, he might point to other aspects of lifestyle that are signs of a lack of genuineness, thus making worship displeasing and unacceptable to God. Amos's point was that "the way people behave in the marketplace or how they judge in the gate" are as much a part of worship as singing and sacrifice.[239] Religious activity is no substitute for national or personal righteousness. It may even sometimes be a hindrance. As Andersen and Freedman observe, "It was because they were so religious that they did not repent."[240] This may have been the way Israel responded to the Lord's discipline (cf. 4:6–11) rather than with true repentance.

"Like a river" is literally "like the waters." The plural form may suggest flood waters that swell with sudden force. A few interpreters take the word translated "justice" (*mišpāt*) to mean "judgment" here and make 5:24 a proclamation of God's overwhelming judgment. However, the combination of "justice" and "righteousness" in Amos elsewhere relates to right relationships and justice in the court. That seems to be the better interpretation here.[241]

The noun translated "stream" (*nahal*) refers to a wadi, which typically is dry or contains only a trickle of water except in the rainy season when it gushes with torrents of water. God demanded that justice and righteousness be produced in Israel like a wadi in the rainy season. But he did not want it to be restricted or sporadic but pervasive, overflowing like a flood, and permanent, like a river that never runs dry (cf. Ps 46:4; Rev 22:1–5). God's expectations of justice and righteousness in society have remained constant generation after generation.

NO SACRIFICES OR OFFERINGS IN THE WILDERNESS (5:25). **5:25** The message of vv. 21–24 is clear that God rejected Israel's false worship, as is the message of v. 27 that he was going to send them into exile. But interpretations

---

[237] Andersen and Freedman note that the "positive thrust" of this central call for justice and righteousness is flanked by two others (5:7; 6:12), which have a negative thrust (*Amos*, 467).

[238] Finley, *Joel, Amos, Obadiah*, 251.

[239] Ibid., 251, 338.

[240] Andersen and Freedman, *Amos*, 529.

[241] Cf. Smith, *Amos*, 187.

abound regarding the difficult intervening two verses, although the general point seems to be that sacrifices and offerings in themselves could not make Israel right with God and so could not keep them from exile.

A rhetorical question such as we find in v. 25 usually assumes a negative answer. No, Israel did not present "sacrifices and offerings" to God during the period of the wilderness wanderings. But there are several interpretative problems with the verse. The first term (*zĕbāḥîm*) refers to animal sacrifices generally, and the second (*minḥâ*) refers to grain offerings. So the two terms together cover presentations at the altar generally. But most would argue that Israel did sacrifice in the wilderness, at least to some extent,[242] and so some kind of qualification is implied. G. Smith, for example, offers the translation, "Did you offer to me *only* sacrifices . . . ?"[243] Others suggest that emphasis is on "me" and that the verse points to the illegitimacy of Israel's worship in the wilderness as being comparable to that of Amos's day. This view, however, violates the emphasis of the grammar, which is on "sacrifices and offerings." Some argue that the implied answer to the question is yes or that Amos's question is in v. 26 dealing with idolatry and that v. 25 is only a subordinate clause giving the circumstances.[244] The point would be that Israel was behaving again as they had in the wilderness when they brought sacrifices and offerings to the Lord while at the same time practicing idolatry. Therefore their attendance at the altar was clearly not a sure sign of their faith or a sufficient way to please God.

There is reason to believe, however, that sacrifices and offerings were severely limited during the wilderness years. Following Israel's rebellion and God's judgment at Kadesh in Numbers 13–14, certain regulations for worship are given but are introduced by "after you enter the land I am giving you as a home" (Num 15:2). D. Stuart explains that neither "slaughtered sacrifices" nor "grain offerings" were "usually" given while Israel was in the wilderness. "The sacrificial system was essentially predesigned for a coming era of normal food production . . . in a landed, settled situation."[245] Though inaugurated at Sinai, "sacrificing and its association with the three yearly festivals became regular only after the conquest."[246] Amos's point in this case would be that in the absence of a regular sacrificial system, God still maintained a

---

[242] Passages often cited demonstrating that at least some sacrifices were offered then are Exod 24; 32; 40:29; Lev 8–10; Num 7–9, but all these are prior to Israel's rebellion and God's judgment at Kadesh in Num 13–14. Andersen and Freedman assert: "The idea that the Israelites had no cult at all in the desert seems *a priori* incredible. The only question is, what kind of cult did they have?" (*Amos*, 531).

[243] Smith, *Amos*, 188.

[244] See Finley, *Amos*, 253. Joüon and Muraoka (*GBH* § 161b) give it an exclamatory nuance and translate, "Indeed, you offered me sacrifices and oblations in the wilderness!" See also Waltke and O'Connor, *IBHS* § 40.3b.

[245] Stuart, *Hosea-Jonah*, 355.

[246] Ibid.

relationship with his people and blessed and cared for them. Therefore the sacrificial system alone is clearly not sufficient to gain God's favor.

Wilderness years were not trouble free, but a close relationship between God and Israel characterized the period (Deut 2:7; Hos 11:1; Jer 2:2–3). Sacrifices and offerings did not maintain that relationship. Amos confronted a people who were eager and extravagant in their sacrifices and offerings, but those activities did not put them right with God. With Hos 6:6 and Mic 6:8 this text stands as one of the great themes in prophetic literature with regard to the nature of sacrifices and true religion. God is not pleased by acts of pomp and grandeur but by wholehearted devotion and complete loyalty.

IDOLATRY (5:26). **5:26** The contrast between the wilderness era and the settled era probably explains the juxtaposition of vv. 25 and 26.[247] Israel's relative obedience to God during the wilderness wanderings degenerated immediately upon their settlement in the promised land, in spite of the beginning of regular sacrifices at that time. Jeremiah made that same point at a later time (Jer 2:2–8). Some interpreters insist that the interrogative particle in v 25 and the expected negative reply also dominate v. 26.[248] This would then suggest that Israel did not practice idolatry after leaving Egypt, a view countered by the incident with the golden calf in the wilderness to which Stephen referred in a context that cites these verses (Acts 7:39–43).

Most scholars consider Amos 5:26 as referring to Mesopotamian astral deities. The phrase translated here "the shrine of your king" is more commonly, and probably more correctly, "Sikkut, your king." The Assyrian war god Adar also was called Sakkut. Likewise, the following phrase translated "the pedestal of your idols" is better (and more literally) rendered "and Kiyyun, your idols."[249] The Assyrians worshiped an astral deity they called Kaiwan, otherwise known as Saturn. "The star of your god [or gods]" apparently refers to the latter.[250] The spelling of these names as *Sikkut* and *Kiyyun* probably is the result of substituting the vowels of the Hebrew word *šiqqûṣ*, "abomination," in the names of the two astral deities.[251] This was the prophet's way of ridiculing these pagan gods. The folly of carrying about such images is that Israel "made" them. Homemade gods regularly disappoint the ones who fashion them (cf. Isa 40:18–20; 41:21–24; 44:12–20; Jer 10:1–16; Hos 8:6). "Therefore" in v. 27

---

[247] It is also possible, however, to understand נְשָׂאתֶם as a future, "and you will carry," thus connecting v. 26 with v. 27 as a prediction of judgment. See Andersen and Freedman, *Amos,* 535; Finley, *Joel, Amos, Obadiah,* 254–55; Harper, *Amos and Hosea,* 137.

[248] Hayes, *Amos,* 176; Wolff, *Joel and Amos,* 265.

[249] Finley notes that the words for "shrine/booth" and "pedestal" would be סִכָּה and כֵּן (*Joel, Amos, Obadiah,* 257).

[250] Mays, *Amos,* 112; Niehaus, "Amos," 1:433.

[251] Andersen and Freedman, *Amos,* 533. For an alternative view of the verse, based on a reconstruction of the text with the aid of the LXX, see C. Isbell, "Another Look at Amos 5:26," *JBL* 97 (1978): 97–99.

indicates that v. 26 speaks of idolatry during Amos's time. But v. 25 would suggest that idolatry also was a problem in the wilderness. This seems to be a point of comparison, then, between the wilderness generation and Amos's Israel.

EXILE (5:27).   **5:27**   God had delivered the people out of their exile in the wilderness (those who did not commit idolatry) into the promised land. Now God was about to drive them back into exile. God's judgment word for Israel was "exile beyond Damascus." This word was for a people who were enthusiastic in their worship but misguided in their devotion. This word would be carried out by Yahweh, the God of hosts. No intermediate agent is named. The absence of justice and righteousness in Israel and the presence of idolatry there meant that the nation could not survive the judgment of God.

(4) A Preeminent Nation (6:1–7)

¹Woe to you who are complacent in Zion,
   and to you who feel secure on Mount Samaria,
you notable men of the foremost nation,
   to whom the people of Israel come!
²Go to Calneh and look at it;
   go from there to great Hamath,
   and then go down to Gath in Philistia.
Are they better off than your two kingdoms?
   Is their land larger than yours?
³You put off the evil day
   and bring near a reign of terror.
⁴You lie on beds inlaid with ivory
   and lounge on your couches.
You dine on choice lambs
   and fattened calves.
⁵You strum away on your harps like David
   and improvise on musical instruments.
⁶You drink wine by the bowlful
   and use the finest lotions,
   but you do not grieve over the ruin of Joseph.
⁷Therefore you will be among the first to go into exile;
   your feasting and lounging will end.

Amos 6:1–7 is another woe oracle.[252] The first element is the woe-cry

---

[252] G. Wittenberg attributes most of vv. 1–7 to Amos but suggests the addition of certain parts by "the Amos School" and by "the Deuteronomists" ("Amos 6:1–7," *Journal of Theology for South Africa* 58 [1987]: 57–69). J. Mays (*Amos,* 115) took the entire seven verses (vv. 1–7) to be the work of Amos including the reference to "Zion" in v. 1. Amos said his call from God was to go to Israel and prophesy to God's people (7:15). In the prophet's understanding both Israel and Judah were God's people. Thus his inclusion of "Zion" should not be a surprise. Other eighth-century B.C. prophets included both kingdoms in their prophecies (cf. Isa 9:7–20; Hos 6:11; Mic 1:3–16).

itself, "woe" (*hôy*). Eight plural active participles follow the woe-cry, a second identifying mark of the woe oracle. The woe-cry says something is wrong, the participles describe what is wrong, and the judgment word (v. 7) announces God's response to what is wrong.

PREEMINENT IN LEADERSHIP (6:1–3). The first focus of the woe oracle is upon the proud leaders of Judah and Israel. They considered themselves the top men of the top nation. The entire house of Israel came to them in all matters of importance "for advice or in order to petition them against injustice."[253]

6:1 The woe-cry (*hôy*), a funeral lament, was in sharp contrast to the leaders' self-evaluation. The following active participles ("who are complacent" and "who feel secure") function as prophetic accusations in describing their behavior. Zion's (i.e., Jerusalem's) leaders were "complacent." They were at ease and untroubled (cf. Isa 32:9–11). Perhaps that attitude grew from their inflated opinion of their spiritual preeminence.

Samaria's leaders felt "secure."[254] Their confidence was in their own ability to control their destiny. They were "trusting in Mount Samaria," literally. Samaria's topography made it a natural fortress. Their leaders' trust may have been in their political and military preeminence. Both sets of leaders (from Judah and Israel) thought of themselves as the "notable men of the foremost nation." "You notable men" translates the passive participle of a verb (*nāqab*) that can mean to "pierce," "point to," or "designate" (cf. Gen 30:28). The position of "foremost" was self-assigned. The leaders designated themselves the number one nation. "To whom the people of Israel come" describes the pitiable plight of Israel's people, who must depend on leaders whose trust is in Mount Samaria rather than God.

6:2 Amos ordered the self-evaluated preeminent leaders in Zion and Samaria to compare themselves with three nearby city-states. The four verbs are imperatives, perhaps suggesting the urgency of the situation from the prophet's perspective. Amos probably did not expect his audience to travel anywhere. In their mind's eye they were to go to the cities named. Calneh and Hamath were Syrian city-states under Israel's influence. Gath was a Philistine city-state under Judah's control. No was the expected answer to the rhetorical questions. The point of the rhetorical questions was the equality between those city-states and Israel/Judah. Leaders of Israel and Judah were wrong if they thought they were better or bigger than the three city-states.

6:3 Another plural active participle ("you put off") continues the

---

[253] Paul, *Amos,* 201.

[254] The term translated "and to you who feel secure" is וְהַבֹּטְחִים, an active participle that could be translated "the ones trusting." Hebrew participles describe continuous action. Thus the leaders in Samaria day in and day out were trusting in the mountain fortress on which the city was built, not in God on whom the nation was founded.

prophetic accusations. Israel's leaders denied that a day of disaster ("evil," *rāʿ*) was approaching (cf. Jer 17:17–18; 51:2). They refused to learn from the history of their neighboring city-states, who once had been independent. Now they were subject to Israel and Judah respectively. What happened to their neighbors could happen to them.

By consigning to the distant future any day of accounting, Israel's leaders invited "a reign of terror." Amos had a view of reality that differed from the view held by the high society of Israel. The leaders in Israel felt secure in their fortresses and comfortable in their winter and summer houses. They scornfully dismissed any thought of a day of "evil."[255] The term translated "put off" occurs elsewhere only in Isa 66:5, where it means to "exclude" or "reject." Here it means they rejected the idea of "the evil day."[256] They were confident such a day was reserved for God's enemies. What they failed to see was that *they* might be God's enemies. Any thought of a day of disaster for Israel was put off to the distant future.

"Violence" is the usual word selected to render into English the idea in the term translated "terror" (*ḥāmās*; cf. comments at 3:10).[257] The word rendered "reign" (*šebet*) means "sitting" or "seat." To dismiss the concept of punishment for evil tends to promote the practice of violence. Israel's leaders precipitated and accelerated "the very misfortune that they claim will never overtake them."[258]

PREEMINENT IN LUXURY (6:4–6).   The focus of the woe oracle shifts in these verses to the self-indulgence of Israel's leading citizens. Active participles in this section continue to function as prophetic accusations. "Only the best for us" was their philosophy.

6:4   Israel's wealthy citizens slept on the best beds. The poor could not afford a bed, much less one inlaid with ivory. In times past only royalty enjoyed such luxury (cf. "the houses adorned with ivory" in 3:15). "Lounge" (*sĕruḥîm*) may be rendered "sprawling," or "hanging over" with a distinctly negative connotation. Implied in the word is either laziness or drunkenness or both.

Israel's leading citizens ate the best food. Ordinary citizens probably ate meat only three times a year, at the annual festivals. "Fattened calves" is actually "calves from the midst of the fattening pen." "Veal" is the common name

---

[255] Wittenberg, "Amos 6:1–7," 60. The "evil day" is a day of calamity or disaster, not moral evil. Wittenberg thinks it should be equated with the day of darkness in 5:18,20.

[256] Holladay (*CHAL*, 228) gives the meaning here to "believe, suppose" something to be "far away."

[257] Wittenberg concluded that the term translated "terror" (חמס, "violence") usually described the violence practiced by "rulers, the king's officials, the rich and the powerful" ("Amos 6:1–7," 62). Wolff defined the scope and application of the term as "violence perpetrated against human life" (*Joel and Amos*, 232).

[258] Paul, *Amos*, 205.

for this delicacy now. Such a meat diet was for the few in Israel's society, a luxury for the wealthy only.

6:5 The leading citizens of Israel had the luxury of a leisurely lifestyle. They could lounge around eating, drinking, and making up songs, imagining themselves to be little Davids (cf. 1 Sam 16:14–23; 2 Sam 23:1; 2 Chr 5:11– 13; 7:6). "You strum away" translates the active participle of a verb that occurs only here. It may have the idea of composing "some frivolous verbal accompaniment to music."[259] "On your harps" is literally "on the mouth of the harp" and means "to the accompaniment of the harp." These activities would have enlivened their revelry.

6:6 Israel's leading citizens overindulged themselves in drinking. For containers to drink wine they used "bowls" rather than cups. The term for bowls is the one usually used in ritual procedures (Exod 27:3; Num 4:14; 7:13; 1 Kgs 7:50). "Use the finest lotion" is literally "the first [best grade] of oils they anoint." Its purpose could have been medicinal, cosmetic, or cultic. The verb describing its application is the one generally employed in a cultic setting. However, stress in the sentence falls on the grade of oil used, "the finest," which favors the cosmetic or medicinal interpretation.

The indictment in all the accusations of indulgence is that Israel's leading citizens went on in their revelry as if all was well (cf. 4:1). Joseph (Israel) was about to break up as a nation, yet the leading citizens were not sick over it as they should have been. They were "totally self-centered, totally preoccupied with the pleasures of life but blinded to the threatening reality all around them."[260] Life, so they thought, could not be better. According to Amos, it could not have been worse.

PREEMINENT IN LEAVING (6:7).   **6:7**   Again Amos introduced the judgment sentence with "therefore." The word "first" has punctuated this entire woe oracle. Israel's leaders thought Israel was the first of the nations. They demanded first grade oils for cosmetic use. Now they would be first in the line of exiles going into captivity. Amos let them be first all the way. Their "feasting" and "lounging" would come to an end.[261]

God does not tolerate a self-indulgent lifestyle. The history of Israel and Judah brought to literal fulfillment the judgment sentence Amos delivered

---

[259] Niehaus, "Amos," 1:439. See also D. N. Freedman, "But Did King David Invent Musical Instruments?" *BibRev* 1.2 (1985): 50–51.

[260] Wittenberg, "Amos 6:1–7," 67.

[261] Some have argued that the term for "feasting," מַרְזֵחַ, suggests a pagan religious feast known from Akkadian and Ugaritic texts (P. King, *Amos, Hosea, Micah—An Archaeological Commentary* [Philadelphia: Westminster, 1988], 138; H. Barstad, *The Religious Polemics of Amos*, VTSup 34 [Leiden: Brill, 1984], 137–42). But the evidence is insufficient to demonstrate a religious context. See Finley, *Joel, Amos, Obadiah*, 265–67. From the use of the term in Jer 16:5 G. Smith suggests the funeral banquet was the background (*Amos*, 193–94; cf. Andersen and Freedman, *Amos*, 566–68).

against them (2 Kgs 24:11–16; 25:11–12,18–21). When the worship of God's people fails to produce justice and righteousness in society, God's judgment cannot be far behind.

(5) A Doomed Nation (6:8–14)

⁸The Sovereign LORD has sworn by himself—the LORD God Almighty declares:
> **"I abhor the pride of Jacob**
> **and detest his fortresses;**
> **I will deliver up the city**
> **and everything in it."**

⁹If ten men are left in one house, they too will die. ¹⁰And if a relative who is to burn the bodies comes to carry them out of the house and asks anyone still hiding there, "Is anyone with you?" and he says, "No," then he will say, "Hush! We must not mention the name of the LORD."

> **¹¹For the LORD has given the command,**
> **and he will smash the great house into pieces**
> **and the small house into bits.**
> **¹²Do horses run on the rocky crags?**
> **Does one plow there with oxen?**
> **But you have turned justice into poison**
> **and the fruit of righteousness into bitterness—**
> **¹³you who rejoice in the conquest of Lo Debar**
> **and say, "Did we not take Karnaim by our own strength?"**
> **¹⁴For the LORD God Almighty declares,**
> **"I will stir up a nation against you, O house of Israel,**
> **that will oppress you all the way**
> **from Lebo Hamath to the valley of the Arabah."**

A loosely developed theme ties Amos 6:8–14 together. God has not changed. He will not tolerate the self-indulgent lifestyle of his people in any generation. That theme is the explanation for Israel's military defeat under the Lord's direction. In form this is a judgment oracle. Samaria may have been the setting for the message. The term translated "house" (*bêt*) functions as a catchword throughout the oracle (vv. 9–11,14) pinpointing the object of God's judgment, "O, house of Israel" (cf. 3:13–15; 5:1,4,6,25; 9:8–9).

THE LORD'S OATH (6:8).   **6:8**   Three times in Amos the Lord's oath introduces a decree of punishment (4:2; 6:8; 8:7). In 4:2 the Lord swears by his holiness. Here he swears by himself. In 8:7 he swears by the pride of Jacob.

"By himself" (*běnapšô*, "by his soul") means "by the Lord's own person," the most binding form of commitment. The Lord's character, integrity, and power stood behind the oath. Amos identified the message to follow as an oracle (*ně²um*) of "the LORD God of hosts" (literally). God's authority and resources supporting this oracle made it awesome. The target of the three verbs ("abhor . . . detest . . . deliver"), though stated variously, is primarily Samaria.

The first verb is "abhor" (*mĕtā'ēb*), a participle expressing God's continuing attitude toward "the pride of Jacob."[262] Most interpreters take "the pride of Jacob" to be an attribute of the people, their arrogant nationalistic and military self-confidence, or their overconfidence in the mountain of Samaria.[263]

Here in v. 8 and in 8:7, where the Lord swears by "the pride of Jacob," the reference seems to be to the city of Samaria.[264] Two factors favor this interpretation: (1) the "fortresses" possessed by ("his" refers to the pride of Jacob in the previous line) the pride of Jacob, a term typically associated in Amos with capital cities (1:4,7,10,12,14; 2:2,5; 3:9–10), and (2) the judgment word at the close of the verse that designates "the city" as the particular target in view. "The city and everything in it" appears to be parallel to "the pride of Jacob and . . . his fortresses."

The second verb is "detest" (*śānē'*, "hate"), a term used earlier about Israel's festivals (5:21) and about one's outlook toward evil (5:15). Here the object of God's hatred is Samaria's "fortresses." The fortresses served as military fortifications and as storage space for booty taken in warfare, as well as gain from robbery and violence against the poor (3:10). The last named usage of fortresses especially would have aroused God's hatred. Israel had placed their trust in them (cf. Deut 28:52) and made them the center of their lives of luxury and violence. "The mighty fortress is their god. Its security and power make God's protection and blessing irrelevant crutches in the real world of economic and political influence."[265] God hates anything that replaces him in the lives of his people, especially when it is associated with wickedness.

The third verb is "deliver up," which suggests the idea of handing over or surrendering a prisoner. It is used in 1:6,9 of selling captives. Samaria and all its people (or everything in it) is the stated target of God's action. Implied in this judgment word is God's use of an enemy nation to execute the judgment against Samaria (6:14).

DEATH FOR SURVIVORS (6:9–10).   A shift from oracular poetry to narrative prose (vv. 9–10) style may be explained by the shift in focus. Verse 8 is a report of God's oath to destroy the city of Samaria. Verses 9 and 10 contain a report of a hypothetical situation in the wake of the destruction of the city to show how complete that destruction would be.

6:9–10   Survivors of the disaster pictured in v. 8 would have only their certain death as a future prospect (v. 9). "Ten men . . . left in one house" poses

---

[262] A textual error of א for ע is commonly recognized in the root האב, which means to "long for." תעב occurs in 5:10 in parallel with שׂנא.

[263] Paul, *Amos*, 213; Wolff, *Joel and Amos*, 282; Mays, *Amos*, 118; Stuart, *Hosea-Jonah*, 363; R. Smith, "Amos," 121.

[264] Hayes, *Amos*, 188.

[265] G. Smith, *Amos*, 207.

problems for interpreters. The number would be too large for an ordinary family. "House" may designate a royal house or a government building. The survivors could be a large extended family, members of the ruling class, or a unit of soldiers. In any case their survival would be short-lived. Interpreters tend to suppose a plague of some sort as the cause of their death, since otherwise cremation was not the common practice.[266] Perhaps the men had crowded into a house after escaping from a military defeat.

The hypothetical "if" of v. 9, though not repeated in the Hebrew text of v. 10, should be understood as dominating the contents of v. 10 (as the NIV translation makes explicit). Disposal of the remains of the corpses is the activity in view. "And if a relative who is to burn the bodies comes" is literally "and his relative carries him, and one burning him." The NIV interprets "one burning him" as describing the relative's purpose in coming and the one addressed as perhaps a survivor. This is suggested by the question, "Is anyone with you?" But the apparently absolute statement in v. 9, "they too will die," leads some to conclude that there were no survivors in the house. In this case the relative is accompanied by a cremator, who could be the one addressed. The phrase "anyone still hiding there" is literally "one inside the house," and perhaps the question simply means, "Is anyone alive?"[267]

But the main point is not who is removing the remains or how they are doing it. Whether a survivor is found and what the appropriate response is to the disaster are the matters of pressing interest. The imperative ("Hush!") and the instruction not to mention the name of the Lord perhaps anticipate a possible response to prayer or lamentation in the face of the disaster. S. Paul explains that to invoke the name of the Lord in prayer or lamentation would risk additional disaster by the Lord's appearance in response to the mention of his name.[268] Or perhaps the idea is that funerary rites in the Lord's name would be inappropriate since these have apparently died under the judgment of God.[269] Another interpretation is that it is too late to pray for deliverance since all the men are dead ("we must not mention" is an interpretation of the negated infinitive "not to mention").[270]

TOTAL DESTRUCTION (6:11).   **6:11**   Israel's God was the one in charge of the nation's destruction. He was giving the orders. He was smiting the houses. "Great house" and "small house" left in "pieces" and "bits" is a picture of complete destruction. "Great house" may refer to the royal house or to the houses of the wealthy. "Small house" may designate lesser government buildings or the houses of the poor. The primary thought is that the result of

[266] R. Smith, "Amos," 7:121; Wolff, *Joel and Amos,* 282; Mays, *Amos,* 119.
[267] Cf. G. Smith, *Amos,* 208; Andersen and Freedman, *Amos,* 572.
[268] Paul, *Amos,* 213.
[269] Andersen and Freedman, *Amos,* 573–74.
[270] G. Smith, *Amos,* 209.

the Lord's command will be to reduce all houses to rubble.

AN ABSURD HAPPENING (6:12).   **6:12**   The two rhetorical questions expect negative answers. No one in their right mind runs horses on rocky crags.[271] The second question is literally, "Does he plow with oxen?" Either the object is understood to be the "rocky crags" mentioned in the first question or the word translated "with oxen" (*bbqrym*) may be divided into two words (*bbqr ym*), which would mean "with oxen the sea."[272] The prophet's audience would have understood the absurdity of either scenario. What Israel had done in turning justice into poison and the fruit of righteousness into bitterness was equally absurd (see 5:7). Such perversion of right relationships and of justice in the courts was self-destructive.

OPPRESSION FOR A PROUD PEOPLE (6:13–14).   Also absurd was Israel's arrogant dependence on their own strength (cf. Jer 9:23–24; 17:5–8). The principle at work in these two verses is that pride in national accomplishments would precede the nation's fall. With plural participles the prophet described the people responsible for the absurd perversion of justice and righteousness (v. 13). Then he set the Lord's announcement of judgment over against their prideful boasting (v. 14).

6:13   Israel had recovered previous losses east of the Jordan as a result of the campaigning of Jeroboam II (2 Kgs 14:25). Two of the cities he recovered were "Lo Debar" (probably a pun on the name of the Gadite city of Debir), which means "not a thing," and Karnaim (*qarnāyim*), which means "a pair of horns." Amos used the names to engage in biting sarcasm. Their rejoicing over "not a thing" and their saying (or thinking) they had by their own strength taken "a pair of horns" were alike prideful boastings. The horns of an animal were symbols of power or authority in Old Testament times. Perhaps Israel thought that by taking Karnaim they had doubled their strength. Actually Karnaim was a relatively insignificant city.

6:14   A nation boasting of its power faced a judgment word of God. Israel's God was arousing a nation as his instrument of judgment. Though not named in this oracle, Assyria eventually executed God's judgment word against Israel. The prophet's authority for such a strong word of judgment was the fact that he brought an oracle of the Lord God of hosts. God's judgment word was that the whole land north to south would be oppressed. "Lebo Hamath" was Israel's northernmost border. "The valley of the Arabah" (better, "the brook" or "wadi of the Arabah") was the southernmost boundary. The emphasis in v. 14 and in the larger passage (vv. 8–14) is total defeat for Israel. The proud would be humbled, the oppressor oppressed.

---

[271] A. Cooper's proposal that בַּסֶּלַע is a place name, Sela, and his emendation of the text to get "valley" (which he equates with modern Beqa', a place name) represents forced and unwarranted handling of the text ("The Absurdity of Amos 6:12a," *JBL* 107 [1988]: 727).

[272] G. Smith, *Amos,* 197.

III. THE VISIONS OF AMOS (7:1–9:15)
   1. Visions of Israel's Imminent Destruction (7:1–8:3)
      (1) First Vision: The Locusts (7:1–3)
         The Vision Revealed (7:1)
         The Prophet's Intercession (7:2)
         The Lord's Response (7:3)
      (2) Second Vision: The Fire (7:4–6)
         The Vision Revealed (7:4)
         The Prophet's Intercession (7:5)
         The Lord's Response (7:6)
      (3) Third Vision: The Plumb Line (7:7–9)
         The Vision Revealed (7:7)
         The Lord's Question (7:8a)
         The Prophet's Response (7:8b)
         The Lord's Explanation (7:8c)
         The Coming Destruction (7:9)
      (4) Who Is in Charge? (7:10–17)
         Jeroboam? (7:10–11)
         Amaziah? (7:12–13)
         Amos? (7:14)
         The Lord! (7:15–17)
      (5) Fourth Vision: A Basket of Summer Fruit (8:1–3)
         The Vision Revealed (8:1)
         The Lord's Question (8:2a)
         The Prophet's Response (8:2b)
         The Lord's Explanation (8:2c)
         The Coming Destruction (8:3)
   2. Oracles and a Vision of Israel's Future Destruction and Ultimate Restoration (8:4–9:15)
      (1) Indictment of Greedy Merchants (8:4–6)
         Social Injustice (8:4)
         Superficial Worship (8:5a)
         Specific Charges (8:5b–6)
      (2) The Lord's Oath against Greedy Merchants (8:7–10)
         Determined to Remember Their Deeds (8:7)
         Dire Consequences of the Lord's Oath (8:8)
         Days of Gloom and Grief (8:9–10)
      (3) The Lord's Threat of Famine (8:11–14)

A Famine of Hearing the Words of the Lord (8:11)
A Futile Search for the Word of the Lord (8:12)
A Fainting from Thirst for the Word of the Lord (8:13)
A Failure of False Religion (8:14)
(4) Fifth Vision: The Lord Standing by the Altar (9:1–4)
Seeing the Awesome Lord (9:1a)
Hearing the Awful Judgment (9:1b)
No Hiding Place (9:2–4)
(5) The Lord Almighty (9:5–6)
(6) Destruction of the Sinful Kingdom (9:7–10)
No Special Immunity for Israel (9:7)
Observed by the Sovereign Lord (9:8)
Judgment of Israel Commanded (9:9)
Death Sentence (9:10)
(7) Future Restoration of Israel (9:11–15)
The Lord's Promise of Restoration (9:11–12)
The Lord's Promise of Plenty (9:13–14)
The Lord's Promise of Security (9:15)

III. THE VISIONS OF AMOS (7:1–9:15)

The two major sections of Amos are (1) the words of Amos (1:3–6:14) and (2) the visions of Amos (7:1–9:15). By "words" reference is made to the oracles of Amos. By "visions" attention is called to the primary motif in the latter part of the book, although the first section of the book contains some materials other than oracles, and the second section contains some oracles scattered among the visions. The visions may be thought of as God's revelations to the prophet, and the words may be thought of as the prophet's proclamation to Israel of those revelations.

The second major section of the Book of Amos contains five vision-reports. Visions one and two are event visions (7:1–3,4–6). Visions three and four are wordplay visions (7:7–9; 8:1–3). The fifth vision is distinct in form and content (9:1–4).

All of the first four vision-reports follow a pattern found in other prophetic literature (Jer 1:11–12,13–19; Zech 5:1–4). Each one begins with an introductory formula: "This is what the Sovereign LORD showed me." The vision content follows the introductory formula. A dialogue between the prophet and God concludes the report.

In the event visions God showed Amos an event that needed no interpretation. Amos began the dialogue with God in the first two visions, interceding for Israel, and then God relented. God initiated the dialogue with Amos in the second two visions, interpreted the object shown, and then announced judgment.

The fifth vision-report is of a theophany. Amos saw the Lord beside the altar. His appearance there was to announce the destruction of Israel, not to bless them. Dramatic movement to a terrifying climax is discernible in the five vision-reports.

The prophet interceded after each of the first two reports, and God stayed the announced judgment. After each of the next two reports prophetic intercession is noticeably absent. Instead, God's announcement of coming judgment closes each of these two reports after an explicit denial of room for prophetic intercession: "I will spare them no longer" (7:8; 8:2). In the final vision-report even the element of dialogue is missing. The earlier vision-reports had announced that Israel's destruction was coming. This final report tells how the destruction will come about. God himself will execute his judgment word. The vision-reports function in the same manner as the oracles. Both convey the message of God to Israel through Amos. While form-critical analysis has uncovered some unique aspects of the visions,[1] the central point is theological: the end of Israel is at hand.[2] As D. A. Hubbard has shown, the main theme is the sovereignty of the Lord. The Lord reveals the visions and is the foundation of Amos's dispute with Amaziah. But Hubbard stresses that the sovereignty of the Lord is "seasoned by compassion." The final theological theme Hubbard points out is the prophetic word, which "mediates the sovereignty and compassion of the Lord."[3] God, in sovereignty and with compassion, gives his word and is faithful to its content.

1. Visions of Israel's Imminent Destruction (7:1–8:3)

(1) First Vision: The Locusts (7:1–3)

[1]This is what the Sovereign LORD showed me: He was preparing swarms of locusts after the king's share had been harvested and just as the second crop was coming up. [2]When they had stripped the land clean, I cried out, "Sovereign LORD, forgive! How can Jacob survive? He is so small!"

[3]So the LORD relented.

"This will not happen," the LORD said.

All the vision accounts follow the first-person style of reporting. Advantages of the style include (1) enhancement of the claim to authority, (2) estab-

---

[1] J. D. W. Watts, *Vision and Prophecy in Amos* (Leiden: Brill, 1958); J. L. Mays, *Amos,* OTL (Philadelphia: Westminster, 1969), 123–27; H. W. Wolff, *Joel and Amos,* Her (Philadelphia: Fortress, 1977); S. Paul, *Amos,* Her (Minneapolis: Fortress, 1991), 222–25.

[2] Paul, *Amos,* 225.

[3] D. A. Hubbard, *Joel and Amos,* TOTC (Downers Grove: InterVarsity, 1989), 204–5.

lishment of rapport between the prophet and his audience, and (3) a more powerful emotional appeal. The report form enabled the audience to identify with what Amos reported, and it enabled Amos to identify with the audience as an intercessor.

THE VISION REVEALED (7:1).   **7:1** The introductory formula, "This is what the Sovereign LORD showed me," is the prophet's way of crediting God with the vision. What Amos saw was no hallucination. He was not daydreaming. God was at work revealing an imminent, potentially devastating event. The introductory formula is similar to the divine-speech and oracle formulae of Amos 1–6 in that it reveals the source and the authority of the message. The term sometimes rendered "behold" that follows the introductory formula in Hebrew (in each of the first four visions) is left untranslated. It is a flag word alerting the listener/reader to some important or startling statement about to be made.

God was "forming" (*yôṣēr*) a swarm of locusts. The word "forming" is found in 4:13, a hymn fragment about the creative activity of God. God creates mountains and wind, darkness and light. He also creates forms of destruction, that is, locusts, to punish his people (cf. 4:9; Deut 28:38; 2 Chr 7:13–14; Joel 1:4), a great concern of the prophet. Two temporal clauses are used to pinpoint the time of the locust swarm. The king had his share of the crop, but the people as yet had none; they would have to wait for the threatened second crop. The term translated "the second crop" (*leqeš*) occurs twice here but nowhere else in the Bible.[4] In the Gezer Calendar[5] the term *leqeš* designates the fifth and sixth months of the year. Since the list of months begins in the fall, the fifth and sixth months would be in March-April of the Western calendar.

A locust swarm at the end of the rainy season, as the grass used the last available moisture for final growth, would result in tragedy for the farmers and their livestock. The onset of the dry season would allow no more growth until the next rainy season. No grass would be available for grazing or for making hay.[6] God gave Amos a vision of a locust swarm at a critically important time. If the locust plague went on unchecked after the end of the rainy season, the result would be tragic indeed.

THE PROPHET'S INTERCESSION (7:2).   **7:2** In his vision Amos watched the locust plague with anguish. The clause translated "when they had stripped the land clean" begins with the verb literally rendered "and it will be," (*wĕhāyâ*). Translating it as a past tense requires an emendation. It also is fol-

---

[4] The related word מַלְקוֹשׁ refers to the "latter rains" of March-April. It occurs in Deut 11:14; Jer 5:24; Joel 2:23. See T. J. Finley, *Joel, Amos, Obadiah* (Chicago: Moody, 1990), 282.

[5] *ANET,* 320.

[6] The term rendered "had been harvested" (גֵּז) usually refers to sheepshearing (Gen 31:19; 2 Sam 13:23), not grass mowing. Only in Ps 72:6 does the term refer to mown grass.

lowed by a particle (*ʾim*) usually meaning "if." Furthermore, such a translation as the NIV (also NRSV) makes difficult the Lord's promise, "This will not happen" (v. 2). Thus a translation is required that conveys the potential nature of the disaster. Stuart explains it as Amos's vision of a *potential* future and translates, "It seemed as if they would completely devour the earth's vegetation."[7] Andersen and Freedman explain the initial verb as giving the clause a modal sense and translate, "When they were about to devour the vegetation of the land entirely."[8]

In desperation Amos interceded with God on Israel's behalf. The double title for God, "Sovereign LORD,"[9] suggests his absolute exaltation and, at the same time, his close relationship with the prophet. "Forgive" (*sĕlaḥ*) is an imperative of entreaty, probably expressive of the prophet's sense of urgency about the situation he observed in the vision. The verb "forgive" has no object and may not have its usual meaning of "pardon for sin." Perhaps the prophet's appeal was for God to exercise forbearance[10] and turn the threatened locust plague away from Israel.

The basis for the prophet's plea was that "Jacob" (Israel) was small. The word "small" (*qāṭōn*) may refer to helplessness rather than to size. During the time of Jeroboam II the nation and its army was not especially small or weak, except before God.[11] "How can Jacob survive?" reveals the prophet's assessment that the nation could not survive the potential plague. The nation's survival hinged on the prophet's intercession and God's response to it.[12]

THE LORD'S RESPONSE (7:3). **7:3** God's positive response to Amos's appeal is in line with the consistent revelation of God in the Old Testament (Gen 18:22–23; Exod 34:6–7; Josh 7:6–13; Jer 18:1–10; Jonah 3:10). The prophet's report of God's response is a straightforward narrative declaration, "So the LORD relented." What the term translated "relented" (*niḥam*) means in the context is expressed by the Lord's promise, "This will not happen."

---

[7] Stuart, *Hosea-Jonah*, 370–71.

[8] Andersen and Freedman, *Amos*, 739, 742–43. Finley considers the clause to express an interrupted thought, the protasis of a conditional sentence without an apodosis (*Joel, Amos, Obadiah*, 282–83). It could perhaps be rendered, "What if they completely devour the land's vegetation!"

[9] Most of the occurrences of יְהוָה אֲדֹנָי in Amos are rendered simply by κυριος in the LXX. H. N. Richardson proposes, "In late Judaism the Hebrew word for Lord (*ʾádōnāy*) was added either before or after Yahweh in order to remind the reader not to pronounce the ineffable name of God" ("Amos's Four Visions of Judgment and Hope," *BibRev* 5 [1989]: 19). But certain patterns in the occurrence of the compound name render this explanation unlikely (e.g., cf. Andersen and Freedman, *Amos*, 614, 617–18). Amos also may have used the double name for God to make emphatic the source and authority for his message.

[10] The first meaning in Holladay, *CHAL*, for סלח is "practice forbearance." In the context that seems to be the meaning of the appeal from Amos.

[11] Paul, *Amos*, 229. G. Smith suggests that Amos may have been thinking of the farmers who with no harvest would be helpless against their wealthy oppressors (*Amos*, 223).

[12] Cf. *IBHS* § 320, n.10.

God canceled the threat of the locust plague. *Niham* with *ʿal* means "to allow oneself a change of heart regarding something."[13] In this case God changed his plan to destroy Israel's plant life with a locust plague.

God gave a positive response to the prophet's intercession. One person made a big difference because God is approachable and merciful. Prophets have been identified traditionally as spokespersons for God to God's people. Another important aspect of their service was as intercessors, speaking to God for God's people.[14] Abraham, the first person in the Bible identified as a prophet, is described as follows: "He is a prophet, and he will pray for you and you will live" (Gen 20:7; cf. also Gen 18:16–33).

(2) Second Vision: The Fire (7:4–6)

⁴This is what the Sovereign LORD showed me: The Sovereign LORD was calling for judgment by fire; it dried up the great deep and devoured the land. ⁵Then I cried out, "Sovereign LORD, I beg you, stop! How can Jacob survive? He is so small!"

⁶So the LORD relented.

"This will not happen either," the Sovereign LORD said.

The form of the second vision-report is almost identical to the first one.[15] The difference is in the method of the coming judgment. While in 7:1–3 judgment would come by locusts, here in vv. 4–6 the instrument is fire. Nevertheless, just as in vv. 1–3, God relented after Amos interceded.

THE VISION REVEALED (7:4). **7:4** What Amos saw under divine guidance was the Sovereign Lord calling for a "judgment" (*rib*) by fire. Some translators want to realign the consonants and obtain a different reading: "calling for a rain of fire" or "calling for a flame of fire."[16] The most important word in the phrase is "fire," often in the Bible described as coming from God, usually in judgment.[17] Fire "dried up" (*toʾkal*) the great deep and "devoured" (*weʾakēlâ*) the land (using two forms of the same verb).[18]

---

[13] For an excellent study of this term see H. Parunak, "A Semantic Survey of *NHM*," *Bib* 56 (1975): 512–32. Also see Andersen and Freedman, *Amos,* 638–79, which finds in Moses a model or precedent for Amos's intervention (cf. Exod 32).

[14] Richardson, "Amos's Four Visions of Judgment and Hope," 16.

[15] See the helpful chart in Andersen and Freedman, *Amos,* 620.

[16] Richardson, "Amos's Four Visions of Judgment and Hope," 17–19; D. R. Hillers, "Amos 7:4 and Ancient Parallels," *CBQ* 26 (1964): 221–25; Stuart, *Hosea-Jonah,* 370; G. Smith, *Amos: A Commentary* (Grand Rapids: Zondervan, 1989), 220.

[17] Cf. Gen 19:23–28; Num 11:1; 16:35; Deut 9:3; 1 Kgs 18:24,38; 2 Kgs 1:10,12; 1 Chr 21:26; 2 Chr 7:1; Job 1:16; Ps 21:9; Isa 29:6; 30:30,33; 66:15–16; Lam 4:11; Ezek 39:6.

[18] The verb translated "dried up," וַתֹּאכַל, is a consecutive imperfect, while the verb "devoured," וְאָכְלָה, is a perfect with *waw.* Andersen and Freedman argue that the two cannot be translated as though they were the same form. Thus they render the first "had consumed" and the second "was consuming" (*Amos,* 745–46).

"Fire" is a symbol here of a severe drought that the Sovereign Lord was summoning against Israel (cp. 4:7–8; but here the vision appears to describe a much more devastating drought). "The great deep" refers to subterranean waters that feed the springs.[19] So intense was God's fire in the prophet's vision that it dried up (lit., "devoured") the great deep (cf. Deut 32:22). The "land" (*ḥēleq*, "portion") the fire devoured (or was devouring) was either the land of Israel (Mic 2:4) or may have been the people themselves (Deut 32:9).[20] Richardson's comment is a fitting summary of the meaning of v. 4: "If Yahweh rained down this fire, it would eventually dry up the fathomless waters of the deep that fed the springs and would consume the entire land."[21]

THE PROPHET'S INTERCESSION (7:5). **7:5** The threat in the second vision needed no interpretation. Amos perceived the danger to Israel and interceded immediately. Again his plea was cast in the imperative form of the verb. He asked God to "stop" the fire. The basis for his request was Israel's need: "How can Jacob survive? He is so small." Israel's leaders thought of themselves as the top leaders of the top nation. Amos saw the nation in its weakness and vulnerability, not "the foremost nation" (6:1) but "small" (7:5). No one should overlook the prophet's solidarity with the people of Israel when he interceded in their behalf.

THE LORD'S RESPONSE (7:6). **7:6** Again the Lord "relented" (*niḥam*). He promised, "This will not happen either." As in the previous vision-report, the account ended with the messenger formula, "the Sovereign LORD said." Twice the prophet's intercession gained a positive response from God to turn away threatened judgment.

(3) Third Vision: The Plumb Line (7:7–9)

[7]This is what he showed me: The LORD was standing by a wall that had been built true to plumb, with a plumb line in his hand. [8]And the LORD asked me, "What do you see, Amos?"

"A plumb line," I replied.

Then the LORD said, "Look, I am setting a plumb line among my people Israel; I will spare them no longer.

[9]"The high places of Isaac will be destroyed
and the sanctuaries of Israel will be ruined;
with my sword I will rise against the house of Jeroboam."

The third and fourth vision-reports vary somewhat from the first and

---

[19] Cf. Gen 1:2; 7:11; 8:2; 49:25; Deut 8:7; Ezek 31:4. Also see R. L. Harris, תהם, *TWOT,* 965–66.

[20] Finley suggests the term חֵלֶק alludes to the close relationship between the Lord and the land he had "apportioned" (*Joel, Amos, Obadiah,* 285). The related verb occurs in 7:17.

[21] Richardson, "Amos's Four Visions of Judgment and Hope," 19.

second reports. As in the first pair, an introductory formula is followed by a report of the vision content. But while in the first pair of visions the prophet initiated the dialogue and did most of the speaking, in the second pair God initiated and concluded the dialogue, and Amos said only one or two words.[22] Although in the first pair the prophet was shown a horrifying sight of judgment, which in response to the prophet's intercession did not occur, in the second pair of visions God asked Amos to identify a common object, which God then explained represented terrible judgment. And in the second pair Amos was given no more opportunity for intercession. God announced the end of Israel's day of grace. While the horror of the locusts and the fire give way to compassion, an ordinary plumb line and a basket of fruit are used to stress the certainty of judgment. Perhaps, as Andersen and Freedman suggest, some period of time elapsed between the first two visions and the next, during which the calamities of 4:6–13 occurred. But the Lord's discipline and Amos's preaching met no repentance on the part of Israel.[23] At any rate, "judgment, terrible and drastic" was on its way, "certainly not because God wills it, though he does, but because the people deserve it and their persistently wicked behavior demands it."[24]

THE VISION REVEALED (7:7).   **7:7**   After the introductory formula, Amos described what he saw: the Lord standing by a wall. But his attention was drawn to a "plumb line"[25] in the Lord's hand. That is made clear by the answer Amos gave to the Lord's question (v. 8). Though Richardson has argued that *ʾănāk* means "tin" based on the Akkadian term *ʾanāku*,[26] the NIV translation "plumb line" is better considering the context. H. G. M. Williamson agreed with this conclusion: "Contextual considerations favour the interpretation of *ʾănāk* as 'plumb line' and . . . philological arguments do not rule this out."[27] The reason interpreters want to take *ʾănāk* as "tin" is to build a case for this vision (like the first two visions) to be an overt judgment message. To accomplish this goal interpreters are forced to emend the received text.[28] Such a step should be taken only after exhausting every available avenue to make sense of the received text. Williamson built an attractive case for identifying the prophet as the plumb line in the hand of God.[29]

THE LORD'S QUESTION (7:8a).   **7:8a**   The Lord's question required

---

[22] See Andersen and Freedman, *Amos,* 624.

[23] Ibid., *Amos,* 630.

[24] Ibid.

[25] אֲנָךְ appears in the OT only in this vision-report. The context seems to favor "plumb line" as its meaning.

[26] Richardson, "Amos's Four Visions of Judgment and Hope," 20.

[27] H. G. M. Williamson, "The Prophet and the Plumb-line: A Redaction-Critical Study of Amos vii," *OTS* 26 (1990): 121.

[28] Wolff, *Joel and Amos,* 300.

[29] Williamson, "The Prophet and the Plumb-line," 121.

Amos to concentrate on the vision in order to identify its contents. "What do you see" is more accurately "what are you seeing," since the verb is a participle. The prophet was in the process of observing what God was showing him. How Amos understood what he was seeing seems to be the intent of the Lord's question.

THE PROPHET'S RESPONSE (7:8b). **7:8b** Amos's reply consisted of only one word (ʾănāk). He made no reference to seeing the Lord, or to the fact that he was standing beside (or upon) a wall, or that the plumb line was in the Lord's hand. The prophet's focus was on the plumb line. That must have conveyed the intended message to Amos; at least it was the focus of the Lord's explanation. Did Amos understand that he was the instrument in God's hand to test Israel for uprightness?

THE LORD'S EXPLANATION (7:8c). **7:8c** What the prophet saw was in accord with what the Lord was about to do to Israel. The Lord was setting an ʾănāk in the midst of Israel. A builder used an ʾănāk to erect a straight wall. The Lord with an ʾănāk in his hand was checking a wall (Israel) that had been built true to plumb. Based on the outcome of the check, either the wall would be approved or it would fail the test and have to come down. All of this is implied, not stated explicitly.

The Lord explained to Amos that he was "setting" (or about to set, a frequent sense of the participle) a plumb line in the midst of Israel. "My people" is an allusion to the covenant between God and Israel.[30] God was checking his own people, who had been built true to plumb, to see if they would stand the test or have to come down. On the basis of that test the Lord announced a new policy of the end of grace: "I will spare them no longer." Israel could not stand the test. The Lord's threatened intervention would not be directed by arbitrary motives but by an incorruptible test, the plumb line.

THE COMING DESTRUCTION (7:9). The targets of the coming destruction were religious sites and the ruling dynasty. Destruction of these targets would be the consequence of the plumb-line vision. Use of a passive verb ("will be destroyed") and a stative verb ("will be ruined") leaves open who or what the agent of destruction might be, but God's control of the agent is implied.

7:9 Two types of religious sites targeted for destruction were "the high places" (bāmôt) and "the sanctuaries" (miqdaš). High places were shrines on the hills in the open country. Sanctuaries were temples usually located in cities such as Bethel and Dan. Together the two terms cover all the religious sites in Israel. "Isaac" (yiśḥāq, usually spelled yiṣḥāq) is an alternate name for the Northern Kingdom. Why use "Isaac" here? As Hubbard points out, "Amos seems to have in mind the special veneration for Isaac which members of the

---

[30] Andersen and Freedman argue that in Amos the name "Israel" when combined with "my people," "house of," or "sons of" includes the people of the Southern Kingdom (*Amos*, 631–38).

Northern Kingdom displayed in making pilgrimages south to Beersheba (cf. (5:5; 8:14), Isaac's birthplace."[31] Nowhere could religious purity be found, neither in established sanctuaries nor in the high places where the people resorted to worshiping pagan deities.

Nothing in this vision-report even hints at intercession by the prophet. A reprieve for corrupt Israel was excluded by the announcement, "I will spare them no longer" (v. 8c). Nearly a century and a half later in Judah the prophet Jeremiah received God's order: "Do not pray for this people nor offer any plea or petition for them, because I will not listen when they call to me in the time of their distress" (Jer 11:14). It is still possible to sin away the day of God's grace.

Typical of these visions, the reason for the judgment is not given. This is assumed from the oracles in chaps. 1–6 (affirming the unity of the book). While Hosea focuses on Israel's corrupt worship (1:2; 2:8,13; 4:10–19), Amos's focus is on the corrupt people (2:6–8; 5:10–13). But Amos also makes clear that a corrupt lifestyle makes worship corrupt as well (3:14; 4:4–5; 5:4–6,21–24). Thus Israel's worship centers would be an object of destruction.

In the case of the action against the house of Jeroboam, God himself would wield the sword. "The house of Jeroboam" refers to the dynasty of Jeroboam, which came to an end when Jeroboam's son and successor Zechariah was assassinated (2 Kgs 15:8–10). The prophecy that God would rise against the house of Jeroboam may have been heard by Amos's audience as a call for the assassination of Jeroboam and his family. This part of v. 9 functions as a transition to the account of conflict between Amos and Amaziah in 7:10–17 (see v. 11). The reference to Jeroboam in v. 9 probably is why the narrative of Amos (vv. 10–17) follows.

(4) Who Is in Charge? (7:10–17)

[10]Then Amaziah the priest of Bethel sent a message to Jeroboam king of Israel: "Amos is raising a conspiracy against you in the very heart of Israel. The land cannot bear all his words. [11]For this is what Amos is saying:

"'Jeroboam will die by the sword,
   and Israel will surely go into exile,
   away from their native land.'"

[12]Then Amaziah said to Amos, "Get out, you seer! Go back to the land of Judah. Earn your bread there and do your prophesying there. [13]Don't prophesy anymore at Bethel, because this is the king's sanctuary and the temple of the kingdom."

[14]Amos answered Amaziah, "I was neither a prophet nor a prophet's son, but I was a shepherd, and I also took care of sycamore-fig trees. [15]But the LORD took

---

[31] Hubbard, Joel and Amos, 210.

me from tending the flock and said to me, 'Go, prophesy to my people Israel.'
^{16}Now then, hear the word of the LORD. You say,
  "'Do not prophesy against Israel,
  and stop preaching against the house of Isaac.'
^{17}"Therefore this is what the LORD says:
  "'Your wife will become a prostitute in the city,
  and your sons and daughters will fall by the sword.
  Your land will be measured and divided up,
  and you yourself will die in a pagan country.
  And Israel will certainly go into exile,
  away from their native land.'"

The shift to third-person narrative in this section is commonly interpreted as a mark that it was written by one of Amos's disciples.[32] It is thus referred to as biographical narrative. Some consider this section a digression or later insertion.[33] Viewing the verses as autobiographical, however, also is possible. J. Niehaus argues that the covenant lawsuit genre pervades the book and that the two third-person sections, 1:1 and 7:10–17, are in keeping with that style. He illustrates shifts between third and first person in second millennium Hittite treaties and in the Book of Deuteronomy and argues that such shifts should be expected in the Old Testament prophets that employ the covenant lawsuit form.[34] Such third-person narratives as we have in 7:10–17, then, can be autobiographical rather than biographical. Such sections employing the third person occur, for example, in Jeremiah, where they conclude with the notation "the words of Jeremiah end here."[35]

Furthermore, although it appears to interrupt the visions, the brief narrative functions significantly in pinpointing the two main reasons for Israel's fall: its government (King Jeroboam) and its misguided religion (the priest Amaziah).[36] Particularly does it illustrate the hardened attitude of the religious leaders to the word of the Lord and thus shows why God would "spare them no longer" (7:8; 8:2).[37] The issue in the narrative of the encounter between Amos and Amaziah was one of authority.[38] Who was in charge of the people called Israel? Was it Jeroboam the king, or Amaziah the priest at Bethel, or

---

[32] See, for example, Wolff, *Joel and Amos,* 295; Stuart, *Hosea-Jonah,* 370.

[33] See Hayes, *Amos,* 230–31.

[34] J. Niehaus, "Amos," in *The Minor Prophets: An Exegetical and Expository Commentary,* ed. T. E. McComiskey (Grand Rapids: Baker, 1992), 1:318–22.

[35] Ibid., 460. See also Finley, *Joel, Amos, Obadiah,* 112.

[36] For other arguments that these verses are vital to their context, see Smith, *Amos,* 232; Andersen and Freedman, *Amos,* 763–65.

[37] See J. de Waard and W. A. Smalley, *A Translator's Handbook on the Book of Amos* (New York: UBS, 1979), 150; G. Smith, *Amos,* 233.

[38] See G. Tucker, "Prophetic Authority: A Form Critical Study of Amos 7:10–17," *Int* 27 (1973): 423–34.

Amos the prophet of God, or God himself? The prophet's report of his vision of a plumb line (7:7–9) ended with a strong judgment word against Israel's religious sites, such as Bethel, and against the nation's ruling dynasty, represented by Jeroboam II.

Amaziah's loyalty was to Jeroboam, who probably appointed him as priest at Bethel. Amos's loyalty was to God, who sent him to prophesy against Israel. Conflict between Amaziah and Amos was inevitable since their loyalties were in conflict. Primary loyalty to God in their service to Israel would have eliminated conflict between the king, the priest, and the prophet. The answer to conflict among God's people is always to place loyalty to God above all else.

JEROBOAM? (7:10–11).   **7:10**   Amaziah is identified as "the priest of Bethel." He probably was the high priest there. His action to send word to Jeroboam implies that he was in charge of the Bethel sanctuary. "Sent" suggests a runner with a written (or verbal) message from the priest to the king. The distance between Bethel and Samaria was approximately twenty-five miles. Assuming that Jeroboam was in Samaria, a response from him would have taken at least two or three days.[39] Amaziah did not claim royal authority for the order and instructions he issued to Amos (vv. 12–13). The text does not indicate that he received a response from Jeroboam. He probably was acting on his own authority as priest of Bethel.

Amaziah charged Amos with treason (cf. Jer 26:7–11; 37:11–38:4). The verb ($q\bar{a}\check{s}ar$) means "tie up," "be allied together," or "form a conspiracy." Nothing in the text of Amos suggests that he was in league with anyone except God in his mission to Israel. But Amaziah accused him of operating on a purely human plane, with human motives and means, assuming perhaps that Amos was a man like himself. As G. Smith observes, Amaziah perverted Amos's words by treating them as political propaganda rather than the words of Yahweh.[40] Those who oppose the ways of the world with divine truth always run the risk of just such an attack. Furthermore, Amaziah had Israel's history as a basis for concern over the possible outcome of the messages Amos preached. Internal revolt had followed other such prophetic predictions (1 Sam 16:1–13; 1 Kgs 11:29–39; 19:15–17; 2 Kgs 8:7–15; 9:1–28; 10:9).

"In the very heart of Israel" is actually "in the midst of the house of Israel." That phrase may refer to the rulers of Israel who had listened to Amos's oracles and vision-reports. Revolt would more likely have arisen from such people than from ordinary citizens. The phrase may, on the other hand, refer to the sanctuary at Bethel where Amos was speaking.[41]

---

[39] J. H. Hayes supposes that Jeroboam was in Bethel for the fall festival (*Amos* [Nashville: Abingdon, 1988], 231–32).

[40] G. Smith, *Amos,* 237.

[41] Andersen and Freedman, *Amos,* 635.

"The land cannot bear all his words" implies a considerable time and range for the prophet's preaching ministry. "Bear" is a verb (*kûl*) that means to "hold," "contain," or "endure" (cf. Jer 2:13; 6:11; 10:10). Amaziah wanted Jeroboam to know his assessment of the prophet's ministry. He felt that the people had heard about all they could stand from Amos.

> Amaziah, like another priest who conveyed truth he was not clearly aware of (John 12:49–52), is uttering a profound truth the force of which he would resent and resist. Amos' words have already penetrated the defenses of Bethel and Israel, and it is already too late to do anything about them. The leaders may silence Amos now and forever, but the damage has begun and will increase. The words cannot be neutralized or contained; they burst the bonds and restraints, and work in the city and the state, bringing about the reality of which they speak. They are self-fulfilling because they have the power to produce results in conformity with their contents.[42]

7:11 Amaziah picked out two items from Amos's words sure to get the king's attention.[43] Amaziah presented them as a direct quote from Amos, introduced with the words, "For this is what Amos is saying." Nowhere, however, does the text of Amos contain the exact words of Amaziah's quotation. And while Amos clearly prophesied Israel's exile (5:5,27; 6:7; 7:17; 9:4), it was Jeroboam's house (family or dynasty) that he said would die by the sword (7:9). Although it would be natural to assume the prophecy included Jeroboam, we do not know how he died. Especially significant is what Amaziah left out—that God himself would be the agent of death. Amos was not engaged in a personal attack on Jeroboam but was proclaiming the divine response to a corrupt ruling dynasty. God would come against the house of Jeroboam with the sword.

AMAZIAH? (7:12–13). **7:12** Amaziah's use of the term "seer" (*hōzeh*, whose root meaning "to see" is used of visions and dreams; cf. Num 24:2,4,16[44]) rather than "prophet" (*nābî*) may have no particular significance since the terms are virtually synonymous (cf. Isa 29:10). Many consider the former a category of the latter.[45] Stuart suggests that "seer" is used because "it was the vision of vv 7–9 that had proved to be the last straw in offensiveness."[46] Some, however, believe the term is derogatory, referring perhaps to a diviner like Balaam, who was available for hire (Num 22:1–6).[47] Others

---

[42] Ibid., 793.

[43] Stuart, *Hosea-Jonah*, 375.

[44] The word for "vision," חָזוֹן, is from the same root. Note also the verb חָזָה in 1:1.

[45] J. Mays, *Amos*, OTL (Philadelphia: Westminster, 1969), 136. Wolff concluded that חֹזֶה was "probably considered a 'prophet' (*nābî*) in preexilic times, but that a 'prophet' was not necessarily a 'visionary'" (*Joel and Amos*, 311).

[46] Stuart, *Hosea-Jonah*, 376; so also Andersen and Freedman, *Amos*, 788.

[47] E. Hammershaimb, *The Book of Amos: A Commentary* (Oxford: Blackwell, 1970), 116.

believe that *hōzeh* designated seers attached to the court, the so-called "court-prophets."[48] Z. Zevit argued that "the role difference [between *hōzeh* and *nābîʾ*] appears to have been that those *nĕbîʾîm* who enjoyed or depended on royal patronage also were called *hōzîm*."[49] From this argument he concluded:

> Thus, when Amaziah addressed Amos as a *hozeh*, he was not challenging the authenticity of his oracles nor was he casting a disparaging remark on his office; rather he was emphasizing the impropriety of Amos, whom he believed to be patronized by the king of Judah, in delivering oracles against Jeroboam at Bethel, an Israelite sanctuary.[50]

Amaziah's treatment of Amos may have been respectful, but his ultimate goal was self-serving and political. He took Amos's words as a threat to Bethel, which he considered to be his personal territory, and to the king, his sovereign.

Stacking two imperatives together, "get out" (*lēk*, "go," or "walk") and "go back" (*bĕrah*, "flee," i.e., "run for your life"), reveals Amaziah's sense of urgency in dealing with the problem Amos created by his preaching. He wanted Amos out of Bethel, back in Judah, and out of his way. Except for the context, his urgency could be interpreted as motivated by a desire to protect Amos from the wrath of the king (cf. Jer 26:20–23).[51] But he was in fact rejecting the Lord's prophet, the Lord's word, and thus the Lord himself. "Earn your bread there" is literally "eat bread there." The meaning is "make your living there" (cf. Gen 3:19; 2 Kgs 4:8), that is, from fees for prophetic ministry. This may imply a charge that Amos was being paid to prophesy against the establishment in Israel (cf. Mic 3:11). Amos later explained that he made his living as a "shepherd" and by taking care of "sycamore-fig trees" (v. 14). Amaziah did not care whether Amos continued to prophesy as long as he did not do it in Israel. By sending him away, however, Amaziah was guilty of the accusation against Israel in 2:12 of commanding the prophets not to prophesy. Amos, on the other hand, could not cease his prophetic ministry (3:8).

7:13 On his own authority Amaziah ordered Amos to leave Israel and never prophesy at Bethel again (the prohibition is expressed in absolute and emphatic terms). According to Amaziah, Bethel (whose position in the sentence makes it emphatic) was not an appropriate place for Amos to preach. The reason Bethel was off limits to Amos was that the sanctuary there

---

[48] D. L. Petersen, *The Roles of Israel's Prophets* (Sheffield: JSOT, 1981), 56–57; S. Paul, "Prophets and Prophecy," *EncJud* 13:1155. Paul bases that conclusion on the fact that הֹזֶה (not רֹאֶה or נָבִיא) is found when reference is made to a king (חֹזֵה הַמֶּלֶךְ, "seer of the king").

[49] Z. Zevit, "A Misunderstanding at Bethel: Amos VII 12–17," *VT* 25 (1975): 787.

[50] Ibid., 789.

[51] Contra Wolff, *Joel and Amos*, 311. Andersen and Freedman think that the account is not given chronologically, that Amaziah tried to order or scare Amos away first. Then when that failed, he sent word to the king, which would have made it necessary for Amaziah to place Amos in custody (*Amos*, 780–94).

belonged to King Jeroboam. The parallel phrase "the temple of the kingdom" designates the sanctuary as a royal shrine. Amaziah felt that as high priest of the royal sanctuary he had every right to expel Amos from Bethel. Whether he was successful in removing Amos from Israel is debated, but Amos was not likely allowed around Bethel again.[52] Andersen and Freedman suggest that like the apostle Paul (Acts 28:17–21), Amos would have welcomed an opportunity to present God's word to the highest authority in the land. "We do not know what may have happened after word was sent to the king, but it is most unlikely that Amos merely returned to Tekoa to tell his disciples about his adventures or to write his memoirs."[53]

AMOS? (7:14). **7:14** Amos's reply in v. 14 has been the source of much discussion and disagreement. In Hebrew it consists of three verbless clauses, for which English translation requires a form of the verb "to be." What tense is required must be determined by the context. Although the NIV chose the past tense (following the LXX), indicating that Amos had not been a prophet until God called him, a present tense may fit the context better.[54] Amos seems to have been disclaiming professional status as a prophet and denying that it was his livelihood. Yet he performed the activity of a prophet when God called him to do so (v. 16).[55]

If the first two verbless clauses should be rendered (literally) in the present tense ("I am not a prophet and I am not a son of a prophet"), then Amos was acknowledging that he had no authority based on professional status as a prophet. "Prophet" and "prophet's son" are parallel designations of an official office of prophet.[56] If the third verbless clause should be rendered (literally) in the present tense ("but rather I am a cattle breeder and a slitter of figs"), then Amos was giving his occupation or professional status. Two participles describe his profession: *bôqēr,* "one tending cattle," and *bôlēs,* "scratching open," with the object *šiqmîm,* "sycamore-fig trees." The latter activity is

---

[52] Cf. G. Smith, *Amos,* 216, 238.

[53] Andersen and Freedman, *Amos,* 792.

[54] T. J. Finley notes that "most (though not all) examples of sentences without a verb that are also contained within a *conversation* are best translated with a present tense." Thus "the translator can assume that the sentence in such a case refers to the present tense unless there are special factors from the context to indicate otherwise" (*Joel, Amos, Obadiah,* 293).

[55] Zevit understood Amos's response when Amaziah called him a *hozeh* to be: "No! I am not a prophet enjoying royal patronage (i.e., a הזֶה); I am an independent prophet—my own man; nor am I a disciple of any prophet, working under his aegis and doing his bidding" ("A Misunderstanding at Bethel," 790).

[56] The term "son of a prophet" may refer to a prophet's disciple or membership in a prophetic guild, i.e., a "professional prophet." Stuart sees the professional sense in the latter term but not the former. He translates: "No! I am a prophet, though I am not a professional prophet because . . ." (*Hosea-Jonah,* 374, 376). Niehaus ("Amos," 1:462–63) supports the NIV translation and rejects Stuart's as unnecessary. See also Finley, *Joel, Amos, Obadiah,* 294. But the sense is essentially the same, that Amos was in some sense a prophet (cf. 3:7–8) but was not a prophet for hire.

uncertain (see also "Amos, the Man" on p. 22).[57] That it was related to sycamore-figs is clear. That fact would have required Amos to journey to elevations lower than Tekoa, perhaps to the Jordan Valley, the coastal plains, or the Shephelah (1 Kgs 10:27). Sycamore-figs did not grow in the higher elevations around Tekoa.

Jeroboam claimed authority in Bethel as the king of Israel. Amaziah claimed authority in Bethel as the high priest there. But Amos claimed no authority. He had no official title. Neither a *bôqēr* nor a *bôlēs* of sycamore-figs had any professional clout in Bethel. Nevertheless he did not flee before Amaziah (cf. 1 Kgs 19:2). The only authority Amos needed rested in the God who took hold of him for service as his spokesman. Wolff considered it notable that "the first classical and canonical prophet stresses that he is a layman." He observed that Amos denied three times "the connection between his own self and what he proclaims: I—no prophet! I—no prophet's disciple! I—a livestock breeder!" Then Amos gave a threefold pointer to Yahweh as the way Amaziah and Israel should hear what he had to say: "But Yahweh took me from following the flock, and Yahweh said to me: 'Go, prophesy unto my people Israel! Now therefore hear the word of Yahweh!'" The prophet explained that he could not resist God's word and that Amaziah and Israel should not resist God's word.[58] Only those chosen and sent out by God have authority to speak God's message.

THE LORD! (7:15–17).   Amos testified that his normal profession had been interrupted by the Lord's action and commission. The prophet's only authority in Bethel was his commission from the Lord to go and prophesy to the Lord's people Israel. By contrast Jeroboam and Amaziah were holding office by their own authority, which was set against God's.

7:15 "The LORD took me" means the Lord intervened to take Amos away from his normal business of "tending the flock" (cf. 2 Sam 7:8; 1 Kgs 11:37; Ps 78:70–71).[59] Then the Lord ordered him to "go" (*lēk*, the same term Amaziah used to order him out of Bethel) and "prophesy" (*hinnābē*, the same verb Amaziah used with a negative particle in v. 13) to Israel. What Amos described was an activity, not an office. His authority was the action and com-

---

[57] KB[3] (Eng. ed., 1:134) explains the verbal meaning as "to scar the unripe sycamore figs (with fingernail or iron tool) in order to promote ripening" and translates the phrase "picker of sycamore figs." Stuart suggests Amos was a "traveling consultant/specialist" whose service was "making a small cut in figs early in their maturation so as to produce a sweeter, softer final fruit" (*Hosea-Jonah,* 377). See also Wolff, *Joel and Amos,* 314; T. J. Wright, "Amos and the 'Sycamore Fig,'" *VT* 26 (1976): 363–65; P. King, *Amos, Hosea, Micah—An Archaeological Commentary* (Philadelphia: Westminster, 1988).

[58] H. W. Wolff, "The Irresistible Word (Amos)," *Currents in Theology and Mission* 10 (1983): 4–13.

[59] Amos may have used such language earlier applied to David to imply that "a true prophet, like a true king, became so by divine election" (Niehaus, "Amos," 1:463).

mission of God.[60] "Amos reveals himself as a lone figure, one who is unclassifiable but with a unitary focus and guided by a personal vision."[61] "My people" meant that Amos was to address his audience as God's covenant people, not as the breakaway kingdom of Israel. They were not Jeroboam's people or Amaziah's or even Amos's. They still owed their allegiance first to God, and Amaziah was wrong to try to stop God's prophet from preaching to them. Interfering with the word of God proved disastrous for Amaziah and remains today a dangerous activity.

7:16 The message in vv. 16–17 is cast in the usual form of an oracle of judgment. It is introduced by a climactic marker in Hebrew (*wĕʿattâ*) translated "now then," followed by a summons to "hear the word of the LORD." Then follows the contrast between what Amaziah was saying and what the Lord says. Amos, like others in the Bible (cf. 1 Kgs 13:11–25; Acts 4:18–20) and still today, was faced with two messages—one from the world and one from God. He does not appear to have hesitated in deciding which one he should follow.

Amos accused Amaziah of countermanding the Lord and thus thinking that his authority superceded God's. He quoted Amaziah's instruction in v. 13 not to prophesy and added something that Amaziah either said or intended—"stop preaching against the house of Isaac."[62] "Preaching" is from a verbal root (*nāṭap*) meaning "drip," as the heavens drip rain (Judg 5:4), as mountains drip wine (Amos 9:13). The image is used of words of counsel in Job 29:22, of words of love in Song 4:11 and 5:13, and of words of enticement in Prov 5:3. In the causative stem used here "preaching" is a synonym for *nābāʾ*, "prophesy" (cf. Ezek 20:46; 21:2 [Heb., 21:1–2]). In Mic 2:6,11 it is used in a derogatory sense as here.[63]

7:17 The Lord's judgment against Amaziah begins typically with "therefore" (*lākēn*) and the messenger formula. The one in charge at Bethel and in Israel from the prophet's perspective was the Lord, not Amos, not Amaziah, not Jeroboam. The authority for the indictment of Amaziah was the word of the Lord that Amos spoke.

In defiance of Amaziah's order, Amos delivered God's judgment word against the priest, his wife, his children, and his nation (cf. Jer 11:21–23; 20:1–6). The emphatic words in the judgment (occurring first in the clauses) are the subjects: "your wife," "your sons and your daughters," "your land," "you," and "Israel." Suggestive of the judgment's main theme of forfeiture of land,

---

[60] Andersen and Freedman argue that the term "my people Israel" applies to both kingdoms (cf. 7:8c, note). Therefore, "Amos was called as a prophet to the larger entity in common with all of the prophets of whom we know enough to be able to form an opinion" (*Amos,* 636–37). This explains his oracle against Judah in 2:4–5.

[61] Andersen and Freedman, *Amos,* 790.

[62] Cf. ibid., 782, 787.

[63] Cf. M. R. Wilson, נָטַף (*nāṭap*), *TWOT,* 576.

the term *'ădāmâ,* translated "land" or "country," occurs three times in the verse. Deprived of husband and children, Amaziah's wife would be forced to support herself as a prostitute. Amaziah's sons and daughters would fall by the sword. The priest's land would be divided and given to others. Amaziah would be taken along with others away from the land of Israel, and there in an unclean land he would die (cf. Jer 6:12). The fact that Amaziah was a priest would make God's judgment even more humiliating than for ordinary citizens.

The narrative of the encounter between Amos and Amaziah settled the issue of authority. Jeroboam was king of Israel, but he was supposed to rule the Lord's people under the Lord's authority. As a high priest Amaziah's concern should have been to serve the Lord's people under the Lord's authority. As God's prophet, Amos spoke to the Lord's people under the Lord's authority. The Lord was in charge in Israel because the people there were the Lord's people. The same is true in the church, where leaders as well as congregations all serve under the Lord's authority. Each one is accountable directly to God, and each one has accountability to the others in the church.

(5) Fourth Vision: A Basket of Summer Fruit (8:1–3)

¹This is what the Sovereign LORD showed me: a basket of ripe fruit. ²"What do you see, Amos?" he asked.

"A basket of ripe fruit," I answered.

Then the LORD said to me, "The time is ripe for my people Israel; I will spare them no longer.

³"In that day," declares the Sovereign LORD, "the songs in the temple will turn to wailing. Many, many bodies—flung everywhere! Silence!"

The format of the fourth vision-report is the same as the third vision-report. Only the object of the vision changes. Amos saw a basket of summer fruit. In the previous visions Amos observed someone doing something, expressed with a participle. Here the participle is missing, but the object being viewed follows the alert word "behold" (*hinnê*) as in the other visions. In the third vision-report the name of the object seen and the word explained are the same (*'ănāk,* "plumb line"). Here the object seen (*qāyiṣ,* "ripe fruit") and the word explained (*qēṣ,* "end") only have a similar sound.[64]

---

[64] Finley noted that in the northern dialect pronunciation of the two words may have been identical (*Joel, Amos, Obadiah,* 299). A. Wolters explained that the wordplay and pun in 8:1–2 had its basis in the "difference between Judahite and Israelite dialects" ("Wordplay and Dialect in Amos 8:1–2," *JETS* 31 [1988]: 407–10). He proposed that the difference between Judahite and Israelite pronunciation makes the wordplay work: "The point is that the LORD mimics the Israelite pronunciation of *qāyiṣ* and in so doing brings into play the entirely different meaning 'end.' The word *qēṣ* thus has two levels—parody and double entendre—with the first making possible the second." The prophet's preparation to receive and understand this vision may have included his experiences in Israelite markets. Perhaps he sold ripe sycamore-figs there and heard Israelite vendors calling out their wares, "*qāyiṣ,*" which sounded to his Judahite ears like a prophet proclaiming "*qēṣ,*" the end!

THE VISION REVEALED (8:1).   **8:1**   The fourth vision-report contains a full introductory formula. The reader/listener learns that Amos saw what God enabled him to see. The name of the object refers in other contexts both to the season (Gen 8:22; Amos 3:15) and to the fruit of the season (2 Sam 16:1). Since "basket" precedes the word here, reference must be to the fruit.

THE LORD'S QUESTION (8:2a).   **8:2a**   In the third vision-report a full introduction to the question is used, "And the LORD asked me" (7:8). Here the introduction is only one word in the Hebrew text, "he asked" (*wāyyōʾmer*).[65] The question is the same as before, "What do you see, Amos?"

THE PROPHET'S RESPONSE (8:2b).   **8:2b**   Amos was clear-eyed. He saw precisely what God showed him, "a basket of ripe fruit (*qāyiṣ*)."

THE LORD'S EXPLANATION (8:2c).   **8:2c**   The Lord's explanation employs a wordplay as in the almond rod vision in Jer 1:11–12. The Lord's words are literally, "The end [*qēṣ*] has come for my people Israel." Based on the prediction that temple songs would turn to "wailing" (Amos 7:3) as a result of the end coming (cf. v. 9), the message must be that the end of Israel's life as a nation had come.[66] The Lord's explanation closes with the same announcement found in the third vision-report that Israel's day of grace was over: "I will spare them no longer."[67]

THE COMING DESTRUCTION (8:3).   **8:3**   Both the oracle formula and the contents of the verse mark v. 3 as a judgment oracle. Two lines in the verse describe Israel's response to catastrophic destruction. "Wailing" (*hêlîlû*) will be the first response, a term that refers to "an inarticulate, shattering scream such as is found in primitive funerary laments and in the face of sudden catastrophe."[68] "Songs in the temple"[69] were usually joyous and celebrative. But

---

[65] Andersen and Freedman note a pattern in the three-quote formulae used in each of the second pair of visions that forms an "envelope construction." Both the first quote formula in vision three and the last quote formula of vision four are "And Yahweh said to me" (*Amos*, 616, 623).

[66] Hayes interpreted הַקֵּץ to mean that "Israel was in its last days," taking the term to be a reference to the last month in the Gezer calendar (*Amos*, 207–8). The implication would be that Israel's end had not come but that it was close.

[67] Smith reminds that "the absoluteness of the end of the nation must be integrated with earlier messages of hope for the remnant . . ., the existence of many people in exile . . ., and specific references to God's plans to fulfill his promises and reestablish his people" (*Amos*, 251).

[68] A. Baumann, "יָלַל *yll*," *TDOT* 6.82. In the Bible the term is not used for mourning an individual but in "expressing affliction in the face of unimaginable catastrophe, moving everyone to pity." It is thus "the ultimate degree of lamentation, an extraordinary wail of agony" (p. 84).

[69] Interpretations of the first three words of v. 3 (וְהֵילִילוּ שִׁירוֹת הֵיכָל) vary. The noun phrase could be the grammatical object ("They shall wail the hymns of the temple" [Mays, *Amos*, 140]) except that elsewhere this verb does not take an object. Finley understands it as the figurative subject, translating essentially with the NIV. "One should imagine beautiful songs of joy and gladness that suddenly burst into somber wailing" (Finley, *Joel, Amos, Obadiah*, 298). Wolff has repointed שִׁירוֹת to שָׁרוֹת and renders, "Then the songstresses of the palace will wail" (*Joel and Amos*, 317; so also Andersen and Freedman, *Amos*, 798). Hayes emends it to שׁוּרוֹת and has "and the walls of the palace shall wail" (*Amos*, 196). More important, God's severe judgment upon Israel would call for national mourning.

in the day of God's intervention the songs will "turn to wailing." "Silence"[70] (*hās*) is the second response, which would be the appropriate response to such devastation (cf. 6:10). The reason for the two responses will be the "many bodies—flung everywhere," suggesting a fierce attack on Israel leaving death and destruction in its wake. "In that day" is a way of referring to the day of the Lord (cf. 2:16; 3:14; and especially 5:18 and comments there). The judgment would be for God's enemies, and the blessing would be for his people.

2. Oracles and a Vision of Israel's Future Destruction and Ultimate Restoration (8:4–9:15)

(1) Indictment of Greedy Merchants (8:4–6)

⁴Hear this, you who trample the needy
  and do away with the poor of the land,

⁵saying,

"When will the New Moon be over
  that we may sell grain,
and the Sabbath be ended
  that we may market wheat?"—
skimping the measure,
  boosting the price
  and cheating with dishonest scales,
⁶buying the poor with silver
  and the needy for a pair of sandals,
  selling even the sweepings with the wheat.

Just as nonvisionary material (7:10–17) follows the third vision in 7:7–9, so also this section of nonvisionary material follows the fourth vision in 8:1–3. Since the internal structure of the first four visions shows that they are paired, it is appropriate that the external structure should confirm that visions three and four go together.[71]

The indictment of Israel's greedy merchants follows a summons to hear. Charges of wrongdoing closely parallel earlier accusations (2:6–7; 4:1; 5:10–12). These charges give the reason for the coming destruction announced in the vision-reports and in the judgment oracles associated with those reports.

SOCIAL INJUSTICE (8:4).   **8:4**   "Hear this" is a herald's summons to his audience to give heed to the message about to be announced (cf. 3:1; 4:1; 5:1;

---

[70] Wolff translated הַס as "Hush!" He described it as "an exclamatory imperative demanding strictest silence" (*Joel and Amos*, 320). The reason he gave for silence was that "any sound might attract the enemy of the living."

[71] G. Smith, *Amos*, 227, 244. Andersen and Freedman propose that 8:4–14 continues and completes the "Book of Woes" in 5:1–6:14 (*Amos*, 795).

Ps 49:1 [Heb., v. 2]). By "trample" he referred to the harsh and unjust treatment of unprotected members of society (vv. 4–6). "Do away with" is literally "cause to cease." It is from the root *šbt* and perhaps is a play on the word *šabbāt*, "Sabbath," in v. 5. It is an infinitive in Hebrew (as are the verbs "skimping," "boosting," "cheating," and "buying" in vv. 5–6) suggesting effect if not intent. Such harsh policies toward the poor were the opposite of the Lord's. Rather than eliminating the poor, Israel's law called for an open hand of generosity to be extended to them (Deut 15:7–11; Ps 72:12–13). To be on God's side, God's people must choose the side of the poor and needy. God requires his people to work for the best interests of the unprotected members of society, which included orphans, widows, aliens, and the poor (Deut 10:14–26; 24:19–21).

SUPERFICIAL WORSHIP (8:5a).   **8:5a**   Amos quoted the merchants to reveal their basic attitude toward worship. They dutifully closed their shops to obey the law related to New Moon and Sabbath observances. In Israel commercial activity was forbidden on the Sabbath (Neh 13:15–22). However, the merchants' own testimony betrayed their real motives and their primary concern. "That we may sell grain" and "that we may market wheat" express their true aims, supplemented by the four following infinitives translated "skimping," "boosting," "cheating," and "buying." Merchants begrudged the merchandising time lost because of monthly and weekly worship days. Their worship was formal and superficial. Merchandising was their priority—selling, not worshiping. Those who focus intently on what they will do after worship is over are not apt to be engaged in true worship and enter into "the joy of these festive occasions."[72]

SPECIFIC CHARGES (8:5b–6).   The specific charges against the merchants reveal how greedy they were, what deceptions they used to increase profits, and the effect the whole business had on the poor. They counted nothing sacred, not worship days, not honesty, and not fellow human beings. Their god was profit, and they willingly sacrificed everything for it.

8:5b   "Skimping the measure" is literally "to make small the ephah." The ephah was a standard unit of dry measure, a half bushel. Using a container that would hold less than half a bushel in measuring bulk commodities allowed the merchants to cheat the customers.

"Boosting the price" is literally "to make large the shekel." Before the use of minted coins, a shekel served as a standard weight by which to measure the silver used to purchase commodities. An enlarged shekel on the scale weighed against the customer's silver meant that he was paying more than he ought to pay for his purchase.[73]

---

[72] Wolff, *Joel and Amos,* 326.
[73] Cf. Niehaus, "Amos," 1:470–71.

"Cheating with dishonest scales" was another method the merchants used to deceive their customers. They fixed the balance beam on the scales and made them into "dishonest scales."

8:6 In 2:6 (see comments there) Amos condemned selling the poor. Here he condemned buying the poor and confiscating their property. The greedy merchants in Israel profited from deceptive methods of buying and selling marketable goods. That was bad enough, but profiting from the purchase and sale of poor people was reprehensible indeed. The merchants took over property belonging to the needy as payment of debts. This greedy practice often resulted in slavery of the needy.

The last line of v. 6, literally, "Even the sweepings of wheat we sell," sounds as if it should be at the end of v. 5. But this return to a first-person verb after the four infinitives binds vv. 5–6 together, and the effect of its following the description of debt slavery is to show "these people regarded cereals and human beings equally as stock for sale. Their practices were both dishonest and inhumane."[74] To sell the sweepings with the wheat was as low as greedy merchants could go in their oppression of the poor. Putting chaff and trash with good grain to sell to desperately hungry poor people was the ultimate in greed. Human greed for profit at the expense of the innocent brings down a society in the just desserts of divine recompense.

(2) The Lord's Oath against Greedy Merchants (8:7–10)

[7]The LORD has sworn by the Pride of Jacob: "I will never forget anything they have done.

[8]"Will not the land tremble for this,
　　and all who live in it mourn?
The whole land will rise like the Nile;
　　it will be stirred up and then sink
　　like the river of Egypt.
[9]"In that day," declares the Sovereign LORD,

"I will make the sun go down at noon
　　and darken the earth in broad daylight.
[10]I will turn your religious feasts into mourning
　　and all your singing into weeping.
I will make all of you wear sackcloth
　　and shave your heads.
I will make that time like mourning for an only son
　　and the end of it like a bitter day.

As G. Smith notes, "Ideas of mourning and death, songs and festivals, and

---

[74] Andersen and Freedman, *Amos,* 804.

the events of 'that day' unite the vision in 8:1–3 with the fuller explanation in 8:7–10."[75]

DETERMINED TO REMEMBER THEIR DEEDS (8:7). **8:7** The Lord indicated his determined stand against the greedy merchants by putting himself under oath. Earlier he swore by his holiness (4:2) and by himself (6:8). Now he put himself under oath by "the Pride of Jacob." One swears by something precious or unalterable (cf. the full oath formula in Ps 137:5). "The Pride of Jacob" may refer to the city of Samaria here as it does in 6:8. Samaria was Israel's most prized possession. But the Lord was about to destroy it, so he could not swear by it, unless the expression is broadened to refer to the land generally as Israel's promised inheritance (Ps 47:4; Isa 58:14).[76] The oath could be ironic and refer to Israel's unalterable pride. Some argue that since elsewhere the Lord swears by himself or one of his attributes (Gen 22:16; Pss 89:35,49; 95:11; Jer 44:26), that is likely the intent here (cf. Gen 49:24; 1 Sam 15:29).[77] Whereas Israel's pride was in themselves and their own accomplishments, it should have been in the Lord, the Pride of Jacob (cf. 8:14).[78]

The Lord bound himself never to forget the deeds of Israel's greedy merchants. What that meant was that he was determined to punish them. Their deeds would always be before the Lord calling for judgment. This is the opposite of God's promise in Jer 31:34 to forgive iniquity and remember sin no more.

DIRE CONSEQUENCES OF THE LORD'S OATH (8:8). **8:8** The rhetorical question anticipates a positive answer. The Lord's solemn oath not to forget the deeds of Israel's merchants would result in the land trembling and all its inhabitants mourning. "For this" (or "on account of this," occurring at the beginning of the Hebrew verse) points back to the Lord's oath as the cause of the trembling and mourning. "Tremble" does not necessarily refer to an earthquake (cf. 1:1). It could describe a trembling in fear (2 Sam 7:10), or joy (Jer 33:9), or grief (2 Sam 18:33 [19:1]). The fear that God would never forget their deeds is the probable meaning here. "Mourn" is an appropriate response for Israel's inhabitants, who await God's dreaded judgment.

The rhetorical question is followed by the rhetoric of judgment. The language found here occurs in several other judgment passages (cf. Isa 24:1–7; Jer 4:27–28; Joel 2:1,10) and anticipates the ultimate judgment to come with the return of Christ (Matt 24:29–30; Rev 1:7). The disturbance and agitation in Israel is compared to the rising and falling of the Nile River in the flood season.[79] Since the rise and fall of the Nile usually extended over a few

---

[75] G. Smith, *Amos*, 249.

[76] Stuart, *Hosea-Jonah*, 385; Niehaus, "Amos," 1:472.

[77] Finley, *Joel, Amos, Obadiah*, 302–3.

[78] G. Smith, *Amos*, 254–55.

[79] Note all but the first line of v. 8 is repeated in 9:5.

months, some national upheaval lasting a considerable period of time is implied by the analogy. Sometimes the flooding of the Nile was highly destructive. Amos may have been comparing the destructiveness of social injustice, civil strife, economic exploitation, and religious shallowness in Israel to the destruction caused by the inundation of the Nile. The flooding of the Nile occurred repeatedly, as did the social, civil, economic, and religious problems of society. The image of water and justice (judgment) is used in 5:21–24. Here, as there, the flow of justice is the goal of society as the proper response to the will of God. It may also refer to the flood of God's judgment.

DAYS OF GLOOM AND GRIEF (8:9–10).   The first-person verbs in this brief oracle make clear that it will be the Lord's actions against Israel that will bring about their dismal future. Those persons on the receiving end of the Lord's actions would include more than the greedy merchants described in 8:4–8. Return to the day-of-the-Lord motif introduced in 5:18 signals the widened target. All Israel would experience the darkness (v. 9), and all Israel would engage in the mourning (v. 10).

8:9   "In that day" points forward to a time of the Lord's intervention to bring additional disasters on Israel. The first word in v. 9 is *wĕhāyâ*, usually translated "and it shall come to pass." It marks what follows as occurring in the future.[80] Israel needed to know that what was going to happen to them was the day of the Lord. For them it would be a day of darkness that the Lord would create.

Amos used the imagery of a solar eclipse as an example of the awesome dread and the startling suddenness of the calamity about to fall on Israel. Two solar eclipses had been visible in the region, on February 9, 784 B.C. and on June 15, 763 B.C.[81] An eclipse suddenly transformed things into their opposite: sundown at midday, darkness in broad daylight. The calamity awaiting Israel would come with awesome dread and startling suddenness. As Niehaus points out, Israel had been warned of such judgment in covenant curse of Deut 28:29—"At midday you will grope about like a blind man in the dark." God's intention to "make the sun go down at noon" when it was at its brightest was an especially appropriate image for Israel at the height of its power under Jeroboam II. Similar images of the Lord bringing darkness is used in other judgment passages such as Isa 59:10; Jer 13:16; 15:8–9; Joel 2:10,31; 3:15; Mic 3:6. "The imagery here not only builds on the covenant curse, but expresses symbolically the sudden, unexpected setting of Israel's sun and the darkening of her day, just when the sun seemed at its zenith of prosperity and power."[82]

---

[80] For other examples of the prophetic introductory formula וְהָיָה בַיּוֹם הַהוּא, see Isa 7:18; Jer 4:9; Ezek 38:18; Hos 1:5; Joel 4:18 (Eng., 3:18); Mic 5:9 (Eng., 5:10). This is the only place it occurs in Amos.

[81] Hayes, *Amos,* 210; Wolff, *Joel and Amos,* 329.

[82] Niehaus, "Amos," 1:473.

8:10 This verse is marked by careful and concise poetic parallelism and is an "ironic litany of reversals."[83] The Hebrew verse consists of three lines with two parts to each line. The first part of each line has a verb that functions for both parts of the line. This style is difficult to translate into English and retain its uniqueness. Literally, the verse reads:

> I will *turn* your religious festivals to mourning,
> and all your praises to dirges.
> I will *place* upon all of you sackcloth
> and upon (your) head baldness.
> I will *make it* like mourning an only child
> and the end of it like a bitter day.

Consequently, all three verses convey a similar message: mourning comes because judgment has come. Because Israel had turned God's justice and righteousness into bitterness and poison (cf. 5:7; 6:12), he would turn their joy into grief.

On that solar eclipse-like day the Lord would turn Israel's religious festivals into mourning. Festivals usually characterized by joyous celebrations of the Lord's blessings would become rituals of mourning (cf. 5:21). The Lord's intervention would turn all of Israel's songs (*šîrîm*) into lamentation (*qînâ*). Israel's songs of praise and exultation celebrating life would become dirges for the dead (cf. 8:3).

"Sackcloth" (*śāq*) was a rough garment (usually made of hair) worn at the hips as a symbol of mourning (cf. Joel 1:8,13). So widespread would be the calamity and grief that all Israel would don these garments. Shaving the head was another symbol of mourning (cf. Ezra 9:3; Isa 22:12; Jer 48:37). Baldness on every head suggests that every person in Israel would be touched by the grief-causing calamity.

The Lord vowed to make the coming grief "like mourning for an only son" (cf. Jer 6:26). No grief was as great as that caused by the death of an only son (cf. Zech 12:10). One reason loss of an only son created such great sorrow was that all hope for the future was gone as well as provision for one's old age. The day that starts out with mourning an only son is sure to end as bitter as it began. A bitter day is a hopeless day. The bitterest part of this entire scene is that it would be brought about by the Lord. Niehaus also notes that such a day is "a type of what one day will occur when the Lord judges not one nation, but all the earth," when there will be "weeping and gnashing of teeth" (Matt 8:12) on the part of those "who had the opportunity to obey their Lord, but went their own way instead."[84]

---

[83] Ibid., 1:474.
[84] Ibid.

(3) The Lord's Threat of Famine (8:11–14)

[11]"The days are coming," declares the Sovereign LORD,
  "when I will send a famine through the land—
not a famine of food or a thirst for water,
  but a famine of hearing the words of the LORD.
[12]Men will stagger from sea to sea
  and wander from north to east,
searching for the word of the LORD,
  but they will not find it.

[13]"In that day

"the lovely young women and strong young men
  will faint because of thirst.
[14]They who swear by the shame of Samaria,
  or say, 'As surely as your god lives, O Dan,'
  or, 'As surely as the god of Beersheba lives'—
they will fall,
  never to rise again."

This oracle of doom continues the theme of approaching calamity but changes the imagery. Famine belonged to the standard list of sanctions God used against Israel's unfaithfulness. Amos cited the Lord's use of famine and drought as chastisement of Israel in the past, but Israel failed to return to God (4:6–8; see comments there). Now they would experience a worse kind of famine, a famine of the word of God.

A FAMINE OF HEARING THE WORDS OF THE LORD (8:11). **8:11** In Hebrew this verse begins with *hinnê,* "behold," alerting Amos's audience to an important message. Together with the following temporal formula, "days are coming," it is found often in prophetic announcements (especially in Jeremiah) of the Lord's future intervention.[85] This phrase is one of several ways Amos referred to the day of the Lord.

Again first-person verbs reveal that the Lord would be the force behind the famine. But what the Lord declared he would send was no ordinary famine, "not a famine of food or a thirst for water." "Food" (bread) and "water" formed the absolute essentials to sustain life physically. But Israel would languish from an even more severe deprivation—"hearing the words of the LORD." D. A. Hubbard wrote: "No one could live without the power and guidance of the divine words any more than anyone could live without the nourishment of bread and the refreshment of water."[86] In fact, as Jesus responded to the tempter in his quote of Deut 8:3, "Man does not live on bread alone, but on every word that comes from the mouth of God" (Matt

---

[85] See 4:2; 9:13; 1 Sam 2:31; Isa 39:6; Jer 7:32; 9:25; 16:14; 23:5; 30:3; 31:27,31,38; 33:14.
[86] D. A. Hubbard, *Joel and Amos,* TOTC (Downers Grove: InterVarsity, 1989), 223–24.

4:4). It is better to be deprived of food and drink than of God's word.

Physical famine was brought on by drought, which produced a lack of food as well as water.[87] The famine envisioned would consist not only of the absence of the Lord's revelation through his prophets but of the Lord himself, whose presence and care brought about the prophetic word. As S. Paul says, "The absence of prophecy depriving man of the divine word, is regarded throughout the Bible as a dire portent of God's wrath (cp. 1 Sam 14:37; 28:6,15–16)."[88] This experience is mentioned as a possibility in Jer 18:18; Ezek 7:26; and Mic 3:6–7, but it became a reality in the fall of Jerusalem (Lam 2:9).[89] Amaziah and Israel would have their wish (2:12; 7:12–13). Worse than strong words of judgment from the Lord is no word from the Lord, an ominous and foreboding silence. To receive no word from God in response to cries for help meant that God had hidden his face from them, rejected and abandoned them to their enemies.[90]

A FUTILE SEARCH FOR THE WORD OF THE LORD (8:12). **8:12** "Stagger" suggests the famished condition of the ones searching for the "words of the LORD" (cf. 4:8). The implication is that the searchers would be so weakened by the famine they would be unsteady and aimless in their movements.[91] From "sea to sea" and from "north to east" covered the points of the compass and indicated search everywhere. Probable reference is from the Dead Sea in the south to the Great Sea (Mediterranean) in the west. Weary searchers for the words of the Lord would wander (or "rove") everywhere, but their search would be in vain (cf. Isa 55:6).[92]

A FAINTING FROM THIRST FOR THE WORD OF THE LORD (8:13). **8:13** The imagery of famine continues to function in this verse as a metaphor of hunger and thirst for the words of the Lord. Again Amos used the temporal formula "in that day" to refer to the day of the Lord. The beautiful virgins and the young men would be the least likely ones to faint because of thirst for water. They were looked upon as the strongest and most durable segment of society. Their fainting indicates the severity of the thirst for the words of the Lord. D. A. Hubbard questioned, "What can this mean but the end of the nation, since those on whom its future population depended have collapsed in 'faint'?"[93]

---

[87] Andersen and Freedman, *Amos,* 823.

[88] Paul, *Amos,* 265.

[89] Ibid.

[90] See Deut 31:17–18; 32:20; Pss 13:1; 22:24; 27:9; 44:24; 88:14; 102:2; Isa 8:16–17; 54:8; 59:2; Ezek 39:23; Mic 3:4.

[91] Andersen and Freedman, *Amos,* 825.

[92] For an argument that the search would encompass the "uttermost boundaries of the earth" see Wolff, *Joel and Amos,* 330–31; Niehaus, "Amos," 1:475. Against this see Finley, *Joel, Amos, Obadiah,* 306–7.

[93] Hubbard, *Joel and Amos,* 224.

A FAILURE OF FALSE RELIGION (8:14).   **8:14**   This verse contains many problems of interpretation. Who are the ones swearing? What is meant by the "shame [ʾašmat] of Samaria"? Who is the god of Dan and "the god [derek, "way"] of Beersheba?" But enough is clear in the verse to draw some conclusions.

Whether the ones swearing by false gods are the young people searching for a word from the Lord, the greedy merchants, or the citizens of Israel generally, their behavior testifies to the practice of idolatry in Israel; and God affirms that he will put an end to it. Swearing had to do with taking an oath before the god that one worshiped, inviting his punishment if what was affirmed was not true (cf. Gen 14:22; 21:23; 24:3; Exod 22:11; Num 5:21; Josh 9:20; 2 Sam 3:35; Ezek 17:19). It also involved allegiance to the god by whom the oath was taken, and so Israel was to swear by no one but the Lord. To swear by any other amounted to forsaking the Lord (cf. Deut 6:13; 10:20; Josh 23:7; Ps 24:4; Jer 12:16).

The "shame of Samaria" apparently refers to false gods worshiped there. While the Lord swore by the "Pride of Jacob" (8:7), the people of Israel swore by false gods to their shame and guilt. In 2 Chr 24:18 and 33:23 ʾašmâ, "guilt," refers to idolatry. Use of the oath formula "as he lives" related to Dan and Beersheba indicates swearing by false gods. Reference to Dan and Beersheba, the northern and southern extremities of the whole land, may suggest the extent of the practice and/or an intent to include all the false gods worshiped in the whole land.[94] The expression "as the LORD lives" is found frequently in oaths in the Bible (cf. Ruth 3:13; 1 Sam 14:45; 19:6; 28:10; 1 Kgs 1:19–30). Hubbard followed a commendable principle of interpretation in using what seems to be clear in the context as a key to interpreting what is not altogether clear: "First, if we take our cue from the second clause whose wording seems clear—'And they say, "As your god lives, O Dan"'—then it seems likely that both the Samaria and the Beersheba clauses contain references to swearing by a deity."[95] The expression "by the shame of Samaria" may be a veiled reference to Ashimah, the idol made by the citizens of Hamath in Samaria (2 Kgs 17:29–30). "The way [derek] of Beersheba" has been understood as the pilgrimage of Beersheba (cf. 5:5), as Derketo (Ashkelon's fish-goddess), and as dōrĕkā, "your circle" or company of gods.[96] What seems clear in all three clauses is that Israel was taking oaths and making promises in the names of foreign deities. As Andersen and Freedman put it, "So we can speak of the whole circle of gods worshiped everywhere in Israel (and Judah), from Dan to Beer-sheba."[97] Israel's trouble was theologi-

---

[94] Andersen and Freedman, *Amos,* 830.
[95] Hubbard, *Joel and Amos,* 225.
[96] See the summary in G. Smith, *Amos,* 257–58.
[97] Andersen and Freedman, *Amos,* 830.

cal. Their false gods could never raise them up if they fell down. Only the Lord could do that.

Andersen and Freedman point out the apparent overlap of the groups referred to in 8:4–6,14. The trampling of the poor may have been "confirmed and validated by the abominable oaths in v. 14."[98] "Whether the groups are identical or only overlap and interlock is immaterial, though one may easily imagine that cheating merchants will swear to their honesty by false gods, and that those who worship those gods would deal treacherously with their fellow human beings. . . . Together they combine the ethical and the theological aspects of covenant violation."[99] God's oath never to forget their misdeeds (v. 7) and his malediction that they will "fall never to rise again" (v. 14) signal certain divine judgment on their oppressive actions and foolish oaths in the name of pagan deities. Such judgment forces us to ask: What are our oppressive acts, and what are our pagan deities? and then forces us to answer honestly and quickly.

(4) Fifth Vision: The Lord Standing by the Altar (9:1–4)

[1]I saw the Lord standing by the altar, and he said:

"Strike the tops of the pillars
 so that the thresholds shake.
Bring them down on the heads of all the people;
 those who are left I will kill with the sword.
Not one will get away,
 none will escape.
[2]Though they dig down to the depths of the grave,
 from there my hand will take them.
Though they climb up to the heavens,
 from there I will bring them down.
[3]Though they hide themselves on the top of Carmel,
 there I will hunt them down and seize them.
Though they hide from me at the bottom of the sea,
 there I will command the serpent to bite them.
[4]Though they are driven into exile by their enemies,
 there I will command the sword to slay them.
I will fix my eyes upon them
 for evil and not for good."

The climactic fifth vision is unlike the other four from start to finish. Among the differences are the following: no introductory formula declaring divine enablement of the prophet to see (cf. "This is what the Sovereign

---

[98] Ibid., 832.
[99] Ibid., 802.

LORD/he showed me," 7:1,4,7; 8:1"), no symbolic component as an interpretive key, and no words of Amos.[100] There is a progression of the Lord's control in the visions and a receding of Amos's involvement. In the first pair of visions Amos spoke more than the Lord; in the second pair Amos spoke only a word or two; here Amos is silent. The Lord's words in first person dominate the report (9:1b–4). No escape from divine retribution is the unrelieved theme.[101]

SEEING THE AWESOME LORD (9:1a). **9:1a** The location of the altar is unspecified. It may have been the Bethel shrine[102] or perhaps only a symbol in light of the previous four symbolic vision-reports.[103] The report contains no explanation of why the Lord was standing beside (or upon) the altar. The verb translated "standing" (*niṣṣāb*) in some contexts refers to the one in charge (Ruth 2:5).

The altar was the place of communion with God, which was assured when offerings were accepted there. Upon hearing the prophet's announcement that he saw the Lord at the altar, worshipers would expect to hear that the Lord had accepted their offerings and looked with favor upon them.[104] What they actually heard from Amos must have shocked them.

HEARING THE AWFUL JUDGMENT (9:1b). **9:1b** The first word from the Lord is a command employing a singular verb, "Strike the tops of the pillars." No indication is given of the intended recipient of the command, but the magnitude of the action would suggest an angel (cf. 2 Sam 24:15–17).[105] The remainder of the monologue magnifies the action of God. Some interpreters suggest an earthquake as the response to the Lord's command (the verb *rāʿaš* is from the same root as the noun for "earthquake" in 1:1). If so, by implication God was the one who struck the tops of the pillars. A strike against the support pillars would shake "the thresholds," the cut-stone

---

[100] Hubbard (*Joel and Amos*, 226) observed four drastic changes in form. This final vision-report is more audition than vision.

[101] Andersen and Freedman suggest that "the even greater intransigence shown by Amaziah in forbidding prophecy altogether at Bethel and, by inference, in all of Jeroboam's domains," leads to the "even more drastic messages of the fifth vision and its accompanying oracles" (*Amos*, 795).

[102] Mays, *Amos*, 152; Wolff, *Joel and Amos*, 338; Hayes, *Amos*, 216; Andersen and Freedman, *Amos*, 835; Smith, *Amos*, 261.

[103] D. Stuart's conclusion that while identity of the altar with the one at Bethel that Josiah destroyed in 622 B.C. was tempting, "the vision seems as easily symbolic as literal, especially in light of the four symbolic visions that precede it" (*Hosea-Jonah*, WBC [Waco: Word, 1987], 391).

[104] The surprise element in the prophet's vision of the Lord at the altar was that his "presence now is a guarantee not of protection but of destruction," as S. Paul put it (*Amos*, 274).

[105] While favoring the view that an angelic agent is involved, Andersen and Freedman point out that "it is essential to the understanding of the message from God that his word is immediately self-effectuating. The command is the deed, and ultimately in the OT the word is itself its fulfilling event" (*Amos*, 839). G. Smith thinks the imperative is just "a rhetorical device to emphasize the certainty of the destruction of the temple" (*Amos*, 266).

bases for the doorposts (cf. Isa 6:4). Collapse of the sanctuary would be the result of the strike. Destruction would be total, from top to bottom.[106]

Worshipers and worship leaders would be crushed by the collapsing sanctuary. "Bring them down" (also a singular command, lit., "cut them off") is a second order following the command to "strike." The object is the "pillars" coming down on the heads of "all the people" (lit., "all of them").[107] Emphasis again is on the completeness of the devastation. When the temple is shaken from top to bottom, "all" the people will suffer from its collapse. But in case any escaped its fall, the Lord vowed to slay them with the sword. "Sword" suggests death at the hands of men, but the verb is first-person singular (note the Lord's reference to "my sword" in 7:9, but the sword is commanded in 9:4).[108] Word order in this line makes emphatic the reference to "those who are left."

The assurance that no one would escape is made at the close of v. 1 with two synonymous clauses that employ wordplay. The two lines could be rendered literally, "No fugitive [nās] from them will flee [yānûs]; no escapee [pālîṭ] from them will escape [yimmālēṭ]." Finley suggests the first clause refers to those trying to flee at the time of the devastation; the second refers to survivors of the initial catastrophe who think they are now safe.[109]

NO HIDING PLACE (9:2–4).   Five conditional sentences in vv. 2–4a, each introduced by the Hebrew particle ʾim, cover five possible hiding places for escaped Israelites seeking to avoid divine retribution. The connection here with Psalm 139 (esp. vv. 7–12) and the biblical theme of the inability to escape from God is apparent. More so, the Book of Jonah is dominated early on by this same theme. No one can escape God's presence.

The Lord's action would guarantee the failure of every effort to elude his grasp. S. Paul aptly described the futility of Israel's efforts to find a hiding place from God's judgment: "Amos unconditionally declares that all possible escape routes are blocked off."[110] Earlier Amos urged Israel to seek good and

---

[106] Hubbard took the description of collapse from top to bottom to be "a further sign that a divine act like an earthquake is in view rather than a military assault" (*Joel and Amos,* 229).

[107] Hubbard thought it best to "translate the second verb as 'shatter' and to 'make its object the capitals of the temple pillars rather than the heads of the people'" (*Joel and Amos,* 229). Andersen and Freedman were content to let the reader decide whether to connect וְרֹאשׁ ("heads") with "the top of the column" or with the heads of the people (RSV) or the first of them (*Amos,* 836). The antecedent for the pronominal suffix in the expression "all of them" is uncertain. Does the pronoun point to all the columns or all the people? The answer may be found in the extended context where the pronoun occurs four times (vv. 1–4). Linked with 8:14 and 9:10 the reference of the pronouns appears to be "all the sinners among my people" (ibid.).

[108] Andersen and Freedman suggest that "the Sword" could be "the name of a heavenly agent who is the sword wielder par excellence" (*Amos,* 836, 838). It may also be simply a personification in v. 4.

[109] Finley, *Joel, Amos, Obadiah,* 315.

[110] Paul, *Amos,* 277.

not evil (5:14). Because of their failure to do so, he asserted the Lord's determined purpose to set his eyes upon them for evil and not good (9:4).

9:2–3 Two sets of extremities reveal how thorough the Lord's pursuit of
Israelite escapees would be. The two sets signify totality, especially with the
chiastic arrangement:

> depths of the earth
>   heavens
>   top of Carmel
>   bottom of the sea

"The depths of the grave" ($\check{s}\check{e}^\jmath\hat{o}l$)[111] and "the heavens" ($ha\check{s}\check{s}\bar{a}may\hat{i}m$) represent the limits of the universe. No matter how deep the Israelites dug or how
high they climbed, God's "hand" (power, authority) would overtake them.
"The top of Carmel" and "the bottom of the sea" represent the limits of the
nearer world. No terrestrial hiding place could conceal them from God's determined pursuit (cf. Ps 139:7–12; Rev 6:15–17). As G. Smith points out, "If neither heights nor depths can separate people from the love of God (cf. Rom.
8:38–39), they are also unable to hide them from the wrath of God."[112]

The continued use of the first person indicates that the Lord's personal
involvement would insure that no one would succeed in hiding from him. His
hand would "take" anyone who dug into Sheol (v. 2a). He would personally
cause to come down anyone who climbed up to heaven (v. 2b). He would
"hunt" and "seize" anyone who tried to hide in the forests and caves of Mount
Carmel (v. 3a; cf. 1:2). He would command the serpent to bite anyone who
sought refuge in the bottom of the sea (v. 3b). Hubbard tied this vision-report
to the day of the Lord oracle in Amos 5: "The account of the serpent's bite
seems deliberately to echo the punch-line of the parable in 5:19: No place is
safe when the day of darkness has been decreed."[113]

9:4 The fifth hypothetical place to hide would be as unsuccessful as the
previous four places. Even captivity would not grant immunity from the
Lord's determined pursuit. The "sword" under his command would slay
them.[114] Mention of the term "sword" in vv. 1,4 encloses the chiastic struc-

---

[111] שְׁאוֹל is the place of the departed dead. At first it designated the burial place. In later development it referred to the general collecting place of all the dead. In some OT texts Sheol is considered a realm beyond the reach of God's sovereignty (Job 10:20–22; Isa 38:18). Apparently
Amos did not share that perspective. The God he had encountered "was stranger to no part of his
creation" (Hubbard, *Joel and Amos,* 230).

[112] Smith, *Amos,* 268.

[113] Hubbard, *Joel and Amos,* 231.

[114] S. Paul commented: "For those who naively think that safety lies in fleeing the borders of
Israel into an alien land and thereby being beyond the reach of the Lord, there comes a rude awak-
ening. No geographical realm is beyond the sovereignty of the God of Israel, whose absolute control extends over all nations" (*Amos,* 279). In the land of their captors, the sword under the Lord's
command would slay them.

ture and stresses that Yahweh's sovereign control extended to every possible hiding place an Israelite escapee might consider.

The reason no one could escape the judgment of God was his decision to turn against them (v. 4b). Usually God's gaze was upon his people for good. His decision to set his eyes upon them for "evil" (*rāʿâ,* here "calamity") and not "good" (*tōbâ*) represented a radical departure from the norm. Andersen and Freedman concluded that "the Bethel sanctuary and its personnel were the direct target of this unparalleled onslaught and that both the sanctuary and its priests would be obliterated, regardless of attempts to escape."[115]

The fifth and final vision-report carried a message of doom for the altar at Bethel and for the cultic personnel associated with the altar. Earthquake and sword would serve as God's agents to bring about total destruction. God's sword would rise against the house of Jeroboam (7:9), Amaziah's sons and daughters (7:17), those left after the initial judgment (9:1), exiles hoping to escape from God's judgment (9:4), and all the sinners of God's people (9:10). Destruction of the altar at Bethel marked the end of that site as a place of communion and reconciliation with God. Excavations aimed at locating the site and remains of the Bethel sanctuary have been unsuccessful. Its destruction meant that the priests and the people accustomed to meeting God in reconciliation at Bethel could no longer do so. Worse than that, the Lord they expected to meet at Bethel would be there, but not to receive them favorably. His presence would be for evil and not good. When God's people steadfastly refuse to seek good rather than evil (5:14), they can expect God's gaze to be upon them for evil, not good (9:4).

(5) The Lord Almighty (9:5–6)

⁵The Lord, the LORD Almighty,
   he who touches the earth and it melts,
   and all who live in it mourn—
the whole land rises like the Nile,
   then sinks like the river of Egypt—
⁶he who builds his lofty palace in the heavens
   and sets its foundation on the earth,
who calls for the waters of the sea
   and pours them out over the face of the land—
   the LORD is his name.

For the third time Amos included a hymn fragment following a strong judgment oracle (cf. 4:13; 5:8–9). Whether this hymn fragment was placed here by Amos or by an editor, the impact is the same. As S. Paul put it, this "hymnic doxology of judgment glorifies the majesty of the Lord, affirming

---

[115] Andersen and Freedman, *Amos,* 841.

that he has the consummate power to carry out his threats of retributive punishment and chastisement just described."[116] The theme of each one is the
Lord's creative nature, his power over nature and, by implication, over events
in Israel. Each of the three hymns has been placed strategically by the author
to illustrate the sovereignty of God in the midst of judgment.

9:5   Much of the language and imagery found here was introduced in 8:8.
The hymn reveals God's power, creativity, and control. Participles punctuate
the piece with descriptions of the Lord's actions: "he who touches"
(*hannôgēaʿ*, v. 5), "he who builds" (*habbôneh*, v. 6a), and "who calls"
(*haqqōrēʾ*, v. 6b).[117]

The hymn begins with the title "the Lord [*ʾădōnāy*], the LORD [Yahweh]
Almighty" (*haṣṣĕbāʾôt*, "of the hosts"). This title stresses the sovereignty of
the Lord, his covenant relationship with Israel, and his power through leadership of the heavenly hosts (angels) and the army of Israel.[118]

This is the last of several possible references or allusions to an earthquake
in the book (cf. 1:1; 2:13; 4:11; 6:11; 8:8; 9:1).[119] An earthquake is an illustration of the power of God, who can touch the earth and melt it. The verb translated "melts" (*mûg*) probably is better rendered "trembles" or "quakes," since
the rest of the hymn contains earthquake imagery (cf. Ps 75:3 [Heb., 75:4];
Nah 1:5).[120] Earthquakes cause so much death and destruction that entire
populations may be thrown into mourning. The land reacts to an earthquake
like the Nile reacts during a flood. It rises and sinks by the Lord's touch. The
language of the verse is found in theophanic passages elsewhere in the Old
Testament (Pss 18:7; 46:6; 97:4–5; 144:5; Mic 1:3–4).[121]

9:6   The creative activity of God is found in the verbs "builds"
(*habbôneh*) and "sets" (*yĕsādāh*). A palace in the heavens whose foundation
is on the earth speaks of a transcendent sovereignty over both earth and
heaven.[122] Both heaven and earth are his domain where he has sovereign

---

[116] Paul, *Amos*, 279–80.

[117] All three participles are *qal* active masculine singular verbs with the definite article prefixed. "The one who . . ." is the usual translation of the form.

[118] This is the fourth use of the term צְבָאוֹת ("hosts") in the book (cf. 3:13; 4:13; 5:16). In each
case but in 4:13 it occurs with אֲדֹנָי ("Lord"). In each case but here it occurs with אֱלֹהֵי ("God
of"). On its structural significance see Andersen and Freedman, *Amos,* 617–18.

[119] Smith, *Amos,* 91.

[120] See Finley, *Joel, Amos, Obadiah,* 316. He notes that Amos adapted the line for use in 8:8
and substituted the verb רָגַז ("tremble, shake").

[121] Hubbard, *Joel and Amos,* 232.

[122] The term אֲגֻדָּתוֹ, translated "its foundation," is of uncertain meaning, but the verb יָסַד
means to "lay a foundation." A structure is described that reaches from earth to heaven. Andersen
and Freedman suggest that two sanctuaries are in view, one heavenly and the other earthly, which
together represent the divine abode (*Amos,* 845). Also see their discussion of the translation problem on pp. 845–54.

authority. This is why escape from him is futile.

The hymn attributes to the Lord[123] the control of rainfall. He has authority to call for "the waters of the sea" and the power to pour those waters out "over the face of the land." That is the God of the fifth vision who will judge his people.

(6) Destruction of the Sinful Kingdom (9:7–10)

> [7]"Are not you Israelites
>   the same to me as the Cushites"
>   declares the LORD.
> "Did I not bring Israel up from Egypt,
>   the Philistines from Caphtor
>
> and the Arameans from Kir?
> [8]"Surely the eyes of the Sovereign LORD
>   are on the sinful kingdom.
> I will destroy it
>   from the face of the earth—
> yet I will not totally destroy
>   the house of Jacob,"
>   declares the LORD.
> [9]"For I will give the command,
>   and I will shake the house of Israel
>   among all the nations
>   as grain is shaken in a sieve,
>   and not a pebble will reach the ground.
> [10]All the sinners among my people
>   will die by the sword,
> all those who say,
>   'Disaster will not overtake or meet us.'

Amos 9:7–10 contains the prophet's final oracle of the coming judgment upon Israel. Yet it contains a note of hope that is elaborated in the book's last message in 9:11–15. The result of the announced judgment will be the destruction of "the sinful kingdom" and death by sword for "all the sinners" among God's people. First-person speech characterizes the oracle as a divine saying. At the same time the rhetorical questions in v. 7 mark it as disputation speech. The Lord himself, not Amos, defends the message of his spokesman.

G. Smith explains that the dispute was regarding the vision of complete destruction in vv. 1–4, just as the dispute in 7:10–17 was brought about by the third vision in 7:7–9 of God's destruction of Israel's false worship and wicked

---

[123] יְהוָה שְׁמוֹ, "Yahweh is his name," is the common refrain in the three stanzas of the hymn, 4:13; 5:8–9; 9:5–6.

king.[124] Such devastation as Amos just announced, from which "none will escape," contradicted Israel's understanding of its history and its relationship with God. Amos 9:7–10 is God's correction of that understanding. In that sense this passage is an echo of 3:1–2, which responded to objections regarding Amos's first judgment speech in which he announced Israel's humiliating defeat from which none would escape (2:13–15). There as here the issue was seen against the background of God's delivering Israel from Egypt (2:9–12; 3:1–2). Israel thought their history with God meant he would always protect them and do good for them. But in 3:1–2 the prophet explained that their special relationship with God ("You only have I chosen of all the families of the earth") was the very reason for their punishment ("therefore I will punish you for all your sins"). With Israel's unique relationship with God came a special responsibility of loyalty to him and accountability for their sins.

The problem of Israel's false understanding, however, is approached differently in 9:7–10. Here the answer to Israel's objections focused on two points: (1) Israel's similarity to the other nations before God (cf. 1:3–2:15) and (2) the purpose of God's judgment of Israel.

NO SPECIAL IMMUNITY FOR ISRAEL (9:7).   **9:7**   The subject of both rhetorical questions is the relationship between Israel and Yahweh. Both are intended to affirm that Israel was no less accountable before God than any other nation. Cush was the territory of Ethiopia and Nubia in Old Testament times. The Cushites were the tribes inhabiting the territory south of the second cataract on the Nile River.[125] They were the remotest of peoples in Israel's experience, and reference to them may have been intended as inclusive of all nations. The point was that Israel shared something in common with all nations.[126] The nature of that similarity begins to be clarified in the second question, with two examples.

In Deuteronomy 2 Moses had affirmed God's involvement with other nations, declaring that he had given Edom the land of Seir, from which he had driven the Horites (2:5,12,22); he had given Moab the land of Ar, from which he had driven the Emites (2:9–11); he had given Ammon their land, from which he had driven the Zamzummites (2:19–21); and he had given the Caphtorites (Philistines) the villages that included Gaza, from which he had driven the Avvites (2:23). In the same way the Lord was about to give Israel the land of the Amorites (2:24). In Amos 9:7 this same concept is in view but is seen from the perspective of God's declared judgment against the Arameans in 1:3–6 and the Philistines in 1:6–8. As God had brought the people of Aram

---

[124] G. Smith, *Amos,* 269–70.

[125] Stuart, *Hosea-Jonah,* 393.

[126] Hayes argued that v. 7 served to "desacralize Israel and to deny the nation any claim on special privilege" (*Amos,* 218). Israel was like the Cushites (Ethiopia in the LXX) to God, a remote and insignificant people (Hubbard, *Joel and Amos,* 233).

from Kir[127] (9:7), he also had declared his intention of driving them back to Kir (1:5) for their sins. And as he had brought the Philistines from Caphtor[128] (9:7) to the villages of Gaza, Ashdod, Ashkelon, and Ekron, he had also determined to destroy them for their sins (1:6–8). The messages of judgment in Amos 1–2, then, are assumed in 9:7, where the point is that God's involvement with Israel does not immunize them from judgment any more than his involvement with any nation immunizes it from judgment.

Again Amos must have left his audience in shock. Israel's elect status did not excuse their sins or make them superior to other peoples. Rather it gave them a responsibility to reveal God to the nations (Gen 12:1–3; Isa 42:6), which they had not done; and thus it gave them greater accountability before God, for which they would most assuredly be judged.

OBSERVED BY THE SOVEREIGN LORD (9:8).   **9:8**   The Lord's gaze upon his people "for evil and not for good" in v. 4 is echoed in v. 8. The identity of "the sinful kingdom" is not made explicit here. The phrase occurs nowhere else. The context at least places the focus on the people to whom Amos preached, namely Israel, the Northern Kingdom, and especially the rulers. Furthermore, the second line specifies that it was the entity God was going to destroy. Amos used the alert word "surely" (*hinnê,* often rendered "behold" or "look") to introduce the announcement about the Lord's observance of "the sinful kingdom," the basis for his destroying it "from the face of the earth." The latter phrase is often found in announcements of judgment and may be an allusion to the flood (Gen 6:7; 7:4,23; Exod 32:12; 1 Kgs 13:34; Jer 28:16; Zeph 1:2–3).

But 9:8c, introduced by "yet" (*'epes kî,* lit., "only that") limits the judgment. "The house of Jacob" would not suffer total destruction. Apparently, then, "the sinful kingdom" and "the house of Jacob" are not identical. Israel, the sinful Northern Kingdom, would cease to exist as a nation, but a remnant of the people who were descendants of Jacob would survive.[129] While the sinful nation would be removed from the face of the earth, the people whom God had chosen out of all the peoples on the face of the earth (Deut 7:6; 14:2) would survive according to the covenant.

A surviving remnant accords with the general thrust of the prophet's message of disaster. The target of judgment usually is the rulers of Israel or the rich, not the population as a whole. The poor and the needy who were abused and oppressed by the rulers and by the rich were not condemned by Amos.

---

[127] It may have been in Mesopotamia. The exact location is unknown (2 Kgs 16:9; Isa 22:6).

[128] Usually considered to be Crete. Cf. Zeph 2:5; Ezek 25:16; 1 Sam 30:14.

[129] D. Hubbard made a distinction between "Israel's political existence" and their "social existence." He asserted, "The political structures were to be toppled. . . . The personal survival of some Israelites was promised" (*Joel and Amos,* 234). See also Andersen and Freedman, *Amos,* 870–71.

They would be more likely to survive a military defeat than the rulers and the rich, since conquerors tended to kill or exile the ruling upper class, the skilled, and the rich (6:7). Complete extermination of God's people was not God's plan. God's vigil in watching his people usually has positive implications. The positive or negative nature of God's gaze depends on what he sees in his people (see comments on 3:2).

JUDGMENT OF ISRAEL COMMANDED (9:9).   **9:9**   The first line may be translated literally, "For behold, I am commanding (or about to command)." God was in the process of issuing the command. To whom God issued the command and what the command was remain unexpressed. But its purpose was for the shaking of Israel among the nations.[130]

God's shaking of Israel is compared to one shaking grain in a sieve. The function of the grain sieve was to trap what was undesirable so that it could be thrown away.[131] Undesirable elements would include pebbles, husks, and pieces of stalks. The grain would fall into a container. Just as no pebble would fall to the ground, so thorough would be the screening process of God's judgment that none of the "sinners" (v. 10) would escape. God's judgments sift his people to remove the bad from the good.

DEATH SENTENCE (9:10).   **9:10**   Here is the last of eight references to the "sword" in Amos. "By the sword" occurs first in the verse, perhaps echoing its last occurrence in the final vision in vv. 1,4. Some warring nation would serve as God's agent of judgment. "All the sinners among my people" implies that all the people of Israel were not sinners and thereby were not destined for death by the sword. "The sinful kingdom" (v. 8) was made sinful by "all the sinners among my people." The purpose of judgment was to remove them.

They are further specified as "all those who say, 'Disaster will not overtake or meet us.'" Some in the prophet's audience were contradicting his message. They were saying that "disaster" (rāʿâ, "evil," or "calamity;" cf. 3:6; 9:4) was not their destiny. Thus they were ones who rejected the word of God (cf. 2:12; 7:16). Amos was saying that only a remnant could hope to survive the coming disaster.

---

[130] Hayes understood the command as "giving the surrounding enemy the order to invade" (*Amos*, 222).

[131] Mays, *Amos*, 161; Hubbard, *Joel and Amos*, 235; Paul, *Amos*, 286; Stuart, *Hosea-Jonah*, 394; Wolff, *Joel and Amos*, 349. Most interpreters agree that the sieve trapped undesirable and worthless debris to be thrown away. Andersen and Freedman vacillated on the question of whether it was the grain that slipped through the sieve leaving coarse particles to be cast aside or the grain that was caught in the sieve allowing fine dust and chaff to be removed. Either way, the "purpose of sifting is to separate the good from the bad" (*Amos*, 871).

(7) Future Restoration of Israel (9:11–15)

[11]"In that day I will restore
David's fallen tent.
I will repair its broken places,
restore its ruins,
and build it as it used to be,
[12]so that they may possess the remnant of Edom
and all the nations that bear my name,"
declares the LORD, who will do these things.

[13]"The days are coming," declares the LORD,

"when the reaper will be overtaken by the plowman
and the planter by the one treading grapes.
New wine will drip from the mountains
and flow from all the hills.
[14]I will bring back my exiled people Israel;
they will rebuild the ruined cities and live in them.
They will plant vineyards and drink their wine;
they will make gardens and eat their fruit.
[15]I will plant Israel in their own land,
never again to be uprooted
from the land I have given them,"

says the LORD your God.

First-person verbs mark this final passage in Amos as divine speech. It completes the book on a positive note, a note radically different from most of what precedes it. For that reason and others, interpreters commonly assign the final pericope to the disciples of Amos after the fall of Judah in 587 B.C.[132] Many interpreters, however, conclude that this final message is from Amos.[133] S. Paul, for example, concluded that arguments for a late date for Amos 9:11–15 based on linguistic and ideological grounds are "seriously open to question."[134] Wendland also supports the integrity of 9:11–15, saying that to dismiss it in any way is to miss "the essential thrust of the prophet's message. . . . it represents the striking consummation of a thematic potential that was already planted much earlier in the prophecy . . . (i.e., 5:4,6,14 and 15) but also by its very structure subtly prefigures the tremendous physical

---

[132] Mays, *Amos,* 164; R. L. Smith, "Amos," BBC 7 (Nashville: Broadman, 1972), 140; Wolff, *Joel and Amos,* 352.

[133] Hayes, *Amos,* 223–28; Stuart, *Hosea-Jonah,* 397; J. D. W. Watts, *Vision and Prophecy in Amos* (Grand Rapids: Eerdmans, 1958), 25–26; Andersen and Freedman, *Amos,* 894; Hubbard, *Joel and Amos,* 238–39; Paul, *Amos,* 288ff.; G. Smith, *Amos,* 277–80.

[134] Paul, *Amos,* 288. I agree with G. Hasel's conclusion: "There is no compelling reason why the final section of Amos could not derive from the historical Amos himself" (*Understanding the Book of Amos* [Grand Rapids: Baker, 1991], 118).

and spiritual reversal to come."[135]

The message of hope and restoration following repeated oracles of doom may be startling to some, but the typical pattern of oracles in the other eighth-century B.C. prophets is that of hope for salvation following oracles of judgment. Hosea 1:2–9 is a message of judgment followed by a message of hope in 1:10–2:1. Hosea 2:2–13 is a message of judgment followed by a message of hope in 2:14–23. This pattern of alternate messages of judgment and salvation is visible throughout the prophecies of Hosea. Micah 1:3–16 is a message of judgment followed by a message of hope in 2:12–13. A similar pattern of judgment in Mic 3:8–12 is followed by a message of salvation in 4:1–5. The messages of Isaiah 1–5 alternate between judgment and salvation.

Furthermore, there are words of hope throughout Amos before this point; so this final oracle of salvation is but a melody produced from those earlier notes (cf. 3:2,12; 5:3–6,14–15; 9:8–10). Our God always manifests his grace as greater than all our sin. God's sending Amos to condemn Israel's sins in itself indicates that God had not given up on his people. Messages threatening judgment were aimed at Israel's redemption, not their destruction. Reference to Israel's chosenness (3:2) suggests a permanent relationship already established. God's threat of punishment for their sins meant that with the privilege of being chosen came the responsibility of maintaining a proper relationship with God.

In direct address Amos described Israel's current relationship with God: "Prepare to meet *your* God, O Israel" (4:12; italics added). The calamities God brought on Israel were meant to be restoration measures (4:6–11). Israel's response to each God-directed calamity was the same. They failed to return to God (vv. 6,8,9,10,11). The message in the middle chapter of Amos is a strong call to seek the Lord and live (5:4–6,14–15).

Twice Amos interceded for Israel, and twice God "relented" (7:3,6). Israel could have found some hope in God's responsiveness to a faithful prophet. However, from these two vision-reports to the hint of hope in the oracle preceding the final passage (9:8–10), the messages grew more and more harsh with threats of judgment and destruction.

Amos's rhetoric here inspires hope for a restored future. Its two parts are marked by the introductory references to the Lord's future interventions to accomplish restoration for his people (9:11, "in that day;" 9:13, "the days are coming"). Nothing in the passage indicates the specific time and place of its delivery. The audience may have included the people of the land but most assuredly did not include the king, the religious leaders, and the socio-economic elite of the country. The faithful in the prophet's audience must have been encouraged to know that the Lord's judgments against Israel did not mean total rejection of his people. This is the function of the final message.

---

[135] Wendland, "The 'Word of the Lord' and the Organization of Amos," 31–32.

THE LORD'S PROMISE OF RESTORATION (9:11–12). "In that day" (v. 11) and "the days are coming" (v. 13) alert the reader that the promises contained in these two sections of the final pericope are for the (in)definite future. The hopeful tone of this passage is the direct result of the Lord's actions in Israel's behalf.

9:11 The four verbs in v. 11 describe the actions the Lord promises to take in the future. "David's fallen tent" (*sukkat dawîd hannopelet*, lit., "the booth of David, which is falling") was the object of the these actions. But what was David's "tent," and in what sense was it "fallen" (or falling)?

Most interpreters agree that David's *sukkat* (from *sukkâ*) is a metaphor for Davidic rule or some aspect of it.[136] The word translated "tent" is not the common word *'ohel* but a term usually referring to a hut of branches and mats used as a temporary shelter from the elements (Isa 4:6) by a watchman in a vineyard (Isa 1:8), livestock (Gen 33:17), travelers (Lev 23:43), or a king in battle (2 Sam 11:11; 1 Kgs 20:12). The plural *sukkôt* also is the Hebrew name for the Feast of "Booths" or "Tabernacles," named for the shelters in which Israel lived during their desert wandering under God's care. Their observance of the feast was to include living in "booths" for seven days (Lev 23:42–43; Neh 8:14–17). While a *sukkâ* was a humble temporary structure, the term is sometimes used in the Old Testament for the abode of God, where the NIV translates it "pavilion" or "canopy" (Job 36:29; Ps 18:11; see also Pss 61:4; 76:2–3, which use the term *'ohel*, "tent").

T. J. Finley explains the use as a figure based on the shelter of a king in battle. This sense, he says, is also appropriate for our passage, where the following verse uses war imagery in the phrase "possess the remnant of Edom." The idea would be that Israel is in a state of defeat or near defeat by their enemies, the sign of which is that their king's *sukkâ* is fallen. Israel, having been "mercilessly assaulted by the nations" according to 9:1–10, is here promised deliverance under the banner of David, a reference to the coming messianic Davidic king who will establish universal dominion (Zech 9:9–10).[137]

Finley's view sees the term *sukkâ* in the passage as a symbol of royal presence and military success and thus of the military success of Israel. It is better, however, to see the term as a reference to David's dynasty, which in 2 Sam 7:5–16 is referred to as his "house" (*bayit*). In Amos's time it was tottering

---

[136] Stuart thinks the reference is to the ancient city named Succoth, the base for David's control of Israel's neighbors to the east and south (*Hosea-Jonah*, 398). סֻכַּת is a feminine construct form. To vocalize as Stuart suggests so as to make the form refer to a place name, Succoth, seems forced. The unique construction found here, סֻכַּת דָּוִיד, should be rendered "booth of David." Then the interpreter's task is to ferret out the meaning of the construction in the context.

[137] Finley, *Joel, Amos, Obadiah*, 323.

and in need of stabilization.[138] Judah was subordinate to Israel most of the 150 years from the reign of Omri to the reign of Pekah in 734 B.C. Judah's King Azariah (Uzziah) regained some stature for the Southern Kingdom during his reign (787–747 B.C.). But leprosy ended his influence prematurely as his son Jotham became coregent in 759 B.C. Matters deteriorated rapidly in Judah under Jotham's rule. David's "tent" was falling. "The Davidic dynasty had fallen so low that it could no longer be called a house."[139]

The Lord promised to "restore" (*ʾaqîm*, "I will cause to rise, or establish") David's tottering rule (cf. *qûm*, "lift up," at 5:2). National life would be secure again as a direct result of God's action. To accomplish this Yahweh promised to "repair its broken places" (lit., "their broken places," referring to growing insurrection in Israel[140]). The verb *gadar* rendered "repair" means "erect a wall," or "wall up a breach." The related noun (*gader*) refers to a stone wall (Ps 62:4; Mic 7:11). The "broken places" should be understood figuratively to refer to "the basic shambles which the descendants of David have made" in ruling Israel.[141] God promised to wall up such breaches in the future.

Another promise the Lord made was to "restore its ruins" (same verb as in the first line). Reference here could be to the destroyed city of Jerusalem, with its breached walls and burned buildings, at the hands of Nebuchadnezzar in 587 B.C. But the term translated "ruins" can also refer to "removal from authority" (Isa 22:19). If that is the connotation of the noun used here, then the Lord promised to restore those who had repudiated the authority of the Davidic king.[142]

Yet another promise the Lord made was to "build it as it used to be." The pronoun object of the verb "to build" (*banâ*, here probably "rebuild") is third feminine singular. The most logical reference is to the feminine noun *sukkat* and thus to Davidic rule. The falling booth of David would be more than stabilized. It would be built "as it used to be." Use of the verb "build" seems to confirm reference to the Lord's promise to David to build a house (dynasty) for him that would endure forever.[143] The Davidic dynasty would be reestablished "in that day," that is, some time following the sifting process of God's judgment spoken of in 9:9. McComiskey explains that according to the prophets this period was seen as continuing until the coming of Messiah,

---

[138] S. Paul denied the common interpretation of "David's fallen tent" as reference to the fall of Judah to the Babylonians in 587 B.C., insisting David's fallen booth was "a dilapidated, unstable, precarious state of affairs" (*Amos,* 290). M. Braun concluded that "fallen tent" referred to "the Davidic kingdom, which was rent after Solomon's death" ("James' Use of Amos at the Jerusalem Council," *JETS* 20 [1977]: 114).

[139] T. E. McComiskey, "Amos," EBC 7 (Grand Rapids: Zondervan, 1985), 329.

[140] Hayes, *Amos,* 225.

[141] Hubbard, *Joel and Amos,* 240.

[142] W. C. Kaiser, Jr. interprets the phrase "restore its ruins" as a reference to David himself and specifically a messianic reference to the restoration of the Davidic line of rulers in Christ (*The Use of the Old Testament in the New* [Chicago: Moody, 1985], 182).

[143] Contrast with 7:9, where God will "raise" up the sword against the "house" of Jeroboam.

thus including the Christian era. The Messiah, coming from the lineage of David, would be the fulfillment of the Davidic Covenant (cf. Isa 9:6–7; 16:5; Jer 23:5; 30:9; 33:15–17; Ezek 34:23–24; 37:24–25; Hos 3:5; Mic 5:2; Zech 12:8–13:1).[144]

9:12 The question before the Jerusalem Council (Acts 15:6–21) was how to receive Gentile converts into a largely Jewish Christian church. Peter, Barnabas, and Paul told how God had worked through them among the Gentiles (Acts 15:7–12). James quoted Amos 9:11–12 in support of God's work in "taking from the Gentiles a people for himself" (Acts 15:14). He quoted from the Septuagint (LXX), the Greek translation of the Old Testament made between 250 and 150 B.C., rather than the Hebrew text (MT). So different are the two versions that the LXX may reflect an interpretive reading of the MT.[145] Even so, the way James used the LXX translation of Amos 9:11–12 to argue for inclusion of believing Gentiles in the community of God is not in conflict with the meaning of the MT of Amos 9:11–12.

Restored Davidic rule (dynasty) would include "the remnant of Edom" and "the nations" (*haggôyim*) according to the MT of Amos 9:12 (cf. Ezek 36:3–5).[146] In the Hebrew text the subject of the verb "possess" is undesignated, but the implied subject is the people of the restored Davidic kingdom. In Amos's focus on that future day, the people of the restored Davidic kingdom will possess those of Edom who survive God's judgment upon them and all the nations (Gentiles) over whom the name of the Lord is called. "That bear my name" is literally "over whom my name is called." It implies God's ownership of the unnamed nations and their submission to him (cf. Mal 1:11).[147] A secondary implication is that God's character is manifested in the people named. In this case reference is to "the nations" included as people of God. The LXX version changes the verb from "possess" to "seek," has "the remnant of men [for Edom]" and "all the nations" as subjects, and does not have an object. The implied object is God. Both the MT and the LXX imply the inclusion of Gentiles among the people of God.[148]

---

[144] McComiskey, "Amos," 7:329.

[145] D. M. King, "The Use of Amos 9:11–12 in Acts 15:16–18," *Ashland Theological Journal* 21 (1989): 8.

[146] J. B. Polhill interpreted the reference in Amos 9:12 to Edom and the nations to mean that they "once again would be gathered into Israel" (*Acts,* NAC [Nashville: Broadman & Holman, 1992], 329). The restored people of God would consist of both Jew and Gentile.

[147] W. C. Kaiser, Jr., "The Davidic Promise and the Inclusion of the Gentiles (Amos 9:9–15 and Acts 15:13–18): A Test Passage for Theological Systems," *JETS* 20 (1977): 103; G. van Groningen, *Messianic Revelation in the Old Testament* (Grand Rapids: Baker, 1990), 473.

[148] יִרְשׁוּ, "possess," in the MT may have been misread by the LXX translators as דָּרְשׁ, "seek." Similarly אֱדוֹם: , "Edom," may have been misread as אָדָם , "man" (singular) but understood as "men" (collective). Whether the LXX resulted from a textual error, the product was an equivalent expression that focused on the experiential aspect of the same truth. Since Edom probably represents the nations once set against God, the change to "man" would make little difference.

The LXX and the MT of Amos 9:11 agree that David's fallen tent will be raised. Verse 12 in the MT has the restored Davidic kingdom possessing Edom and the nations, while the LXX in v. 12 indicates that restoration of the Davidic kingdom would stimulate the nations to seek God.[149] The result in both verses supports Gentile inclusion as the people of God along with the restored Davidic kingdom. The possession of Edom should not be understood as military subjugation but as "spiritual incorporation into the restored kingdom of David."[150]

Some have counted Acts 15:13–18 among the most important passages in the New Testament to support the idea that Israel will be restored alongside an eschatological body of Gentile believers. The focus of James's concern, however, was not prophecy of future events but how to handle the current problem of Gentile inclusion in the church. James argued that earlier prophecy (from Amos and others) was in process of fulfillment as the Gentiles turned to God through Christ and thus joined the body of Christ, the church.

Restoration of Davidic rule is assured by the prophet's use of the oracle formula, "declares the LORD." Another word of assurance that the promised restoration would occur and that the Gentiles would be included in the people of God is the statement that the Lord is the one doing it. The prophecy of Amos concerning the Gentiles continues to be fulfilled.

THE LORD'S PROMISE OF PLENTY (9:13–14).   The ideal future conditions contained in 9:13–15 are also found in other prophetic literature (cf. Isa 11:6–9; Hos 14:4–7). Themes dominating vv. 13–14 are the bounty of the land and restoration to a stable society. Although Amos had prophesied famine and drought (4:6–8), the future was one of "plenty."

9:13   The introduction to the promise of plenty sets the time frame in the future: "The days are coming" (see 8:11 and comments there). That such a day about to be described was sure to come is indicated by the prophet's use of the oracle formula, "declares the LORD."

Four participles define four agricultural activities in Amos 9:13: plowing, reaping, treading, and planting. Plowing began the agricultural year after the first rains in October-November. Reaping ended the agricultural year in April-May. Usually a gap of six months separated these two activities. Here a compression of time has the one plowing overtaking the one reaping. It is a picture of harvests so abundant that the gathering of one crop will not be finished before time to begin the next crop.

---

[149] E. Richard explained Luke's addition of the verb translated "I will return" (Acts 15:16) in relation to God's visitation (v. 14; 14:11–18) and to the Gentiles' "turning to God" (v. 19; "The Creative Use of Amos by the Author of Acts," *NovT* 24 [1982]: 48). Then he concluded: "In effect God returns to his people (the Jews) so that the Gentiles may turn to him."

[150] Kaiser, "The Davidic Promise and the Inclusion of the Gentiles," 103.

The next part of the verse has the grape treader close on the heels of the planter. Pressing grapes was an activity performed during the months of August-September, and planting was a job for November-December. Again, a time lapse usually separated these two activities. Here a compression of time has their work overlapping. This picture of vigorous activity reflects the abundance of a new era.[151] Word pictures at the end of v. 13 enable the reader to envision the enormous harvest of grapes resulting in new wine dripping from the mountains and flowing from the hills. No one in the new day would want for food and drink. With God's blessing upon it, the land would truly become the land that was promised, flowing with milk and honey.

9:14 The Lord promised to reverse the fortunes of his people Israel (*šabtî ʾet-šebût*), restoring them to their former state of well-being.[152] The NIV translation "I will bring back My exiled people Israel" (cf. NJB, NKJV) refers most directly to a return from Assyrian or Babylonian captivity. However, this language probably describes a reversal of fortunes (cf. REB, NRSV), a concept suitable to many settings even in or before the time of Amos. In contrast to the phrase "I will not *turn* it [i.e., "my wrath"; italics added] back" (*loʾ ʾašîbenû*) in 2:4,6, what would now *return* (*wešabtî*) to Israel was God's blessing.

The basis for God's future shift from wrath to mercy in his relationship to Israel[153] will be Israel's renewed faith in and loyalty to the Lord. This is made clear in Deut 30:1–3, where the verb *šûb* is used in vv. 1–2 of Israel's return to faith; and the expression *wešab šebûteka*, "he will restore your fortunes," is given as the result in v. 3 (see also Jer 29:12–14).[154] According to Amos the evidence of the shift and the reversal of fortunes will be the rebuilding of "ruined" (or "desolate") cities so that the people may live in them. Another evidence will be the planting of vineyards and such stability of life as to enjoy the produce of those vineyards. The opportunity to plant gardens and eat their fruit are promises of blessings that reverse the earlier threat of curses (5:10–11).[155]

THE LORD'S PROMISE OF SECURITY (9:15). **9:15** God's forgiveness of Israel will be permanent. His blessing will be constant. Restoration of covenant blessings is an unconditional promise. Once and for all time God promised to

---

[151] Andersen and Freedman, *Amos,* 921. S. Paul referred to the bounty promised in the new age as "the forthcoming unconditional blessing of abundant fertility that will be bestowed upon the land" (*Amos,* 292).

[152] See the use of the expression in Jer 29:14; 30:3,18; 31:23; 32:44; 33:7,11,26; Ezek 39:25.

[153] Mays, *Amos,* 167.

[154] Cf. E. H. Merrill, *Deuteronomy,* NAC (Nashville: Broadman & Holman, 1994), 386–90; F. B. Huey, Jr., *Jeremiah, Lamentations,* NAC (Nashville: Broadman & Holman, 1993), 260–61, 296.

[155] Hubbard, *Joel and Amos,* 243.

plant Israel on their ground, never to be uprooted again.[156] The land would be theirs as a gift from God. "Says the LORD your God" is the closing messenger formula, guaranteeing the promises based on the sure word of Israel's covenant God. This permanent possession of the land in the future represents a reversal of the destiny expressed in 5:2, "fallen . . . never to rise again."

Although the postexilic community experienced a partial fulfillment of such promises as are made in 9:11–15,[157] their ultimate fulfillment awaited New Testament times. Jesus Christ in the line of David was the manifestation of God at work to change the word of wrath to the word of mercy. He founded the church, a God-blessed people, the Israel of God (Gal 6:16). He charged them to make disciples of "all the nations." This part of the promise (Amos 9:12) is in process of fulfillment. The text, with its first-person verbs referring to God's actions, makes clear that God is the one who restores, builds, plants, and blesses. It will not be by political coup, social revolution, or military maneuvers that Israel will regain its ascendancy. It will be by the coming of the Lord, who will heal his people and their land.

---

[156] S. Paul interpreted v. 15 to be an "unconditional and unqualified promise" of "the permanent possession of the land of Israel" (*Amos,* 295). Andersen and Freedman concluded their discussion of v. 15 with the strong assertion that "the land promised of old is now to be given once more in perpetuity" (*Amos,* 926).

[157] Cf. M. Breneman, *Ezra, Nehemiah, Esther,* NAC (Nashville: Broadman, 1993), 56–58.

Obadiah

____ INTRODUCTION OUTLINE ____

1. Canonical Position
2. The Date
3. The Book
4. The Author
5. Edom and the Edomites
6. The Message

_____ **INTRODUCTION** _____

Obadiah is the shortest book in the Old Testament, consisting of only twenty-one verses. In the Book of Joel, Edom is accused of violence against the people of Judah (3:19). When this particular violent action occurred is uncertain, considering Edom's long-term antagonism to Israel that began with the struggle of Esau and Jacob in Rebekah's womb (Gen 25) and continued into the Babylonian captivity of Judah. Here in Obadiah, Edom receives a prophetic announcement of impending judgment.

1. Canonical Position

Obadiah stands between Amos and Jonah, both of whom prophesied in the eighth century B.C. Since Obadiah's date appears to be early in the sixth century B.C. (see discussion in next section), a catchword or theme may explain the canonical position of the book. The approaching day of the Lord is one such theme. The statement that Israel will "possess the remnant of Edom" in Amos 9:12 is another (cf. Obad 17,19–20).

2. The Date

Nothing in the title verse (v. 1) offers help in dating the book. Prophets who ministered during the reigns of the kings of Israel and Judah often have preserved in the title verse of their collected prophecies a reference to the king (or kings) contemporary with their ministry. The absence of such a reference in Obadiah may serve as a clue that no king reigned at the time. One such time was the period following the fall of Judah in 587 B.C.

The usual method of determining the date of Obadiah is to look for a period when Judah and Jerusalem were destroyed and Edom behaved in a hostile manner toward their Judahite brothers. B. C. Cresson lists six such events: (1) Absalom's revolt, (2) Shishak's invasion, (3) the Philistine-Arabian invasion, (4) the Israelite invasion, (5) Nebuchadnezzar's invasion in 597 B.C., and (6) Nebuchadnezzar's invasion in 587 B.C.[1] The last event is the most likely. A short time after the fall of Judah to the Babylonians (587 B.C.) fits the situation and perspective of the book. H. W. Wolff argued that in the Book of Obadiah only vv. 11–14 can be "unequivocally dated." He concluded that the remarks made there "can refer only to the period immediately after the Babylonian conquest of Jerusalem in 587 B.C."[2]

Although vv. 12–14 are in the form of prohibitions that might suggest the events have not yet occurred, the intent is commonly recognized not as prophetic but rhetorical (note the past tense in vv. 10–11,15). As Finley explains: "The prophet portrays the past event of Edom's transgressions against Jerusalem more vividly by placing himself at the scene and demanding, as it were, that the Edomites cease their wicked behavior."[3] Since Edom's fall prophesied in the book had occurred by about 500 B.C.,[4] Obadiah was written sometime between 587 and 500 B.C.

3. The Book

The book begins with a brief title, "the vision of Obadiah" (v. 1a). A messenger formula follows the title (v. 1b), ending with an introduction to the addressee, or the subject of the oracle (Edom). Only the title and the introduction are in prose. The rest is poetry.

The first oracle concerns the pride of Edom and God's vow to bring the nation down (vv. 1c–4). It ends with an oracle formula. Edom's sure defeat is the theme of the second oracle (vv. 5–10). The third oracle focuses on Edom's mistreatment of Judah (vv. 11–14). Edom's conduct toward Judah was unbrotherly. The theme of the fourth oracle is the day of the Lord (vv. 15–21).

---

[1] B. C. Cresson, "Obadiah," BBC 7 (Nashville: Broadman, 1972). The date of 587 B.C. is defended by J. Limburg in his commentary, *Hosea-Micah*, IBC (Atlanta: John Knox, 1988), 130. L. C. Allen holds the same date as the likely setting for the book. See his commentary on *The Books of Joel, Obadiah, Jonah, and Micah*, NICOT (Grand Rapids: Eerdmans, 1983), 129. J. R. Lillie concluded that "Obadiah 11–14 refers to the catastrophic fall of Jerusalem to Babylon in 587/86 B.C. and to the treachery which Edom displayed against Jerusalem in that fateful day" ("Obadiah—A Celebration of God's Kingdom," in *Currents in Theology and Mission* 6 [1979]: 18).

[2] H. Wolff, *Obadiah and Jonah*, trans. M. Kohl (Minneapolis: Augsburg, 1986), 18.

[3] T. Finley, *Joel, Amos, Obadiah* (Chicago: Moody, 1990), 340.

[4] Cf. Mal 1:2–5. See also J. R. Bartlett, "The Rise and Fall of the Kingdom of Edom," *PEQ* 104 (1972): 36–37.

4. The Author

The title contains only the name of the author. "Obadiah" means "servant of Yahweh" or "worshiper of Yahweh," an expression of "the faith of the parents and of their hopes for the child."[5] Thirteen different people are named Obadiah in the Old Testament. Because of the absence of genealogical information in the book, efforts have been made to identify the Obadiah named here with one of the Obadiahs referred to elsewhere in the Old Testament. One suggested is the servant of Ahab who saved the lives of a hundred prophets during Jezebel's persecution (1 Kgs 18:4), but the evidence does not warrant that identification.

With the limited information in the book, not much can be said about the author. His family, hometown, and date are not given. About all that can be said is that a certain man named Obadiah served as prophet of God at a time of calamity in Judah.[6] Through him God sent a strong message of condemnation for Edom (who participated in Judah's defeat) and words of hope for Judah. Obadiah was a prophet to whom God gave a word to speak against Edom for the encouragement of Israel. He did so, and the book's prophetic origin led to its becoming Scripture to Israel. There is little reason to believe that Obadiah went to Edom to deliver his message as Jonah went to Nineveh. As with the other oracles against the nations, there is no explicit statement that the message was delivered to anyone outside of Israel, and the message's interpretation does not require it.[7] Normally the prophetic judgment speeches against the nations were intended for the ears of God's people.[8] According to G. V. Smith, Obadiah's audience was a remnant of Jews left in Jerusalem who were wondering whether God would judge Edom for their "spiteful hatred."[9]

5. Edom and the Edomites

Most of the available information on Edom and the Edomites exists in the literature of their neighbors and enemies. Prominent among their neighbors

---

[5] J. Thompson, "The Book of Obadiah," IB (New York: Abingdon, 1956), 857.

[6] Based on an argument from function, some refer to Obadiah as a cult prophet, i.e., one "who performed prophetic functions within established ritual." See J. D. W. Watts, *Obadiah: A Critical Commentary* (Grand Rapids: Eerdmans, 1969), 23. It is a theory we cannot prove or disprove.

[7] See F. B. Huey, Jr., *Jeremiah, Lamentations,* NAC (Nashville: Broadman, 1993), 374–75.

[8] C. H. Bullock notes that Jer 27:1–11 offers a precedent for a prophet communicating with a foreign people but concludes that "in view of the loss of national status and diplomatic channels, it is not likely that Judah could send ambassadors to the nations" (*An Introduction to the Old Testament Prophetic Books* [Chicago: Moody, 1986], 261).

[9] G. V. Smith, *The Prophets as Preachers: An Introduction to the Hebrew Prophets* (Nashville: Broadman & Holman, 1994), 243.

and enemies were the Israelites, Egyptians, Assyrians, and Babylonians.[10] Biblical writers referred to Edom and the Edomites frequently. The entire Book of Obadiah is an anti-Edomite oracle. Obadiah's description of Edom's behavior (vv. 11–14) is the most specific of all the biblical polemics against Edom.[11] The Genesis account of the origin of Edom clearly identifies Edom with Esau, Jacob's (Israel's) twin brother (Gen 25:25–26; 36:1,9,19,40–43). The relationship of Israel and Edom as "brothers," however, is more complex than the record that Jacob and Esau were born as twin sons of Isaac.[12]

Tensions evident between Jacob and Esau in the story of their birth continued and accelerated, according to the record of their relationship preserved in the Old Testament. Edom denied Israel's request for permission to pass through Edomite territory on their way from Egypt to Canaan (Num 20:14–21). Saul fought against Edom (1 Sam 14:47), and King David conquered it (2 Sam 8:13–14). Hadad, however, a young member of the Edomite royal family, escaped, fled to Egypt, and returned after David's death to plague Solomon (1 Kgs 11:25).

At times in Edom's history they were subject to Judah. At other times they were independent. During the reign of King Jehoram of Judah (848–841 B.C.), Edom rebelled and became an independent monarchy (2 Kgs 8:20–22; 2 Chr 21:8–10). In the fourth year of Zedekiah, king of Judah (594 B.C.), Edom had put aside its hostility toward Judah and was one of the small states allied with Judah against Babylon (Jer 27:2–7).[13] Edom must have committed some hostile act against Judah shortly after that diplomatic conference, however, which would explain Judah's impassioned prophecies against Edom (Jer 49:7–22; Ps 137:7; Lam 4:18–22; Ezek 25:12–14; 35:1–15).

The statement in Lam 1:2 that "all her [Judah's] friends have betrayed her; they have become her enemies" may include Edom. In a reference to the rebuilding of the Jerusalem temple, *1 Esdr* 4:45 identifies one enemy as Edom

---

[10] S. Cohen, "Edom," *IDB*, 24. J. R. Bartlett, describing the paucity of evidence on the history, geography, and society of Edom, wrote: "As we have no extant Edomite texts to lighten our darkness, we are left dependent on two important, if limited, resources. The first is archaeological evidence, and second is the existence of a few possible allusions to Transjordan in the Egyptian records" (*Edom and the Edomites,* JSOTSup 77 [Sheffield, Eng.: Sheffield Academic Press, 1989], 67).

[11] For the most recent and thorough study of Edom in the prophetic literature and in the OT in general, see the work by B. Dicou, *Edom, Israel's Brother and Antagonist: The Role of Edom in Biblical Prophecy and Story,* JSOTSup 169 (Sheffield: JSOT Press, 1994). Also see the article by J. Muilenburg, "Obadiah, Book of," *IDB,* 578.

[12] R. J. Coggins, *Israel among the Nations: A Commentary on the Books of Nahum and Obadiah,* ITC (Grand Rapids: Eerdmans, 1985), 70–71.

[13] J. M. Myers, "Edom and Judah in the Sixth-Fifth Centuries B.C.," in *Near Eastern Studies in Honor of William Foxwell Albright,* ed. H. Goedicke (Baltimore: The Johns Hopkins Press, 1971), 379–80.

in the expression "the temple, which the Edomites burned when Judea was laid waste by the Chaldeans." Even though the trustworthiness of this text is doubted and it contradicts *1 Esdr* 1:55, which says the Babylonians burned the temple, still the statement lends support to the generally hostile attitude of Edom toward Judah as this is reflected in Old Testament materials. The Peshitta and Arabic versions of 2 Kgs 24:2 read "Edomites" instead of "Arameans" among those going against Judah to destroy it in 598 B.C. However, this textual evidence is not sufficient to emend the MT.[14]

The territory occupied by Edom from about 1300 B.C. was situated to the south of the Dead Sea. A mountain range overlooking the Arabah served as its western border. The desert functioned as the eastern and southern borders. The brook Zered separated Edom from Moab to the north. Reddish (cf. Gen 25:25) colored rocks and cliffs were the most striking feature of the area. Edom's territory was relatively small, about seventy miles from north to south and only fifteen miles from east to west.[15]

6. The Message

The Book of Obadiah is one of several polemics in the Old Testament against Edom. Similar messages are located in Isaiah (21:11–12), Jeremiah (49:7–22; this text has striking similarities to Obadiah), Ezekiel (25:12–14; 35), Amos (1:11–12), and Malachi (1:2–5). Obadiah's message from beginning to end concerns the Lord's judgment of Edom. But its role in the book also extends to that of representative of the nations of the world that oppose God and his people (cf. Ps 2).[16] The basis of the judgment was Edom's pride (vv. 1–4) and their participation in Judah's downfall (vv. 10–14). The prophet pictured Edom (the house of Esau) as stubble that would burn and leave no survivors (v. 18). Ultimately deliverers on Mount Zion would govern the mountains of Esau (Edom, v. 21).

The message, however, concerns more than Edom. It is placed in the context of a day of judgment on all nations when they receive just recompense for all their deeds (vv. 15–16). Thus the deliverance on Mount Zion will be final, the inheritance they regain will be theirs forever (v. 17), and the Lord's kingdom (v. 21) will be a universal one. Obadiah's word against Edom, then,

---

[14] J. R. Bartlett evaluated *1 Esdr* 4:45 as "the most explicit and probably least accurate reference to Edomite behavior in 587 B.C." ("Edom and the Fall of Jerusalem, 587 B.C.," *PEQ* 114 [1982]: 22–23). He concluded his treatment of the long-standing complaints against Edom with the judgment that "Edom has been falsely maligned" and that the prophets "owe Edom an apology." I think Bartlett has outrun his own evidence. Objective judgment of the biblical evidence about Edom will conclude that Edom was culpable in that nation's relationship to Judah.

[15] Limburg, *Hosea-Micah,* 129.

[16] See Amos 9:12 and the comments on that verse in the present volume.

may be interpreted in light of Isaiah's more general prophesy that "the LORD will punish the powers in the heavens above and the kings on the earth below" (24:21); and as a result "the people of the world learn righteousness" (26:9), "he will remove the disgrace of his people from all the earth" (25:8), "cities of ruthless nations will revere" the Lord (25:3), "the LORD Almighty will prepare a feast of rich food for all peoples" (25:6), and he "will reign on Mount Zion and in Jerusalem and before its elders, gloriously" (24:23; cf. Mic 4:7).

Obadiah's God is sovereign over the nations of the earth. They may create chaos by mistreating God's people; they may seem to get by with impunity, but the day of the Lord will come and set things right. The Lord's sovereign reign will be established. J. Limburg identified some of the relevance of Obadiah to modern readers with his statement that "the Book of Obadiah brings an important message about oppressors and the oppressed, betrayers and those who have been betrayed. Arising out of a time of national crisis, it has a word for 'innocent bystanders' and also for survivors."[17] What at first glance can appear to be pure, primitive hate can be seen more correctly, upon close examination, to be God's punitive justice.[18]

───────────── *OUTLINE OF THE BOOK* ─────────────

I. The Lord's Pledge to Bring Edom Down (vv. 1–4)
1. Title (v. 1a)
2. Introduction (v. 1b)
3. Call to Battle (v. 1c)
4. Cut Down to Size (v. 2)
5. Deceived by Pride (v. 3)
6. Brought Down to Earth (v. 4)

II. The Lord's Promise to Destroy Edom (vv. 5–10)
1. Edom Completely Ransacked (vv. 5–6)
2. Edom Deceived by Allies (v. 7)
3. Edom's Wise Men Destroyed (v. 8)
4. Edom's Population Decimated (v. 9)
5. Edom Destroyed Forever (v. 10)

III. Edom's Wrongs against Judah (vv. 11–14)

---

[17] Ibid., 127.
[18] Wolff, *Obadiah and Jonah*, 22.

1. Acted Like a Foreigner Toward Judah (v. 11)
2. Rejoiced over Judah's Destruction (v. 12)
3. Looted Judah's Wealth (v. 13)
4. Sold Judah's Fugitives into Slavery (v. 14)

IV. The Coming Day of the Lord (vv. 15–21)
   1. A Day of Judgment on All Nations (vv. 15–16)
   2. A Day of Deliverance for the House of Jacob (vv. 17–18)
   3. A Day of Restoration of Israel (vv. 19–21)
     (1) On Expanded Territory (vv. 19–20)
     (2) Under the Lord's Rule (v. 21)

I. THE LORD'S PLEDGE TO BRING EDOM DOWN (vv. 1–4)
1. Title (v. 1a)
2. Introduction (v. 1b)
3. Call to Battle (v. 1c)
4. Cut Down to Size (v. 2)
5. Deceived by Pride (v. 3)
6. Brought Down to Earth (v. 4)

I. THE LORD'S PLEDGE TO BRING EDOM DOWN (vv. 1–4)

Whereas many prophetic books contain prophecies against foreign nations, the entire Book of Obadiah is a prophecy against Edom. Its components are typical of other prophecies against foreign nations:[1] (1) naming the enemy nation (v. 1), (2) warning about the coming doom of the enemy nation (vv. 2–18), (3) the Lord's intervention and punishment of the enemy (throughout the book), and (4) Israel's future ascendancy over the enemy (vv. 19–21). These first four verses introduce the prophecy and give the first announcement of Edom's doom.

1. Title (v. 1a)

[1]The vision of Obadiah.

1a In Hebrew the title is two words, *ḥăzôn ʿōbadĕyâ* (cf. Nah 1:1). The noun translated "vision" (*ḥăzōn*) is from a verbal root meaning "to see," or "to envision." The name "Obadiah" is from a root meaning "to serve," with a shortened form (*yâ*) of the covenant name for Israel's God, Yahweh. Thus the name means "servant (or worshiper) of Yahweh." "Vision" may describe the manner of reception of the message of God or simply the genre. What follows is a report of the word of the Lord concerning Edom, not accounts of prophetic visions about Edom.[2] The only other books called a *ḥăzôn* are Isaiah and

---

[1] See the chart in L. E. Cooper, Sr., *Ezekiel*, NAC (Nashville: Broadman & Holman, 1994), 244.

[2] R. Robinson, "Levels of Naturalization in Obadiah," *JSOT* 40 (1988): 88. H. Wolff commented that "חָזוֹן no longer means the process through which the prophet arrives at his perception or knowledge; it is simply the content of that knowledge itself: the revealed word" (*Obadiah and Jonah*, trans. M. Kohl [Minneapolis: Augsburg, 1986], 44).

Nahum. D. Stuart translated the term *ḥăzôn* as "revelation."[3] The two-word title, then, describes the contents of the book as a written record of a revelation from God received by the prophet Obadiah. Readers from ancient and current times have understood the Book of Obadiah to be more than a human product. Although God is not mentioned in the title, "vision" or "revelation" implies a message whose source is beyond the person named. The very next line in the verse gives the source as "the LORD." "Vision" as a genre designation alerts the reader to the theological significance and divine purpose of the book.

2. Introduction (v. 1b)

This is what the Sovereign LORD says about Edom—

1b The source of Obadiah's message was "the Sovereign LORD."[4] This divine title is not used anywhere else in the book. Among the prophets only in Ezekiel and Amos is it a rather common title. The placement of Obadiah after Amos in the canon may be based in part on this catchword,[5] although a more obvious linkage is provided by the mention of "the remnant of Edom" in Amos 9:12.

The subject of Obadiah's vision was Edom, and the dominant tone of his message was outrage. The preposition (*lĕ*) preceding the noun Edom may mean "for," "belonging to," "about," or "to" Edom,[6] but the direct address style in subsequent verses (vv. 2–16) argues for "to Edom" as the correct translation. This, however, is only a rhetorical device. In reality Obadiah was functioning as an emissary sent with the message of God to the Judahites concerning Edom.[7] Why? As Finley says, "As a part of Scripture, though, this small book is both a warning to nations and individuals who do not serve the Lord and a lesson for those who follow Him."[8]

3. Call to Battle (v. 1c)

We have heard a message from the LORD:
    An envoy was sent to the nations to say,
    "Rise, and let us go against her for battle"—

---

[3] D. Stuart, *Hosea-Jonah,* WBC (Waco: Word, 1987), 410.

[4] The term אֲדֹנָי, meaning "Lord," "Master," or "Sovereign," precedes יְהוָה, the personal name of Israel's covenant God.

[5] Stuart, *Hosea-Jonah,* 416.

[6] Similar to the NIV, Wolff translated the expression "concerning Edom" and understood the meaning to be a collection of sayings relating to Edom (Wolff, *Obadiah and Jonah,* 45). If "concerning" or "about" were the idea, however, we would expect the preposition עַל as in Mic 1:1.

[7] See Introduction, "The Author" on p. 169.

[8] T. Finley, *Joel, Amos, Obadiah* (Chicago: Moody, 1990), 354.

1c Here begins a passage (vv. 1c–4) that also is largely duplicated in Jer 49:14–16. Slight differences, however, show that one author adapted rather than quoted the other, or that both adapted earlier traditional material.[9] Since this third segment of v. 1 does not yet begin the Lord's message to Edom but is another level of introduction, the NIV has punctuated it as parenthetical.[10] The revelation Obadiah received began with a message he overheard the Lord sending to the nations surrounding Edom.[11] The message was entrusted to an envoy. It consisted of a call to attack Edom, which coming from the Lord amounted to an invitation (or command) to join him in the judgment of Edom for that nation's behavior against Judah.[12] With the first-person plural "we," Obadiah identified himself with the congregation in the circumstances faced after the fall of Jerusalem or with fellow prophets who also had heard a call to battle against Edom (Jer 49:14 reads "I have heard a message").[13] The call was from the one rallying the nations for service as his instrument to judge Edom.[14] The tense of the verb "was sent" indicates to the suffering community of Judah that the work of the "envoy" was already underway and, therefore, that God was at work. Already he had gone to the nations to rally support against Edom.

The Lord's call employs two different command forms (imperative and cohortative) of the same verb, *qûm*, meaning "to rise." It could be translated literally, "Rise! and let us rise!" The command reveals the urgency of the situation and a strong desire to secure a coalition of forces to wage war on Edom.[15] The setting for Obadiah's sermon may well have been a gathering of God's suffering people among the ruins of the temple in Jerusalem in 586 B.C.

4. Cut Down to Size (v. 2)

[2]**"See, I will make you small among the nations;**
you will be utterly despised.

---

[9] See the discussion in Finley, *Joel, Amos, Obadiah,* 342–45.

[10] B. C. Cresson suggested putting it in parentheses. See "Obadiah," BBC 7 (Nashville: Broadman, 1972), 146.

[11] According to M. B. Dick the content of the message or report that Obadiah heard is that "an envoy was sent to the nations." The *waw* of וְצִיר "introduces what was heard." See M. B. Dick, "A Syntactic Study of the Book Obadiah," *Semitics* 9 (1984): 8.

[12] According to Finley, Jer 49:14 gives the content of the envoy's message ("Assemble yourselves to attack it!"), and Obadiah gives the nation's response (*Joel, Amos, Obadiah,* 344).

[13] Wolff, *Obadiah and Jonah,* 46.

[14] צִיר is the word for messenger here. A plural form of the noun is rendered "envoys" in Isa 18:2. There it is in parallel with the more common word for messenger (מַלְאָךְ).

[15] The feminine suffix "against her" is curious since elsewhere Edom is regarded as masculine. Finley (*Joel, Amos, Obadiah,* 356) suggests that the feminine is used of the country and the masculine of the people, whereas Dick thinks the feminine may have been used "for its -*āh* assonance" ("A Syntactic Study of the Book Obadiah," 8).

This verse begins Obadiah's direct address to Edom. Essentially it is a message of Edom's destruction. The Lord himself pledged to bring Edom down from their lofty perch. Of course the message addressed to Edom was for Judah's ears.

2 The alert word translated "see" (*hinnê*) calls attention to a startling prophecy concerning Edom's destiny. "Small" is in the emphatic position preceding the verb.[16] The verb translated "will make" is a grammatical form normally used for past tense.[17] But in a context that deals with divine acts in the future, it can be understood to express that God has *determined* to do something. His divine nature thus assures the accomplishment of such actions as certain. In many cases the use of this tense can be understood in the context of the prophetic vision, in which the prophet has been transferred in his revelation into the future. From that perspective he views events as completed that for his audience are still unfulfilled. The implication is that the events so described are sure to occur.[18] Because of the context the NIV translators rendered it in future tense.

The first-person verb "I will make you" describes God's action. Edom's destiny under God's punishment would be to become small, decimated in population, and to be "utterly despised" (lit., "despised exceedingly"). They were destined to become insignificant, in sharp contrast to their exalted opinion of themselves. The Lord who controls all nations was the source of the call to rally the nations against Edom and the one whose actions would reduce Edom to insignificance. The word "small" (*qāṭōn*) is the same word used to describe Israel in Amos 7:2,5, where Amos pleads with God for mercy on Israel because of their helplessness. For Edom, however, there would be no intercession and no way to escape God's impending judgment. The Lord will reduce all who consider themselves great in their own right.

5. Deceived by Pride (v. 3)

³The pride of your heart has deceived you,
you who live in the clefts of the rocks
and make your home on the heights,

---

[16] It is ironic that Obadiah is also the smallest of the prophetic books.

[17] The function of verb tenses in Hebrew is a complex issue. The form referred to here is the *qātal* form, the perfective conjugation usually simply called the "perfect." For a summary of the issues see R. Buth, "The Hebrew Verb in Current Discussions," *JTT* 5 (1992): 91–105.

[18] This use of the verbal tense, then, has been traditionally referred to as the "prophetic perfect." See Robinson, "Levels of Naturalization in Obadiah," 90. R. J. Coggins suggested that the stress in so-called prophetic verbs is on "the inevitability of what is announced" (*Israel among the Nations: A Commentary on the Books of Nahum and Obadiah,* ITC (Grand Rapids: Eerdmans, 1985), 78). See also Waltke and O'Connor, *IBHS* § 30.5.1e (which mentions the term "prefective of confidence"); G. L. Klein, "The Prophetic Perfect," *JNSL* 15 (1990): 45–60.

you who say to yourself,
  'Who can bring me down to the ground?'

3 Edom's problem was pride. "The pride of your heart" is emphatic in the sentence by virtue of its placement ahead of the verb. The Edomites' haughty pride tricked them into believing they were self-sufficient. Pride was their preeminent sin, giving them false hope of being secure in their mountain fortress.

Edom's source of pride was where they lived, "in the clefts of the rocks" and in their "home on the heights." The two expressions suggest hiding places among their rocky settlements and secure location high in the mountains. They thought they were out of sight and out of reach. The term translated "rocks" (*sela*ᶜ) may be a pun on the name of Edom's capital city, Sela (cf. 2 Kgs 14:7; Isa 16:1; 42:11). Identification of Sela with Petra cannot be established absolutely for lack of adequate evidence.[19] Individuals, nations, and religious bodies must guard against the dangers of pride, which often creates the illusion of self-sufficiency. Edom affords an excellent illustration of Prov 16:18: "Pride goes before destruction, a haughty spirit before a fall."

God knew what the people of Edom thought of themselves, as reflected in their haughty boast, "Who can bring me down to the ground?" "No one" is the answer they expected, but Edom had failed to reckon with the knowledge of God and the judgment of God. The nation thought no one could conquer them, but God vowed to bring them down. Lillie commented, "Drunk on pride and deceived by a false sense of security, Edom will tumble from its heights and become an object of derision among the nations."[20] The real answer to the question is "God can!" And God did.

6. Brought Down to Earth (v. 4)

⁴Though you soar like the eagle
  and make your nest among the stars,
 from there I will bring you down,"
            declares the LORD.

4 Obadiah compared Edom with the eagle, a bird known to soar high in the air and to nest in the mountain heights. From such lofty heights the eagle customarily launched deadly attacks on its victims below. Edom had been accustomed to doing that. Like the eagle Edom felt secure, even unconquerable. Obadiah's God had no fear of heights and had no difficulty scaling the heights. "From there" means "from the very places Edom counted safe and

---

[19] Ibid., 79; W. M. Fanwar, "Sela," *ABD* 5.1073–74.
[20] J. R. Lillie, "Obadiah—A Celebration of God's Kingdom," in *Currents in Theology and Mission* 6 [1979]: 19.

out of reach." To those very places God vowed to go and to bring Edom down. The authority and power behind Edom's fall would be God, though he might choose to use some military force to bring about Edom's destruction. Cresson referred to such a prideful attitude as "spiritually suicidal."[21] Similarly, God vowed to cast down the king of Babylon from his starry heights (Isa 14:12–15).

The message directed to Edom begins with the messenger formula (v. 1b) and ends with the oracle formula, "declares the LORD" (v. 4). Obadiah was the messenger. His message came from God with the authority of God. In spite of its formal address to Edom, the message was designed to assure Judah that God would deal effectively with Edom and that Judah would rise to ascendancy over Edom.

---

[21] Cresson, "Obadiah," 7:147.

II. THE LORD'S PROMISE TO DESTROY EDOM (vv. 5–10)
  1. Edom Completely Ransacked (vv. 5–6)
  2. Edom Deceived by Allies (v. 7)
  3. Edom's Wise Men Destroyed (v. 8)
  4. Edom's Population Decimated (v. 9)
  5. Edom Destroyed Forever (v. 10)

II. THE LORD'S PROMISE TO DESTROY EDOM (vv. 5–10)

Following the first announcement of Edom's doom in vv. 1–4, the extent and manner of their destruction is described in vv. 5–7. Then a second announcement of doom, this time focusing on the people of Edom, is given in vv. 8–9. Verse 10 serves as a bridge from the subject of Edom's destruction to the subject of Edom's wrongs against Judah. The first part of the verse introduces the theme of Edom's wrongs against Judah. Edom's complete destruction is the closing thought in the verse. The prominent name for Edom in this section of the text (vv. 5–10) is the eponymous ancestor Esau.

1. Edom Completely Ransacked (vv. 5–6)

> **5"If thieves came to you,**
>   **if robbers in the night—**
> **Oh, what a disaster awaits you—**
>   **would they not steal only as much as they wanted?**
> **If grape pickers came to you,**
>   **would they not leave a few grapes?**
> **6But how Esau will be ransacked,**
>   **his hidden treasures pillaged!**

Verses 5–6 consist of a comparison in the form of a how-much-more argument. Thieves and grape pickers left more behind than Edom would have after it had been completely ransacked.

5 Verse 5 consists of two rhetorical questions introduced by the conditional particle (ʾ*im*, "if"). The term is used three times in the verse, but the first two uses go together to express one conditional question. The questions present two hypothetical cases of typical experience. They call for the

185

Edomites to reflect upon their own knowledge of what thieves would do if they broke into their homes and what grape pickers would do if they went into the vineyards. What do night robbers (lit., "robbers of the night") do? Do they steal everything in the house? No! They take only what they consider valuable and can carry away. The owner would suffer only partial loss.

The prophet could not wait to describe the complete destruction of Edom. He had to insert a hint of it before he finished his rhetorical questions. "Oh, what a disaster awaits you" is an exclamation of imminent judgment. The introductory particle *ʾēk* is typically a cry of mourning (2 Sam 1:19). The only other word in the parenthetical expression in Hebrew is a verb meaning "it has been destroyed." Edom will meet a violent end (cf. Isa 15:1; Jer 47:5; Hos 4:6; Zeph 1:11).[1] Grammatically, the verb here is a prophetic perfect, meaning that the outcome is certain (see comment at v. 2). The expected answer to the rhetorical question is yes: thieves would steal "only as much as they wanted." The purpose of the two conditional questions is to set up the contrast with what Esau would experience. Edom would be totally sacked, not partially.

The second conditional question concerns the habit of grape pickers. Harvesters of grapes do not strip the vineyards clean. They "leave a few grapes" here and there. Some grapes would be left on purpose, perhaps, as gleanings for the poor. Or in haste to get the harvest in, some grapes would be missed.

6 In contrast with the partial loss to thieves and the partial harvest of grapes, Edom would be stripped clean. This verse begins by repeating the exclamatory particle (*ʾēk*). The verbs are still prophetic perfects describing the certainty of what will happen to Edom in the future. Having been brought down from their lofty perch (v. 4), Edom would be "ransacked" (*neḥpěśû*). The verb means to "search out" (cf. Amos 9:3). This language along with the subsequent descriptions imply warfare as the way God would judge Edom. An enemy nation would search out Edom, making a thorough check.

The purpose of the search of Edom would be to locate the nation's "hidden treasures." Edom's mountains afforded numerous places to hide the loot taken in raids or the tax from transporting goods along roads controlled by Edom. Edom thought their treasures were secure. But the prophet said such treasures would be "pillaged."[2]

2. Edom Deceived by Allies (v. 7)

> [7]All your allies will force you to the border;
> your friends will deceive and overpower you;

---

[1] T. Finley, *Joel, Amos, Obadiah* (Chicago: Moody, 1990), 359–60.

[2] According to KB[3] (Eng. ed., 1:141) the verb בָּעָה (I) is found elsewhere only in an oracle against Edom in Isa 21:12. There it is a *qal* meaning "ask."

those who eat your bread will set a trap for you,
but you will not detect it.

7 This verse explains how God would lure the Edomites down from their
secure heights. He would have their allies turn against them and "deceive"
them (note the same verb is used in v. 3).[3] Edom's loss of material wealth
(v. 6) would not be as damaging as loss of support from allies. "All your
allies" is literally "all the men of your covenant." It is parallel to "your
friends," which is literally "men of your peace," and "your bread," a figurative expression translated "those who eat your bread."[4] Reference here is to a
nation or nations with whom Edom had a treaty of peace. One would expect
such nations could be depended upon to be loyal, at least to the point of carrying out the agreements entered into with the covenant partner. But that would
not be the case for Edom's covenant partners. Edom would have no one to
answer their appeals for help. The answer of covenant partners would be to
send Edom to the border empty-handed. "Will force you" is from an intensive
form of the verb meaning "send out" (cf. Gen 3:23). J. R. Bartlett concluded
that "the allies and confederates of v. 7 can hardly be any other than the Babylonians."[5]

The term translated "trap" (*māzôr*) probably came from the Hebrew verb
zûr, "be a stranger," or "be a foreigner."[6] Nouns of this form are usually
abstracts or nouns of place. *Māzôr* probably means "place of foreigners." The
idea in context seems to be that Edom would be displaced by foreigners.

Archaeological and biblical evidence point to some time in the sixth cen-
tury B.C. for the fulfillment of Obadiah's prophecy of Edom's destruction.
N. Glueck based his dating of the final Edomite period on his work at Tell el-
Kheleifeh.[7] Obadiah prophesied deportation for Edom (v. 7). Nabonidus,
Babylonian ruler from 555 to 539 B.C., campaigned in southern Transjordan
and northern Arabia in 552 B.C. He may have been the ally-turned-enemy. By

---

[3] M. B. Dick believes that "deceive" and "overpower" form a hendiadys as similar verbs do in
Jer 38:22 ("A Syntactic Study of the Book Obadiah," 9).

[4] C. E. Armerding, "Obadiah," EBC 7, ed. F. E. Gaebelein (Grand Rapids: Zondervan, 1985),
345–46.

[5] J. R. Bartlett, *Edom and the Edomites,* JSOTSup 77 (Sheffield: JSOT Press, 1989), 159. Others suggest the Persians (Finley, *Joel, Amos, Obadiah,* 360).

[6] P. K. McCarter, "Obadiah 7 and the Fall of Edom," *BASOR* 221 (1976): 87–88. Finley
derives it, however, from מזר, "to weave" or "twist" (*Joel, Amos, Obadiah,* 360).

[7] N. Glueck, *The Other Side of the Jordan* (Cambridge, Mass.: American Schools of Oriental
Research, 1970), 126. McCarter concluded his discussion of dating the destruction of Edom with
these observations: "The precise date of the final expulsion of the Edomites is undetermined, but
is placed late in the sixth century by general agreement. The archaeological evidence, still regret-
tably meager, shows the last part of that century to have been a period of general collapse in
Edomite culture" ("Obadiah 7 and the Fall of Edom," 89). He rejects the prophetic character of
the book, however, and uses the destruction of Edom referred to there to date Obadiah.

the latter third of the fifth century B.C., or perhaps earlier, the destruction of Edom was complete (Mal 1:3–5), and their homeland was occupied by the Nabatean Arabs.

Finley has pointed out the irony in the final line, which is literally "and there is no understanding in it." "Understanding" is often used as a synonym for "wisdom," for which Edom was well known (cf. Job 2:11; Jer 49:7).[8] God is able to confound worldly wisdom and show the folly of those who reject him (cf. v. 8; 2 Sam 15:31; Isa 29:14; Jer 8:9; 9:23–24; 1 Cor 1:18–31; 3:19; Jas 3:13). B. Dicou interprets the final clause to mean that "the Edomites do not even realize that their end is near."[9]

3. Edom's Wise Men Destroyed (v. 8)

> [8]"In that day," declares the LORD,
>   "will I not destroy the wise men of Edom,
>   men of understanding in the mountains of Esau?

8 The rhetorical question raised in v. 8 demands a yes answer. "In that day" is prophetic language for a future intervention of God in human affairs (cf. Amos 2:16; 8:3,9,13; 9:11). Here it refers to the time of God's judgment of Edom (cf. v. 15). B. Dicou observes that the "day" of Edom's judgment is retaliation for their part in the "day" of Israel's doom referred to ten times in vv. 11–14.[10] R. B. Robinson has correctly understood "day" to be a reference "not to an actual day in realistic [historical] time, but to the eschatological day, that envisioned and visionary day when God will judge all nations."[11] Edom's failure to understand the deception of their allies (v. 7) would be associated with God's destruction of the nation's wise men (v. 8). "Men of understanding" is translated to parallel "the wise men" in the second line, but there is no word for "men of" in the Hebrew. More than just the wise men, God will destroy all pretense of wisdom and understanding in Edom.

4. Edom's Population Decimated (v. 9)

> [9]Your warriors, O Teman, will be terrified,
>   and everyone in Esau's mountains
>   will be cut down in the slaughter.

9 Teman, the name of a major city and of the northern district in Edom, is

---

[8] Finley, *Joel, Amos, Obadiah*, 361.

[9] B. Dicou, *Edom, Israel's Brother and Antagonist: The Role of Edom in Biblical Prophecy and Story*, JSOTSup 169 (Sheffield: JSOT Press, 1994), 27.

[10] Ibid.

[11] R. Robinson, "Levels of Naturalization in Obadiah," *JSOT* 40 (1988): 91.

a synonym of Edom in v. 9 (cf. Jer 49:20). The verb translated "terrified" (*ḥattû*) can also mean "be shattered" or "dashed to pieces" (cf. 1 Sam 2:10; Isa 7:8). Either physical or psychological destruction in the face of imminent disaster is the idea of the verb. Those to be so affected were Edom's mightiest, bravest men, their best soldiers (*gibbôrêkā*, "your mighty men"). The result is given in the remainder of the verse, which is introduced in Hebrew by the conjunction *lĕmaʿan*, "so that" (translated here "and").[12] Jeremiah compared the dismay of Edom's warriors to that of a woman in labor (Jer 49:22). The word translated "everyone" is the word for "each" (*ʾîš*) and emphasizes the thoroughness of the slaughter of those who are not driven out of Edom (v. 7). After shattering the army, Edom's whole population would be decimated.[13]

5. Edom Destroyed Forever (v. 10)

[10]Because of the violence against your brother Jacob,
    you will be covered with shame;
    you will be destroyed forever.

Verse 10 may close the pericope beginning with v. 5, or it may open the passage concerned with Edom's mistreatment of "Jacob,"[14] here meaning the Southern Kingdom of Judah (vv. 11–14). The verse provides a transition from a description of the judgment of God upon Edom to the citation of various wrongs Edom committed against Judah. This may be emphasized by the formal similarity between the last word of v. 9, *miqqāṭel,* literally "from slaughter," which describes Edom's penalty, and the first word in v. 10, *mēḥāmas,* literally "from violence," which describes Edom's sin. The earlier detailed linkage with Jeremiah 49 is absent from this point on with only a partial exception in v. 16, where the theme corresponds with Jer 49:12.[15]

10 The charge of "violence" may be an accusation of general hostility against Jacob's descendants rather than of some recent atrocity. But whatever the nature of the offense, Edom's penalty would be utter humiliation. Proud Edom would be "covered with shame." And worse even than total shame, the

---

[12] See *IBHS* § 38.3b.

[13] Finley (*Joel, Amos, Obadiah,* 362–63) notes that v. 9 may be hyperbolic. He points to such apparent hyperbole in 1 Kgs 11:15–16, which says that under David's command Joab "struck down all the men in Edom." Yet there continued to be men in Edom after this (1 Kgs 22:47; 2 Kgs 3:9,26; 8:20–22).

[14] Use of "Jacob" here reminds the reader/listener of the struggle of the twins, Jacob and Esau. Esau's line became Edom, and Jacob's line became Israel/Judah. See Finley, *Joel, Amos, Obadiah,* 363–64.

[15] Cf. R. J. Coggins, *Israel among the Nations: A Commentary on the Books of Nahum and Obadiah,* ITC (Grand Rapids: Eerdmans, 1985), 84.

nation would "be destroyed forever." The verb here is from the same root (*kārat*) as the verb translated "cut down" in v. 9. To be cut down forever would mean no future as a nation. The kinship between Jacob and Esau made Edom's violence against Judah even more reprehensible.[16] "Brother" refers to blood relationship between Judah and Edom rather than a contractual relationship between partners to a treaty.[17]

As it will become clear in v. 15, theologically Edom represents the enemy of God's people in all generations, as well as perpetual world power over against God. The ultimate destiny of such enemies is destruction. God is unalterably opposed to such enemies. No mountain is high enough, no fortress is strong enough, no military force is large enough, and no hiding place is dark enough to secure such an enemy from the judgment of God.

---

[16] B. K. Smith, "Obadiah," LBBC 13 (Nashville: Broadman, 1982), 134.

[17] Wolff, *Obadiah and Jonah,* trans. M. Kohl (Minneapolis: Augsburg, 1986), 52. Dicou observes that Obadiah is "the only one of the four major oracles against Edom [the others being Isa 34; Jer 49:7–22; Ezek 35] in which Edom is called Israel's brother (*Edom, Israel's Brother and Antagonist,* 16). It is mentioned, however, in Hos 12:3 and Amos 1:9,11.

III. EDOM'S WRONGS AGAINST JUDAH (vv. 11–14)
1. Acted Like a Foreigner toward Judah (v. 11)
2. Rejoiced over Judah's Destruction (v. 12)
3. Looted Judah's Wealth (v. 13)
4. Sold Judah's Fugitives into Slavery (v. 14)

III. EDOM'S WRONGS AGAINST JUDAH (vv. 11–14)

What Edom was told not to do to Judah is just what they had done.[1] Edom's attitudes and actions displayed toward Judah during a time of calamity in Judah and Jerusalem were unbrotherly at best. In fact the stance they took and the deeds they performed were beastly. Yet the forefathers of Judah and Edom were indeed brothers.

The most likely time of Edom's atrocities against Judah was during and/or just after Nebuchadnezzar's siege and destruction of Jerusalem and Judah in 587 B.C.[2] For brothers to fight under any circumstances is bad enough. But for Edom to pounce on Judah after Babylon had flattened them and left them helpless and undefended was reprehensible.

1. Acted Like a Foreigner toward Judah (v. 11)

¹¹On the day you stood aloof
while strangers carried off his wealth
and foreigners entered his gates
and cast lots for Jerusalem,
you were like one of them.

11 "Day" (*yôm*) is the dominant word in vv. 11–14, used (in the Heb. text) ten times ("while" in v. 11 is lit., "on the day"). This term designates a historical time when Jerusalem fell to the Babylonians. The climax of Obadiah's use of the term "day" comes with the announcement that this day is

---

[1] The NRSV and GNB translate the prohibitions here "you should not have . . ." See also R. J. Coggins, *Israel among the Nations: A Commentary on the Books of Nahum and Obadiah,* ITC (Grand Rapids: Eerdmans, 1985), 87. But D. J. Clark suggests: "Could it be that the prophet pictures the people of Edom as mentally reliving their moment of vindictive triumph . . . and tells them to stop doing it?" ("Obadiah Reconsidered," *BT* 42 [1991]: 333).

[2] See Introduction.

the "day of the LORD" (v. 15), which in the prophets is a time when God's
enemies (including unbelieving Israel) will be judged and his people restored
and blessed (cf. Amos 5:18–20 and comments there).[3]

The first word of indictment against Edom pictures them in a stance of non-
involvement. They "stood aloof." The term translated "aloof" (*minneged*, lit.,
"from opposite") suggests not only distance but also opposition (cf. 2 Sam
18:13, "kept *your distance*"). J. A. Thompson suggests the meaning "stood in
opposition."[4] This interpretation fits with the closing phrase describing Edom
as "like one of them." Edom acted like Babylon, an enemy, not like a brother.
Help was needed because strangers were carrying off the wealth of Jerusalem,
but Edom did not lift one finger to help. Their behavior showed that they were
on the side of their brother's enemies. Refusing to come to the aid of someone
in need is the same as rendering the harm yourself (cf. Luke 10:30–37).

As vv. 13–14 show, Edom acted like buzzards circling a dying animal,
waiting until Babylon soundly defeated Judah and Jerusalem. The siege of
Jerusalem lasted about eighteen months (2 Kgs 25:1–8). When the city fell,
Nebuchadnezzar's forces moved in with a vengeance to destroy, kill, and pil-
lage. Then when they were finished, Judah's kinsmen moved in to loot, to capture fugitives to sell as slaves, and to kill those who fled from the destruction.

2. Rejoiced over Judah's Destruction (v. 12)

[12]**You should not look down on your brother**
     in the day of his misfortune,
  nor rejoice over the people of Judah
     in the day of their destruction,
  nor boast so much
     in the day of their trouble.

12 This verse begins a series of eight prohibitions in vv. 12–14 (lit., "do
not . . ."). They employ the form of an immediate prohibition (using the negative particle *'al*) rather than that of a general prohibition (using the negative
particle *lō'*). This does not imply that there are times when such an attitude is
acceptable, however, but that a specific instance is in view.[5] Only three of the
prohibitions are translated "you should not" (at the beginning of vv. 12,13,
and 14).[6] Translating all of them the same and lining them up would give a
similar effect in English to the effect of the Hebrew text:

---

[3] Coggins, *Israel among the Nations*, 85.

[4] J. A. Thompson, "The Book of Obadiah," *IB* VI (New York: Abingdon, 1956), 863–64.

[5] D. Stuart, *Hosea-Jonah,* WBC (Waco: Word, 1987), 419.

[6] The translation of the other prohibitions is "nor," twice in v. 12, twice in v. 13, and once in
v. 14.

You should not look down on your brother . . .
You should not rejoice over the people of Judah . . .
You should not boast so much . . .
You should not march through the gates of my people . . .
You should not look down on them in their calamity . . .
You should not seize their wealth . . .
You should not wait at the crossroads to cut down their fugitives . . .
You should not hand over their survivors . . .

J. Lillie described the impact Obadiah's repeated language pattern may have had on the listeners: "The cadence is that of the incessant beat of a drummer leading troops into battle."[7] Surely Obadiah's Judahite audience would have applauded to hear their God call the Edomites to account for their treacherous actions. If in self-pity Israel had wondered before whether the Lord had noticed the wrongs they were suffering, surely Obadiah put an end to their feelings of abandonment.

The three prohibitions in v. 12 unveil Edom's outrageously smug and presumptuous attitude toward Judah. The first is literally "do not look on the day of your brother in the day of his misfortune." The term "misfortune" (*nōker,* related to the word translated "foreigners" in v. 11) occurs only here and in Job 31:3, where it is parallel to a word meaning "disaster" (cf. v. 13; Deut 32:35). Here the parallel with words for "destruction" and "trouble" make the sense quite clear. In the context the verb "look" (*rā'â*) implies more than simple observation (cf. Gen 9:22), as reflected in the translation "look down on" (NIV) or "gloated over" (RSV). The word "boast" translates an expression, "make great your mouth," whose sense probably is to "make yourself out to be great with your mouth." It involves an attitude of superiority having compared oneself to someone else. Such an attitude based upon the misfortune of others is bad enough in itself, but toward a brother it is worse. Unfortunately, there is a sinful human tendency toward such self-evaluation based on external circumstances. God's judgment was to demonstrate that Edom's opinion of itself was premature and inaccurate.

3. Looted Judah's Wealth (v. 13)

[13]You should not march through the gates of my people
   in the day of their disaster,
nor look down on them in their calamity
   in the day of their disaster,
nor seize their wealth
   in the day of their disaster.

---

[7] J. Lillie, "Obadiah—A Celebration of God's Kingdom," in *Currents in Theology and Mission* 6 (1979): 20.

13 Three more prohibitions are given in v. 13. Babylon had battered down the gates of Jerusalem and entered to plunder the city (v. 11). Edom took advantage of Judah's vulnerable position and entered ("marched" is the same verb translated "entered" in v. 11) the city with the same evil intent. They gloated over (lit., "looked on," as in v. 12) Judah's "calamity," greedy for their wealth. They chose a day of disaster for Judah to express their gloating attitude and to perform their greedy act. Three times in the verse the phrase "in the day of their disaster" punctuates the account. The wordplay in the Hebrew text between the term translated "their disaster" (ʾêdām) and Edom is lost in English translations. The point of the wordplay may be that what appeared to be a day of disaster for Israel would ultimately prove to be a day of disaster for Edom.[8] When Edom looked upon Judah's disaster, they were in effect looking into a mirror.

Not only was Edom's act barbarous and inhuman; not only was it treacherous; it was also sacrilege. When they entered the gates of "my people," they were violating God's own possession by covenant. Judah was not just any people. They were special. They were the "apple of his eye" (Deut 32:10; Zech 2:8), and God would not take lightly this violation on the part of foreigners or of Edom.

4. Sold Judah's Fugitives into Slavery (v. 14)

[14]You should not wait at the crossroads
to cut down their fugitives,
nor hand over their survivors
in the day of their trouble.

14 The two prohibitions in v. 14 are that Edom was not to "wait" (from ʿāmad, "stand") in ambush to kill those Judahites fleeing Jerusalem, nor were they to capture them to "hand over" (causative of sāgar, "shut") to the Babylonians or to slave traders (cf. Amos 1:6,9).[9] The victims of Edom's actions were citizens or soldiers (or both) fleeing from Jerusalem in the wake of Nebuchadnezzar's attack. Judeans would have been panic stricken and helpless to defend themselves.

What Edom did to others would be done to them (v. 15). They too would be "destroyed" (v. 10, the same verb as the one here translated "cut down"). Edom deserved the judgment of God because of their deplorable attitudes and actions toward their brothers, who were in addition God's people.

---

[8] Coggins, *Israel among the Nations*, 88.
[9] B. C. Cresson, "Obadiah," BBC 7 (Nashville: Broadman, 1972), 149. Thompson pointed out that this was not the first time for Edom to be involved in Israelite slave trade ("The Book of Obadiah," 864).

IV. THE COMING DAY OF THE LORD (vv. 15–21)
1. A Day of Judgment on All Nations (vv. 15–16)
2. A Day of Deliverance for the House of Jacob (vv. 17–18)
3. A Day of Restoration of Israel (vv. 19–21)

IV. THE COMING DAY OF THE LORD (vv. 15–21)

Amos had clarified what the day of the Lord would mean for the eighth-century nation of Israel (Amos 5:18–20). The day would not bring deliverance and blessing to them as they supposed. Rather, the day would be dark with defeat and destruction. But for sixth-century Judah, Obadiah presented the eschatological significance of the day. The day of the Lord's intervention would result in the destruction of all God's (and Israel's) enemies, represented by the paradigm nation of Edom,[1] and the exaltation of God's people, Israel. Obadiah set God's judgment of Edom in a broad context of judgment upon all nations. As C. E. Armerding has written, v. 15 "provides a theological framework for the preceding verses: the localized disasters befalling Edom and Jerusalem are not merely isolated incidents in a remote and insignificant theater of war, for they mark the footsteps of the Lord himself as he approaches to set up a 'kingdom that will never be destroyed' (Dan 2:44)."[2]

The widespread opinion that the two parts of v. 15 are in the wrong order[3] is not well founded. To follow vv. 11–14, which emphasizes the "day" of Judah's disaster, with this announcement that "the day of the LORD is near" seems completely logical.[4] Neither does the changed emphasis require a different author. The book is best interpreted as the work of one author (see the Introduction).

The day of the Lord will bring about two things. First, judgment will come

---

[1] D. W. Baker, *Obadiah: An Introduction and Commentary,* TOTC (Downers Grove: Inter-Varsity, 1988), 39. According to M. H. Woudstra, Edom had this significance for Ezekiel as well ("Edom and Israel in Ezekiel," *CTJ* 3 [1968]: 21–35). See also J. R. Bartlett, *Edom and the Edomites,* JSOTSup 77 (Sheffield, Eng.: Sheffield Academic Press, 1989), 184–86.

[2] C. E. Armerding, "Obadiah," EBC 7 (Grand Rapids: Zondervan, 1985), 353.

[3] Cf. L. C. Allen, *The Books of Joel, Obadiah, Jonah, and Micah,* NICOT (Grand Rapids: Eerdmans, 1983).

[4] See D. J. Clark, "Obadiah Reconsidered," *BT* 42 (1991): 331. He explains that vv. 15b–16 describe "the specific application" of the general principle of the day of the Lord to the Edomites. He also notes a chiasmus in vv. 15–16: of all nations / you / you / all nations.

195

on those who do not acknowledge Yahweh's lordship over all creation and submit to him in faith. Second, the "kingdom" of God will be established.[5]

1. A Day of Judgment on All Nations (vv. 15–16)

[15]"The day of the LORD is near
   for all nations.
As you have done, it will be done to you;
   your deeds will return upon your own head.
[16]Just as you drank on my holy hill,
   so all the nations will drink continually;
they will drink and drink
   and be as if they had never been.

15 Verses 15 and 16 both begin with the Hebrew particle *kî*, "for," indicating that they give the reason Edom would regret their behavior toward Judah—the approaching day of the Lord. The first feature of the day of the Lord that Obadiah mentions is its imminence. The day was "near." That fact was good news for sixth-century Judah with its implications of reversal for their plight. They had suffered a humiliating defeat at the hands of the Babylonians. Edom's attitudes and actions had added to Judah's sorrows, so they yearned for the Lord's intervention in their behalf.[6] But the day would not be welcome news for the enemies of God.

The second feature of the day of the Lord in Obadiah's treatment of it was its universal dimension. "All nations" would be affected by the day. With this emphasis Obadiah set Edom's judgment in the larger context of judgment upon all the nations. Worthy of note are the striking parallels between Obadiah 15–21 and Joel 3. The judgment of God in both contexts is against "all nations," and the outcome of judgment in both is the destruction of God's enemies and the exaltation of God's people.

Third, their punishment would fit the crime.[7] A review of what Edom had done to Judah would form a mirror image of what God's judgment would be like.[8] The singular verbs and pronouns in v. 15 may state a general principle applicable to all nations;[9] however, they seem to point specifically toward Edom's mistreatment of Judah. What Edom did to Judah would be done to

---

[5] T. Finley, *Joel, Amos, Obadiah* (Chicago: Moody, 1990), 370.

[6] This message is similar to that found in Isa 13:6; Ezek 30:3; Joel 3:14, which also announce the nearness of the day of the Lord. But its nearness is announced in Joel 1:15; Zeph 1:7,14 in a context of judgment against Israel.

[7] Cf. D. Stuart, *Hosea-Jonah*, WBC (Waco: Word, 1987), 420.

[8] H. W. Wolff, *Obadiah and Jonah* (Minneapolis: Augsburg, 1986), 57.

[9] See P. D. Miller, Jr., *Sin and Judgment in the Prophets* (Chico, Cal.: Scholars Press, 1982), 130–31.

Edom. "Your deeds" (a singular noun taken collectively with a second mascu-line singular pronominal suffix) in the larger context refers to Edom's mis-treatment of Judah. But the typical usage of the word (gemûl) affirms the general principle that divine retribution awaits those who commit iniquity and that it will match their deeds.[10] There will be no "unrequited wickedness," nor will punishment exceed the crime.[11] Obadiah does not reveal who would administer the returning deeds on the head of Edom, but clearly the Lord would be in charge of whoever did it.

Edom represents all nations in every generation that are opposed to God and to God's people. Ultimately all attacks of the nations against God and his people will meet with defeat. God will judge all such nations with the same atrocities those nations have inflicted upon God's people.

16 Apparently Edom drank in celebration of Babylon's victory over Jerusalem.[12] Actually two different images have converged in the verse[13] that continue the theme from v. 15 of just recompense: just as the nations stag-gered with drunkenness from the wine of victory as they celebrated their con-quest of God's people, they will stagger from the wine of God's judgment (cf. Ps 75:8; Isa 51:17,22; Jer 25:17; Hab 2:15–16; Mark 14:36; Rev 14:10; 16:19).[14] The cup Jerusalem drank would pass into the hands of their torment-ers.[15] "My holy hill" (lit., "the mountain of my holiness") refers to Mount Zion (vv. 17,21), in a narrow sense the temple mount in Jerusalem and more broadly the city where God had chosen to "dwell" (cf. v. 17; Ps 2:6; Isa 8:18; Joel 2:1; 3:17; Zeph 3:11). Just as the nations had violated God's special pos-session, Israel (v. 13), they had also profaned his special place, Jerusalem, and celebrated their victory there.

The term "continually" and the expression to "drink and drink" points to wave after wave of God's punishment. As Jeremiah assured Judah in Lam 4:21–22, Edom's time of rejoicing was over. Although Judah's punishment

---

[10] Cf. Judg 9:16; Pss 28:4; 59:2; Isa 3:11; 35:4; 59:18; 66:6; Jer 51:6,56; Joel 3:4,7. See also K. Seybold, גָּמַל gamal, TDOT 3.23–33. He defines the term as "an act that one performs inten-tionally and deliberately toward his fellow man" (p. 28) and "a responsible and significant act which ought to be repaid" (p. 29).

[11] Baker, Obadiah, 38.

[12] Armerding, however, interprets the switch to second-person plural "you drank" as the sole address to Judah ("Obadiah," 7:353; see also GNB). But it more likely refers to Edom and the nations, especially in view of the logical connection to the previous prohibitions by the particle כִּי. See Clark, "Obadiah Reconsidered," 330–31; J. D. W. Watts, Obadiah: A Critical Exegetical Commentary (Grand Rapids: Eerdmans, 1969), 56; Baker, Obadiah, 39.

[13] R. J. Coggins, Israel among the Nations: A Commentary on the Books of Nahum and Oba-diah, ITC (Grand Rapids: Eerdmans, 1985), 91.

[14] Watts, Obadiah, 58.

[15] Wolff, Obadiah and Jonah, 65; B. C. Cresson, "Obadiah," BBC 7 (Nashville: Broadman, 1972), 150.

and exile would end, such would not be the case when the cup passed to
Edom and they suffered shameful exposure and judgment for their sins. As
the "clamor" and "uproar" of God's enemies had risen, mocking him "continually" (Ps 74:23), so they would endure lasting punishment. The second verb
for "drink" in the expression (*lāʿû*) means "slurp" or "drink noisily"[16] and
"underlines the torture of having to drink without stopping."[17] The end for
Edom and all the nations is spelled out in the final line of v. 16: they will "be
as if they had never been." This does not refer to an unbeliever's loss of personal existence but to the complete destruction of the national entities that had
opposed the Lord (cf. Jer 25:9,18). After Israel received their just punishment
from the Lord, Edom and the nations would experience the day of the Lord
(cf. Isa 10:12).

2. A Day of Deliverance for the House of Jacob (vv. 17–18)

> [17]But on Mount Zion will be deliverance;
>   it will be holy,
>   and the house of Jacob
>   will possess its inheritance.
> [18]The house of Jacob will be a fire
>   and the house of Joseph a flame;
>   the house of Esau will be stubble,
>   and they will set it on fire and consume it.
>   There will be no survivors
>   from the house of Esau."
>   The LORD has spoken.

Judahites attempting to escape the Babylonian attack were intercepted by
Edom and mistreated. No escape was allowed them. But in the day of the
Lord, their roles would be reversed. Mount Zion (God's "holy hill" in v. 16),
where Judah received judgment from God and their "fugitives" (*pĕlîṭāyw*)
were cut down (v. 14), would be the very spot where "deliverance" (*pĕlêṭâ*, a
related word) would come.

17 Mount Zion, which God loved (Ps 78:68), had become the scene of
destruction for Judah (cf. Lam 5:18), but it would now become the place of
Judah's deliverance (cf. Joel 2:32). The place of God's dwelling, desecrated
by foreigners (cf. Ps 74:7), would "be holy" again. The Lord would answer
the psalmist's prayer and "remember the people you purchased of old, the
tribe of your inheritance, whom you redeemed—Mount Zion, where you
dwelt" (Ps 74:2). Mount Zion also would be restored to the house of Jacob as

---

[16] *CHAL*, 178.
[17] Wolff, *Obadiah and Jonah*, 65.

the center of their rightful inheritance,[18] once again "beautiful in its loftiness, the joy of the whole earth" (Ps 48:2); and "Mount Zion, which cannot be shaken but endures forever" (Ps 125:1), where the Lord "bestows his blessing, even life forevermore" (Ps 133:3; cf. Heb 12:22).

18 Fire is one means of divine punishment in the Old Testament (cf. Exod 15:7; Isa 10:17; Joel 2:5; Amos 1:4,7,10,12,14; 2:2,5). The house of Jacob will serve as God's "fire," and the house of Joseph (Jacob's prominent son) will serve as God's torch ("flame").[19] These parallel lines identify God's reunited people (Judah and Israel) as the instrument of judgment on Edom (cf. Pss 77:15; 81:4–5; Jer 3:18; Ezek 37:16–28). The house of Esau will be "stubble," subject to the flame of God's judgment. "Set . . . on fire and consume" describes the thoroughgoing judgment God would execute on Edom. "No survivors" for Esau is a dismal prospect.[20] The authority for Obadiah's harsh message of judgment against Edom was that the Lord had "spoken." Just as the word of God created in the beginning (Gen 1:3), the word of God would now destroy.

God punished Judah for turning from him. He does not countenance sin in his people. At the same time God will provide a way of escape for those who will hear and heed his word (cf. Isa 37:32).[21] Judah's deliverance and Edom's destruction are matching sides of the whole picture of the coming day of the Lord.

3. A Day of Restoration of Israel (vv. 19–21)

[19]People from the Negev will occupy
     the mountains of Esau,
and people from the foothills will possess
     the land of the Philistines.
They will occupy the fields of Ephraim and Samaria,

---

[18] A textual variant, מוֹרִישֵׁיהֶם, "those dispossessing them," for the MT מוֹרָשֵׁיהֶם, "their possessions" ("its inheritance"), is reflected in the versions and followed by some (REB, Wolff, Stuart, *Hosea-Jonah,* 411–13). Though this reading is supported by the scroll of the Minor Prophets found at Murabba'at near the Dead Sea and may be right, it is rejected by many. See Watts, *Obadiah,* 60; M. B. Dick, "A Syntactic Study of the Book of Obadiah," *Semitics* 9 (1984): 10; Finley, *Joel, Amos, Obadiah,* 378–79. B. Dicou (*Edom, Israel's Brother and Antagonist: The Role of Edom in Biblical Prophecy and Story,* JSOTSup 169 [Sheffield: JSOT Press, 1994], 23) notes that the word מוֹרָשָׁה, a feminine noun with the same meaning as מוֹרָשׁ, "possession," occurs in Ezek 26:2,3,5 in a similar context: "land taken from the Israelites by the neighbouring nations will be returned (cf. Ezek 36:8–12)."

[19] Cf. Coggins, *Israel among the Nations,* 93.

[20] For a discussion of the historical end of Edom, see Armerding, "Obadiah," 7:354–55. Clark ("Obadiah Reconsidered," 331) considers the announcement that Edom will have no survivors to be the "climactic final point" of vv. 1–18.

[21] B. C. Cresson, "Obadiah," BBC 7 (Nashville: Broadman, 1972), 151.

and Benjamin will possess Gilead.
²⁰This company of Israelite exiles who are in Canaan
   will possess [the land] as far as Zarephath;
the exiles from Jerusalem who are in Sepharad
   will possess the towns of the Negev.
²¹Deliverers will go up on Mount Zion
   to govern the mountains of Esau.
And the kingdom will be the LORD's.

The day of the Lord would mean different things to different people. For Edom and the nations it would be a day of judgment. For the house of Jacob it would be a day of deliverance. For the people of Israel it would be a day of restoration and expansion under the Lord's rule.

19   The first emphasis in the final three verses (vv. 19–21) is that of repossession of lands formerly occupied by Judah and Israel.[22] Neighboring countries had spread out to control sections of Canaan vacated by Israel and Judah when they fell to Assyria (722 B.C.) and Babylon (587 B.C.), respectively. These neighbors included Edom, Philistia, Samaria, and Ammon.

There are only two verbs in the elliptical Hebrew text of v. 19. The verb translated "will occupy" (from *yāraš*) also occurs in v. 17, where it is translated "will possess," which is the basic meaning. There is no verb in Hebrew corresponding to "will possess" in v. 19. In each clause where it occurs the reader is expected to supply the same verb as in the previous clause. "The house of Jacob" and "the house of Joseph" in vv. 17–18 are the likely antecedents of the subject "they" in the third clause. Whereas the NIV has taken the subjects of the other clauses to be "the Negev," "the foothills," and "Benjamin," supplying "people from" and "the land of," some (e.g., REB, Wolff) consider those to be the objects and Israel to be the subject of every clause. In this case "the mountains of Esau," "the Philistines," and perhaps "Gilead" and "the fields of Samaria" are in apposition.[23] As the text stands, Judahites in the Negev[24] will capture Mount Esau, those living in "the foothills" (the Shephelah) will capture the land of the Philistines to the west, some unspecified

---

[22] Based on his excavations in the Negev, I. Beit-Arieh concluded that "Edom invaded and conquered extensive territory that belonged to Judah in the eastern Negev some time near the fall of Jerusalem. . . . This Edomite invasion . . . was a prelude to the further expansion of Edomite settlement into the Hebron highlands, the southern Shephelah and the northern Negev" ("New Light on the Edomites," *BAR* 14.2 [1988]: 41).

[23] Dicou, *Edom, Israel's Brother and Antagonist,* 23; J. A. Bewer, *A Critical and Exegetical Commentary on Obadiah and Joel,* ICC (Edinburgh: T & T Clark, 1948), 44; Baker, *Obadiah,* 41–42. The editor of the Hebrew text considers "the mountains of Esau," "Philistines," "Samaria," and "Benjamin" to be later explanatory glosses. Cf. Coggins, *Israel among the Nations,* 96; Allen, *Obadiah,* 169–71; Wolff, *Obadiah and Jonah,* 61.

[24] The mention of the Negev at the beginning of v. 19 and the end of v. 20 forms a literary envelope that groups these two verses. See Baker, *Obadiah,* 41.

people (presumably the remnant of the northern tribes[25]) will occupy the territory of Ephraim and Samaria, and people from the Benjamin tribe will possess Gilead in the hills of northern Transjordan.[26] The people involved in repossessing old Israelite and Judean territory were either returning exiles or those still living in the land of Canaan.

20 The focus of v. 20 is on exiles returning to the promised land. They will be responsible for the expansion of the occupied territory to its ideal limits. Israelite exiles will push the northwestern limit to Zarephath just south of Sidon (Josh 19:28). Jerusalem exiles will return to occupy southern Judah (the Negev). The location of Sepharad from which Jerusalemite exiles returned is uncertain. Probably Sepharad was located northwest of Media, beyond the Babylonian Empire.[27]

21 The "deliverers" probably are returned exiles who make Zion (Jerusalem) the center of government in the day of the Lord (cf. v. 17). A contrast is drawn between Zion, the holy mount, and Mount Esau, the mount of profanation. The word translated "govern" (from *šāpaṭ*) usually means "to judge, to administer justice," or "to punish," but during the period of the judges the judges also were deliverers (cf. Judg 3:9,15; Neh 9:27). Obadiah's point may be that "just as the Lord raised up the judges of old to rescue His people, so in the future similar leaders will arise to save Israel from the oppression of the nations."[28] Clearly, in the restoration era Judah will be dominant over Edom, either judging, administering justice, or punishing them.[29]

More important than the establishment of Mount Zion as the center of government and more important than Judah's elevation over Edom is Obadiah's assertion that finally the Lord's supreme rule over the nations and the earth will be manifest. The day of the Lord will mean the defeat of God's enemies, the restoration of his people, and the establishment of his universal rule. God's people may suffer temporary defeat for their sins, but God will intervene to rescue them, to judge his enemies, and to establish his kingdom. In the end God's kingdom will come, and he will reign over all peoples of the earth (cf. Isa 4:5; 18:7; 24:23; Mic 4:7).

---

[25] Finley, *Joel, Amos, Obadiah,* 375.

[26] Finley (ibid.) notes that Saul's son Ishbosheth, a Benjamite, was king of Gilead and Israel (2 Sam 2:8–11).

[27] Stuart, *Hosea-Jonah,* 421.

[28] Finley, *Joel, Amos, Obadiah,* 378.

[29] Coggins suggests that Edom here stands for all who oppose God. See his comment in *Israel among the Nations,* 98.

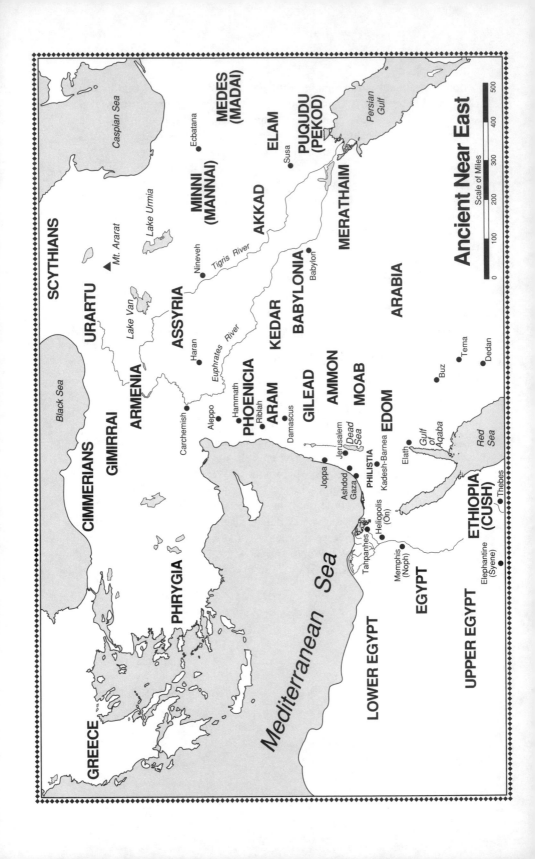

Ancient Near East

Scale of Miles

0 100 200 300 400 500

GREECE

PHRYGIA

CIMMERIANS

GIMIRRAI

ARMENIA

SCYTHIANS

URARTU

Black Sea

Lake Van

Caspian Sea

Lake Urmia

▲ Mt. Ararat

MINNI
(MANNAI)

MEDES
(MADAI)

● Ecbatana

ELAM

● Susa

PUQUDU
(PEKOD)

Persian
Gulf

AKKAD

MERATHAIM

ASSYRIA

● Nineveh

Tigris River

Euphrates River

● Haran

Carchemish ●

● Aleppo

Hammath ●

● Riblah

PHOENICIA

ARAM

● Damascus

KEDAR

BABYLONIA

● Babylon

ARABIA

GILEAD

AMMON

MOAB

EDOM

● Buz

● Tema

● Dedan

Mediterranean Sea

● Joppa

Jerusalem ●

Dead
Sea

PHILISTIA

Ashdod ●
Gaza ●

Kadesh-Barnea ●

Elath ●

Gulf
of
Aqaba

Red
Sea

Heliopolis
(On) ●

Tahpanhes ●

Memphis
(Noph) ●

LOWER EGYPT

EGYPT

UPPER EGYPT

ETHIOPIA
(CUSH)

Elephantine
(Syene) ●

● Thebes

Jonah

―――――― *INTRODUCTION OUTLINE* ――――――

1. Author
2. Date
3. Genre and Purpose
    (1) Midrash
    (2) Allegory
    (3) Didactic Fiction
    (4) History
4. Structure

―――――― **INTRODUCTION AND BACKGROUND** ――――――

The Book of Jonah is small in size (a mere forty-eight verses) but great in its impact and extremely significant in light of its controversial interpretive history. The character, Jonah, has intrigued believers for many centuries. Unfortunately, he has become caricatured by many who miss the positive results of an objective examination of his life. The Book of Jonah is a case study of "missed blessings" because so many readers focus upon its supposed difficulties rather than upon its rich teachings. J. H. Kennedy laments this reality. He states that "to some people Jonah is only a hocus-pocus term which conjures up thoughts about bad luck and personal misfortune. . . . To many people, Jonah suggests an ancient literary myth, a fantastic tale about a man's being swallowed by a whale and surviving the ordeal. The story is marked by the usual fictional extravagance of folk tales and especially by biblical supernaturalism."[1]

This author hopes that all readers might see the inherent spiritual truths of Jonah, sense its deep message for humankind, and recognize its important portrayal of the character of God and his purpose. There are important lessons in this small book. One needs to realize that the "fish" is a relatively minor part of the story, mentioned in only three verses. R. T. Kendall is on target in stating, "The Book of Jonah is one of the most relevant books for the present time."[2] Its message is abidingly relevant for the modern-day reader.

---

[1] J. H. Kennedy, *Studies in the Book of Jonah* (Nashville: Broadman, 1956), x–xi.
[2] R. T. Kendall, *Jonah: An Exposition* (Grand Rapids: Zondervan, 1978), 11.

The Book of Jonah is the fifth of the so-called Minor Prophets. But in content and form it resembles the narratives concerning the prophets in the historical books of the Old Testament (cf. 1 Kgs 17–19) more than it does the other prophetic books. It details a segment in the ministry of Jonah, the son of Amittai. According to 2 Kgs 14:25, Jonah was from Gath Hepher in the territory of Zebulun (cf. Josh 19:13) in the Northern Kingdom, and he prophesied during or shortly before the time of Jeroboam II (793–753 B.C.). Before that king's reign, Israel was being tormented by the Syrians, whose successes against them were the result of Israel's sins (cf. 2 Kgs 13:1–3). Israel was protected from conquest, however, in response to the pleas of King Jehoahaz (814–798 B.C.) when God sent "a deliverer" (2 Kgs 13:5), whom many interpret to have been King Adad-nirari of Assyria (810–783).

Problems with the Syrians continued, however, into the reign of Jehoash, king of Israel. It was to Jehoash whom the prophet Elisha promised victories from his deathbed (2 Kgs 13:14–19). The prophet Jonah, a successor of Elisha, then promised that these victories would continue for Jehoash's son Jeroboam II, whom the Lord would enable to restore Israel's ancient boundaries. But Israel's successes, the author of Kings explains, came not as a result of their faithful obedience but rather the Lord's compassion (2 Kgs 13:4,23; 14:26–27) in spite of Israel's sin (2 Kgs 13:2,6,11; 14:24).

From the Book of Jonah we learn that the Lord's compassion extended even beyond his people Israel. The same Jonah (evident from his father's name) received a command from the Lord to go to Nineveh and announce the destruction of that city because of its sins. The book relates in simple prose (1) Jonah's rebellion against the call; (2) the Lord's retrieval and recommissioning of Jonah; (3) Jonah's preaching in Nineveh and its successful result; (4) the prophet's complaints at the Lord's compassion toward Nineveh; and (5) the reproof God administered to the pouting prophet.[3]

Given the knowledge of Jonah's general period of ministry, we can ascertain that the story occurred during a time of Assyrian weakness. In the first half of the eighth century B.C., especially between the death of Adad-nirari III[4] (810–783 B.C.) and the crowning of Tiglath-Pileser III (745–727 B.C.), Assyria was fighting to defend itself against the Arameans and Urartians. The Assyrian

---

[3] C. F. Keil and F. Delitzsch, "Jonah," COT (Grand Rapids: Eerdmans, 1978), 10:380. Many Jewish traditions of no historical value arose around Jonah, including one that made him the son of the widow at Zarephath whom Elijah restored to life (1 Kgs 17:17–24). See R. K. Harrison, *Introduction to the Old Testament* (Grand Rapids: Eerdmans, 1969), 905. There is also a tradition that the prophet's grave is in Meshad of Galilee and another that it is in Nineveh.

[4] Adad-nirari III has been suggested as the king during Jonah's preaching ministry because of a recorded inscription attributed to him: "On Nabu wait: Do not trust in another god." This statement of supposed monotheistic belief, however, is contradicted by numerous other statements by Adad-nirari III. See D. D. Luckenbill, *Ancient Records of Assyria and Babylonia* (Chicago: University of Chicago Press, 1926), 1:260–64, for examples.

Eponym Chronicle records that Assyria's troubles were aggravated by famine (in 765 and 759 B.C. and perhaps the years between) and internal revolts (763–760 and 746 B.C.), all of which explain the "increasing impotence of the Assyrian monarchs towards the middle of the eighth century BC."[5]

According to G. Roux, "for thirty-six years (781–745 B.C.) Assyria was practically paralysed."[6] W. W. Hallo observes that "even the central provinces maintained only a tenuous loyalty to Assyria, for the various governors ruled in virtual independence."[7] This could explain the otherwise unknown expression "king of Nineveh" (rather than "king of Assyria" found elsewhere) in 3:6. Nineveh was at this time virtually the extent of the king's domain. It also could explain the unusual phrase in 3:7, "By the decree of the king and his nobles." As P. J. N. Lawrence has demonstrated, the precarious position of the king may have necessitated his acknowledging in his decree the power and influence of surrounding provincial governors.[8]

The *Chronicle* also mentions that during the reign of Ashur-dan III (771–754 B.C.) there was a full eclipse of the sun (in 763 B.C.), which some have suggested would have increased Nineveh's receptivity to Jonah's preaching if it occurred not long before he arrived.[9] The period finally culminated in a revolution that installed on the throne the famous Tiglath-Pileser III. He reestablished Assyrian supremacy, annexing the Aramean kingdoms and subjugating Israel and Judah (cf. 2 Kgs 15–16).

The following king, Shalmaneser V (727–722 B.C.), conquered Samaria in 722 B.C. and deported its inhabitants (cf. 2 Kgs 17). Thus Jonah's prophetic mission to this languishing foreign nation resulted not only in their repentance and deliverance but ultimately also in Israel's destruction. This fact must surely contribute to the canonical significance of the book.

1. Author

The Book of Jonah contains no explicit reference to an author or to a chronological setting. In fact, if it were not for 2 Kgs 14:25, we would know almost nothing about the historical situation or the prophet. Therefore it is impossible to know whether the book is *by* Jonah or only *about* him. While

---

[5] T. D. Alexander, *Obadiah, Jonah, Micah: An Introduction and Commentary,* TOTC (Downers Grove: InterVarsity, 1988), 80.

[6] G. Roux, *Ancient Iraq* (Baltimore: Penguin, 1966), 274.

[7] W. W. Hallo and W. K. Simpson, *The Ancient Near East: A History* (New York: Harcourt Brace Jovanovich, 1971), 131. See also A. K. Grayson, "Assyria: Ashur-dan II to Ashur-Nirari V (934–745 B.C.)," *CAH* III/I, 273; P. J. N. Lawrence, "Assyrian Nobles and the Book of Jonah," *TynBul* 37 (1986): 126–32.

[8] Lawrence, "Assyrian Nobles and Jonah," 131.

[9] D. J. Wiseman, "Jonah's Nineveh," *TynBul* 30 (1979): 42–51.

most scholars doubt authorship by Jonah,[10] some affirm his contribution, at least in supplying information.[11]

The issue of authorship is somewhat related to how the book is to be interpreted. A parabolic or allegorical interpretation invariably accompanies the view that the book was a late anonymous composition. But if it is a historical account (as I later argue), then at least some of the historical data could have come from the prophet.

D. Stuart, however, while understanding Jonah as a historical account, thinks it unlikely that the main character would have written such a book "so consistently critical" of himself.[12] The book does not claim authorship by Jonah, nor does it contain use of the first-person singular. There is also no statement elsewhere in Scripture that can be used to determine the author. The most that can be said is that since Jonah was a prophet of the Lord (2 Kgs 14:25), and following the lead of other prophets, he could have written this book.

Whoever the author was, the book's inclusion in canonical Scripture indicates that the community of Israel acknowledged its divine inspiration and prophetic character. Although the author possessed certain information otherwise unknown to Jonah at the time of the event, such as the sailors' conversation in Jonah 1:5, he could have obtained the information later from the sailors themselves or by someone else. In the final analysis we do not know *how*, only *that* God enabled the recording of his Word for the benefit of his people.

2. Date

The debate regarding authorship has more especially been about when the Book of Jonah was written. It was already written by at least 200 B.C., for "the twelve prophets" is mentioned in *Sir* 49:10, an apocryphal book written shortly after 200 B.C.[13] The earliest date would be the time of Jonah's ministry, which 2 Kgs 14:25 places in the first half of the eighth century.

Perhaps the majority of scholars, while recognizing the paucity of evidence on the date of authorship, favor a date in the exilic or postexilic periods, between the sixth and fourth centuries B.C.[14] There are four main arguments.

---

[10] See, e.g., L. C. Allen, *The Books of Joel, Obadiah, Jonah and Micah*, NICOT (Grand Rapids: Eerdmans, 1976), 186; G. M. Landes, "Linguistic Criteria and the Date of the Book of Jonah," *ErIsr* 16 (1982): 147–70; J. Magonet, "Jonah, Book of," *ABD* 3.941; J. A. Soggin, *Introduction to the Old Testament*, 3d ed. (Louisville: Westminster/John Knox, 1989), 415–16.

[11] H. L. Ellison, "Jonah," EBC (Grand Rapids: Zondervan, 1985), 7:362.

[12] D. Stuart, *Hosea-Jonah*, WBC (Waco: Word, 1987), 432.

[13] Jonah is also mentioned in the Codex Sinaiticus of *Tob* 14:4,8, a fourth- or third-century B.C. book. But the same passage in Codex Vaticanus contains no such reference.

[14] See, e.g., Magonet, *ABD* 3.940–41; J. M. Sasson, *Jonah: A New Translation with Introduction, Commentary, and Interpretation*, AB (New York: Doubleday, 1990), 26–27. The latter speculates "that a collection of narratives was given unity and focus by importing the name of this prophet from its context in Kings and inserting it rather frequently (eighteen times) into the resulting text" (p. 27).

The first is based on linguistic data. It is held that Jonah uses several words and expressions that are characteristic of at least an exilic if not a postexilic context. That is, they are typically found in the latest Old Testament books (a problematic issue itself, since all do not agree on the date of such books as Ecclesiastes and Daniel). Several of these are Aramaisms (words that are common Aramaic words but that have been adapted into Hebrew usage) found nowhere else but in biblical or nonbiblical Aramaic texts.[15] G. M. Landes examined these in detail, however, and concluded that most of the linguistic data does not demand a postexilic origin but is found in preexilic texts as well.[16] It may reflect a northern Israelite dialect influenced by Canaanite-Phoenician rather than later Aramaic. He also notes the presence of other linguistic evidence that favors a preexilic date. His conclusion is that "there is relatively little in the language of the book that supports its composition after the 6th century BCE."[17] T. D. Alexander subjects to further analysis Landes's remaining linguistic indicators of a late date and finds that even they are inconclusive: "It is, therefore, not inconceivable that the book of Jonah could have been written prior to the sixth century, possibly even in the eighth century BC, especially if one envisages a north Israelite provenance."[18]

Second, the author's supposed denunciation of Jewish nationalism and exclusivism, as supposedly exhibited by Ezra and Nehemiah, was at one time claimed to be most appropriate in a postexilic context.[19] This argument, however, is generally rejected today. R. E. Clements, for example, points out that Jonah does not deal with any of the issues such as mixed marriages, "which we know deeply affected the relationships of Jews with non-Jews in the postexilic period." Furthermore, "the so-called separatism of Nehemiah and Ezra was not so much concerned with making a distinction between Jew and Gentile, . . . but with a division between Jews and those who laid claim to being Jews."[20] Besides, so-called universalistic concepts appear throughout the Old Testament (cf. Gen 12:3; Pss 9:8; 22:27–28; 72:17; 96; Isa 2:2–4; 11:10; 25:6–8; 52:15; 56:7; Mic 4:1–3).

Third, many commentators claim that the book shows signs of consider-

---

[15] See Allen, *Joel, Obadiah, Jonah and Micah,* 186–88. While recognizing regarding the linguistic data that "it is possible to counter a number of them, their cumulative effect conveys an impression of lateness." He favors a date in the fifth or fourth century (p. 188). J. Limburg agrees that "these connections with postexilic vocabulary do not prove that Jonah was composed in the postexilic period, but the evidence surely points in that direction" (*Jonah: A Commentary,* OTL [Louisville: Westminster/John Knox, 1993], 29).

[16] Landes, "Linguistic Criteria," 147–70. In this regard his study agrees with and extends that of O. Loretz, "Herkunft und Sinn der Jonah-Erzählung," *BZ* 5 (1961): 18–29.

[17] Landes, "Linguistic Criteria," 163.

[18] T. D. Alexander, "Jonah and Genre," *TynBul* 36 (1985): 55.

[19] O. Eissfeldt, *The Old Testament: An Introduction* (New York: Harper & Row, 1965), 405.

[20] R. E. Clements, "The Purpose of the Book of Jonah," *VTSup* 28 (1975): 19. Not all agree on the presence of a universalistic theme in Jonah. See Sasson, *Jonah,* 25.

able distance from the prophet's era by its alleged historical inaccuracies. According to L. C. Allen, the book portrays Nineveh as the capital of Assyria, which it was not until the seventh century.[21] It also speaks of the city as much larger than it was, requiring three days to cross (according to Allen's translation of 3:3). And the phrase "king of Nineveh" in 3:6 is unattested in Assyrian annals. These clues suggest to some a time of composition well after the fall of Nineveh in 612 B.C., which is thought to be confirmed by the past tense in 3:3: "Now Nineveh *was* a very important city."[22] Furthermore, it is thought that reference to animals in mourning and to a decree sent from "the king and his nobles" in 3:7–8 reflects Persian rather than Assyrian customs.[23] Allen concludes, "These phenomena are all quite consistent with a later author who had no intention of teaching a history lesson but employed contemporary tradition as basic material for a didactic parable."[24]

If it is assumed that "a journey of three days"[25] in 3:3 means that either crossing the city or circumscribing it on foot would take three days, then Nineveh would have to have been fifty to sixty miles either in diameter or in circumference. All agree, however, that cities in ancient Mesopotamia were not this large in the eighth nor the third centuries.[26] Regardless of when the book was written, then, this interpretation of the phrase would demand that it be understood as an exaggeration, which seems to be ruled out by the next verse, "On the first day, Jonah started into the city."[27] The phrase in 3:3, however, may mean that Jonah had to preach in Nineveh for three days in order to get the message to the entire population.[28] Alternatively, the reference may be to a day of arrival, followed by a day of preaching, then a day of departure.[29] Another possibility is to define "Nineveh" as "Greater Nineveh" comprising the territory between Nineveh, Asshur, Calah, and Dur-Sharrukin.[30] This may find confirmation in the phrase "the great city of Nineveh" in 1:2; 3:2; 4:11 (cf. Gen 10:11–12).[31] This view is rejected by Allen because 4:11 gives Nin-

---

[21] H. W. Wolff, however, sees Nineveh portrayed in Jonah not as the capital of the Assyrian empire but as "a huge city-state" (*Obadiah and Jonah: A Commentary*, trans. M. Kohl [Minneapolis: Augsburg, 1986], 77, 99).

[22] On the interpretation of this clause, see the comments on 3:3.

[23] Regarding the decree see p. 205.

[24] Allen, *Joel, Obadiah, Jonah and Micah*, 186. For his comments on 3:3 see p. 256. See also Smith, *Prophets and Their Times*, 272; Wolff, *Obadiah and Jonah*, 147–49.

[25] The Hebrew מַהֲלַךְ שְׁלֹשֶׁת יָמִים , which the NIV translates "a visit required three days," is literally "a journey/distance of three days."

[26] Sennacherib (704–681 B.C.) enlarged the city from a circumference of about three miles to seven miles. See Alexander, "Jonah," 56.

[27] Ibid., 57.

[28] J. Walton, *Jonah,* BSC (Grand Rapids: Zondervan, 1982), 66.

[29] Wiseman, "Jonah's Nineveh," 38.

[30] Ibid., 38–39.

[31] Alexander, "Jonah," 57–58.

eveh's population as 120,000, which would be a more likely number for the population of Nineveh proper.[32] D. J. Wiseman, however, has revised his population estimates upon which Allen relies, resulting in 120,000 being a reasonable number for the population of "Greater Nineveh."[33]

The phrase "king of Nineveh" has been shown to reflect Assyria's diminished realm during the time of the prophet (see p. 198). It also is parallel to the designation "king of Samaria" used of Ahab in 1 Kgs 21:1, whereas he is called "king of Israel" elsewhere.[34] Whether Nineveh was the capital of Assyria in Jonah's day, it was at least a chief city and a royal residence during the time of Tiglath-Pileser I (1114–1076), Ashurnasirpal II (883–859), and Sargon II (722–705). Besides, we know so little about Assyria during this time of Assyrian weakness that it would be unwise to argue from silence.[35]

The fourth line of argumentation sometimes used to demonstrate an exilic or postexilic date of composition is that of biblical parallels. Some think that verbal and thematic parallels to passages in Kings, Jeremiah, Joel, and other books are sufficient to argue for dependency of Jonah on those books.[36] Arguments based on literary dependency, however, are seldom convincing because of the difficulty of proving the direction of dependency. Also it is possible that both works under analysis are dependent upon an earlier source. Sasson believes that "such comparisons are often superficial and do not adequately recognize how ideas and phraseology are transmitted in ancient Israel."[37]

Arguments, then, for a date of composition after the fall of Nineveh in 612 B.C. are inconclusive. Furthermore, if the book is a historical account (see the following section), it is more likely that its origin was before that time.[38] Perhaps the most convincing argument for the probability of a preexilic date is to recognize that Jonah's ministry was clearly in the vein of preclassical prophecy. His writings and prophecy preserved the tensions present in the prophetic community of the eighth century B.C.[39]

3. Genre and Purpose

While the message of Jonah to Nineveh was clearly one of judgment, scholars have had many different views of the canonical purpose of the book,

---

[32] Allen, *Joel, Obadiah, Jonah and Micah,* 222.

[33] Wiseman, "Jonah's Nineveh," 41–42. Cf. Alexander, "Jonah," 59.

[34] Stuart, *Hosea-Jonah,* 441.

[35] Ibid., 442.

[36] See, e.g., Wolff, *Obadiah and Jonah,* 77; Limburg, *Jonah,* 23, 30.

[37] Sasson, *Jonah,* 23. See also Stuart, *Hosea-Jonah,* 433.

[38] K. Almbladh points out, however, that "in case the accuracy of a historical or biographical document was solely dependant on when it was written, much of that which we read in our history books would rest on a shaky ground indeed" (*Studies in the Book of Jonah* [Uppsala: University Press, 1986], 41).

[39] Walton, *Jonah,* 71–72.

which is closely related to the issue of genre. The first question is whether to treat the Book of Jonah as a historical account. While at one time this involved only the issue of whether the events occurred, this question is now usually subordinated or sidestepped by asking whether the author even intended to describe actual events at all. The trend in this century has been to answer this question negatively and to understand the book as some form of didactic fiction. J. Limburg, for example, describes it as "a fictitious story developed around a historical figure for didactic purposes."[40] He agrees with the statement of B. Childs that "by determining that the book of Jonah functions in its canonical context as a parable-like story, the older impasse regarding the historicity of the story is by-passed as a theological issue." While Jonah, like the parable of the good Samaritan, has "historical features," it is "theologically irrelevant" whether the events occurred.[41]

This attempt to remove the Book of Jonah from the historian's probe has resulted in various designations of its genre (some overlapping and several almost identical): midrash, allegory, parable, legend, novella, satire, etc.[42] Frequently involved in the discussion is a false dichotomy between history and literature or history and prophecy, as if a work cannot relate historical events in a rhetorically sophisticated fashion for didactic purposes.[43] But the Bible is full of literature that does this very thing.[44] To understand the nature of the Book of Jonah, it is necessary to consider some of the major views.

(1) Midrash

First suggested by K. Budde,[45] this designation for the Book of Jonah has more recently been advocated by P. Trible. She explains that a midrash is a

---

[40] Limburg, *Jonah,* 24.

[41] B. Childs, *Introduction to the Old Testament as Scripture* (Philadelphia: Fortress, 1979), 426. See also Sasson, *Jonah,* 327–28. For an argument on the importance of biblical historicity for biblical relevance, see V. P. Long, *The Art of Biblical History* (Grand Rapids: Zondervan, 1994), 88–119.

[42] For citations listing advocates of each view see T. D. Alexander, "Jonah and Genre," *TynBul* 36 (1985): 36–37. A more thorough survey may be found in P. Trible, *Studies in the Book of Jonah* (Ph.D. diss., Columbia University, 1963), 126–77. The "lack of standard nomenclature" and the "elusive character" of the book, she says, explains why "no fewer than ten different *Gattungen* have been applied" (p. 127).

[43] On the other side of this argument is Trible's claim that scholars who view Jonah as historical fail to distinguish between *Historie* and *Geschichte* (ibid., 129). Trible, however, is imposing a nineteenth-century dichotomy that is foreign to Hebrew thought.

[44] See, e.g., Long, *The Art of Biblical History,* 73–75; T. Longman III, "Storytellers and Poets in the Bible: Can Literary Artifice Be True?" in *Inerrancy and Hermeneutic: A Tradition, a Challenge, a Debate,* ed. H. M. Conn (Grand Rapids: Baker, 1988), 137–49; E. Yamauchi, "The Current State of Old Testament Historiography," in *Faith, Tradition, and History,* ed. A. R. Millard, J. K. Hoffmeier, D. W. Baker (Winona Lake, Ind.: Eisenbrauns, 1994), 28–30

[45] K. Budde, "Vermutungen zum 'Midrasch des Buches der Könige,'" *ZAW* 11 (1892): 37–51.

commentary on a portion of ancient Scripture whose purpose was to adapt it to an immediate situation. While it can comprise legal material, it is usually in the form of "tales which exalted the acts of God."[46] Various passages have been offered as the basis for the book, including 2 Kgs 14:25 (Budde's view) and scattered portions of Isaiah, Jeremiah (18:8), Ezekiel, Joel (2:13–14), Amos (7:9,11), or Obadiah.[47] Trible argues that Jonah is a midrash based on the declaration of God's mercy in Exod 34:6 (cf. Jonah 4:2).[48] More precisely, however, she says the midrash takes the form of a legend, which is a narrative with a historical core embellished by imagination.[49] The historical core is the prophet Jonah and the geographical locations referred to. The story "may have grown out of some incident(s) in the life of Jonah," being gradually "embellished considerably by mythological and folk-tale motifs."[50] It may even have "originally existed as a folk-tale independent of the prophet Jonah"[51] and then been associated with him by a Hebrew storyteller.

Although many have recognized that Jonah may have a midrashic element,[52] few scholars have been satisfied with this label for the genre. As Trible herself acknowledges, even if Jonah is postexilic it would be one of the earliest examples of midrash. The only other example is from two references in 2 Chronicles (13:22; 24:27), the nature of which is unknown. Another problem with the designation is the difficulty of getting agreement on what passage is being expounded. Yet as Trible explains, the text should be "evident in the midrash itself."[53] As Stuart says, "By its nature Jonah appears far more likely to be not the midrash but the primary material, so that any midrash would be secondary, i.e., a discussion of the truth contained in Jonah."[54]

Regarding Trible's proposal to read Jonah as a legend, Wolff objects that "what we have here is not really a story about Jonah at all. It is a story about Yahweh's dealing with Jonah."[55] Furthermore, if the story recounts actual incidents in Jonah's life, as we shall argue, then it is not "embellished by imagination." Nor is it a fanciful commentary on some other passage, designed to extol the greatness of Israel's God of history by means of a fictitious story.

[46] Trible, *Studies in the Book of Jonah,* 163.

[47] See, for example, G. A. F. Knight, *Ruth and Jonah: Introduction and Commentary* (London: 1966), 51–52; R. Coote, *Amos among the Prophets* (Philadelphia: Fortress, 1981).

[48] Trible, *Studies in the Book of Jonah,* 168.

[49] Ibid., 169–70.

[50] Ibid., 174.

[51] Ibid.

[52] Cf. Wolff, *Obadiah and Jonah,* 81. Wolff believes the term "midrash" does not sufficiently account for the story's "artistic form."

[53] Ibid., 167.

[54] Stuart, *Hosea-Jonah, 435.*

[55] Wolff, *Obadiah and Jonah,* 81.

(2) Allegory

This approach to Jonah understands that the features of the book represent certain aspects in the life of Israel. It is usually connected with the meaning of Jonah's name, "dove," taken as a reference to Israel (cf. Ps 74:19; Hos 7:11; 11:11). The fish usually is supposed to represent Babylon (cf. Jer 51:34,44), who swallowed up Israel during the exile as a punishment for their refusal to carry out God's mandate to the world at large (represented by Nineveh). The flight of Jonah to Tarshish symbolizes Israel's specific default with respect to its call from God. The fish's regurgitation of Jonah corresponds to the Hebrew people's restoration from the period of exile.[56] W. Neil leans toward allegory as he sees here a message of the readiness of Israel's neighbors to respond to the knowledge of God. The prophet is pictured, he says, "sulking in his flimsy shelter" as he "depicts the Nehemiahs, Ezras, Joels, and Obadiahs of his day, sheltering under the precarious protection of their recently rebuilt temple, uncompromising in their hatred of the Gentiles, hoping for the apocalyptic judgment of God to fall upon them, and still unwilling to recognize the purpose of God to save the whole world and not only the Jews."[57]

There are several reasons why the allegorical view of Jonah must be rejected. First, allegories in the Old Testament (e.g., Ezek 17; 23; Zech 11:4–17) are rather brief and unmistakable in their allegorical nature. As Stuart explains, "Figures in an allegory are patently symbolic and fictional, and the audience must realize this at once if the allegory is to be effective."[58] The Book of Jonah does not meet this requirement. Particularly it should be noted that the point of a biblical allegory or parable is to clarify a spiritual or heavenly truth on the basis of analogy with common earthly experience. Having God as a main character in such a story would be counterproductive. Second, the identification of Israel with the dove can in no way be considered standard (cf. Jer 48:28; Nah 2:7). One work associates the "dove" with Nineveh, the chief sanctuary of the goddess "Ishtar," whose sacred bird was the dove.[59] Third, in the Old Testament it is evident that the exile of Judah occurred not for failure to carry the message of God to the Gentiles but for unfaithfulness to the covenant by acts of idolatry and immorality. Fourth, if the Book of Jonah were intended to be allegorical in nature, it would make more sense that a prophet from Judah be selected instead of one from Galilee. Fifth, the

---

[56] The most elaborate example is found in C. H. H. Wright, "The Book of Jonah Considered from an Allegorical Point of View," in *Biblical Essays* (1886): 34–98. See the summary in Trible, *Studies in the Book of Jonah,* 153–56.

[57] W. Neil, "Jonah, Book of," *IDB* 3.967.

[58] Stuart, *Hosea-Jonah,* 436. Cf. Harrison, *Introduction to the Old Testament,* 911–12; G. C. Aalders, *The Problem of the Book of Jonah* (London: Tyndale, 1948), 16.

[59] Oesterly and Robinson, *Introduction to Books of the Old Testament,* 377.

fish is portrayed in 2:1–11 not as a means of punishment but of deliverance. Sixth, many of the details of the story do not fit the supposed allegory. It makes no sense for one of the figures in the allegory, Nineveh, to be itself figuratively portrayed in 4:10–11 by the plant. In fact, it is difficult to find a function in the allegory for chap. 4 at all. Also, Jonah's invitation to be thrown into the sea in 1:12 does not correspond to Israel's experience. As M. Burrows states, "The greatest weakness of this kind of exposition is that it is only to a small degree controlled by the text."[60]

(3) Didactic Fiction

Under this category may be considered the various other proposals for Jonah's form that include parable and novella or short story. While allegorical interpretation seeks to find meaning in almost every detail, parabolic interpretation focuses on the story as a literary whole and usually finds one basic point.[61] According to J. Bewer, the tale was intended to oppose the narrow, nationalistic tendency among postexilic Jews who believed that they alone were Yahweh's peculiar people, the sole object of his love and care.[62] Landes, on the other hand, views it as a call to repentance, whose parabolic message is that "Yahweh is unswerving in offering his pity and compassion to repentant sinners."[63] G. I. Emmerson argues that the parable probes the problem of unfulfilled prophecy and proclaims the "absolute freedom of Yahweh," especially his freedom to be gracious.[64] Wolff reads the book as an "ironically didactic novella." That is, it belongs to the genre novella, its aim is instructive, and "the unique beauty of the story and its liberating power is to be found in its *comedy*."[65] Its purpose, he says, is to help those who are struggling to reconcile the Lord's mercy with his justice and to combat the "despairing theology" that "serving Yahweh seems pointless" since he no longer seems to distinguish between Israel and foreigners.[66]

P. Trible has argued cogently that the many themes proposed for the Book

---

[60] M. Burrows, "The Literary Category of the Book of Jonah," in *Translating and Understanding the Old Testament*, ed. H. T. Frank and W. L. Reed (Nashville: Abingdon, 1970), 89.

[61] C. Blomberg, however, presents a cogent argument that the parables of Jesus have as many lessons as they have main characters. See *Interpreting the Parables* (Downers Grove: InterVarsity, 1990).

[62] J. A. Bewer, *A Literature of the Old Testament*, rev. ed. (New York: Columbia University Press, 1933), 403. Allen similarly sees the audience as a postexilic community "embittered by its legacy of national suffering and foreign opposition" and the theme as Yahweh's universal power and concern (*Joel, Obadiah, Jonah and Micah*, 190–91).

[63] G. M. Landes, "Jonah, Book of," IDBSup 2:490.

[64] G. I. Emmerson, "Another Look at the Book of Jonah," *ExpTim* 88 (1976): 87.

[65] Wolff, *Obadiah and Jonah*, 84–85.

[66] Ibid., 85–86.

of Jonah demonstrate that it is not a parable, which is a simple story designed to clarify a central point that "can be readily grasped by the listener."[67] Its multiple elements and the complexity of its themes are not characteristic of the parabolic form.

Limburg is content to describe the book simply as didactic fiction, which "portrays the God who creates, sustains, and delivers," and it invites and models for "both the people of God and the peoples of the world" the response of praise.[68] His list of six theological themes in Jonah is a helpful summary of the book's teaching: (1) God's sovereignty over the natural world, (2) his deliverance of those who call upon him in need, (3) his concern for all people, (4) his freedom to alter his plans for judgment, (5) his uniqueness as the one true God, and (6) the appropriateness of "thanksgiving, witness, and praise."[69] But such a list raises a question: Is a book of fiction an appropriate medium and one where we would expect to find Scripture teaching such lessons? As Stuart has written: "People act more surely upon what they believe to be true in fact, than merely what they consider likely in theory. . . . If it really happened, it is really serious. If this is the way God works in history, then a less narrow attitude toward our enemies is not just an 'ought,' it is a must; it is not simply a narrator's desire, it is God's enforceable revelation."[70]

Bewer's primary reason for treating Jonah as unhistorical is the supposed incredibility of its account. To believe "that Jonah should have remained in the fish for three days and three nights and should have prayed a beautiful psalm of thanksgiving inside, exceeds the limits of credibility."[71] He has the same opinion of Jonah's ejection from the fish, the size of Nineveh, Jonah's ability to communicate with Assyrians, Nineveh's conversion, and the extraordinary growth of the plant. In fact, to suppose that Jonah is intended as a record of actual historical events would be a sin against the author. "It is a prose poem, not history."[72] Besides, he says, far from being unique and unparalleled, the story of Jonah turns out to be a common story the world over. By this he means that the miraculous tale of deliverance is similar to many other stories told along the coast of Palestine.

The Book of Jonah is in fact full of extraordinary acts of God that could be called miracles. Other miracles in the Book of Jonah include the following:

---

[67] Trible, *Studies in the Book of Jonah,* 159.

[68] Limburg, *Jonah,* 36.

[69] Ibid., 33–36.

[70] Stuart, *Hosea-Jonah,* 440.

[71] J. A. Bewer, H. G. Mitchell, and J. M. P. Smith, *A Critical and Exegetical Commentary on Haggai, Zechariah, Malachi, and Jonah,* ICC (New York: Scribner, 1912), 4–6. Bewer shares some of the better known monster-deliverance stories that possibly were circulated in the area of Palestine.

[72] Ibid.

1. the sudden providential storm (1:4)
2. the falling of the Lot upon Jonah (1:7)
3. the immediate calming of the storm (1:15)
4. the divinely appointed fish (1:17)
5. the divinely appointed vine (4:6)
6. the divinely appointed worm (4:7)
7. the scorching wind (4:8)

Most of these miracles, however, have parallels elsewhere in the Bible.[73] Several involve natural forces that God manipulated from time to time to fulfill his purposes. One is especially reminded of Christ's stilling the storm on the Sea of Galilee. God's sovereignty over the beasts and other parts of his creation is declared in Job 38–41.

So what does one mean by "credibility" (or probability) when speaking of events usually described as miracles? Would not Bewer's approach result in most biblical literature being relegated to the category of didactic fiction? But this would cut the heart out of the biblical message.[74] We might argue that any situation in which God deals with mere human beings contains the element of miracle. As Walton says: "If these be miracles, it is useless to discuss the gullet sizes and geographical habitats of dozens of species of whales, or the chemical content of mammalian digestive juices and their projected effect on human epidermis over prolonged periods. If we wanted to discuss this sort of thing, we would have to begin with first things first, and ask whether or not God could talk to man, as he did in Jonah 1:1."[75]

Furthermore, it is commonly recognized that there is much similarity between the Book of Jonah and the account of Elijah (cp. Jonah 1:1–2 and 3:1–2 with 1 Kgs 17:2: "Then the word of the LORD came to Elijah: 'Leave . . .'"), which is full of "incredible" events. But can we seriously consider the explanation that the author intended the account of Elijah as a parable? As Alexander writes, "If ancient Israelites believed that God had sent ravens to feed Elijah, could they not also accept as historically probable the sojourn of Jonah inside the belly of a great fish?[76]

Also, if one of the lessons of Jonah, as most would admit, is that God is sovereign over and responsive to human actions, how can we employ a method in its explication that denies that message by ruling out the possibility of miracles? The miraculous or unexpected events in the book may be understood, rather, as a vital part of the message. Applying J. Goldingay's question of the patriarchal narratives to Jonah, we may rightly ask, What kind of

---

[73] D. W. Hillis, *The Book of Jonah: Jonah Speaks Again* (Grand Rapids: Baker, 1967), 12.

[74] Cf. S. Greidanus, *The Modern Preacher and the Ancient Text* (Grand Rapids: Eerdmans, 1988), 33.

[75] Walton, *Jonah*, 75.

[76] Alexander, "Jonah and Genre," 46.

"implied vested interest" does it have in the historicity of the events it narrates? And as he asks further:

> Are they the kind of stories that could be completely fictional but still be coherent and carry conviction? A parable is fictional, but nevertheless carries conviction on the basis of who it is that tells it and of the validity of his world-view as it expresses it. A gospel, however, invites commitment to the person portrayed in it, and in my view this implies that it cannot be both fictional and true. The kind of response it invites demands that the events it narrates bear a reasonably close relationship to events that took place at the time. Without this it cannot be coherent and carry conviction. In the absence of reference, it cannot even really have sense.[77]

Jonah, however, is not a story told by a prophetic teacher who introduces it with "Listen to this parable," or even with "Thus says the LORD." Nor does it conclude with any words that would suggest to the reader that something other than actual events have been recounted. The book, in fact, does not exhibit the form of a parable. Even B. Childs must admit that it is only "parable-like."[78] Even this is too much to grant, however, except in the broadest sense. For one of the main characters of the book, "the person portrayed in it"[79] to whom commitment is invited, is actually God. And should we suppose that ancient Israel would have accepted as Scripture a fictional story in which God was only a character? The story of Jonah, then, does have an "implied vested interest" in the historicity of the events described.

In response to claims that the book's alleged reliance on exaggeration and surprise categorizes it as didactic fiction,[80] Alexander demonstrates that "the characteristics of exaggeration and surprise are not inherent features of the story; rather they are the products of modern imaginations."[81] Allen proposes that an unhistorical quality is shown in that the events in Jonah are based in part upon the stories of Sodom and Gomorrah (Gen 19:25) and the flood (Gen 6:11,13), and much of the discourse echoes the words of Elijah (1 Kgs 19:4), Joel (2:13–14), and Jeremiah (18:7–8,11).[82] This argument, however, is based

---

[77] J. Goldingay, "The Patriarchs in Scripture and History," in *Essays on the Patriarchal Narratives,* ed. A. R. Millard and D. J. Wiseman (Winona Lake, Ind.: Eisenbrauns, 1983), 27.

[78] He avoids the term "parable" because of (1) the difficulty of defining the term, (2) the presence of nonparabolic features in the book, and (3) a desire to avoid "an overly rigid formal classification" (*Introduction to the Old Testament as Scripture,* 421–22).

[79] Note the quotation by Goldingay. Alexander asks: "Is it not highly improbable that a Jewish author of the period 780 to 350 BC would have dared create a fictional account with God as a central character? Would not this have been viewed by devout Jews of that time as tantamount to blasphemy?" ("Jonah and Genre," 58).

[80] Cf. Allen, *Joel, Obadiah, Jonah and Micah,* 176.

[81] Alexander, "Jonah and Genre," 49.

[82] Allen, *Joel, Obadiah, Jonah and Micah,* 176–77.

on a problematic late date for Jonah and a questionable interpretation of the author's purpose in reflecting these passages in his account (if one exists).[83]

T. Fretheim claims that Jonah's "concern for structure and symmetry is not as characteristic of straightforward historical writing," and that "the pervasiveness of the didactic element . . . far exceed[s] that which is to be found in other historical narratives in the Old Testament."[84] But even if Jonah is more literary and didactic than Kings, for example, can such a quantitative difference mark such a qualitative distinction as that between history and fiction? Who is to say how much of a literary or didactic element a narrative may have and still be classed as history? Alexander notes the growing recognition that Hebrew narrative characteristically employed literary structures such as chiasmus. For him the evident didactic emphasis of Jonah suggests the label "didactic history" rather than didactic fiction.[85]

(4) History

If Jonah is so "clearly non-historical,"[86] as many claim, it only became so in the nineteenth century. Prior to that virtually every biblical scholar and reader of the book assumed that it at least claimed to recount actual events. Those who continue to affirm the historical interpretation of Jonah point to several facts. First, everyone recognizes that the story has a historical setting, with the main character, "Jonah son of Amittai," known to have been a prophet in eighth-century Israel, and with places known to have existed at that time. Trible even grants that much of the information about Nineveh probably is historically accurate.[87]

Second, the opening verses show no signs that the book should be read as anything other than (didactic) history. As Alexander has explained: "If the opening lines are stylistically in keeping with other historical narratives, it is only natural that [the reader] should treat the text as factual. However, if he begins by believing that these events took place, only to discover later, perhaps in Chapter 3, that this is pure fiction, he will feel mislead, if not actually deceived, and this is something which any competent author would clearly avoid."[88] The fact that we are not also told where Jonah was when God first spoke to him, where the great fish deposited Jonah on the shore, when the

[83] Cf. Alexander, "Jonah and Genre," 49–52.

[84] T. Fretheim, *The Message of Jonah: A Theological Commentary* (Minneapolis: Augsburg, 1977), 66. J. Licht argues that Jonah's didactic element is more decisive for its unhistorical quality than its "fondness for wonders" (*Storytelling in the Bible* [Jerusalem: Magnes, 1978], 124).

[85] Alexander, "Jonah and Genre," 52–55. On the false dichotomy between literature and history see p. 204.

[86] See, e.g., Trible, *Studies in the Book of Jonah*, 176.

[87] Ibid., 128, 175–76.

[88] Alexander, "Jonah and Genre," 57.

events occurred, etc. can hardly be sufficient, as Trible and others claim,[89] to overturn the conclusion that we are reading a historical account. Historical narrative always involves the elimination of much detail, especially when its purpose is primarily to teach and to persuade, as is the case in biblical history.

Third, ancient tradition regarded the book as historical. The Jewish scholar Josephus, for example, used it in his first-century account of Jewish history (*Ant.* 9.12.2). R. H. Bowers demonstrates how the church fathers, while recognizing the remarkable nature of the events, nevertheless treated the book not only as history but also as prophecy confirming the power of God to raise the dead.[90] He cites Cyril of Jerusalem (ca. 370), for example, as arguing that "if the resurrection of Christ be credible so is that of Jonah, and vice-versa."[91] As Alexander asks, "Were these earlier generations completely blind to features which we are asked to believe are immediately apparent?"[92]

Finally, there is the witness of Jesus Christ, which apparently was the basis for the early church's linking the historicity of Jonah's experience with that of Jesus, especially his resurrection. Although it would be conceivable that Jesus might have been merely illustrating in Matt 12:40 when he associated his prophesied resurrection with Jonah's experience in the fish, it is much more difficult to deny that Jesus was assuming the historicity of the conversion of the Ninevites when he continued in v. 41 (cf. Luke 11:32).

> The men of Nineveh will stand up at the judgment with this generation and condemn it; for they repented at the preaching of Jonah, and now one greater than Jonah is here.

This is confirmed in the following verse (cf. Luke 11:33) when Jesus parallels the "men of Nineveh" with the "Queen of the South," whose visit to Jerusalem is recounted in 1 Kings.

> The Queen of the South will rise at the judgment with this generation and condemn it; for she came from the ends of the earth to listen to Solomon's wisdom, and now one greater than Solomon is here.

Clearly Jesus did not see Jonah as a parable or an allegory. As J. W. McGarvey stated long ago, "It is really a question as to whether Jesus is to be received as a competent witness respecting historical and literary matters of the ages which preceded His own."[93]

Therefore, since this author believes very strongly in the veracity of God's

---

[89] Trible, *Studies in the Book of Jonah,* 129, 175. She also cites "miraculous features of the story," the "lack of any biblical or extra-biblical confirmation of the events," and the absence of "the historical mode of writing" (p. 129). The first we have already dealt with, the second we object is unnecessary, and the third we deny.

[90] R. H. Bowers, *The Legend of Jonah* (The Hague: Martinus Nijhoff, 1971), 20–32.

[91] Ibid., 24.

[92] Alexander, "Jonah and Genre," 58.

[93] J. W. McGarvey, *Jesus and Jonah* (Cincinnati: Standard, 1896), 18–19.

Word and in the power of God to act in extraordinary ways, and because there are no compelling reasons to view the story otherwise, the position affirmed here is that the Book of Jonah is a skillfully written narrative recounting a series of actual events from the life of the prophet Jonah. Its purpose is to instruct God's people more fully in the character of their God, particularly his mercy as it operates in relation to repentance. Price and Nida are correct in stating, "The message of the book may be summed up as 'What is likely to happen when people repent.'"[94] This does not deny that there are many other lessons to be found in the Book of Jonah. There are messages concerning such subjects as monotheism, obedience, and motivation that will be uncovered in the exegesis of the text. One aspect of the book's canonical and continuing significance has been expressed in the comment that "the mission of Jonah was a fact of symbolical and typical importance, which was intended not only to enlighten Israel as to the position of the Gentile world in relation to the kingdom of God, but also to typify the future adoption of such of the heathen, as should observe the word of God, into the fellowship of the salvation prepared in Israel for all nations."[95]

4. Structure

In recent studies of the literary character of the Old Testament the verdict is unanimous that the Book of Jonah exhibits a high degree of literary excellence. K. M. Craig, Jr. describes it as "enormously varied, rich, and complex. Even the choice of what might appear to be 'small' words is calculated."[96] L. C. Allen calls it a "model of literary artistry, marked by symmetry and balance."[97] H. C. Brichto says it is "from beginning to end, in form and content, in diction, phraseology, and style, a masterpiece of rhetoric." Regarding the existing text of Jonah he also says, "As an esthetic achievement the marvel of its creation is surpassed, if anything, by the marvel of its pristine preservation and transmission over a period of twenty-five centuries and more."[98]

The book divides into two halves, each spanning two chapters. R. E. Longacre and S. J. J. Hwang have applied a textlinguistic analysis to the book and describe it as comprising two parallel embedded discourses, each having a stage (1:1–3; 3:1–4), a prepeak episode (1:4–16; 3:5–10), and a peak (point of highest tension) episode (2:1–11; 4:1–11). The peak of the first discourse is marked by its poetic form, which has a higher prominence in narrative than

---

[94] V. F. Price and E. A. Nida, *A Translator's Handbook on the Book of Jonah* (N.Y.: UBS, 1978), 1.

[95] Keil and Delitzsch, "Jonah," COT, 10:383.

[96] K. M. Craig, Jr., *A Poetics of Jonah: Art in the Service of Ideology* (Columbia, S.C.: University of South Carolina, 1993), 2.

[97] Allen, *Joel, Obadiah, Jonah and Micah*, 197.

[98] H. C. Brichto, *Toward a Grammar of Biblical Poetics* (New York: Oxford University Press, 1992), 68.

prose. The peak in the second discourse is marked by the dialogue exchange between Jonah and God.[99] The Lord and Jonah are indicated as the two main characters of the story by being the only ones who are named; the other characters are anonymous. Phenomena of nature also serve in each half as props: wind, storm, sea, dry land, and fish in the first half; and herd and flock, plant, worm, sun, and wind in the second half.[100] When placed side by side, chaps. 1 and 3 and chaps. 2 and 4 can be seen as parallel. Chapters 1 and 3 begin with Jonah receiving a word from the Lord consisting of a call to go to Nineveh.

> 1:1–2   The word of the LORD came to Jonah son of Amittai:
> "Go to the great city of Nineveh and preach against it, because its wickedness has come up before me."

> 3:1–2   Then the word of the LORD came to Jonah a second time:
> "Go to the great city of Nineveh and proclaim to it the message I give you."

The similarity in the form of the two calls highlights the contrast between Jonah's response to each.

> 1:3   But Jonah ran away from the LORD and headed for Tarshish.

> 3:3   Jonah obeyed the word of the LORD and went to Nineveh.

Jonah's response to the two calls leads in each case to an encounter with a group of non-Hebrews: the sailors and their captain in chap. 1 and the Ninevites and their king in chap. 3. A parallel between these two groups is set up by their similar responses to threatened disaster. The sailors' response to the storm is expressed in 1:5 by three verbs.

> All the sailors *were afraid* and each *cried out* to his own god. And they *threw* the cargo into the sea to lighten the ship.

The Ninevites' response to Jonah's warning of disaster is also expressed by three verbs (3:5).

> The Ninevites *believed* God. They *declared* a fast, and all of them, from the greatest to the least, *put on* sackcloth.

In both cases there is an inward response, then an articulated response, and finally an outward response.[101] Similar statements of hope also are given by the captain (1:6b) and the king (3:9).

> 1:6b   "Maybe he will take notice of us, and we will not perish."

> 3:9   "Who knows? God may yet relent and with compassion turn from his fierce anger so that we will not perish."

---

[99] R. E. Longacre and S. J. J. Hwang, "A Textlinguistic Approach to the Biblical Hebrew Narrative of Jonah," in *Biblical Hebrew and Discourse Linguistics,* ed. R. D. Bergen (Dallas: Summer Institute of Linguistics, 1994), 342–43.

[100] Trible, *Rhetorical Criticism,* 109.

[101] Ibid., 112. Trible also explains the favorable portrait of the foreigners as a contrast to Jonah.

In chaps. 2 and 4 Jonah is alone with God. The second chapter consists almost entirely of Jonah's prayer in which he thanks the Lord for his deliverance. But in the fourth chapter his initial words of anger against God for delivering Nineveh begin a dialogue between Jonah and God that ends with a divine question. Such lack of an explicit resolution may lead the reader to assume Jonah's repentance. It may also be intended to invite the reader to respond.

Many scholars believe that the psalm in chap. 2 is a later addition to the book.[102] As J. S. Ackerman humorously puts it, "Biblical scholars have had as much difficulty digesting Jonah's song as the great fish had with Jonah."[103] First, the situations of the prayer and of its context in Jonah seem different. The psalm mentions the setting of "the depths of the grave" (2:2), "the deep" (2:3), and the temple (2:4,7,9), but not the fish. And the one who hurled the psalmist into the sea was the Lord (2:3) rather than the sailors. Second is a difference in vocabulary. For example, the verb "hurled" (*šlk*) is used in v. 4 (Heb. v. 3) rather than "threw" (*twl*) in 1:15. Third, although the narrative leads the reader to expect Jonah to pray for deliverance, the psalm is one of thanksgiving. Finally, although Jonah is viewed unfavorably in the book as a whole, he is presented in the psalm as a consistent man of faith. Parallels also are noted between Jonah's prayer and passages from the Psalms. Even though some scholars deny that the psalm was an original part of the book, many critical scholars have recently been adding their voices to those of conservatives in maintaining that while the author of the book might not have composed the psalm himself, it formed a vital part of the original composition.[104]

Response has been made specifically to the arguments for disunity (see the comments on chap. 2), but many have concentrated on the literary examination of the book's structure based on the integrity of the text as it stands. Allen, for example, points out that three key words referring to the Lord's grace (*hesed*) and Jonah's life (*hay* and *nepeš*) in the psalm (2:5–8, Heb. vv. 6–9) have parallels in Jonah's prayer in 4:2–3. "The themes that drew forth Jonah's praise in the psalm are ironically the very ones that cause him grief in

---

[102] See Bewer, *The Book of the Twelve Prophets,* 21; Neil, "Jonah," 2:967; S. Sandmel, *The Hebrew Scriptures* (New York: Knopf, 1963), 495; Eissfeldt, *The Old Testament,* 406; Wolff, *Obadiah and Jonah,* 78–79, 128–31; Trible, *Rhetorical Criticism,* 160–61, 172–73.

[103] J. S. Ackerman, "Satire and Symbolism in the Song of Jonah," in *Traditions in Transformation: Turning Points in Biblical Faith,* ed. B. Halpern and J. Levenson (Winona Lake, Ind.: Eisenbrauns, 1981), 213.

[104] See E. J. Young, *An Introduction to the Old Testament,* rev. ed. (Grand Rapids: Eerdmans, 1960), 281; Harrison, *Introduction to the Old Testament,* 915; G. M. Landes, "The Kerygma of the Book of Jonah," *Int* 21 (1967): 3–31; J. Magonet, *Form and Meaning: Studies in Literary Techniques in the Book of Jonah* (Bern/Frankfurt: Herbert Lang/Peter Lang, 1976), 39–63; Ackerman, "Satire and Symbolism in the Song of Jonah," 213–46; D. L. Christensen, "The Song of Jonah: A Metrical Analysis," *JBL* 104 (1985): 217–31; K. M. Craig, Jr., "Jonah and the Reading Process," *JSOT* 47 (1990): 103–14; A. Brenner, "Jonah's Poem out of and within Its Context," in *Among the Prophets,* ed. P. R. Davies and D. J. A. Clines, JSOTSup 144 (Sheffield: JSOT, 1993), 183–92.

his second prayer." This, he notes, supports the structural parallel between chaps. 2 and 4.[105]

On the basis of a metrical analysis, D. L. Christensen argues that the psalm is an integral part of the book: "At the very point in the narrative where Jonah makes his final descent to the depths of hell itself, the language soars to lyrical heights. And once the GREAT FISH 'turns Jonah around' en route to Nineveh, the language of the poet returns to the level of narrative poetry."[106] H. C. Brichto argues that the psalm fits its context perfectly and was composed by the narrator from various passages in the Psalter. To suppose that the evidence for incongruity shows that it was borrowed or composed for insertion later "is simply to solve the conundrum of a narrator's idiocy by attributing that idiocy to a supposed editor."[107] Limburg's conclusion is that "there are no compelling reasons for considering the psalm as a later addition to Jonah," and it is "such an essential part of the narrative that it is difficult to imagine a version of the Jonah story without it."[108]

─────────── *OUTLINE OF THE BOOK* ───────────

I. God's First Call and Jonah's Response (1:1–16)
    1. God's Instruction and the Prophet's Flight (1:1–3)
    2. The Storm at Sea (1:4–6)
    3. Unveiling of Responsibility and Identity (1:7–10)
    4. Stilling of the Storm (1:11–16)
II. God's Rescue of the Rebellious Prophet (1:17–2:10)
    1. God's Protection and Jonah's Prayer (1:17–2:9)
    2. The Prophet's Deliverance (2:10)
III. God's Second Commission and Jonah's Obedience (3:1–10)
    1. God's Renewal of His Commission (3:1–2)
    2. The Prophet's Preaching and Nineveh's Response (3:3–9)
    3. God's Response (3:10)
IV. Jonah's Displeasure and God's Response (4:1–11)
    1. The Prophet's Displeasure (4:1–3)
    2. God's Response (4:4–11)

───────────────────────────────

[105] Allen, *Joel, Obadiah, Jonah and Micah,* 198–99. See also Landes, "The Kerygma of the Book of Jonah," 16–17.

[106] D. L. Christensen, "Narrative Poetics and the Interpretation of the Book of Jonah," in *Directions in Biblical Hebrew Poetry,* ed., E. R. Follis, JSOTSup 40 (Sheffield: Academic Press, 1987), 45.

[107] Brichto, *Toward a Grammar of Biblical Poetics,* 73 (also see pp. 74, 267–68).

[108] Limburg, *Jonah,* 32–33. This is also the conclusion of Stuart (*Hosea-Jonah,* 438–40) and Alexander ("Jonah," 63–69).

I. GOD'S FIRST CALL AND JONAH'S RESPONSE (1:1–16)
  1. God's Instruction and the Prophet's Flight (1:1–3)
  2. The Storm at Sea (1:4–6)
  3. Unveiling of Responsibility and Identity (1:7–10)
  4. Stilling of the Storm (1:11–16)

───────── **I. GOD'S FIRST CALL AND** ─────────
JONAH'S RESPONSE (1:1–16)

1. God's Instruction and the Prophet's Flight (1:1–3)

¹The word of the LORD came to Jonah son of Amittai: ²"Go to the great city of Nineveh and preach against it, because its wickedness has come up before me."

³But Jonah ran away from the LORD and headed for Tarshish. He went down to Joppa, where he found a ship bound for that port. After paying the fare, he went aboard and sailed for Tarshish to flee from the LORD.

The Book of Jonah begins in an exciting fashion, with God's self-revelation to the prophet Jonah. It does not begin with a title, as do most of the prophets (e.g., Isaiah, Jeremiah, Hosea, Joel, Amos, Obadiah). The expression "the word of the LORD came to . . ." *(wayhî dĕbar yhwh ʾel)* does not open another biblical book. It is found many times, however, opening an episode in a larger book (cf. 1 Sam 15:10; 1 Kgs 6:11; 16:1; 21:17,28; 2 Chr 11:2; Isa 38:4; 29:30; 32:26; 33:19,23; 34:12; 35:12; 37:6; Zech 7:8). It gives the impression that we are reading the continuation of an account already underway (the beginning word *wayhi* is often translated "then . . . came"). However, there is no need to presume that the Book of Jonah consists of "episodes plucked from many Jonah adventures that apparently circulated in ancient Israel"[1] or that it was part of a larger work no longer extant. Instead, it is more appropriate to understand that the author referred to God's continuing work with his people.[2] More important, Jonah begins as an account of events in the life of the historical prophet Jonah. It shows no signs of being a work of "didactic fiction."

---

[1] J. M. Sasson, *Jonah: A New Translation with Introduction, Commentary, and Interpretations,* AB (New York: Doubleday, 1990), 85.
[2] A. J. Glaze, Jr., "Jonah," BBC 7 (Nashville: Broadman, 1972), 159. Other books that begin with the word וַיְהִי are Joshua, Judges, Samuel, Ezekiel, Ruth, and Esther.

1:1 The phrase "the word of the LORD" is mentioned seven times in this book. The exact manner in which God relayed his desires and/or message to Jonah is not given. God chose to speak to prophets in diverse ways. At times God spoke through dreams, and at other times he spoke more directly. On some occasions God chose to speak through a "still, small voice" (1 Kgs 19:9–13) or through rather sensational means, such as the whirlwind (Job 38) or earthquake. The words of J. H. Kennedy are significant at this point: "This is the essence of divine privilege, purpose, and perogative—to speak to man, so bringing him into voluntary and intelligent participation in the divine plan for his life and for the peoples of the world in which he lives."[3]

"Jonah, son of Amittai" was the designated recipient of God's revelation. Little is known about Jonah outside of this book. The one designation in 2 Kgs 14:25 gives us a general time frame for his ministry.[4] Nothing is known about his father, Amittai. While some have seen great significance in the meaning of "Amittai" ("truth") and the name "Jonah" ("dove"), we must be careful not to interpret these in a way that goes beyond the book's obvious intent.

1:2 The Hebrew text of v. 2 begins with two imperatives, "Arise, go" (*qûm lek*). The first imperative functions adverbially to give the command to go a sense of immediacy (cf. NRSV "go at once").[5] This is a definite and firm call from the Lord. The prophet was given traveling orders, and the destination was Nineveh.

Nineveh was a city whose reputation called for direct action from the Lord. The term "great" designates nothing more than its size (see Introduction, p. 203, and notes on 3:3).[6] Nineveh was situated on the eastern bank of the Tigris River, opposite the modern city of Mosul, north of the city of Zab. It was an old city, dating back to approximately 4500 B.C., and one of the principal cities of ancient Assyria. According to Gen 10:11, the city was built by the "great hunter" Nimrod. It became an extremely important city in the reign of the Assyrian monarch Sennacherib (705–681 B.C.). During his reign he strongly fortified the city and for a time made it the capital of Assyria.

H. L. Ellison suggests that the translation "preach against it" may imply

---

[3] J. H. Kennedy, *Studies in the Book of Jonah* (Nashville: Broadman, 1956), 3–4.

[4] T. D. Alexander, "Jonah," TOTC (Downers Grove: InterVarsity, 1988), 97–98.

[5] Sasson, *Jonah*, 69–70. There is no indication that the person in question is lying down. קוּם is a command to take action (cf. Gen 19:15; 27:19). It is often found in a prophetic summons (cf. Num 22:20; Deut 10:11; Josh 7:10; 1 Kgs 17:9; Jer 13:4,6). The root occurs three times in chap. 1 (vv. 2,3,6) and three times in the structurally parallel chap. 3 (vv. 2,3,6).

[6] The word גָּדוֹל ("great") occurs thirteen times in the small Book of Jonah, six times in the first half and seven in the second half. It is found qualifying a "great city" (1:2; 3:2–3; 4:11), a "great wind" (1:4), "great fear" (1:10,16), a "great storm" (1:12), a "great fish" (1:17), the most influential citizens ("great ones," 3:5,7), Jonah's "great displeasure" (4:1), and his "great joy" (4:6).

that Jonah was more personally involved in the message than the Hebrew expression (qara᾽ plus ῾al) justifies. He prefers the JB translation: "Inform them that their wickedness has become known to me." In a nondirective fashion "Jonah had merely to announce imminent judgment, leaving it to his hearers' conscience to judge why it was coming."[7] Wherever the verb qara᾽, "cry out, proclaim," occurs with the preposition ῾al, however, it describes an appeal for or an announcement of the Lord's judgment against someone or something (cf. Deut 15:9; 24:15; 1 Kgs 13:2,4,32; 2 Kgs 23:17).[8] We are not given any further details at this point about the exact nature of Jonah's "marching orders." While one may speculate about the content of the message based on later words from God, at this point it is sufficient to say that the evil of the city incensed the Lord; and he commanded his servant Jonah to proclaim a message of judgment against it.[9]

"Because its wickedness has come before me" is paraphrased interestingly in TLB as "it smells to highest heaven."[10] While all sin is abhorrent to God, in some instances a specific group of people had become so wicked that God issued a special call of localized judgment. So it was with Nineveh. Archaeology confirms the biblical witness to the wickedness of the Assyrians. They were well known in the ancient world for brutality and cruelty. Ashurbanipal, the grandson of Sennacherib, was accustomed to tearing off the lips and hands of his victims. Tiglath-Pileser flayed victims alive and made great piles of their skulls.[11] Jonah's reluctance to travel to Nineveh may have been due to its infamous violence.[12]

---

[7] H. L. Ellison, "Jonah," EBC 7 (Grand Rapids: Zondervan, 1985), 369.

[8] When קְרָא carries the meaning "summon," the combination describes physical antagonism (cf. Isa 31:4; Jer 25:29; 49:29; Ezek 38:21; Ps 105:16; Lam 1:15). According to Sasson the expression קְרָא עַל means "imposing an (unpleasant) fate upon something" (Jonah, 75). But in the expression קְרָא צֹום , "proclaim a fast," the preposition עַל identifies the location or participants (2 Chr 20:3; Ezra 8:21).

[9] The verb קְרָא ("preach, proclaim, call, cry out, declare") occurs four times in the first half of Jonah and four times in the second half: three times in chap. 1 (vv. 2,6,14), once in chap. 2 (v. 3 [Eng., v. 2]), and four times in chap. 3 (vv. 2,4,5,8).

[10] The word רָעָה, "evil, wickedness, calamity, trouble," occurs nine times in the book (1:2,7,8; 3:8,10 [twice]; 4:1,2,6), and its two senses create a wordplay that relates the concepts of wickedness and trouble. J. Magonet explains, "Although the author could have chosen a different word each time to express different shades of meaning, by retaining this one, he allows each usage to interact with the other, multiplying the levels of correspondence and contrast between the respective subjects or contexts related to the word" (Form and Meaning: Studies in Literary Techniques in the Book of Jonah, 2d ed. [Sheffield: Almond, 1976], 22). Sasson notes that all the occurrences of the noun are in the absolute form except the first and last, which have a pronominal suffix. "If not coincidental, this condition can be labeled 'grammatical inclusio'" (Jonah, 76).

[11] F. I. Gaebelein, The Servant and the Dove: Obadiah and Jonah (New York: Our Hope, 1946), 65.

[12] T. E. Fretheim, The Message of Jonah (Minneapolis: Augsburg, 1977), 22.

Many people in the world today ignore God and assume that he also
ignores them. Many believe that God set the world into motion and allows it
to continue along unnoticed. This text portrays God as one who notices, as a
God who is active, and as a God who takes sin seriously.

1:3 Verse 3 relates a tragic decision by Jonah. God commissioned the
prophet to carry a divine message to the people of Nineveh, but Jonah decided
differently. Instead of traveling approximately five hundred miles northeast of
Palestine to Nineveh, Jonah went to Joppa, the nearest seaport. There he took
a ship for Tarshish, probably a Phoenician port in Spain, some two thousand
miles due west.[13] The contrast between God's command and Jonah's response
is accentuated by the structure of v. 3 (seen through a literal translation),
which places the stress on "to Tarshish."

> So Jonah rose
> > to flee *to Tarshish from before Yahweh.*
> > He went down to Joppa,
> > > he found a ship going *to Tarshish,*
> > > he paid its fare
> > and he went down into it
> > to go with them *to Tarshish from before Yahweh.*[14]

Some have taken the expression "from before [*millipnê*] Yahweh" to indicate that Jonah believed it possible to escape God's presence. Many other Old
Testament passages prior to Jonah's time, however, show conclusively that the
Hebrew did not think of Yahweh as a local deity, and Jonah himself in v. 9
confesses his belief in the Lord's universality as Creator. The clearest passage
denying the possibility of escape from (or being lost by) the Lord is Psalm
139, especially v. 7 (which uses an almost identical expression): "Where can I
go from your Spirit? Where can I flee from your presence [*mippaneyka*]?"

What does it mean, therefore, to go "away from the LORD"? In Gen 4:16
the expression (*millipnê*) is used to describe Cain's broken relationship with
the Lord—his rebellion against the Lord and the Lord's displeasure with him.
D. Alexander suggests that we interpret the phrase in light of its use in the
expression to "stand before [*lipnê*] the LORD," which is an idiom used of
being in the Lord's service (cf. 1 Kgs 17:1; 18:15; Jer 15:19). "By fleeing
from the Lord's presence Jonah announces emphatically his unwillingness to

---

[13] We are uncertain of its location, but an identification with Tartessos on the southwestern
coast of Spain is attractive. It was a known source of precious metals that the Bible associates with
Tarshish (cf. Ps 72:10; Isa 23:1,10; 60:9,19; Jer 10:9; Ezek 27:12,25; 38:13). See Alexander, who
quotes an Assyrian inscription of King Esarhaddon (680–669 B.C.): "All kings who live in the
midst of the sea, from Cyprus and Javan as far as Tarshish, submit to my feet" (*Jonah,* 99–100).

[14] The chiastic structure of the verse has been recognized by several scholars. See N. Lohfink,
"Jona ging zur Stadt hinaus (Jon 4,5)," *BZ* 5 (1961): 201.

serve God. His action is nothing less than open rebellion against God's sovereignty."[15]

The surprising nature of Jonah's disobedience is highlighted by the syntax of v. 3 and by the repetition of the verb *qûm* from v. 2. God had commanded his prophet, "Arise, go to Nineveh." Verse 3 begins (literally), "So Jonah rose," as if Jonah were about to obey the Lord as prophets were expected to do (cf. Gen 12:1,4; 22:2–3; 1 Kgs 17:9–10; 18:1–2; 2 Kgs 1:15; 1 Chr 21:10–11,18–19). But the verse continues surprisingly, "to flee to Tarshish from before the LORD." As H. C. Brichto wrote:

> One would be hard put to imagine a narrative beginning better designed to strike an ancient Israelite audience as discordant, incongruous, absurd. A monarch charges a deputy, trusted and long in his service, with a mission which, altogether in the line of his duty, will take him to one end of his lord's far-flung empire. Without a word of demurral, without a suggestion of motive, the deputy proceeds—and ever so casually—to head in the opposite direction.[16]

The reader is given no clue at this point why Jonah chose to act so foolishly. One wonders whether Jonah paused to consider the consequences of his action or if he merely reacted on the spur of the moment. If he had stopped to consider seriously what he was doing, would he have continued in his westerly direction?

Is it possible that Jonah ran from the presence of the Lord because of fear? After all, Nineveh had taken up the sword more than any other group. T. Fretheim observes that while prophets had commonly been called on to speak against other nations, no other prophet had been called on to put in a personal appearance (although the Judahite prophet Amos did go to Israel). "To speak was one thing. To actually go there and deliver was another."[17] While the issue of personal safety may have been a factor, it certainly was not the predominant one. The reason for Jonah's disobedience in flight, while not given in this verse, is explicitly stated by the author in 4:2. The issue *was* fear—fear that the Ninevites might repent and be spared the disaster they deserved.

In view of Israel's characteristically stubborn refusal to repent in response to the Lord's prophets, it is surprising that this possibility would have motivated Jonah to act so rashly. But the result of such a repentance on the part of these pagans would have made Israel's continued stubbornness and perseverance in sin appear all the more heinous and worthy of punishment and inevita-

---

[15] Alexander, *Jonah*, 101.

[16] H. C. Brichto, *Toward a Grammar of Biblical Poetics: Tales of the Prophets* (New York: Oxford University Press, 1992), 68.

[17] Fretheim, *Message of Jonah*, 76. J. Magonet explains that "Nineveh, for Jonah, was the Berlin of the Third Reich" (*Form and Meaning*, 175).

ble ruin. Some think that Jonah's fear of repentance from Nineveh was based on his belief that a spared Nineveh would eventually mean the destruction of Israel. Thus Ellison states:

> If Israel were to be spared now, it could only be that the doom pronounced at Horeb to Elijah should go into full effect. Sick at heart from the foreshortened view of the future so common to the prophets in foretelling the coming judgments of God, Jonah wished to escape, not beyond the power of God, but away from the stage on which God was working out his purposes and judgments.[18]

Thus perhaps Jonah, in an act of rebellion and disobedience, had the "capacity" to second-guess God's plan. But like many through the ages who have sought to thwart God's plans, Jonah was to learn by experience that such actions are ill-advised.

"Joppa" was the seaport of Jerusalem and corresponds to the modern Jaffa, which is now a part of Tel Aviv. There Jonah found a ship going to Tarshish. That he was prepared to risk his life at sea rather than face up to God's call is another point to verify his determination, for Hebrews were basically a "people of the land." Allen states that the hearers of the story of Jonah would see such a venture as proof positive of his "mad determination."[19] The narrative may also suggest that Jonah hired the whole ship,[20] which if true would have taken a considerable sum of money. J. Magonet suggests that "to flee from God, Jonah must have sold his home, left everything behind and set off at the risk of his life."[21] The ship on which Jonah traveled was most likely a merchant ship and probably of Phoenician registry. The Phoenicians were responsible for most of the sea traffic in the Mediterranean during this period of time. They pioneered exploration and trade by sea. But Jonah tragically played the fool when he chose to pit their seafaring skills against the Creator and Lord of the sea.

J. Limburg asks what these first three verses say about God.[22] This is a significant question. Although Limburg delves unnecessarily into a discussion of ecumenical thought, there are three basic answers to his question. First, God calls people to his service. Here Jonah is called to preach to a foreign city, Nineveh. Second, God cares enough about sinners to send a word of hope, love, and grace. Finally, implied here and told later in the story, no one can run from God. "You hem me in—behind and before; you have laid your hand upon me" (Ps 139:5). And certainly if our misdeeds are never hidden from him, so also are our needs ever before him (cf. Isa 40:27).

---

[18] Ellison, "Jonah," 369.

[19] L. C. Allen, *Joel, Obadiah, Jonah, and Micah* (Grand Rapids: Eerdmans, 1976), 205.

[20] Wolff, *Obadiah and Jonah,* 102; Sasson, *Jonah,* 83.

[21] Magonet, *Form and Meaning*, 175.

[22] J. Limburg, *Jonah,* OTL (Louisville: Westminster, 1993), 46–47.

2. The Storm at Sea (1:4–6)

⁴Then the LORD sent a great wind on the sea, and such a violent storm arose that the ship threatened to break up. ⁵All the sailors were afraid and each cried out to his own god. And they threw the cargo into the sea to lighten the ship.

But Jonah had gone below deck, where he lay down and fell into a deep sleep. ⁶The captain went to him and said, "How can you sleep? Get up and call on your god! Maybe he will take notice of us, and we will not perish."

1:4 The word order of this verse, with the subject first (rather than the verb-first order normal for Hebrew), places emphasis on the Lord's acts over against those of Jonah.[23] This is enhanced by the fact that v. 4 ends with the same word, *yhwh* ("the LORD"), that ends v. 3. As Brichto has written, "The flight of Jonah must stand out, as the author intended, in all its existential absurdity."[24] Jonah thought he could just walk away from a divine assignment. But the Lord was to make Jonah's voyage into a "teachable moment." The plans of a sovereign God are not so easily thwarted by the stubborn will of a puny prophet. Jonah was to learn that it was not so easy to resign the Lord's commission.

There is nothing uncommon about a storm at sea, but we are informed that this storm had a special purpose. It was caused by a "great wind" that God's hand hurled like a spear to stop the fleeing prophet in his tracks. The verb translated "sent" (*tûl*) is elsewhere used of hurling an object such as a spear (cf. vv. 5,12,15, "throw"; 1 Sam 18:11; 20:33; Isa 22:17; Jer 22:26–28). Persons at sea often experience feelings of isolation, but Jonah would find such feelings misleading. The eyes of the Lord were continually upon him (cf. Prov 15:3), and the sea is God's dominion. As the psalmist wrote, "The earth is the LORD's, and everything in it, the world, and all who live in it; for he founded it upon the seas and established it upon the waters" (Ps 24:1–2).

The last clause of the verse is striking because of its imagery and syntax. The verb translated "threatened" (*hašab*) means to "consider" or "plan" when it occurs with a human or divine subject (cf. 1 Sam 18:25; 2 Sam 14:13–14; Esth 8:3; 9:24; Jer 26:3; 29:11). Thus the ship is here personified.[25] It was determined to break apart. The drama of the situation is heightened by the syntax, which sets off this clause parenthetically from the others. This might be better expressed by translating, "Now the ship was determined to break apart." In contrast to the disobedient prophet, the wind, the sea, and even the ship were tuned in to the Lord's purposes (cf. Lev 18:25). As Sasson describes, "The ship is first to realize the brutality of the storm, and its own

---

[23] The verse begins with וַיהוה, which should be translated either 'Now the LORD" or "But the LORD," recognizing the use of a *waw* disjunctive.

[24] Brichto, *Toward a Grammar of Biblical Poetics*, 69.

[25] Sasson, *Jonah*, 96.

terror at breaking up is quickly communicated to the sailors."[26] As v. 5 will explain, Jonah was the last one to respond.

1:5 Verse 4 shows the initiator of the storm; v. 5 tells of the results of this frightening tempest. The response of the seamen was to cry out to their own gods. Apparently this was "an international, polytheistic crew."[27] These sailors had experienced storms before, so why did this storm invoke a "religious response"? Perhaps there was a vague uneasy feeling or a recognition that the suddenness of this storm involved a divine reaction. How they discerned this is not stated, but to their credit they recognized a divine reaction to some sin. Of course, their crying out to other deities was ineffective. The ancient Near East's religious environment included devotion to a multitude of "protecting spirits, patron deities, lower echelon gods and goddesses and senior members of the Pantheon," which gave rise to an extremely confusing situation.[28] Perhaps the sailors felt that they had not reached their god or had gone through the wrong "channels" to contact their particular patron deity. Thus they also "threw the cargo into the sea to lighten the ship" (cf. Acts 27:18–19), practicing the advice penned many years later, *Pray like everything depends upon prayer, and work like everything depends upon work.*

The storm's frightening intensity along with the sailors' frantic activities stood in stark contrast to Jonah's state; he had gone "below deck," literally "into the inmost part of the ship," as far away from God and his duty as he could go.[29] There he sank into an extremely deep sleep, almost a hypnotic sleep (cf. Gen 15:12; Judg 4:21; 1 Sam 26:12; Jer 51:39; Dan 8:18; 10:9). The same root (*rdm*) is used in Gen 2:21 for the sleep of Adam that allowed for "surgery."[30] Even through the roaring of the wind and the tossing of the ship, Jonah remained asleep, as dead to the world as he was to God (cf. 1 Thess 5:6).

How could anyone remain asleep through a storm of this magnitude? Perhaps Jonah was exhausted from the taxing journey. Being glad to relax, he was lulled into deep slumber by the action of the waves.[31] H. L. Ellison suggests a different physiological reaction as contributing to this deep sleep: "The storm that can terrify the sailor can reduce the landsman to physical

---

[26] Ibid., 105.

[27] J. Baldwin, "Jonah," in *The Minor Prophets: An Exegetical and Expository Commentary,* ed. T. E. McComiskey (Grand Rapids: Baker, 1993), 2:556.

[28] J. Walton, *Jonah,* BSC (Grand Rapids: Zondervan, 1982), 17. Cf. E. R. Clendenen, "Religious Background of the Old Testament," in *Foundations for Biblical Interpretation,* ed. D. S. Dockery, K. A. Mathews, R. S. Sloan (Nashville: Broadman & Holman, 1994), 274–305.

[29] As the syntax at the beginning of v. 4 spotlighted the Lord's actions, so here the spotlight is shifted to Jonah.

[30] The root דד , used with either the verb or the noun, indicates a special state of deep or hypnotic sleep. See D. Stuart, *Hosea-Jonah,* WBC (Waco: Word, 1987), 457–58.

[31] Allen, *Joel, Obadiah, Jonah and Micah*, 207.

impotence and unconsciousness."[32] Other commentators point to the extreme emotional exhaustion and depression that is inevitable when a person directly rebels against the revealed will of the Lord. Whatever the cause, Jonah was out of contact for the moment, unaware of the danger from the storm.

1:6 The sailors were working feverishly and praying heartily for their lives, but the cause of the trouble was below decks fast asleep. Not knowing Jonah's connection to the trouble, the captain (lit., "head of the rope pullers") nevertheless saw the incongruity of his sleeping through it all, especially since Jonah would have been the first to drown if the ship had gone down. So he asked him the question, "How can you sleep?" The NRSV more literally renders it, "What are you doing sound asleep?"

The captain of the ship did not recognize Jonah as a Hebrew or as a prophet whose prayer should have been especially effective, nor did he mention the covenant name of Jonah's God.[33] But seeing Jonah as yet another person who might join in the desperate prayer meeting, this heathen sea captain admonished him to pray. In doing so, the captain used two of the verbs Jonah had previously heard from God. "Get up" is the verb *qûm* that begins v. 2 in Hebrew, and "call" is the verb *qara᾽*, there translated "preach." "The captain speaks better than he knows, and the irony cannot have escaped Jonah."[34]

Perhaps the captain did recognize the possibility that Jonah's God, Yahweh, might be the initiator of the storm and, because he was being ignored by Jonah's slumbering, needed to be consulted also. As Allen says, "Grudgingly, one has to admire this enlightened pagan who outshines Jonah in his grasp of divine truth."[35] The captain issued forth the idea that perhaps whatever god was responsible might "take notice of us" (or "spare us a thought"). The verb "take notice" is found only here in the Hebrew Old Testament (and only in Dan 6:4 [Eng., v. 3] in Aramaic, where it is translated "planned"). As Baldwin explains, "The sailors envisage the gods as existing 'somewhere out there,' but apt to be preoccupied." Furthermore, "This man, although an idolater, appreciates that mere humans cannot dictate to their god"[36] (cf. 3:9).

There is extreme irony here: a "heathen sea captain" pleaded with a Hebrew prophet to pray to his God. It is sobering to see one who might be termed an "unbeliever" pleading for spiritual action on the part of a "believer." The "unbeliever" saw the gravity of the situation while the prophet slept. It is a sad commentary when those who are committed to the truth of God's word have to be prodded by a lost world into spiritual activity.

---

[32] Ellison, "Jonah," 7:370.

[33] J. A. Bewer, H. G. Mitchell, and J. M. P. Smith, *A Critical and Exegetical Commentary on Haggai, Zechariah, Malachi, and Jonah*, ICC (New York: Scribner, 1912), 33.

[34] Baldwin, "Jonah," 2:556.

[35] Allen, *Joel, Obadiah, Jonah, and Micah*, 208.

[36] Baldwin, "Jonah," 7:556–57.

3. Unveiling of Responsibility and Identity (1:7–10)

⁷**Then the sailors said to each other, "Come, let us cast lots to find out who is responsible for this calamity." They cast lots and the lot fell on Jonah.**

⁸**So they asked him, "Tell us, who is responsible for making all this trouble for us? What do you do? Where do you come from? What is your country? From what people are you?"**

⁹**He answered, "I am a Hebrew and I worship the LORD, the God of heaven, who made the sea and the land."**

¹⁰**This terrified them and they asked, "What have you done?" (They knew he was running away from the LORD, because he had already told them so.)**

1:7a Having received no direction during their short yet intense prayer meeting, the sailors began to speak among themselves. They recognized some sort of divine initiation in the storm, perhaps because of its unusual intensity or the peculiar appearance of a storm during the sailing season, and they sought yet another way to determine the cause. They wanted to find the individual responsible for incurring this divine wrath, so they purposed to employ the casting of lots to reveal the guilty person. The context relates that Jonah was now on deck. There is no evidence that he joined in the sailors' prayer meeting, but he did come on deck, apparently in response to the captain's rebuke.

The casting of lots was a widely used method in the ancient Near East.[37] The most common word used for "lot" indicates that they were either stones or pebbles[38] that were painted or colored. When the stones were thrown, if two dark sides landed up the usual interpretation was no. If two light sides landed up, that meant yes. A light and a dark side meant throw again. Using this system, the sailors dealt with each individual until the color revealed the guilty person.[39] This specific means of discerning the Lord's will is found many times in Scripture. For example, the casting of lots was the means for determining the guilt of Achan (Josh 7:14–18), for distributing the land to the tribes of Israel (Josh 18:10), and for selecting Saul as king (1 Sam 10:20–22). As Prov 16:33 says, "The lot is cast into the lap, but its every decision is from the LORD."

1:7b–8 It is interesting to imagine the drama of this moment. As the lot found Jonah to be the guilty party, all eyes focused on him. What was his reaction? Did he think that somehow the lot would not show him to be guilty? Did he think "luck" might be on his side in this instance? Regardless, questions were asked very quickly.

---

[37] Sasson, *Jonah*, 108–10.

[38] J. Lindblom, "Lot-Casting in the Old Testament," *Journal of Theology* 12 (1962): 164–78.

[39] Stuart, *Hosea-Jonah*, 459–60.

The first question, "Who is responsible for making all this trouble for us?" is almost identical to the question over which the sailors had just cast lots in v. 7a. Therefore some scholars think it is redundant and should be omitted here, following some LXX manuscripts and two medieval Hebrew manuscripts.[40] This first question may simply have been asked in a rather emotional fashion to set the stage for the remaining questions. Or it may have expressed a desire to corroborate the finding of the lots or to give Jonah an opportunity to deny it.[41] Clearly the sailors were exceedingly cautious and awestruck by the storm and this man.

The slight difference in the framing of the two expressions, however, may suggest a difference in function. Before casting lots the sailors asked (literally) "on whose account this calamity is ours." The expression they used when speaking to Jonah afterwards probably should be understood either as an identification of Jonah or as the reason for their further questions. Therefore it may be rendered, "Tell us, you on whose account this calamity is ours," or perhaps, "Tell us, because it is on your account that this calamity is ours."[42]

Whatever the function of the first question, the answers to the sailors' other questions would clarify the decision of the lot and help them determine what must be done. These mariners wanted answers, and they wanted them quickly. Their lives had been placed in danger, and they wanted to understand why.

1:9 For the first time in the story Jonah speaks. But he responds to all their questions with only two answers, which are simple and relatively short. He knew that his response probably would satisfy the curiosity of the seamen. In describing himself as a Hebrew, he was using terminology they would understand (cf. Gen 39:14; Exod 1:15; 1 Sam 4:6).[43]

In the statement "I worship the LORD" Jonah was answering not an overt question but an essential and perhaps implied one. His answer is a rudimentary confession of faith, perhaps even a word of testimony. "Worship" translates a participle (*yare*') meaning "fearing." Since participles usually are used to identify occupations, it could be understood as answering one of their questions explicitly, but it is almost certainly intended to express a state of affairs that is vital to the problem at hand. Even though Jonah's witness at this time

---

[40] The repetition of the question is found in the margin of a medieval Greek MS (Codex 384) and is regarded by some as a marginal gloss that has crept into the text. The difficulty of the question's recurrence, however, commends the reading of the MT. For a discussion of this rare (for Jonah) textual difficulty, see Price and Nida, *Translator's Handbook,* 17, and Allen, *Joel, Obadiah, Jonah, and Micah,* 209. K. Almbladh notes that the MT reading occurs in a text from Wadi Murabbaat (no. 88; see *Studies in the Book of Jonah* [Uppsala: University Press, 1986], 21).

[41] Baldwin, "Jonah," 2:559.

[42] Sasson, *Jonah,* 112–13; Brichto, *Toward a Grammar of Biblical Poetics,* 69. See also Walton, *Jonah,* 19–25, which also has a rather extensive section on lots and oracles in the OT.

[43] Cf. Sasson, *Jonah,* 115–19.

was anything but consistent (so the irony in his claim),[44] his statement was generally true and to the point (cf. Mal 3:16). The God they were encountering was Yahweh, whom Jonah identified for their benefit as "the God of heaven."

The Phoenician sailors worshiped Baal Shamem, which means "the lord of heaven."[45] The phrase indicates the supreme God who controls the heavens and, therefore, was indeed the initiator of the winds that brought the storm. While the phrase "the God of heaven" is one that became intensely popular in postexilic writings (cf. Ezra 1:2; 5:12; Neh 1:4–5), the phrase also was used earlier (cf. Gen 24:3,7). Jonah added the last phrase, "who made the sea and the land," to identify the Lord as being the Lord of all creation. This gave further proof that the Lord was the initiator of this frightful storm.

Many interpreters have identified vv. 4–16 as a chiasmus, that is, the recurrence of a series of terms and themes in reverse order. In all of these analyses vv. 9–10 are viewed as the center, focus, and turning point. D. Alexander has followed and refined the analyses of Lohfink, Pesch, and Fretheim in producing the following analysis that shows the relationship between the various parts:[46]

A   Yahweh hurls a wind on the sea; the storm begins; sailors fear and cry to their gods (vv. 4–5a)
  B   Jonah sleeps; cry to your god; we shall not perish; divine sovereignty (vv. 5b–6)
    C   that we may know on whose account (v. 7)
      D   the sailors question Jonah (v. 8)
        E   I fear (v. 9)
        E´   the sailors fear (v. 10)
      D´   the sailors question Jonah (v. 11)
    C´   I know that it is on my account (v. 12)
  B´   sailors strive for land; sailors cry to Yahweh; let us not perish; divine sovereignty (vv. 13–14)
A´   sailors hurl Jonah into sea; the storm ceases; sailors fear Yahweh and sacrifice (vv. 15–16)

1:10   At this point in the drama tension heightened. The expression is literally "they feared with a great fear." The seamen not only were horrified that their "numinous dread" had been confirmed (that this was a divinely initiated judgment), but they were now filled with "holy fear" by Jonah's admission

---

[44] L. C. Allen explains that "Jonah's fear is a feeble thing, for all its orthodoxy, compared with the numinous awe of the seamen, which Jonah is deliberately not recorded as sharing. The runaway prophet is shown in a bad light: crew and captain can teach him many a lesson about his own faith (*Joel, Obadiah, Jonah and Micah,* 209).

[45] Bewer, *Jonah,* 36.

[46] Alexander, *Jonah,* 106–9.

that he served a god who controls everything.[47] To know that Jonah was a Hebrew was one thing; to know that he worshiped the supreme God was another. To run away from a god was foolish; but to run from "the God of heaven, who made the sea and the land" was suicidal. Their question, "What have you done?" was not a question about the nature of Jonah's sin but an exclamation of horror. They were frightened to the depths of their beings.

4. Stilling of the Storm (1:11–16)

[11]The sea was getting rougher and rougher. So they asked him, "What should we do to you to make the sea calm down for us?"

[12]"Pick me up and throw me into the sea," he replied, "and it will become calm. I know that it is my fault that this great storm has come upon you."

[13]Instead, the men did their best to row back to land. But they could not, for the sea grew even wilder than before. [14]Then they cried to the LORD, "O LORD, please do not let us die for taking this man's life. Do not hold us accountable for killing an innocent man, for you, O LORD, have done as you pleased." [15]Then they took Jonah and threw him overboard, and the raging sea grew calm. [16]At this the men greatly feared the LORD, and they offered a sacrifice to the LORD and made vows to him.

1:11 With the identity revealed not only of the culprit but also of the angry deity, the sailors demanded a solution from Jonah. This was an increasingly desperate situation, and they knew that something had to be done to placate this angry God. Since they did not know this God's prescription for obedience, they naturally turned to Jonah and asked him, "What should we do to you?"[48]

1:12 Jonah's reply to the sailors is fascinating. If the sailors were looking for a confession, they received it here. Apparently Jonah's reaction of "spiritual greatness"[49] was inspired by the "piety" of the sailors, which had "banished his nonchalant indifference and touched his conscience."[50] Jonah showed a deeper understanding of God, but one would have to recognize that his motives were not the highest. As chap. 4 makes clear, at this point Jonah did not have deep compassion for the pagan. Glaze is right that "it was the voice of his conscience, not compassion, that spoke."[51]

The unnatural ferocity of the storm and the casting of the lot only confirmed what Jonah already knew. So now he resigned himself to his "fate." He

[47] Allen, *Joel, Obadiah, Jonah, and Micah,* 210.

[48] The two sentences of this verse in the NIV are in the reverse order in Hebrew, so that there the effect—the sailor's demand—precedes the cause—the worsening storm.

[49] Ellison, "Jonah," 7:372.

[50] Allen, *Joel, Obadiah, Jonah and Micah,* 210.

[51] Glaze, "Jonah," 7:164.

did not exhibit repentance for fleeing from the Lord but merely resigned himself to the only seeming solution. In v. 6 the captain had already asked Jonah to pray. Jonah did not seem so inclined but gave the sailors instruction on what to do so that they might possibly be saved from the ferocious tempest. It is interesting that Jonah did not offer to jump overboard on his own. Perhaps he was too frightened, or perhaps at this point he was merely asking for them to be the instrument of God's punishment.

1:13 Verses 13–16 portray an emotional, frantic, and tragic scene. The pagan sailors were caught in a dilemma. They did not wish to throw Jonah into the sea. But it was not humanitarian motives that bothered them; it was fear of Jonah's God. Nevertheless, in this increasingly dangerous situation, the sailors came to recognize that Jonah's solution was their only hope.

The sailors' effort "to row back to land" was a valiant one. The word "rowed" literally means "to dig into the water." They did their best to reach land, to rid themselves of this troublesome passenger. But their attempt failed. The further they rowed, the wilder the wind blew and the more tempestuous the sea grew. It became quite obvious to the sailors that Jonah's God was not in favor of their chosen method of dealing with Jonah's predicament. Superficial solutions to the entanglements caused by our rebellion and disobedience seldom work. Repentance often requires radical action.

1:14 Having failed in the "rescue" attempt, there ensued an unusual prayer meeting. The prayers were passionate, but those who prayed were pagan and had only recently come to a commendable respect for Yahweh and his power. This prayer as recorded in v. 14 is a structural counterpart to their earlier prayers to pagan gods in v. 5. Clearly they had come to appreciate the power of Yahweh and now entreated his mercy. The sailors' prayer consisted of three parts.

The petition "O LORD, please do not let us die for taking this man's life" not only indicates a respect for God's power but also a fear of his vengeance. The sailors were fearful that there might be some kind of retribution for what they were about to do. They obviously were aware that the taking of a man's life was a very serious matter, and consequences were involved, especially when the person was a servant of the supreme God.

The second of the two petitions strikes deeper than the first, at the reason why their intentions might place them in danger. The use of the term "innocent" might indicate some uncertainty on their part about Jonah's guilt. Or the term could be used to describe one who had not been judged guilty in a human tribunal.[52] The sailors had not been present during Jonah's "crime" and therefore had no direct evidence by which to judge him. But the intent of the prayer is obvious. They did not wish to be held responsible for what was

---

[52] Ellison, "Jonah," 7:372.

going to happen. They had already seen Yahweh's power, and they wanted no part of punishment by this God who controls the sea.

In their final statement, "For you, O LORD, have done as you pleased," the sailors attempted to establish God's "guilt" in this matter. They wanted the Lord to recognize that they were unwilling pawns in this situation. They were washing their hands, attempting to be released of responsibility. This phrase also indicates the sailors' recognition of the absolute power of Yahweh and is a melody that runs close to the heart of the Book of Jonah. The sovereign Lord acts according to his good pleasure—either in judgment or in grace (cf. Pss 51:18; 115:3; 135:6; Prov 21:1; Isa 55:11; Lam 3:37–39; Matt 11:25; Eph 1:5,9).

1:15 This verse follows logically after v. 12. The verb for "took" (*nasa'*) is the same one Jonah used there (translated "pick me up"), and the phrase "threw him overboard" uses the same words as Jonah's "throw me into the sea." Furthermore, the effect that Jonah predicted—"it will become calm"— came about (but in different words, lit., "the sea stood still from its raging"). From the perspective of narrative artistry, vv. 13–14 serve to heighten the dramatic tension by postponing the inevitable. Although they do not advance the story line, they do include helpful information about the sailors' character and the important statement about the Lord's sovereign will and power.

How much time transpired between vv. 14 and 15? Was the "amen" of the prayer meeting the seizing of Jonah? Could there have been a moment of silence seeking some sort of sign from Yahweh in response to the prayer? The text does not answer these questions. It simply relates the outcome. The effect of the sailors' action seems to have been immediate. The cessation of the raging tempest was proof to them that Jonah had been right and that Yahweh actually did control the sea.

1:16 The verb for "fear" occurs first in v. 5 of the sailors' fear of the storm, then in v. 9 of Jonah's claim to reverence the Lord, then in v. 10 of the sailors' terror of the Lord, and finally here of their profound awe before the Lord (cf. Luke 8:22–25). The expression (literally) "feared the LORD with a great fear" is the same as in v. 10 with the addition of "the LORD." The obvious difference is that fear for their lives had turned to submissive awe, which apparently manifested itself in some degree of repentance. These pagan sailors recognized the awesome capability of the God of Israel (cf. Isa 59:19; Mic 7:17; Zeph 2:11; Mal 1:14; 3:5).

The author does not attempt to explain the type of sacrifice offered by these sailors or the nature of the vows. D. Stuart makes a reasonable point that the sacrifice "could hardly have occurred on board the ship, denuded of its cargo." He explains further that "the transportation of edible animals on ocean-going ships was as infrequent in ancient times as in modern" and that "in all the religions of the ancient Near East, as far as the evidence is known, sacrifices took place at shrines or temples."[53] Therefore they probably made vows to offer sacrifices and fulfilled those vows after they reached land (cf. Pss 76:11; 116:17–18). The Midrash understands this to mean that they threw their idols into the waves, returned to Joppa, went up to Jerusalem, and became proselytes.[54] This is not impossible, but we must be careful not to go beyond the text. While some would associate these actions on the part of the sailors with true worship of Yahweh,[55] it is not clear whether these mariners had a conversion experience to Israel's God. No doubt they became cognizant of the power of the Lord and learned to respect that power. Whether they went further than that we do not know. D. Stuart argues that the statement that they "greatly feared" the Lord "would hardly mean to the ancient audience that the crew had been converted to monotheistic Yahwism. They had, however, been so convinced that Yahweh really could do 'as he wanted' (v. 14) that they added Yahweh to the god(s) they already believed in."[56] It is sad but true that there are some who seem to recognize the power of the Lord but refuse to receive him as Lord and Savior. It would be wonderful to know that these sailors continued in their fear of the Lord and ultimately came to "know" him, but their ultimate end is unknown.

---

[53] Stuart, *Hosea-Jonah,* 464–65.

[54] Ibid., 373.

[55] Glaze, "Jonah," 7:164.

[56] Stuart, *Hosea-Jonah,* 464.

II. GOD'S RESCUE OF THE REBELLIOUS PROPHET (1:17–2:10)
   1. God's Protection and Jonah's Prayer (1:17–2:9)
      (1) The "Appointed" Fish (1:17)
      (2) The Prophet in Prayer (2:1)
      (3) The Psalm of Thanksgiving (2:2–9)
   2. The Prophet's Deliverance (2:10)

II. GOD'S RESCUE OF THE REBELLIOUS PROPHET (1:17–2:10)

1. God's Protection and Jonah's Prayer (1:17–2:9)

(1) The "Appointed" Fish (1:17)

¹⁷But the LORD provided a great fish to swallow Jonah, and Jonah was inside the fish three days and three nights.

1:17 This verse, which begins chap. 2 in Hebrew, is perhaps the most famous verse in the Book of Jonah. Rimmer ironically says: "This is the first of 2 verses which 'ruin' the narrative. If this verse and 2:10 were removed, then the prophecy would be plausible for modern readers."[1] It probably is true but tragic that many point to this verse as their "reason" for not believing God's Word. This miracle is singled out, even though it is simply one of several in the book (see p. 215 in the Introduction).

The text says that "the LORD provided" a great fish to swallow Jonah. The word "provided" (from *manâ*) has been the subject of varying translations. In the KJV it is rendered "prepared." This gives the perception that God created a special creature for the specific purpose of rescuing Jonah and providing a place for his training in humility and submission. But an accurate translation would be "ordained" or "appointed." The word is used four times in the Book of Jonah and always points to the Lord's power to accomplish his will. Here it shows his sovereignty over the creatures of the sea; in 4:6 it shows his power over plants; in 4:7 it shows his power over crawling creatures; and in 4:8 it shows his power over the wind. While God indeed may have prepared a spe-

---

[1] H. Rimmer, *The Harmony of Science and Scripture,* 8th ed. (Berne, Ind.: The Berne Witness Company, 1939), 169.

cial "fish" for Jonah, the text only indicates that God summoned the fish, common or special, to be at that place at the exact moment of need.

Conservative scholars throughout the years have spent a great deal of energy and time describing types of large fish that might have been capable of swallowing a human.[2] But all we know for sure is that it was a "large fish." The word translated "fish," *dag*, is the general Hebrew word for any aquatic creature (cf. Gen 9:2; Num 11:22; 1 Kgs 4:33; Ps 8:8). The LXX uses *ketos*, which means a "huge sea-fish."[3] The KJV causes some misunderstanding, for in Matt 12:40, which quotes Jonah 1:17 (from the LXX), it translates the word as "whale."

Trying to marshal evidence to confirm this Scripture may in fact result in the denigration of the miracle. Searching for historical incidents when people and large animals were swallowed and later recovered from sea creatures[4] shows a posture of defensiveness that is unnecessary, counterproductive, and violates the nature of the biblical account. As D. Stuart says, "A miracle is a divine act beyond human replication or explanation."[5] On the other hand, it is hard to argue that the author invented the tale without presupposing the impossibility of the miraculous, which would be irreconcilable with Hebrew tradition. Also, as D. Alexander and others have observed: "The author's portrayal of this most peculiar event is very low key; it has certainly not been included in order to heighten the dramatic quality of the narrative. This being so, why should the author have invented it, if it did not really happen?"[6]

Why did God use this specific means of returning Jonah to his appropriate place of service? For some the purpose of the fish was solely allegorical. Glaze states: "The literary apparatus rich in metaphors and poetic imagery indicates the broader purpose of the author, and the allusions are evident to the intended audience. The relationship to one of Jeremiah's prophecies was

---

[2] Ibid., 190–91. See also A. J. Wilson, "The Sign of the Prophet Jonah and Its Modern Confirmations," in *The Princeton Theological Review* 25 (1927): 631–32. He discusses at length the physical characteristics of a number of sea creatures capable of swallowing a man.

[3] T. Muraoka, *A Greek-English Lexicon of the Septuagint (Twelve Prophets)* (Louvain: Peeters, 1993), 134.

[4] Many historical instances are cited by Wilson ("The Sign of the Prophet Jonah," 635–37). The most fascinating concerns James Bartley, who supposedly was swallowed by a sperm whale in 1891 and was recovered live but "raving." Rimmer tells of other instances. One man was rescued alive and unhurt from the belly of a rhinodon shark but was "devoid of hair, and patches of a yellowish-brown color covered his entire skin" (Rimmer, *Harmony of Science*, 195–96). See also C. F. Keil and F. Delitzsch, "Jonah," COT (Grand Rapids: Eerdmans, 1978), 10:398. Such stories are doubted by E. B. Davis, who diligently attempted to unearth the facts of the "Bartley" story. He concluded that the story is "a whale of a tale" ("A Whale of a Tale: Fundamentalist Fish Stories," in *Perspectives on Science and Christian Faith*, 43, ed. J. W. Hass, Jr. [Ipswich, Mass.: American Scientific Affiliation, 1991], 224–37).

[5] D. Stuart, *Hosea-Jonah*, WBC (Waco: Word, 1987), 474.

[6] T. D. Alexander, "Jonah," TOTC (Downers Grove: InterVarsity, 1988), 111–12.

clear: Israel, swallowed by Babylon, would be delivered."[7] In other words, the story had to present elements commensurate with the intended teaching lesson.

More fitting of the context is the view that the fish provided time for instruction from the Lord. R. T. Kendall says it well: "The belly of the fish is not a happy place to live, but it is a good place to learn."[8] Jonah was well aware of the numerous Old Testament reflections of chaos, pictured by the sea monster Leviathan (Pss 74:13–14; 104:26). During Jonah's time in the fish he may have reflected on God's dominance over every force in the world. Jonah had to learn that God's purpose was serious and that his concerns as well as his power went far beyond the shores of Palestine.

Jonah was in the fish "three days and three nights," although he would have realized this only after his removal from the fish. This phrase may be intended as an approximation rather than as a precise measure of seventy-two hours;[9] however, the point of the fuller expression rather than simply "three days" would seem to be that Jonah was confined for "three *full* days."[10] Some think the expression reflects the ancient belief that death was permanent only after a body showed no signs of life for three days (cf. John 11:6,14). If this interpretation is applied to the Jonah text, it apparently would mean that the fish was not primarily an agent of Jonah's deliverance but an additional danger to his life. The "three days and three nights" phrase would point to his precarious state of existence, hovering between life and death.[11] This interpretation, however, appears out of step with Jonah's prayer of thanksgiving from inside the fish (2:2–9). Nevertheless, his thanksgiving probably was not solely for deliverance from drowning but was based on his anticipation of deliverance from the fish as well. Therefore the time frame perhaps should suggest that God's power and grace retrieved Jonah as if from the dead (cf. 2:6), and the great fish was the vehicle God used.

A similar interpretation is that the expression alludes to a common motif in the ancient Near East of a three-day journey to the underworld and back. With that notion in mind, the readers of Jonah would have seen the fish as repre-

---

[7] A. J. Glaze, Jr., "Jonah," BBC 7 (Nashville: Broadman, 1972), 166.

[8] R. T. Kendall, *Jonah: An Exposition* (Grand Rapids: Zondervan, 1978), 101; Keil and Delitzsch, "Jonah," COT, 10:398.

[9] Ellison, "Jonah," 375.

[10] Stuart, *Hosea-Jonah,* 474.

[11] G. M. Landes, "The 'Three Days and Three Nights' Motif in Jonah 2:1," *JBL* 86 (1967): 446–50; id., "The Kerygma of the Book of Jonah," *Int* 21 (1967): 11–12. While D. Stuart (*Hosea-Jonah,* 475) accepts this argument that "the Sheol journey motif is probably behind the author's choice of words as a purposeful echo of the reference to the Underworld in the Psalm (v 7[6])," Alexander considers that "there is insufficient evidence within the Old Testament itself to demonstrate that this is how a Hebrew reader would have interpreted the phrase" ("Jonah," 112).

senting God's rescue from the underworld, that is, death.[12] Numerous texts in the Old Testament refer to three days as the period of a journey. For example, Moses asked that Pharaoh permit the Israelites to leave Egypt to go on a three-day journey into the wilderness (Exod 3:18; cf. also Gen 22:4; Num 10:33; Josh 9:17; 1 Sam 30:1; 2 Sam 24; 2 Kgs 2:17). Jonah's preaching tour of Nineveh also took three days (3:3). Jonah later may have pondered regretfully upon his three days in the fish made necessary because he tried to avoid three days of walking and preaching in Nineveh.

Although the phrase "three days and three nights" may have had a variety of connotations both from other Old Testament passages and from extrabiblical writings, no compelling reason exists to disbelieve the literal span of time indicated. In fact, none of the Old Testament allusions of a similar nature are necessarily figurative. The major point is that God, through the fish, could sustain this pouting prophet during "unbelievable" circumstances and return him to the place where he could renew his commission to serve.

(2) The Prophet in Prayer (2:1)

[1]From inside the fish Jonah prayed to the LORD his God.

2:1   The significance of this verse is found in Jonah's willingness to pray. From a near drowning experience he awakened to find himself in a terrifying environment. Nonetheless, his ability to breathe and continue living was a cause for rejoicing. So he prayed (lit.) "from the belly of the fish." We do not know how long Jonah was in the fish before he prayed. No doubt he found his entire experience in the sea overwhelming. That this prophet of few words finally prayed marks a turning point in the book. Although exhorted to pray earlier by the pagan captain, there is no indication Jonah did so.[13] That Jonah prayed not only to the Lord, as the sailors did, but to "the LORD *his God*" is significant.

---

[12] Landes, "The 'Three Days and Three Nights' Motif in Jonah 2:1," 448. In the Sumerian myth "The Descent of Inanna to the Nether World," Inanna instructs her divine minister, Ninshubur, to set up an elaborate lament for her after she has departed for the underworld. Then follows the text of the lament, the account of Inanna's departure and reception into the lower realm, culminating in her death at the hands of the goddess Ereshkigal. At this point the text then reads: "After three days (and) three nights had passed, her minister Ninshubur, her minister of favorable words, her knight of true words, sets up a lament for her by the ruins" (Part II, lines 169–73). The "three days (and) three nights" are intended to cover the time of travel to the realm of the dead. It would appear this is a most promising clue for understanding the full import of the words "three days and three nights" in Jonah 1:17. They are used to indicate the period of time it took the fish to bring Jonah back from the deep, understood more explicitly in the following psalm as the netherworld (cf. 2:6). Thus, just as Inanna required three days and three nights to complete her descent into the underworld, so also the fish is assigned the same time span to return Jonah from "Sheol" to the dry land.

[13] Price and Nida, *Translator's Handbook,* 35. The usual verb for "pray" (*hithpael* of פלל) is used twice in the book, here and in 4:2. Elsewhere the verb is קרא, "call."

(3) The Psalm of Thanksgiving (2:2–9)

2He said:
  "In my distress I called to the LORD,
    and he answered me.
  From the depths of the grave I called for help,
    and you listened to my cry.
  3You hurled me into the deep,
    into the very heart of the seas,
    and the currents swirled about me;
  all your waves and breakers
    swept over me.
  4I said, 'I have been banished
    from your sight;
  yet I will look again
    toward your holy temple.'
  5The engulfing waters threatened me,
    the deep surrounded me;
    seaweed was wrapped around my head.
  6To the roots of the mountains I sank down;
    the earth beneath barred me in forever.
  But you brought my life up from the pit,
    O LORD my God.

  7"When my life was ebbing away,
    I remembered you, LORD,
  and my prayer rose to you,
    to your holy temple.

  8"Those who cling to worthless idols
    forfeit the grace that could be theirs.
  9But I, with a song of thanksgiving,
    will sacrifice to you.
  What I have vowed I will make good.
  Salvation comes from the LORD."

These verses produce consternation in some and worship in others. Some say they are out of place. According to Glaze, "A later scribe, possibly feeling the need for a recorded prayer, probably transposed that which the author had placed following verse 10."[14] Many believe that these verses do not record Jonah's actual prayer at all, but that 2:2–9 was included at a later time to illustrate Jonah's feelings while in the fish. Arguments usually focus on alleged inconsistencies between the psalm and the surrounding narrative and on the

---

[14] Glaze, "Jonah," 167. Another writer who delineates this view in a detailed fashion is J. Magonet, *Form and Meaning* (Sheffield, Eng.: Almond, 1983), 39. See also H. W. Wolff, *Obadiah and Jonah: A Commentary,* trans. M. Kohl (Minneapolis: Augsburg, 1986), 133.

claim that it is not necessary to the plot (see Introduction, p. 221, for arguments on both sides).

A strong case, however, can be made for the genuineness of the psalm. D. Stuart laments the failure of many scholars to recognize that "the occasional citation of poems in prose contexts is an aspect of normal OT narrative style."[15] He also points out that "one can find at least some part of virtually *any* document, ancient or modern, that is not actually required for the sensible flow of logic, and which would not therefore be 'missed' in the strict sense if it were not present. . . . Very few literary works contain the minimum that may be said. . . . The potential for abridgment is therefore a common feature of literary works" and should not be considered evidence of interpolation.[16] He also argues that while the psalm does not refer explicitly to Jonah's situation, this is typical of psalms, especially of thanksgiving, and Jonah's psalm "is as closely related thematically to the rest of the book as a psalm of its type could be."[17] Finally, Stuart argues that if the psalm were absent, the book would have no expression of (1) Jonah's partial change of heart that led to his obedience in chap. 3, (2) Jonah's thankfulness for rescue that "explicitly conveys his realization that to him personally Yahweh has shown the sort of mercy he will also show to Nineveh," and (3) the nature of Jonah's experience in the fish, that he was thinking and learning there.

Also without the psalm the message of the Lord's mercy, love, and forgiveness would be weakened.[18] The book's major irony would also be missing, that Jonah could accept thankfully the Lord's merciful forgiveness but deny it to the Ninevites. Kennedy counters the objection that thanksgiving for deliverance is herein given while Jonah was still inside the fish by pointing out that the deliverance referred to here is not from the fish but from drowning.[19] While some feel that the prayer would have been more suitable after Jonah was safe on land, there is no textual evidence for deleting or moving it.

As many have observed, this prayer resembles other passages of Old Testament Scripture. The opening words of the prayer resemble Pss 18:6; 118:5; 120:1. But this similarity is no reason to doubt the authenticity of Jonah's prayer. Rather, it is a good example of Hebrew psalm-poetry in which the poet drew upon the regular liturgical language common to the Book of Psalms and other poems in the Old Testament to fit the situation.[20] It is a beautiful example of a believer who prayed biblically. Inevitably, those who know the Lord

---

[15] Stuart, *Hosea-Jonah*, 470.

[16] Ibid., 470–71.

[17] Ibid., 471. Stuart presents a chart of these interrelationships.

[18] Ibid., 472–73.

[19] Kennedy, *Studies in Jonah*, 38.

[20] Price and Nida, *Translator's Handbook*, 34. Magonet concurs with this assessment (*Form and Meaning*, 49).

will not only speak to one another using biblical language (cf. Eph 5:19–20) but also to God.

Whether Jonah composed his prayer in this form as a psalm inside the fish or only later, we do not know; neither do we know whether Jonah himself was the one who gave it poetic expression. But there is no adequate cause to doubt that it accurately reflects his thoughts in this unusual situation. The form of the prayer is in accord with the thanksgiving prayers/psalms found elsewhere in the Old Testament. Four typical elements are reproduced: an introductory summary of answered prayer (v. 2), reports of the personal crisis (vv. 3–6a), divine rescue (vv. 6b–8), and a vow of praise (v. 9).[21]

2:2 As Jonah came to his senses, he recognized his preservation alive in the fish's belly as a pledge of his complete deliverance.[22] Jonah's earlier stated belief in God's dominion over all the earth was personalized as he recognized that God heard his prayer even in the midst of this distressing situation.

While most would quickly identify Jonah's sojourn in the fish as his time in the "depths of the grave" and the fish as the cause of distress or even the vehicle of his judgment, Jonah did not regard it so. As this psalm explains, it was while struggling for his life in the sea, with seaweed wrapped around his head (v. 5) and seemingly sinking to his grave "banished" from the Lord's favor that he suddenly had hope and prayed (v. 4). That he now found himself alive even in so terrifying an environment Jonah took to be a miracle of God intended as the means of his eventual deliverance. The fish was a beneficent device for returning Jonah to the place of his commission. Landes states, "It is clearly before Jonah is swallowed by the fish that he is threatened by the sea and in danger of permanent residence in the nether world."[23] Whether Jonah was describing the inward parts of the fish or the engulfing sea, he nonetheless described his distress as the "depths of the grave." Literally, the word for "grave" is "Sheol" (cf. KJV "hell").

The term "Sheol" was used in various ways. It may be said with certainty that in Hebrew thought the term referred to a place of the dead. It was spoken of as located under the earth (Amos 9:2). Normally those who were in Sheol were seen as separated from God (Ps 88:3; Isa 38:18), yet God was shown to have access to Sheol (Ps 139:8). Sheol was used as an expression for being in the grave (Pss 18:6; 30:3; 49:14; Isa 28:15). With this imagery Jonah here described his experience of being "at the very brink of death."[24] Fretheim agrees that the language used here goes beyond the literal sense, especially regarding Sheol: "Inasmuch as Sheol was believed to be under the floor of the

---

[21] L. C. Allen, *The Books of Joel, Obadiah, Jonah and Micah*, NICOT (Grand Rapids: Eerdmans, 1976), 215.

[22] Keil and Delitzsch, "Jonah," COT, 10:399.

[23] Landes, "The 'Three Days and Three Nights' Motif in Jonah 2:1," 449–50.

[24] J. Walton, *Jonah*, BSC (Grand Rapids: Zondervan, 1982), 33.

ocean, Jonah was spatially near the place."[25] It also helps to understand at this point that in the Old Testament death is understood to be more a process than an event. As for Jonah's place in that death process, life had ebbed so much that he could have been reckoned more among the dead than among the living. Similar idioms in modern speech are found regularly.[26]

While the vast majority of modern scholars considers Jonah's situation in this verse to be a close brush with death, a few believe that Jonah was referring to an actual death experience. The miraculous event in this case would be resurrection as well as rescue. The rationale is that Jonah's experience would conform more closely to that of Jesus to which it is compared in the New Testament.[27] Such a view, however, goes beyond the language of the text and violates the nature of its imagery.

The term "my distress" defines Jonah's situation, and its poetic parallel, *beten šeʾôl*, literally, "the belly of sheol" ("the depths of the grave"), would be understood by the reader as metonymy, the use of a term in place of that to which it compares. Jonah believed that he was as good as dead, that he had been "eaten" by death, which was often spoken of as an enemy that devours (Pss 49:14; 55:15; Prov 1:12; 27:20; Isa 5:14). Jesus' comparison of his own coming death to this event in Jonah's life focuses on two elements of correspondence: the time period of three days and the nature of the event as a sign (cf. Matt 12:40; 16:4; Luke 11:29–30). While Jonah's imagery of death supported the comparison, a literal correspondence at this point was not required by the comparison.[28]

2:3 Perhaps the most important aspect of v. 3 is Jonah's testimony to God's sovereignty. He not only recognized God's hand in his being thrown into the sea, but he also saw the "waves and breakers" that swept over him as belonging to God, tools in his hand. He finally came to grips with the author of his life. Martin Luther said: "Jonah does not say the waves and the billows of the sea went over me; but thy waves and thy billows, because he felt in his conscience that the sea with its waves and billows was the servant of God and of His wrath, to punish sin."[29]

It may be that the sea language in this verse and others must be understood

---

[25] T. Fretheim, *The Message of Jonah: A Theological Commentary* (Minneapolis: Augsburg, 1977), 99.

[26] Ibid., 100.

[27] J. V. McGee, *Thru the Bible with J. Vernon McGee* (Pasadena: Thru the Bible Radio), 3:749–50.

[28] On the nature of Jonah's experience as "a sign to the Ninevites" (Luke 11:30), see E. H. Merrill, "The Sign of Jonah," *JETS* 23 (1980): 23–30. He argues that the sign was Jonah's deliverance from the fish, interpreted in light of the name of the city, which meant "fishtown," and the Ninevites' belief that their city was founded by a fish god. Jonah's experience was somehow communicated to the inhabitants, who concluded that he was a divine messenger.

[29] Quoted in Keil and Delitzsch, "Jonah," COT, 10:401.

both figuratively and literally.[30] However, it is an accurate description of Jonah's experience after being thrown overboard.

2:4 In this passage the prophet expressed both the depths of despair and the heights of hope, his plight as well as his deep faith in the results of God's mercy. The syntax (with the pronoun subject expressed first) indicates a contrast with the previous verse. Though overwhelmed by the sea, seemingly banished (from the verb *garaš*) by the Lord, nevertheless (*'ak*) Jonah suddenly said to himself in faith that he would live to pray once again.[31] This verse is formally quite similar to Ps 31:22 (cf. also Lam 3:54). There the psalmist was the object of the Lord's "wonderful love" but said to himself, "I am cut off [from *garaz*] from your sight!" Yet (*'aken*) the Lord heard his cries for help.

The term "banished" is used in Lev 21:7 of a woman whose husband has divorced her.[32] As discussed at 1:3, Jonah was not expressing a belief in the localization of Yahweh to Palestine. He stood with many other Old Testament prophets in believing in the all-present God of Israel. Therefore this phrase must be taken as an expression of emotional consternation at being out of the Lord's favor.

Jonah's expression of confident faith in the latter part of the verse, "yet I will look again toward your holy temple," may refer not to a literal visit to the temple but figuratively to his intention to pray, though he wondered whether his prayer would be heard.[33]

The context of vv. 3,5 has led some to question the appropriateness of an expression of faith at this point. Rather than "yet I will look again" the LXX translates, "Shall I indeed[34] look again," and the Greek translation of Theodotion has "how[35] shall I look again?" Although these renderings would remove the difficulty of Jonah's optimism in such a hopeless situation, the Greek translators had a Hebrew text without vowels.[36] Furthermore, this understanding overlooks the syntax of the verse, which suggests a contrast, as well as the ability of Hebrew poetry to sandwich expressions of faith between descriptions of despair.

---

[30] Fretheim, *Message of Jonah,* 102.

[31] It is possible to translate the verb אָמַרְתִּי as a present perfect, "I have said," and to understand the statement of faith as uttered from inside the fish and expressing "Jonah's confidence that having been rescued by the fish he will again worship in the Temple in Jerusalem" (Alexander, "Jonah," 115).

[32] Ibid., 40.

[33] Fretheim, *Message of Jonah,* 102.

[34] The Greek word is ἆρα, an "interrogative particle implying anxiety or impatience" (J. Lust et al., eds., *A Greek-English Lexicon of the Septuagint* [Stuttgart: Deutsche Bibelgesellschaft, 1992], 59).

[35] The Greek word is πῶς, which can translate Hebrew אֵי , which we may suppose is then a variant of אֵ in this verse.

[36] Price and Nida, *Translator's Handbook,* 41.

One must beware of making textual alterations based upon the supposed unlikelihood of what a character might say or do in a given situation. L. C. Allen agrees that this verse depicts a new Jonah. He states: "He is soon to demonstrate a willing spirit by accepting the commission he formerly had rejected. In line with this change of heart, even now in this testimony to God's grace he looks forward to seeking the special presence of God to offer his praise."[37]

2:5–6 To understand properly the continuity of thought, these two verses are best considered together. Verse 5 is similar to Pss 18:4 and 69:1. As Jonah lay in the great fish, he continued to reflect upon his miraculous deliverance from the sea. Not only had the currents swept him beneath the waves (v. 3); his head was even entangled in seaweed, adding to his peril.[38]

Thus this statement elaborates on Jonah's sense of a spectacular reversal in the miraculous deliverance enabled by the Lord. Indeed, he painted a dreadful picture of the action of the water. The first phrase, "engulfing waters threatened me," uses the term *nepeš* (lit., "waters engulfed me to [my] *nepeš*"), which is often translated in the Old Testament "soul."[39] Here the KJV has "even to the soul" (cf. the NASB "to the *very* soul"), which makes little sense. The word can also refer to the "throat" or "neck" (cf. Pss 69:1; 105:18; Prov 23:2). The REB has "the water about me rose to my neck."

Since Jonah is describing a situation of being under the water (vv. 3,6), however, the idea of the water being up to his neck, at least in a literal sense, seems inappropriate. The NRSV makes good sense in taking it as the equivalent of a personal pronoun, translating, "The waters closed in over me." Finally, the NIV seems to have understood the term as referring to Jonah's life (cf. v. 7; Lev 17:11; Deut 12:23; Ps 30:3; Prov 7:23; 19:8), which the waters were threatening. Some translate the Hebrew *sûp* (the name of the "Red" or "Reed" Sea, the "Yam Suph"[40]) "seagrass," referring to a variety of underwater plant life that grows only at the bottom of the sea. Others see this as referring to seaweed, which grows at many depths.

The phrase "to the roots of the mountains I sank down" echoes the painful event of descending into his grave.[41] "Roots of the mountains" suggests a belief that the foundations of the mountains lie in the depths of the earth,

---

[37] Allen, *Joel, Obadiah, Jonah, and Micah*, 217.

[38] Fretheim states that Jonah's experience with entangling seaweed clearly portrays his presence in the sea, not the fish (*Message of Jonah*, 102).

[39] On the meaning of the word נֶפֶשׁ see H. W. Wolff, *Anthropology of the Old Testament* (Philadelphia: Fortress, 1974), 10–25.

[40] Almbladh mentions a Midrash that speaks of Jonah as taken by the fish on a tour of the Israelites' path through the Sea of Reeds (*Studies in the Book of Jonah* [Uppsala: University Press, 1986], 28).

[41] The verb יָרַדְתִּי in v. 7 (Eng., v. 6) serves as an important link between the psalm and the surrounding narrative (cf. 1:3,5). See Magonet, *Form and Meaning,* 43.

which are covered by the sea (cf. Sir 16:19).[42] Jonah was expressing his feeling of being in the deepest part of the ocean, as far removed from the world of human habitation as it was possible to conceive. Any help or hope was completely out of reach.

The phrase "the earth beneath barred me in forever" has been the cause of a great deal of discussion. It is literally, "The earth, its bars behind me forever." While this phrase is an expression of despair on Jonah's part, it is not certain what "bars" are referring to. In Job 38:10 is found an idea of bolts and doors of the ocean. There it seems the bolts of the sea are the walls of the sea basin, which set bounds to the sea that it cannot pass over. Consequently, the bolts of the earth may be such barriers as restrain the land from spreading over the sea. Jonah felt the weight of the waves or the great masses of water pressing upon him when he sank to the bottom of the sea, refusing him access back to the earth.[43]

The expression also may refer to the gates of Sheol, the underworld, conceived to be a fortified city (cf. Ps 9:13; Isa 38:10). If these bars were closed behind a human being, they remained finally shut.[44] Jonah had a sense of being entombed by the sea. These verses express Jonah's extreme depth of despair, his utter hopelessness. As in v. 2, Jonah may have been expressing his feeling that he was virtually dead. Even beyond the deepest sea, he felt that he had passed into the underworld from which he would never escape.[45]

The phrase "but you brought my life up from the pit, O LORD my God" is the turning point of the prayer.[46] Here is an expression of praise, a recognition of God's sovereign power. Jonah was referring to God's miraculous intervention by way of the great fish. Here begins an extremely strong contrast to the preceding description, since Jonah was acknowledging that he had been brought back alive from the depths of the sea. This is one of the many "but God" verses in the Bible (e.g., Gen 8:1; 45:7; 50:20; Josh 14:12; Pss

---

[42] To achieve greater poetic balance, many would reconstruct vv. 5–6 so that לְקִצְבֵי הָרִי concludes v. 5 rather than beginning v. 6 (following the LXX), yielding the translation (NRSV): "Weeds were wrapped around my head at the roots of the mountains. I went down to the land whose bars closed upon me forever." See Almbladh, *Studies in the Book of Jonah*, 28. This reading is probably secondary, however, introduced to make the poetic structure conform to later standards.

[43] Keil and Delitzsch, "Jonah," COT, 10:402.

[44] Wolff (*Obadiah and Jonah,* 136) opts for this concept while Walton (*Jonah,* 34) thinks the word refers to physical imprisonment.

[45] J. T. Walsh notes the vertical movement in vv. 5–6a (Heb. 6–7a) together with the absence of any reference to God and explains, "No longer upheld by his God, the psalmist feels himself sinking helplessly and hopelessly to the netherworld" ("Jonah 2:3–10: A Rhetorical Critical Study," *Bib* 63 (1982): 227).

[46] According to Walsh (Ibid., 228), "With the verb *watta al*, Yahweh appears on the scene abruptly and actively."

37:13,17,33; 49:15; John 1:18; Acts 2:24; 3:15; 10:40; 13:30; Rom 5:8; 1 Cor 1:27; 2 Cor 7:6; Eph 2:4; Phil 2:27). Jonah had been retrieved by God from a hopeless situation.[47] The God from whom Jonah thought he was banished had reached down and pulled him out of death and despair, showing that he was still "Yahweh my God."[48] Jonah was overcome with praise for his God, who had shown him such compassionate grace.

2:7   While it is obvious from a reading of the entire Book of Jonah that the prophet had not reached spiritual maturity, there were some significant advances in his life. This prayer clearly shows him turning back to the Lord. This verse echoes the initial summary statement in v. 2 of Jonah's distress and his prayer, which the Lord answered.[49]

It is accurate to call Jonah an Old Testament prodigal. L. C. Allen picks up on this theme: "Now the prodigal returns, drawn closer to him than ever before by the cords of redemptive love. Just as dire physical extremity forced the prodigal son to a decision to return home in penitence, so Jonah in his last moments thought of the one who alone could help him as Creator and controller of the sea."[50] As Jonah had said more than once (vv. 2,5,6), his "life" was as good as gone. The word for "life" here is different from the one used in the previous verse. Here it is the word *nepeš* that occurs in v. 5. It was at this desperate moment, he said, when (literally) "Yahweh I remembered." The verb "remember" (*zakar*) refers here to the mental act of focusing attention on something. It is almost always the basis for action (Exod 20:8; Num 15:40; Ezek 6:9). By itself, especially in contrast to "forget" (*šakah*), it often means "to act on the basis of knowledge" (cf. Ps 74:22–23). In 2 Sam 14:11 it is translated "invoke," which would fit here as well.[51]

The last phrase of v. 7 is identical in Hebrew to the final phrase of v. 4. However, there is no proof that the earthly temple in Jerusalem was intended here. For example, Solomon's prayer in 1 Kings 8 shows the ideas of the earthly temple and the heavenly dominion of God as closely related. Simply,

---

[47] The word translated "pit," שַׁחַת, is rendered "corruption" by the early translators (LXX, Syr, Vg). This rendering is unquestionably the correct one in Job 17:14, where the meaning "pit" is quite unsuitable. But it is by no means warranted in the present instance. The word also occurs in Job 33:18,24,30; Pss 16:10; 35:7; 55:24 (Eng., v. 23); 103:4; Isa 38:17. Cf. the use of its synonym בּוֹר in Pss 28:1; 30:4; 88:5,7 (Eng., vv. 4,6); 143:7; Prov 1:12; Isa 14:15,19; 38:18; Ezek 26:20; 31:14–16; 32:18,23–24,29.

[48] As Walsh expresses, "The entire drama of distress, entreaty, and salvation has been played out in the context of that relationship" ("Jonah 2:3–10," 228).

[49] Wolff, *Obadiah and Jonah,* 137.

[50] Allen, *Joel, Obadiah, Jonah and Micah,* 217–18. See also Gaebelein, *Servant and Dove,* 104.

[51] J. T. Walsh explains that Jonah's "last conscious thought had been a remembrance of Yahweh" and that "this thought must have been received as an effective prayer for salvation" ("Jonah 2:3–10," 224).

Jonah knew that his prayer reached God's heart.

2:8–9 These verses that form the concluding strophe of this psalm are words of thanksgiving and praise. Jonah herein declares his conviction that Yahweh alone is the source of salvation, and he bestows it upon those who call on him. On the other hand, those who look to idols will miss "the grace that could be theirs."

There are several difficulties of interpretation in v. 8.[52] Syntactically, it is a sentence, with the subject in the first line, then the object and verb in the second. The subject is literally "those who guard/serve[53] vanities of worthlessness." The latter phrase, as the NIV has translated it, refers to idols. The entire line is found also in Ps 31:6 (Heb., v. 7): "I hate those who cling to worthless idols." The verb in the second line (*ʿazab*) means to "abandon, forsake, forfeit." The primary difficulty in the verse is with the word *hasdam*, translated "the grace that could be theirs." It is made up of a pronominal suffix meaning "of them" and the word *hesed*, which can have several meanings, such as "loyalty, obligation, faithfulness, kindness, grace, mercy." The problem is determining which meaning best fits in this case and whether the pronoun represents the object or subject of the *hesed*. One view is that, as the NIV interprets, idolaters forfeit "their grace" from God. Another is that unlike Jonah, who would "make good" what he had vowed (v. 9), idolaters will abandon "their loyalty" to their supposed gods when they discover how impotent they are.[54]

When we take into consideration the general thought of this strophe, the interpretation of the NIV seems preferable. The overall thought here seems to emphasize the salvation that comes from the Lord (v. 9b). Wolff probably is correct that *hesed* refers here to the divine attitude that in the Psalter is continually extolled as God's faithfulness, goodness, and graciousness, the one true help for human beings (cf. Pss 59:17; 144:2).[55]

The mention of sacrifice and the paying of vows in v. 9 echoes the end of chap. 1, where the pagan seamen celebrated their deliverance through the offering of sacrifices and the making of vows. In this passage Jonah also sang a song of thanksgiving and vowed sacrifice and the fulfillment of covenant vows. Though the essence of the vow is not delineated, it may have been some kind of commitment to live up to his calling as a prophet.

While some doubt the genuineness of this passage, here Jonah dealt with the subject that is the basis of the book, that there is the possibility to forfeit God's offer of salvation. Idols represent not only ineffectiveness, but worship-

---

[52] See the discussion in Price and Nida, *Translator's Handbook,* 46–48.

[53] The *piel* of שׁמר is of uncertain meaning since it does not occur elsewhere. Sasson (*Jonah,* 160, 197) translates "hold to" or "maintain" and notes that it is opposite in meaning to עזב, "forfeit."

[54] Alexander, "Jonah," 117.

[55] Wolff, *Obadiah and Jonah,* 183. Cf. Gaebelein, *Servant and Dove,* 105.

ing them involves a rejection of Yahweh. It may be said that this line of thought is highly ironic. In this text Jonah sermonized during his prayer regarding an issue where he himself had failed. While he advocated total dependence upon the Lord and the forsaking of idols, his recent history showed that he was the one who fled and forsook God. Did Jonah express hypocrisy here? Did he fail to deal honestly with his own life? No, not at all. When we read the first part of chap. 2, we recognize that he was dealing with his own life, his failings, as well as his intent to seek change. Understanding again the context of the whole book, we realize that Jonah had not yet reached a point of total repentance. Nonetheless, he seriously considered the right path and in v. 8 expressed that way of righteousness.

In the words "salvation comes from the LORD," Jonah extolled the work of the Lord as Savior. Here also is an emphasis on the Lord's sole sovereignty in the area of salvation. No one else can provide in such a way, though Jonah already showed in v. 8 how one might reject God's offer. It is correct to say that this line may serve as the key verse in the book. Fretheim is possibly correct in pointing out that salvation does seem to be the key motif in the book, and this verse points to that motif. Salvation for the sailors is emphasized in chap. 1, for Jonah in chap. 2, for the Ninevites in chap. 3; and it is the objective of God's questioning of Jonah in chap. 4.[56] Jonah recognized that he deserved death, not deliverance. He then knew, as we do, that no one deserves deliverance. It is an act of mercy by a gracious God.

2. The Prophet's Deliverance (2:10)

[10]And the LORD commanded the fish, and it vomited Jonah onto dry land.

2:10 In this verse the narrative of 1:17 is resumed. The verse begins with the Lord's speaking to the great fish. God concluded his assignment for this fish by commanding it to relieve itself of its cumbersome cargo. The word translated "vomited" in the NIV is a coarse word and is used in the Old Testament only in images that arouse disgust (Isa 19:14; Jer 48:26; Lev 18:28). While in other versions it is translated "spit" or "spewed," the word used in the NIV is not only graphic but also accurate.[57]

Jonah's expulsion from the ship may have landed him in the coastal area near Joppa, his "starting place." At least one writer makes this assertion based on a probable translation of 1:13, where the seamen rowed hard to bring the ship "back" to the land. This indicated their nearness to the starting port of

---

[56] Fretheim, *Message of Jonah,* 103–4.

[57] A. J. Wilson ("The Sign of the Prophet Jonah and Its Modern Confirmations," 637) relates the sperm whale's practice of relieving itself of awkward and indigestible objects.

Joppa.[58] The point of emphasis here is that Jonah was returned to dry land, thus completing God's rescue.

This chapter may be the "happiest" section in the entire book. These verses contain the story of miracle and grace, praise and thanksgiving, deliverance and renewed hope. In this chapter the poor fish is relieved of its cargo (few ever express sympathy for the difficult days of this marine creature). In these verses are found the education of the pouting prophet and the affirmation of God's sovereignty. It is God who is the most important character. He is the one who affects salvation, and he is the one who enables deliverance. Neither Jonah nor the fish had control. It was God and God alone.

---

[58] Gaebelein, *Servant and Dove,* 107. This point is used to show that when a person rebels, God wishes to bring that person back to the point of departure from fellowship. While this may be true, this text does not contain any such message. Jonah 3:1 may, but 2:10 does not.

III. GOD'S SECOND COMMISSION AND JONAH'S OBEDIENCE
(3:1–10)
1. God's Renewal of His Commission (3:1–2)
2. The Prophet's Preaching and Nineveh's Response (3:3–9)
    (1) The Short Sermon (3:3–4)
    (2) The Response of the People (3:5)
    (3) The Response of the King (3:6–9)
3. God's Response (3:10)

III. GOD'S SECOND COMMISSION AND JONAH'S OBEDIENCE (3:1–10)

1. God's Renewal of His Commission (3:1–2)

¹**Then the word of the LORD came to Jonah a second time:** ²**"Go to the great city of Nineveh and proclaim to it the message I give you."**

This chapter brings resolution to the primary storyline of the Book of Jonah, for it relates the fulfillment of God's word concerning both Nineveh and Jonah. Jonah finally obeys God and preaches in Nineveh, and the greatest miracle in the book takes place: the turning or repentance of an entire nation to God.

Having experienced the miraculous expulsion from the belly of the fish, Jonah found himself on dry land. Verses 1 and 2 do not mention his emotional state, so we are left to conjecture. Did he expect events to occur in this way? Though he had hoped for deliverance, did he expect it so soon? How long did it take him to regain a sense of composure? Did he simply wait in place for God to speak to him again? While the Scripture obviously does not deal with these matters, we may surmise that there was at least a brief period in which Jonah sought to regain a sense of composure and stability.

3:1 If we read the Book of Jonah in one sitting, these words will be familiar, for 3:1–2 is strikingly similar to 1:1–2. In a sense Jonah was back to where he began. However, the Jonah in chap. 3 is somewhat different from the person found in chap. 1. Much had happened, and many lessons were learned, but the process of discipleship obviously was not yet complete. The text simply points out that God spoke to Jonah again. There is no mention of reproach for the prophet's former disobedience. The Lord simply repeated his command. While Jonah had taken quite a detour since the first command, God's will remained steadfast.

Although God's word came to Jonah a second time, demonstrating his forbearance and mercy, examples in Scripture show that not everyone has a second chance to do what God has commanded (cf. Gen 3; Num 20:12; 1 Kgs 13:26). However, this text should bring thanksgiving to the heart of every believer who has been given another opportunity to do what God requires. This text, more than anything else, points to God's sovereignty and his insistence upon the accomplishment of his will. As J. Baldwin has written, "He will not be frustrated by the effrontery of a prophet, nor has he allowed the prophet to wander indefinitely off course."[1]

3:2 This verse is almost identical to 1:2 except for the final clause (see Introduction, "Structure," p. 219). It uses the same three imperatives in Hebrew, literally, "Arise, go . . . proclaim." But in 1:2 the reason for Jonah's mission is given, while in 3:2 the stress is on delivering God's words. Although the precise content of the message Jonah was commanded to preach to this Assyrian city is not yet mentioned, two things are made clear: where he should preach and the source of the message. Jonah was given specific "marching orders" about the destination. He also was reminded that the message would not come from him nor from anyone else, but only from the Lord. His job was to deliver the message, not to critique or revise it.[2]

The clause "I give you" is literally "which I am speaking (or about to speak) to you." The question arises whether the message was the same as given before, a new one God gave at this moment, or one God would give upon Jonah's arrival at Nineveh.[3] Nevertheless, the text confirms that Jonah was assured of God's revelation, and he was commanded to preach that message. The verb used here for "proclaim" is the one that occurs so many times in Jonah meaning either "proclaim" or "call" (see comments on 1:2). It suggests a formal type of announcement, such as one made by an official messenger or ambassador. This lends credence to the importance of the message.

---

[1] J. Baldwin, "Jonah," in *The Minor Prophets: An Exegetical and Expository Commentary,* ed. T. E. McComiskey (Grand Rapids: Baker, 1993), 2:576.

[2] D. Stuart, *Hosea-Jonah,* WBC (Dallas: Word, 1987), 482. Another difference in 1:2 and 3:2 is that in 1:2 the verb קְרָא governs the prepositional phrase עָלֶיהָ, "against it," which ends the main clause, whereas in 3:2 it governs אֵלֶיהָ, "to it," followed by the object אֶת־הַקְּרִיאָה, "the proclamation," with its modifying relative clause. As J. Sasson explains: "The first time around, Nineveh is simply being served with a death warrant. In this case, however, God commissions Jonah with a *qerîʾâ;* Nineveh, therefore, will receive a specific message from Israel's god" (*Jonah,* AB [New York: Doubleday, 1990], 226).

[3] The Hebrew participle is translated as a past in the Septuagint, a present in the Vg, and a future in the Syr. Cf. Price and Nida, *Translator's Handbook,* 52.

2. The Prophet's Preaching and Nineveh's Response (3:3–9)

(1) The Short Sermon (3:3–4)

[3]Jonah obeyed the word of the LORD and went to Nineveh. Now Nineveh was a very important city—a visit required three days. [4]On the first day, Jonah started into the city. He proclaimed: "Forty more days and Nineveh will be overturned."

3:3 The first half of v. 3 stands in stark contrast to 1:3, which begins in Hebrew with the same two words, literally, "So Jonah rose." But whereas 1:3 continues, "to flee to Tarshish from before Yahweh," 3:3 continues, "and went to Nineveh according to the word of Yahweh." The last time God called, Jonah headed west. This time in response to God's call he headed northeast. Depending upon Jonah's starting place, the trip to Nineveh would have been approximately five hundred land miles. According to the usual manner of transport (camel or donkey caravan), it would have taken approximately one month to traverse this distance. Going by foot would have taken even longer.

Several issues are involved in interpreting the clause "Nineveh was a very important city." First is the use of the perfect tense verb *hayĕtâ,* translated "was." As mentioned in the introduction, several scholars point to this as proof that Nineveh had ceased to exist by the time of Jonah's writing. Hebrew has only two so-called tenses, and they do not necessarily mark time, especially in the kind of circumstantial clause found here. The choice of verb form here is determined not by Nineveh's former greatness but by syntax and the past time of the surrounding narrative. It emphasizes the size and importance of the city in Jonah's day.[4]

The phrase "a very important city" is literally "a city great to God."[5] Most versions have rendered the word meaning "to God" (*le'lohîm*) as an adverb such as "exceeding" or "very." L. C. Allen sees this phrase as a striking, biblical way of expressing a superlative by bringing it into relation with God. It is simply saying that Nineveh was "God-sized."[6] Although the word *'elohîm* may serve in this way elsewhere in Scripture,[7] Sasson claims that in such

---

[4] See Sasson, *Jonah,* 228. Allen (*Joel, Obadiah, Jonah and Micah*, 221) is correct, citing G. S. Ogden ("Time and the Verb *hyh* in Old Testament Prose," *VT* 21 [1971]: 453), that this verb only has the stative sense in direct speech and that in narrative it refers to the past (pp. 451–52). But since the entire narrative refers to the past, Allen goes too far in saying that the verb here "indicates that the situation came to an end before the time of the author's statement." As G. C. Aalders states, "We can view the perfect tense as synchronistic; it says no more than that when Jonah went to Nineveh it was a great city" (*The Problem of Jonah* [London: Tyndale, 1948], 10–11).

[5] D. J. Wiseman has noted that Scripture uses the adjective "great" of only four cities: Babylon (Dan 4:30), Jerusalem (Jer 22:8), Gibeon (Josh 10:2), and Nineveh.

[6] Allen, *Joel, Obadiah, Jonah and Micah,* 221.

[7] Cf. Joüon and Muraoka, *GBH* § 142n; Waltke and O'Connor, *IBHS* § 14.5b.

cases it is always paired with a noun, such as "prince of God" in Gen 23:6 or "mountains of God" in Ps 36:6 [Heb., v. 7]. He favors treating the phrase "as a circumlocution whereby 'the large city' is said to 'belong' to God." It thus expresses "God's dominion over the staunchest of Israel's foes."[8] While a literal rendering "great to God" may be unnecessary, clearly God cared deeply about the Ninevites, whom he had created in his image.[9] Therefore he sent this prophet with a message that would ultimately lead to their turning.

Following the phrase "great to God" that modifies "city" is another phrase (literally), "a journey of three days." While some would dismiss this phrase as part of the general hyperbole or exaggeration of the writer,[10] several scholars have shown that it can be understood in a literal sense (see Introduction, "Date," p. 206). In the first century B.C., Diodorus Siculus correlated all the information received from the fourth-century Ctesias that Nineveh's total circumference was approximately fifty-five miles. Given this, a three-day journey would be a reasonable trek around the city.[11] On the other hand, the Assyrian king Sennacherib (704–681) wrote that he enlarged the circumference of the city of Nineveh from 9,300 to 21,815 cubits, or from about three miles to seven miles.[12]

But Wiseman has shown that this phrase can relate not only to Nineveh proper but to the entire administrative district of Nineveh. This metropolitan district included also the cities of Assur, Calah (Nimrud), and even Dur-Sharruken (Khorsabad).[13] This interpretation is supported by Gen 10:11–12, where "that is the great city" seems to refer to the whole district covered by Nineveh, Rehoboth, Ir, Calah, and Resen.

Regardless of the extent of Nineveh, perhaps the best way of understanding this phrase is as a description of the type of visit Jonah made to the city of Nineveh. As the NIV has translated, Jonah's visit to Nineveh was a three-day event. Nineveh was a major diplomatic center of the ancient world, and the message God wanted the city to hear could not be shared hastily. For Jonah to have accomplished his mission, he would have had to travel to various sections, speaking to as many groups as possible.[14] Such a visit could have taken three days. Another suggestion is that the three-day journey refers to the ancient Oriental practice of hospitality in which a visit required three days.

---

[8] Sasson, *Jonah*, 228–29.

[9] Gaebelein describes the significant cultural attainments of Nineveh, verified by modern archaeology (*Servant and Dove*, 112–13).

[10] Fretheim states that "the author's purposive use of exaggeration is especially prominent in this chapter" (*Message of Jonah*, 106).

[11] Allen, *Joel, Obadiah, Jonah and Micah*, 221.

[12] J. Walton, *Jonah*, BSC (Grand Rapids: Zondervan, 1982), 37.

[13] D. J. Wiseman, "Jonah's Nineveh," *TynBul* 30 (1979): 38.

[14] Stuart, *Hosea-Jonah*, 487–88.

The first day was for arrival, the second for the primary purpose of the visit, and the third for return.[15] However the phrase is understood, it does not necessarily refer to the size of the city.

3:4   On this first day of the visit, customarily designed for meetings with city leaders, Jonah made his grand entrance. As Stuart points out, it is not likely that he simply "wandered into Nineveh" virtually unnoticed and then began shouting his message. Perhaps his first day involved meetings with officials and included the presentation of gifts to city dignitaries.[16]

Although Bewer thinks that Jonah did not preach until the end of the first day,[17] all the text says is that he began preaching on the first day of his visit, apparently whenever he found an opportunity or place fitting for his proclamation.[18] Jonah's arrival in Nineveh probably was dramatic. His clothing was no doubt different from the norm, his bearing gave evidence of a different lifestyle, and a possibly bleached skin color provided for much attention.

Many object to the historical reliability of this story because of the alleged unlikelihood that Jonah would have been able to communicate with the Ninevites. Bewer says that "this is another sign of the folktale character of the story."[19] However, if an Assyrian official could speak to the populace of Jerusalem in Hebrew in 701 B.C. (2 Kgs 18:26–28), there is no reason to doubt that a Hebrew prophet could speak to the populace of Nineveh in Aramaic, the lingua franca of the day, fifty years earlier.[20]

Allen describes the situation poetically: "Lost like a needle in a haystack inside this gigantic Vanity Fair, this Sodom of a city, the tiny figure feels he can go no further. He stops and shouts out the laconic message with which he has been entrusted."[21] The message from the Lord, imparted by Jonah, was a relatively short one. In the Hebrew the message was only five words long. While it is not clear that this was all he had to say, the text does suggest that God's message was brief and that Jonah simply preached it repeatedly. If these words were the sum total of the message, no reason for the destruction was given, nor was the manner of destruction described. There was not even an explicit call to repentance.

Jonah's dialogue with God in the fourth chapter suggests that he may have preached this message with the secret hope that Nineveh would be destroyed.

---

[15] Wiseman, "Jonah's Nineveh," 38.

[16] Stuart, *Hosea-Jonah*, 487–88.

[17] Bewer, *Haggai, Zechariah, Malachi, and Jonah*, 52.

[18] Keil and Delitzsch, "Jonah," COT 10:405. Many agree with this conclusion. See Ellison, "Jonah," 381; Kennedy, *Studies in Jonah*, 48.

[19] Bewer, *Haggai, Zechariah, Malachi, and Jonah*, 53.

[20] W. L. Banks states, "He [Jonah] spoke Aramaic, a language known to both Hebrew and Assyrian alike" (*Jonah, The Reluctant Prophet* [Chicago: Moody, 1966], 72).

[21] Allen, *Joel, Obadiah, Jonah and Micah*, 222.

Fretheim states: "Jonah had just experienced the unmerited grace and good-ness of God in his own life. Now he turns right around and makes it as diffi-cult as possible for the Ninevites to experience God's deliverance . . . a graceless message delivered by one living in the shadow of an experience of grace."[22]

Nevertheless, although Jonah apparently did not mention the possibility of deliverance in response to repentance, both he and his audience may have assumed it. At least his audience hoped for it. If this were not so, why had Jonah's deity given them forty days? As Stuart explains, there was ambiguity in the message, for the forty days might be "simply to assure that the divine judgment was not far off." Also the word for "destroy" (*hapak*) carries a cer-tain vagueness, since it can mean either "turn" or "overthrow" (see comments on Amos 5:7 in this volume). It can signify "judgment, a turning upside down, a reversal, a change, a deposing of royalty, or a change of heart." In other words, Jonah's words could mean either that in "forty more days Nineveh would be destroyed" or that "in forty more days Nineveh would have a change of heart."[23] Therefore the ambiguity in these words given by the Lord may have been what opened the door of understanding for the Ninevites and led to their positive response.

This also relates to the charge that Jonah's prophecy was false since his prediction did not occur. If it was a prediction, then it was falsified by the out-come of the situation. However, if it was a warning, then it implied the condi-tion "unless you repent." While Jonah apparently hoped that this was a prediction, it is obvious that God meant it as a warning.[24] Nowhere in the Book of Jonah does God call this message a prophesy. The issue is clarified even further by a reading of Jer 18:7–8, where the Lord carefully delineates the conditions under which he would relent:

> If at any time I announce that a nation or kingdom is to be uprooted, torn down and destroyed, and if that nation I warned repents of its evil, then I will relent and not inflict on it the disaster I had planned.

The discussion of warning and judgment in this passage should lead to the recognition of several key points. First, this passage refers to the seriousness of sin as well as the certainty of God's judgment. Nineveh was an exceedingly wicked and violent city, and this did not escape God's notice. In that age as well as in every age, God recognizes and condemns what is unholy and

---

[22] Fretheim, *Message of Jonah,* 108. See also B. Halpern and R. E. Friedman, "Composition and Paronomasia in the Book of Jonah," *HAR* 4 (1980): 79–92; E. M. Good, *Irony in the Old Tes-tament* (Philadelphia: Westminster, 1985), 48–49.

[23] Stuart, *Hosea-Jonah,* 489. Wiseman notes that the Assyrian equivalent, *abaku,* would have carried the same ambiguity ("Jonah's Nineveh," 49).

[24] G. B. Caird, *Language and Imagery of the Bible* (Philadelphia: Westminster, 1980), 56–57.

unjust. One must also recognize the issue of God's warning to those who are outside his will and his use of believers as messengers. In the Old Testament, Israel was intended to be a light to the nations (cf. Isa 49:6). In the New Testament one reads of the believers' responsibility to be ambassadors in this world and carriers of the good news. This passage in Jonah portrays beautifully God's concern for those who are outside his will and his plan for using his disciples in the grand process of reconciliation. Thus the people of Nineveh were given time, forty days, to recognize the seriousness of the situation and to repent.[25]

(2) The Response of the People (3:5)

⁵The Ninevites believed God. They declared a fast, and all of them, from the greatest to the least, put on sackcloth.

3:5 This verse gives a summary of Nineveh's astounding response to the proclamation of this strange Hebrew prophet, which is then detailed in vv. 6–9. His message, heard by many and no doubt shared with others, spread to every part of the populace. Not only did they hear his message, they believed that it was a serious one. Thus the residents of Nineveh sought to avert their destruction. Like the reaction of the sailors in 1:5, the Ninevites' reaction is conveyed by three verbs: "believed . . . declared . . . put on." These describe three stages of response: inward, articulated, then outward (see Introduction, "Structure," p. 219).

The events of v. 5 portray a whirlwind of activity by the populace. Since no further preaching is mentioned beyond the first day, it is possible that Jonah's planned three-day preaching tour proved unnecessary. The revival broke out in the city on the first day.[26] They accepted en masse the divine source of Jonah's message, believing that what had been threatened might be carried out. The very size of Nineveh enhanced the nature of this miracle. Ellul is correct in stating that "we are here in the presence of a mystery and a miracle."[27] All the odds were against Nineveh's accepting this message. After all, as Baldwin notes, "When Jeremiah preached a century or more later that Jerusalem would be overthrown, he was arrested and imprisoned for treason (Jer 26:8), although he was well known as the prophet of God."[28] One would not expect them to react to this strange prophet in this manner. One would imagine widespread questioning and doubt. If such a situation were to occur today, what would be the response of modern hearers? Who was going to destroy the city? How would it be done? Why should one believe such a message? We

---

[25] Wolff, *Obadiah and Jonah,* 150.

[26] Stuart, *Hosea-Jonah,* 488.

[27] J. Ellul, *The Judgment of Jonah* (Grand Rapids: Eerdmans, 1971), 97.

[28] Baldwin, "Jonah," 2:577.

might expect that the people of Nineveh would have responded to Jonah with an incredulous sneer.[29]

Obviously the Ninevites did "believe." The important question here, however, is what did they believe? The NIV is correct in translating this phrase, "The Ninevites believed God." Although the Hebrew can be translated literally "and the men of Nineveh believed *in God*" (*be'lohîm*), this phrase does not carry the same significance as the modern understanding of "in God," denoting a conversion to faith.[30] The Hebrew phrase means only that they believed what Jonah's God said would happen. It is best to understand the phrase as the NIV (and the NRSV) translates it, "believed God."

In support of this understanding, Jonah did not mention the name *Yahweh* for God at this point. He used the word *Elohim*. The obvious purpose was to bring home that Jonah had not been proclaiming Yahweh to those who did not know him but that the supreme God, whatever his name, was about to show his power and judgment.[31] There is not the slightest indication that Jonah at any point in his sojourn in Nineveh mentioned the God of Israel. There is no indication that the Ninevites turned from their other gods or that they even knew the name of the Lord (Yahweh). The text only states that the message Jonah brought from God was accepted as true.[32]

Some interpret this verse as describing the single greatest revival in history.[33] J. Walton, however, argues that this was not a "saving faith" resulting in a transformation of moral standards but only external actions by which they were spared. He compares their repentance to that of Ahab in 1 Kgs 21:27, which was sufficient to gain only a postponement of judgment.[34] Stuart agrees, stating, "They remained, by all accounts, the same polytheistic, syncretistic pantheists they had been all along."[35] Later history would certainly confirm that if a genuine change took place at Nineveh, it lasted only for a moment.

Jesus' words in Luke 11:32, however, sometimes are used to argue that a genuine conversion must have taken place. Jesus' own testimony is that "they repented at the preaching of Jonah" with the result that they will be present at the judgment condemning those who rejected Jesus' preaching. It is hard, then, to deny that at least some of the Ninevites were genuinely converted.

---

[29] P. Fairbairn, *Jonah, His Life, Character and Mission* (Grand Rapids: Kregel, 1964), 113.

[30] J. Walton, "The Object Lesson of Jonah 4:5–7 and the Purpose of the Book of Jonah," *BBR* 2 (1992): 53.

[31] Ellison, "Jonah," 382.

[32] Walton, *Jonah*, 47. If Num 20:12 is used for comparison, one will note that the same Hebrew construction is used and that the phrase implies no more than the believing of the message.

[33] Gaebelein, *Servant and Dove*, 115.

[34] Walton, *Jonah*, 53–54.

[35] Stuart, *Hosea-Jonah*, 497.

Furthermore, God would not have lifted his hand of judgment if the Ninevites had been acting out of hypocrisy. There can be no question that the change was relatively short-lived, but it seems that at least a few experienced a repentance that led to eternal life.[36] How long the city's submission to the Lord lasted we do not know. If Jonah's visit occurred around the reign of Jeroboam II in Israel, the next subsequent mention of the Assyrian Empire was some thirty to forty years later. In that instance Pul, the king of Assyria, came up against Menahem, king of Israel. After that it was not until Sennacherib's invasion of Judah during Hezekiah's reign that the king and people of Nineveh defied Yahweh. There are lengthy periods of time in which no historical record exists about the moral conduct of the Ninevites.

Even though the Ninevite revival was brief, one must ask how long a revival must last to be genuine, and, "Was there ever a lasting and continuous conversion in the history of Israel?"[37] The conclusion is that although we hope that the Ninevite revival amounted to a genuine conversion to faith in Yahweh, the text does not allow us to determine whether this was the case. We only know that the depth the repentance reached was sufficient for God to relent regarding the judgment he threatened. It is true that Nineveh did make a miraculous turn *toward* a correct faith, but we are uncertain whether they were being converted to Judaism, the Lord, or even monotheism. The response of the people of Nineveh was great, but it may have been primarily just a turning away from violence and wickedness.

A question frequently asked is that if this repentance occurred, why is there no historical record of it? First of all, the greatest of historical documents does speak to this turning. Those who affirm the historical reliability of Scripture would quickly point to the record in question as being sufficient evidence of such a turning. Still others seek extrabiblical evidence. Such evidence is absent from Assyrian records for several reasons. First of all, the extant records are comparatively few. There are large segments of undocumented history. Second, there was a serious, pronounced bias in recording history that gave only the most favorable of impressions. Kennedy points to several instances in which there obviously was little space given for religious experience symbolized by sackcloth and ashes.[38] Still, the questions must be asked: Why did Nineveh respond in such a fashion? What could have caused such a great turning when they heard this message from God? It was not for social and humanitarian reasons nor for reasons of conscience.[39] Could Jonah's demeanor have carried with it an air of authority that prompted belief? Fairbairn wrote of Jonah, "He bears himself as a man deeply in ear-

---

[36] Fairbairn, *Jonah, His Life,* 123.

[37] J. Overduin, *Adventures of a Deserter* (Grand Rapids: Eerdmans, 1965), 113.

[38] Kennedy, *Studies in Jonah,* 55.

[39] Ellul, *Judgment of Jonah,* 97.

nest, and alive to the awful importance of the work he has in hand."[40] Did the Ninevites somehow sense the seriousness of the matter through the confidence of this prophet? Did his unusual skin color prompt questions about why he looked this way? Some have surmised that Jonah's sojourn in the fish was shared with the people before his coming and that it prompted a reverential awe for this prophet.

As discussed earlier (see Introduction, p. 204), Nineveh was in a time of national crisis. In the middle of the eighth century their sense of well being would have been extremely low as a result of famine, enemy attacks, and internal revolts. There was even a full eclipse of the sun in 763 B.C. Assyrians worshiped many gods and believed that a single careless act could offend one of them and cause serious trouble. This caused a great deal of religious uncertainty. As Walton explains, the people of Nineveh would have been looking eagerly for understanding of their situation from the omens. God had apparently been using these factors to prepare them to receive Jonah's message. "Even if Jonah's prediction was not the interpretation of omens that had been read prior to his arrival, it would be normal for the Assyrians to react to his message by checking the omens to see if they agreed."[41]

Apparently Jonah's message was confirmed, for a fast was declared. The phrase "all of them" is not in the Hebrew text, but that is the point of the phrase "from the greatest to the least." Trible explains that it "suggests the riches of inclusivity: from royalty to commoners, nobility to peasants, age to youth, powerful to powerless—indeed, all sorts and conditions of folk."[42] "Sackcloth" (*saq*), a coarse cloth most often made of goat's hair, was the customary dress of the poor and those who were in mourning. In the Old Testament Jacob expressed his grief for the loss of Joseph and Job for his sad condition by putting on sackcloth (Gen 37:34; Job 16:15). Prophets often wore sackcloth, perhaps partly to associate themselves with the poor (who were being abused by the greed of the upper classes) but also as a sign of mourning for the sins of the people.

As Walton explains, the normal response for Assyrians to news that the gods were offended would have been sacrifices, libations, supplications, and prostration.[43] But it is well known that fasting was a symbol for the affliction of the soul or for intense mourning of the heart. Perhaps the Ninevites proclaimed a fast because of their knowledge that fasting was a Hebrew practice. Because this strange prophet was Hebrew, it would be best for them to join in

---

[40] Fairbairn, *Jonah, His Life,* 114.

[41] Walton, *Jonah,* 46. Walton establishes the extremely superstitious nature of the Ninevites in their careful attention to animate or inanimate terrestrial occurrences. For a defense of the historical probability of the Ninevite repentance, see Stuart, *Hosea-Jonah,* 490–92.

[42] Trible, *Rhetorical Criticism,* 181.

[43] Walton, *Jonah,* 47.

a Hebrew ritual that exhibited mourning and contrition. As T. Kirk has said, "Great emergencies demand and justify the use of extraordinary methods. The peril was too awful and near for a moment's delay."[44] The Ninevites, intent on averting disaster, utilized every means possible to show contrition. Like many who have a mistaken view of fasting today, they thought it might be a way to win God's approval and avert disaster.[45] Extraordinarily, God responded with compassion to this show of repentance and for the time being called a halt to the onslaught of his wrath.

The Hebrew prophets and countless preachers since their time who have grieved over the apparent ineffectiveness of their proclamation would have been thrilled at such a response as Jonah received. Here a city was literally shaken by a single sermon from a foreign prophet. Even Jesus noted the contrast between the response to Jonah and that which he received from the scribes and Pharisees. Without asking for a further sign, the Ninevites believed the message of the Lord's prophet, but the scribes and Pharisees demanded that Jesus prove his identity with a sign. In fact, Jesus declared that the Ninevites will stand up in the day of judgment to condemn the scribes and Pharisees for their unbelief (cf. Matt 12:41; Luke 11:30–32). The Ninevites believed after one short sermon without signs, whereas the scribes and Pharisees heard many sermons of Jesus and saw many signs yet still refused to believe.[46]

(3) The Response of the King (3:6–9)

6When the news reached the king of Nineveh, he rose from his throne, took off his royal robes, covered himself with sackcloth and sat down in the dust. 7Then he issued a proclamation in Nineveh:

"By the decree of the king and his nobles:

Do not let any man or beast, herd or flock, taste anything; do not let them eat or drink. 8But let man and beast be covered with sackcloth. Let everyone call urgently on God. Let them give up their evil ways and their violence. 9Who knows? God may yet relent and with compassion turn from his fierce anger so that we will not perish."

3:6 This verse details the royal reaction to Jonah's preaching. The phrase "when the news reached the king of Nineveh" indicates that this turning of Nineveh began with the common people, not with royalty.[47] It may have taken

---

[44] T. Kirk, *Jonah: His Life and Mission* (Minneapolis: Klock & Klock, 1983), 173.

[45] Fasting is to be seen as an expression of such intimate devotion to the Lord that one's physical needs are seen as unimportant, at least for a specific length of time.

[46] Overduin, *Adventures of a Deserter,* 107.

[47] The word for "the news" is הַדָּבָר, "word, matter." Here it can refer to news of the Ninevite revival, the content of Jonah's preaching, or both. The word דָּבָר has occurred previously in 1:1; 3:1,2,3.

some time before the secluded monarch heard the word of God from this Hebrew prophet. The title "king of Nineveh" is not the normal nomenclature used by the Assyrians but is a Hebrew expression to denote the ruling monarch of Nineveh.[48] No mention is made of the specific identity of this ruler, but Stuart presents a strong case for identifying him with Assur-dan III.[49]

The remainder of v. 6 describes the exciting response by this ruler. He rose[50] from his throne, the seat of his royal power, and humbled himself with the common people. He laid aside his robe, which was a large and beautifully embroidered mantle. The word that is used here for robe is the same as that given to the garment found by Achan among the spoils of Jericho (Josh 7:21). In its place the king put on sackcloth as a sign of mourning, and he sat in ashes, a sign of deep humiliation. The radical nature of his repentance is stressed by the literary structure of the clauses:

> he *rose* from his throne,
>   *took off* his royal robes,
>   *covered* himself with sackcloth
> and *sat down* in the dust.

He who was the highest in the empire took the lowest position of abasement.[51] It must also be noted that Ezek 26:16 depicts the mourning of the Tyrians over the ruin of their capital in just the same manner as the king of Nineveh is described here; however, instead of sackcloth they clothed themselves with "terror."

3:7 The previous verse shows the personal response of the ruler of Nineveh. This verse further details the official response. By the issuing of a proclamation the king added official sanction to that which already was underway. In other words the decree of the king amounted to a royal seal of approval on what had already occurred spontaneously throughout the city. It became a part of official government policy.[52] The inclusion of the "nobles" (lit., "the great ones") as the authority for the decree suggests a limited monarchy, confirming

---

[48] Kennedy explains that "the dominance of Israelitish idioms for the expression of Assyrian facts is to be accepted as natural in this story" (*Studies in Jonah,* 52). On the use of the expression "king of Nineveh" see further the Introduction, p. 205.

[49] "A king such as Assur-dan III, during whose reign an agonizing confluence of omens and disasters (eclipse, earthquake, famine, rioting) had occurred, whose capital (or at least common residence) may have been Nineveh, though this cannot be proved, and who was beset by international problems including continuing military failures against Urartu, was certainly the sort of king (among others) who might well have been predisposed to receive Jonah's message sincerely as a chance for respite from his troubles" (Stuart, *Hosea-Jonah,* 492).

[50] Trible notes (*Rhetorical Criticism,* 183) that this verb is used previously with Jonah as the subject in 1:3 and 3:3 to describe his response to the Lord's "word" (דָּבָר).

[51] Kirk, *Life and Mission,* 174–75.

[52] Fretheim, *Message of Jonah,* 111.

that Jonah's visit probably took place during a period of Assyrian weakness.

The decree called for four behavioral responses to Jonah's message: fasting (v. 7), wearing sackcloth, pleading with God, and turning from evil and violence (v. 8). The decree regarding fasting consists of two parts: a general order not to "taste anything," which is then emphasized by a command neither to "eat" (better "graze") nor to drink. The unusual aspect of the decree was the inclusion of animals in the fasting and also the wearing of sackcloth. There is some evidence of the involvement of animals in rites of mourning and humiliation among the Persians, although none has been found among the Assyrians.[53] This is flimsy evidence, however, from which to argue for the Persian period as the time of writing,[54] especially since even the Persian evidence is limited. D. J. Wiseman does cite an Assyrian decree from the early eighth century B.C. that calls for a general state of mourning and prayer by "you and all the people, your land, your meadows."[55]

The inclusion even of animals in this royally mandated fast is the act of a desperate monarch and a desperate people. Fasting and uncomfortable dress represented self-denial. By eschewing normal comforts and making themselves physically miserable, they sought to show the genuineness of their prayers for mercy.[56] This action was an attempt to impress forcibly upon the Lord the sincerity of Nineveh's repentance. It was an attempt to move the heart of God and lead him to relent. In other words, they were using every option available, including superstition. Perhaps they also felt that combining their cries of contrition with the pleading of the animals for water and food would rise as one mighty prayer for mercy to this God who threatened their destruction.

3:8 This verse contains the second, third, and fourth responses called for in the decree. The second response, the wearing of sackcloth, continued the external nature of the first and also its application to animals as well as humans. The inclusion of animals shows again the earnest, almost desperate, plea of the Ninevites. Outwardly, it sounds even more unusual to require animals to wear sackcloth than it did to require them to fast (v. 7). As seen earlier, this odd behavior was not uncommon in ancient cultures.

The next two responses had an internal and spiritual nature. The third com-

---

[53] Many point to the report of Herodotus that the Persian army cut the manes from their war horses as a part of the lamentation ceremony when an esteemed general was lost in battle (Herodotus, *The Histories*, 9.24). To a degree the cases are parallel, for in both instances animals were included in the symbolic expression of distress and sorrow. A nearer parallel to Jonah in ancient literature occurs in the apocryphal book of Judith (4:10–14), where animals were dressed in sackcloth as part of a day of repentance.

[54] Allen uses it to suggest a date of composition in the Persian period, "between the mid-sixth century B.C. and the mid-fourth" (*Joel, Obadiah, Jonah and Micah,* 186).

[55] D. J. Wiseman, "Jonah's Nineveh," *TynBul* 30 (1979): 51.

[56] Stuart, *Hosea-Jonah,* 493.

manded "everyone" (a word only implied in the Hebrew text) to call on God "urgently." This adverb translates a Hebrew word meaning literally "with strength," which perhaps "serves as a device by which to gauge the depth of a worshiper's *conviction*"[57] and prepares us for the radical nature of the last required response. No subject is specified in this third part of the decree. The Hebrew text simply says, "Let them call to God with strength." Some writers persist in extending the subject from the first two parts of the decree, where animals were included in the outward trappings of mourning and repentance. Although Job 38:41 refers to the raven's young who "cry out to God" for food, it is not likely that the Assyrians expected their animals to voice their repentance to God.[58]

The last command, "Let them give up their evil ways and their violence," indicates yet another point of advanced understanding by the ruler. He decreed that the people's lives should match their prayers. The language of this verse is a typically Hebrew way of joining the general and the specific, the individual and the corporate. Anything and everything condemned by law and conscience is included under "evil ways,"[59] but the pronoun is singular. It is literally, "Let them each turn from his evil way," indicating individual responsibility. A generic term is used here and appropriately so, for the sins of the Ninevites would be as diverse as any people of any age. It is interesting to note that the word for "evil" is *ra'â*, occurring nine times in the book in its two senses of "evil" and "trouble, calamity" (see comments on 1:2). The Ninevites were to turn from evil to avoid trouble (cf. v. 10).

The phrase "their violence" is literally "from the violence which is in their hands." It indicates a more specific confession and at the same time a corporate responsibility.[60] Archaeology is unanimous in substantiating the cruelty of the Ninevites. One writer said, "The Assyrian records are nothing but a dry register of military campaigns, spoliations, and cruelties."[61] The term "violence," the arbitrary infringement of human rights, is a term often used by the prophets (cf. Isa 59:6; Ezek 7:23; Hos 12:1; Amos 3:10). It seems to suggest moral misbehavior and aggressive violence toward other nations. Assyria, and therefore Nineveh, was especially guilty of such violence. The wickedness identified by God in 1:2 now becomes a point of self-awareness on the part of the Ninevites. They were urged by the king to change their ways.

3:9 These words of the king echo those of the ship's captain in 1:6 (see

---

[57] Sasson, *Jonah*, 258. See also Trible, *Rhetorical Criticism*, 186.

[58] Cf. Price and Nida, *Translator's Handbook*, 61. Perhaps there is intentional ambiguity here to call attention to the fact that most of the praying in the Book of Jonah seems to have been done by nonbelievers.

[59] Ellison, "Jonah," 383.

[60] Trible, *Rhetorical Criticism*, 186.

[61] Kirk, *Life and Mission*, 184.

Introduction: "Structure," p. 219). The concluding expressions of hope are identical in Hebrew, literally, "that we may not perish"; the opening words, "perhaps" in 1:6 and "who knows?" in 3:9, are equivalent in meaning;[62] and the divine response both men desired was essentially the same. The captain was hoping for a present peril to be removed if Jonah's God should "take notice"; the king was hoping for an anticipated peril to be diverted should he "relent." In both cases these pagans recognized that, as Jonah declared in 2:9, "salvation comes from the LORD." It is in God's hands whether sinners should perish or be delivered. But these pagans correctly rejected determinism, that humans are only actors in a play written and directed by supernatural powers, and that they have no will of their own and no way to affect the outcome.

The word translated "relent" (*niham*) varies in meaning in different grammatical forms and in different contexts, but it always connotes in some sense the feeling of emotional pain.[63] Elsewhere it can mean to "comfort" or "regret." As Sasson explains, here and in its two other uses in Jonah (3:10; 4:2) it refers to "divine actions that are contemplated but are never fulfilled."[64] The meaning "repent" or "change one's mind" is an appropriate translation when the subject is humans (cf. Job 42:6; Jer 31:19). But when it refers to God's decision to change an announced course of action in response to human repentance, prayer, or some other circumstances, the translation "relent" is preferable (see Amos 7:3 and comments in this volume). In this chapter God decided that in light of Nineveh's turning, he would save them rather than follow through on his previous announcement to destroy them.

The word that characterizes vv. 8–10 by its repeated use is *šûb*, whose basic meaning is "return." Other than its use in 1:13 in the causative stem (lit., "the men rowed hard to *return* to dry land"), all its uses in Jonah are in these verses. In v. 8 it is part of the king's decree to *turn* from ("give up") evil and violence. In v. 9 the word occurs twice, as reflected in a literal rendering of the central clause: "God may *turn* so that he relents and *turns* from his burning anger."[65] The last use of the verb is in v. 10, referring again to the repentance of the Ninevites.

We can only imagine the anxiety present in Nineveh at this point. There was hope yet no guarantee that God would indeed relent and turn from his fierce anger and spare Nineveh. Did fear increase as the time neared? Did the prophet Jonah make use of this time by sharing the truth of God's way? The

---

[62] Sasson, *Jonah*, 260. See also J. I. Crenshaw, "The Expression *mî yôdea* in the Hebrew Bible," *VT* 36 (1986): 276, which compares the use here to 2 Sam 12:22 and Joel 2:14.

[63] Ellul, *Judgment of Jonah,* 98–99.

[64] Sasson, *Jonah,* 262.

[65] Sasson is probably correct that the Masoretic accentuation should be disregarded here in favor of that found in the otherwise identical Joel 2:14. The first use of the verb (יָשׁוּב) is an auxiliary governing the two *waw*-consecutive perfects, וְנִחַם and וְשָׁב (*Jonah,* 261).

answers to these questions are not given, but one might imagine the increasing trauma during this interim time.

3. God's Response (3:10)

[10]When God saw what they did and how they turned from their evil ways, he had compassion and did not bring upon them the destruction he had threatened.

3:10 This verse explicitly relates the Ninevites' repentance and God's mercy. Its structure derives from the repetition of two Hebrew roots and the use of two synonyms, translated "turned" (*šûb*) and "had compassion" (*nhm*). The structure can be seen more clearly by a literal translation:

> Then God saw their deeds (*'sh*)
> > that they turned (*šûb*) from their ways of evil (*ra' â*)
> > and God relented (*nhm*) concerning the "evil" (*ra' â*)
> which he had spoken to do (*'sh*) to them, and he did not do (*'sh*) it.

The Ninevites' "turning" from "evil" led to God's "turning" from "evil." It is interesting to note that of all the "deeds" of the Ninevites, the fasting, wearing of sackcloth, calling on God, and turning from evil, only the last is mentioned as explicitly leading to God's relenting. This is perhaps because it was Nineveh's evil that led to Jonah's mission in the first place (1:2).

As the king and people of Nineveh had hoped, God relented. No fire and brimstone fell on this Sodom-like city after all.[66] God pulled back his hand of judgment, though not forever. As prophesied by Nahum, Nineveh later experienced total destruction. There was a period of many years, however, between Jonah and Nahum. Stuart said it well: "When Nineveh repented, God relented."[67] The very thought of God "changing his mind" causes difficulty for some believers. In perfect consistency with his justice, righteousness, and mercy, he spared Nineveh. There is absolutely no contradiction here. God's character and his promises do not change, as Jas 1:17 says (cf. Num 23:19). But many other verses show that God does change his plan of action according to his purposes. In Exod 32:12 Moses prayed that Israel might not be destroyed despite their sinful behavior in making and worshiping the golden calf. He asked God, "Turn from your fierce anger, relent and do not punish your people" (cf. Amos 7:3,6; Jer 18:7–11; 26:2–3). Again and again the Old Testament relays the truth that God is responsive to his creation.[68]

The turning of the Ninevites demonstrated at least a recognition of their condition before the Lord. God's compassionate heart is always sensitive to

---

[66] Allen, *Joel, Obadiah, Jonah and Micah,* 226.

[67] Stuart, *Hosea-Jonah,* 495.

[68] Fretheim, *Message of Jonah,* 114.

those who cry out for mercy. This truth is evidenced powerfully here in v. 10. This passage speaks of the incredible mercy of God's heart, of his incredible love. Here one finds irrefutable evidence that God wishes not for the destruction of the sinner but for the redemption and reconciliation of all his creation. Even if their repentance was not thorough, God's hand of judgment was removed at least temporarily to give this frail flower of searching sufficient time to bloom.

The story of the sparing of Nineveh in chap. 3 parallels Jonah's own experience. He too had been the object of divine anger and later experienced God's miraculous redemption. So too was the experience of the Ninevites. This same truth could be said of every believer who has taken hold of the promises of God through Jesus Christ. Because of sin, which pervades the world, all stand condemned. Only through God's miraculous intervention in the person of Jesus Christ is there any hope. The story of Jonah and Nineveh is the story of every true believer. The pity of this situation, as it is seen in v. 10, is that there was no transference to future generations of the truth learned. The task is not over when repentance occurs but only when the following generations have been discipled with the truth.

IV. JONAH'S DISPLEASURE AND GOD'S RESPONSE (4:1–11)
  1. The Prophet's Displeasure (4:1–3)
  2. God's Response (4:4–11)
      (1) The Probing Question (4:4)
      (2) The Pouting Prophet (4:5)
      (3) God's Methods of Discipline (4:6–8)
      (4) The Rebuke (4:9)
      (5) God's Mercy (4:10–11)

IV. JONAH'S DISPLEASURE AND GOD'S RESPONSE (4:1–11)

1. The Prophet's Displeasure (4:1–3)

¹But Jonah was greatly displeased and became angry. ²He prayed to the LORD, "O LORD, is this not what I said when I was still at home? That is why I was so quick to flee to Tarshish. I knew that you are a gracious and compassionate God, slow to anger and abounding in love, a God who relents from sending calamity. ³Now, O LORD, take away my life, for it is better for me to die than to live."

4:1 Nineveh's repentance led to the reaction of mercy from the Lord and great displeasure from Jonah. What pleased God displeased Jonah. After recognizing that God had relented of his threatened destruction, Jonah reacted in a way many would deem peculiar. One writer says, "Jonah finds that the time-fuse does not work on the prophetic bomb that he planted in Nineveh."[1]

The NIV speaks of Jonah's great displeasure and great anger. The literal translation is, "It was evil to Jonah with great evil." There is a play on words here with the root *ra'â,* which can refer to wickedness on the one hand (see 1:2) or to disaster, trouble, or misery as here. The evil that was characteristic of the people of Nineveh here described the prophet of God.

As we study this verse in context, we find that several emotions were involved: anger and displeasure as well as a lack of understanding. Jonah literally hated what God had done. As God's anger and judgment were averted in chap. 3, Jonah's anger was incited. Why was Jonah's reaction so negative?

---

[1] L. C. Allen, *Joel, Obadiah, Jonah and Micah,* NICOT (Grand Rapids: Eerdmans, 1976), 227.

271

Could his reaction have been due to a narrow-minded nationalism as a Hebrew prophet? Many have supposed that this was the primary reason for Jonah's displeasure and the main target of the book's author.[2] Others have cited as the cause Jonah's awareness that Assyria would be the downfall of Israel. Nineveh was head of a resurgent Assyrian military state. Even in this period of Assyrian history, their imperialistic ambitions had been displayed. Perhaps Jonah foresaw and feared the movement of the Assyrian armies toward Israel. The stigma of being instrumental in the sparing of one of Israel's greatest enemies may have been more than Jonah's emotional makeup could withstand. Still others point to the possibility that Jonah felt his personal reputation was at stake. After all, he had prophesied destruction, and then it did not occur. Calvin said that the reason for Jonah's anger was "because he was unwilling to appear as a vain and lying prophet."[3] This "loss of face" would cause him an embarrassing loss of stature in Nineveh. In addition, what would happen when he returned home to Israel?

Another explanation supposes that Jonah had proclaimed devotion to Yahweh in his native Israel with very little success. Israel was experiencing a time of prosperity and resulting lack of dependence on Yahweh. Perhaps Jonah longed for God's strong hand of judgment to awaken Israel. If God had destroyed Nineveh, what a mighty lesson it would have been to the Hebrews. Jonah recognized that God averted judgment and thereby removed the very weapon from his hand by which he hoped to prevail with his rebellious countrymen.[4]

At the very worst we see a prophet with a shocking disregard for human life and a bitter hatred toward those who had experienced mercy. At the very best he was a prophet who misunderstood God's mercy and had a limited view of God's plan for the redemption of his own people. While there may have been some reasons for Jonah's displeasure, it is sad to see him place limits on the same grace that saved him. While missionaries and evangelists would be delighted at such results, Jonah failed to recognize his privilege of being an instrument of God in a miraculous situation. Failing to recognize God's sovereign plan, he missed the joy of the situation. Much like Elijah (1 Kgs 19:3–18), Jonah sank into a selfish state of mind. Here again the message of the Book of Jonah is seen to be abidingly relevant. Countless numbers of modern-day believers miss much of the joy of being involved in God's wonderful work because of self-centeredness.

4:2 In this verse Jonah shared with the Lord his reason for anger and turmoil. At least Jonah did express this to the Lord in prayer. Instead of complain-

---

[2] D. Stuart, *Hosea-Jonah,* WBC (Waco: Word, 1987), 501–2.

[3] Calvin, quoted in P. Fairbairn, *Jonah, His Life, Character and Mission* (Grand Rapids: Kregel, 1964 [1849]), 148.

[4] Ibid., 156.

ing about God, he complained to God. However, this prayer was quite unlike Jonah's prayer in 2:1. Obviously, differing circumstances call for different kinds of prayers. But often differing kinds of prayers suggest varying stages of maturity or serve as an indication of swings in commitment. In this prayer we find a reversion to the "old Jonah" who ran away from God's stated wish.

The prayer begins with a particle of entreaty, but the petition does not appear until the end. The selfishness of this prayer needs to be noted. The word "I" or "my" occurs no fewer than nine times in the original. Not only does this prayer show an extreme selfishness, but it also indicates Jonah's shortsightedness. As stated in the prayer, he had already told the Lord what he dreaded, and yet the Lord, by his action, had brought it about. This was a grave offense to Jonah. He presumptuously felt that the Lord should have shaped his course according to his (Jonah's) mind. Jonah did not want God to do what was right and proper according to his merciful nature. Instead of bestowing upon Nineveh the kind of grace God had granted to Israel, Jonah wished the Ninevites' destruction without any chance to repent. It is easier to assume that God is with "us" more than he is with our foes. The natural tendency of Jonah and his readers would have been to presume that God could never be "on the side" of the Ninevites.[5] Jonah audaciously stated, in essence, "I told you so." Then he acted as though this was sufficient to excuse his running to Tarshish.

The second half of v. 2 rehearses God's compassionate nature. In this segment Jonah went on to argue with God by complaining about God's goodness! To Jonah the most recent occurrences in Nineveh seemed a theological embarrassment and a divine faux pas.[6] In this sarcastic complaint Jonah cited an ancient formula that is basically a quotation of Exod 34:6–7.[7] The wording used here is descriptive of God's character. First, God is seen as a "gracious" (*hannûn*) God. This word communicates the attitude of the Lord toward those who are undeserving, thereby expressing benevolence in the ultimate sense. The next word used to describe God is the word "compassionate" (*rahûm*). This word is translated in many ways and can mean "loving" or "merciful." It also expresses the understanding and loving compassion of a mother to her child, hence the idea of understanding and loving favor. God is also described as "slow to anger" (*ʾerek ʾappayim*). This speaks to the patience and longsuffering of the Lord. Nineveh was the obvious recipient of this characteristic of the Lord. The next phrase used to describe God in this segment is "abounding in love" (*rab hesed*). The word *hesed* refers to the covenant love of God. This

[5] Stuart, *Hosea-Jonah,* 502.

[6] Allen, *Joel, Obadiah, Jonah and Micah,* 229.

[7] This statement had virtually the status of a creed in ancient Israel. It occurs some ten times (Exod 34:6–7; Joel 2:13; Num 14:18; Neh 9:17; Pss 86:15; 103:8; 145:8; Nah 1:3; 2 Chr 30:9) and is alluded to in many other places (e.g., Pss 111:4; 112:4; 116:8).

attribute expresses itself in redemption from sin. It encompasses the qualities of kindness, loyalty, and unfailing love. No one term in English adequately and accurately expresses the meaning of *hesed*. This this covenant love issues itself in God's being "a God who relents [*niham*] from sending calamity" (*ra'â*). Amazingly, Jonah did not use these words in praise to the Lord but as a tirade against him.

This verse is an extremely disturbing one. It indicates that while Jonah had become obedient, he still lacked a spirit of submission. Lest we judge Jonah too harshly, we should remember the common frailty of murmuring against God's sovereign will. Throughout the pages of history, believers have stood in direct opposition to God's revealed will and sought the implementation of their own wishes.

4:3   Here is the conclusion of Jonah's prayer. While it was commendable for Jonah to have prayed, this prayer stands in stark contrast with the words of Jonah 2:7, where he cried out to the Lord, "My life was ebbing away." Jonah was a man of irony. As he fled from the Lord in chap. 1 only to lament being banished from the Lord in chap. 2, so in chap. 2 he praised God for saving his life only to pray in chap. 4 for God to take his life. In the second instance he cried out for death, which he did not receive. It is true that God always answers prayer, but not always affirmatively. In this case Jonah's answer from the Lord was not affirmative. Believers, however, should always be thankful that God knows the depths of every heart and knows every need better than we may know ourselves.

The words of this verse are remarkably similar to those in 1 Kgs 19:4, where Elijah also cried out wishing to die. The words also are similar to Moses' words in Num 11:15, where he pleaded for an early death. While many have noted the similarity between Jonah's and Elijah's prayers, the situations were entirely different. Elijah's prayer appears to have been founded upon the seeming failure of Yahweh worship in Israel. Israel's sin had depressed him. The underlying cause of Jonah's prayer was not nearly so admirable. Jonah did not wish to live any longer because God had not carried out Nineveh's judgment. Nineveh's redemption had depressed him.

Perhaps Jonah felt that life was horribly out of order. Nineveh was the recipient of God's grace, and his precious Israel was destined to suffer at their hands. One writer states it well: "Here we see how bad theology may also lead to despair. If the Israelites had not had such a limited understanding of their God, an understanding that, among other things, tied together much too closely faith in God and social/political/economic prosperity, they would have been better enabled to cope with the realities of life."[8]

---

[8] T. Fretheim, *The Message of Jonah: A Theological Commentary* (Minneapolis: Augsburg, 1977), 121.

2. God's Response (4:4–11)

(1) The Probing Question (4:4)

⁴But the LORD replied, "Have you any right to be angry?"

4:4 God's response to Jonah came in the form of a probing question. It was not the response many might have imagined. The Lord simply asked a rhetorical question to evoke Jonah's consideration. Instead of a thunderous blast of rebuke, the marvelous image of a tender God is portrayed. Instead of breaking off the dialogue, God reached out to Jonah, encouraging him to pause and reflect. Here is a divine response that is beyond the comprehension of many.

Jonah was asked if it was right or justifiable (lit., "good") for him to be angry. The word for anger here means "to burn" or "to be kindled." The root *harâ* also occurs in 3:9 and 4:1. In an attempt to help Jonah correct his "bad theology," God asked this question. Jonah's anger was not justifiable. It was not the "righteous indignation" mentioned in Eph 4:26. God's dealing so patiently here with Jonah may indicate that Jonah's anger included a deep concern for Israel since Nineveh had been spared. Nonetheless, his anger was inappropriate, and God sought to help Jonah understand his compassion for all people.

(2) The Pouting Prophet (4:5)

⁵Jonah went out and sat down at a place east of the city. There he made himself a shelter, sat in its shade and waited to see what would happen to the city.

4:5 The text is silent about the time span, if any, between vv. 4 and 5. Some believe Jonah left the city as soon as he preached his judgment message. Based on this reconstruction of events, some have argued that this verse has been displaced from its original position after 3:4,[9] while others view these verses as a flashback.[10] There is no syntactical indication, however, that the verses constitute a flashback. A simpler explanation is that just as Jonah fled in 1:1–3 after receiving God's instructions to preach in Nineveh, "Jonah's departure from the city should be seen as his reaction to God's indignant question in the preceding verse."[11]

---

[9] K. Almbladh (*Studies in the Book of Jonah* [Uppsala: University Press, 1986], 37) discusses this and judges that "such a dramatic transposition cannot be reasonably explained except as the result of extreme carelessness, and there is nothing else in the book that makes such a thing likely."

[10] D. Stuart (*Hosea-Jonah,* 500–501) says that the reader is to keep God's question in mind while the writer recounts the story of the gourd. It serves as a coda to conclude the book with a challenge to the reader. The events of vv. 1–4, he says, occurred after the forty days, but the lesson of the gourd was taught after Jonah's brief preaching tour. Stuart thus translates the first two verbs of v. 5 as past perfects.

[11] Almbladh, *Studies in the Book of Jonah,* 37.

There is no recorded answer from Jonah to God's question. This silence may have been a sign of stubbornness and resolve to continue in the way of hatred and anger, or it may have been because he was reflecting on God's ways. Regardless of his intention, when the object lesson was over, Jonah was still angry (v. 9). This suggests to Walton that one of the purposes of the lesson was to help Jonah deal with his anger.[12] Did Jonah go out of the city before the end of the forty-day waiting period? Some feel that God would not have reproved Jonah for his anger before the end of the forty days, nor would the anger have been present before the end of the forty days.[13] On the other hand Jonah had seen the repentance of Nineveh and was inwardly convinced from the merciful character of God that the Lord would, and indeed had, relented prior to the forty days. Perhaps along with Jonah's displeasure was the lingering hope that Nineveh would revert to its violence and experience God's judgment.[14] So Jonah went out and stationed himself at a safe distance from the city. The location of his waiting place lay to the east of Nineveh, perhaps because of the higher elevation there, or perhaps because that is where his preaching tour ended.

Having arrived there, he constructed a shelter such as one the caretaker of a vineyard would use (Isa 1:8; 4:6). This booth or hut was a crude shelter that provided only slight assistance in deflecting the hot Assyrian sun. The same word (*sukkâ;* cf. Amos 9:11, "tent") is used for the structures of leafy branches made for the Feast of Tabernacles, so the making of these booths or huts was a familiar occupation with the Hebrews. The booths were constructed primarily of interlaced branches of trees. After constructing his temporary dwelling place, Jonah sat down under its partial shadow and watched and waited.

What transpired in Jonah's mind during this time? Perhaps it was difficult for him to believe that the repentance of the Ninevites was genuine. Perhaps he had answered the question of v. 4. He may have thought he had convinced God he was right to be angry and that God should carry out his original intention of judgment. Possibly his basic train of thought was morbid anticipation of the Ninevites' reversion to their old ways. Rather than examining himself as the Lord had wished, he examined the city to see if they were the ones who would change. The verb "see" used of Jonah in this verse was used of God in 3:10. While God looked upon Nineveh's turning from evil with delight, Jonah looked upon it and God's consequent reversal of plans with anger and hoped for a return to evil.[15] "Without using any words, his very attitude was a defi-

[12] J. H. Walton, "The Object Lesson of Jonah 4:5–7 and the Purpose of the Book of Jonah," *BBR* 2 (1992): 48.

[13] C. F. Keil and F. Delitzsch, "Jonah," COT (Grand Rapids: Eerdmans, 1978), 10:412.

[14] T. Kirk, *Jonah: His Life and Mission* (Minneapolis: Klock & Klock, 1983), 212.

[15] This verbal parallel is noted in A. Cooper, "In Praise of Divine Caprice: The Significance of the Book of Jonah," in *Among the Prophets: Language, Image and Structure in the Prophetic Writings,* ed. P. R. Davies and D. J. A. Clines, JSOTSup 144 (Sheffield: JSOT, 1993), 155.

ant reply: we shall see whether my anger is justifiable or not!"[16] Perhaps Jonah hoped for a destruction similar to that of Sodom and Gomorrah.

(3) God's Methods of Discipline (4:6–8)

[6]Then the LORD God provided a vine and made it grow up over Jonah to give shade for his head to ease his discomfort, and Jonah was very happy about the vine. [7]But at dawn the next day God provided a worm, which chewed the vine so that it withered. [8]When the sun rose, God provided a scorching east wind, and the sun blazed on Jonah's head so that he grew faint. He wanted to die, and said, "It would be better for me to die than to live."

4:6 The booth Jonah constructed (v. 5) no doubt provided adequate shade for a short time in the oppressive Assyrian heat. The leaves on the brush used for the roof withered quickly, however, and no doubt fell off. It was then that the Lord God provided a vine to minister relief to Jonah.[17] In view of the circumstances, such an act of unmerited favor by the Lord may seem unusual, but God had a lesson in mind for Jonah.

Some words in this text are worthy of note. First, the provision of this vine for Jonah's comfort is ascribed to "Yahweh-Elohim," the "LORD God." This composite name perhaps is chosen here to ease the transition from the use of "Yahweh" in v. 4 to "Elohim" in vv. 7 and 8. The name "Elohim" is used to signify God's divine creative power, which caused the miraculous vine to minister to Jonah.[18] F. D. Kidner, however, notes that prior to this verse Jonah was a "textbook example" of the rule that *Yahweh* is preferred in an Israelite context and *Elohim* elsewhere.[19] Walton picks up this observation and further notes that the use of the compound name in v. 6 introduces the object lesson in which the term *Elohim* is used while Jonah is in focus. This, he argues, signals the reader that God is putting Jonah "in Nineveh's shoes to help evaluate whether his anger is justified."[20] He further notes that in the object lesson, "God then *did* to Jonah what Jonah *wanted* him to do to Nineveh."[21]

The verb "provided" is the same Hebrew word (*manâ*) used in 1:17 to describe the "preparing" of the great fish. Thus both the great fish and the vine are illustrations of God's continuing sovereignty over creation and his intention to be active in the affairs of human beings through his creation.

---

[16] H. W. Wolff, *Obadiah and Jonah* (Minneapolis: Augsburg, 1986), 169.

[17] As H. C. Brichto expresses it, "God provides Jonah's lean-to with a providential layer of natural insulation" (*Toward a Grammar of Biblical Poetics: Tales of the Prophets* [New York: Oxford University Press, 1992], 78).

[18] Allen, *Joel, Obadiah, Jonah and Micah,* 230.

[19] F. D. Kidner, "The Distribution of Divine Names in Jonah," *TynBul* 21 (1970): 126.

[20] Walton, "The Object Lesson of Jonah 4:5–7," 48–49. See also Allen, *Joel, Obadiah, Jonah and Micah,* 233.

[21] Ibid., 51.

The word translated "vine" has been a matter of dispute. The Hebrew word *qîqayôn* designates an unidentified garden plant. Most scholars seem to believe that this plant may be the castor vine, a shrub with large leaves and common in Eastern lands. Possibly the word is equivalent to the Egyptian *kiki,* which is the castor oil tree. However, the textual versions (LXX, Syr, Vg) favor the bottle/gourd plant. It is interesting to note the significance of the controversy over the identification of this plant. When Jerome changed the traditional rendering of this word from gourd to identify it with the castor oil plant, a riot broke out in Oea, a city east of Carthage.[22] This disagreement also caused bitter controversy between Jerome and Augustine. While it is true that the gourd plant is commonly employed in Palestine for shading arbors, either plant could have provided sufficient shelter for one man's relief from the unrelenting rays of the Assyrian sun.[23]

The phrase "to ease his discomfort" is literally "to deliver him[24] from his evil" (*ra'â*). The latter word is the term occurring throughout the book with its two senses, "wickedness" or "trouble, calamity" (see comments at 1:2; 4:1). The translation of the NIV, "discomfort," while perhaps on the side of understatement, does express the general state of Jonah's malcontent. No doubt the heat was a major cause for this discontent. The mean daily maximum temperature in Mesopotamia is about 110 degrees, so the temperature was a factor. Any shade would have been most welcome. Perhaps adding to his discomfort was the sound of mourning and supplication from the city below him. From his overlooking perch he could hear the cries of the cattle and the wailings and earnest beseechings of the human inhabitants.[25] These factors, combined with the restlessness that inevitably occurs when a believer is out of the perfect will of God, accounted for Jonah's discomfort.

The last clause in this verse, "and Jonah was very happy about the vine," is both fascinating and tragic. Literally, the text says that "Jonah rejoiced over the vine with a great rejoicing." He was not just happy; he was deliriously happy. The miraculous growth of this vine caused Jonah to experience an emotion that is otherwise unrecorded in the book. In other words, for the first time Jonah was happy. He did not experience this emotion either in his own deliverance from certain death or from the mass turning of the people of Nin-

---

[22] J. N. D. Kelley, *Jerome: His Life, Writings and Controversies* (London: Deckworth, 1975), 266.

[23] For a detailed discussion of the probable plants and their characteristics, see Kirk, *Life and Mission,* 219–21, or B. P. Robinson, "Jonah's *Qiqayon* Plant," *ZAW* 97 (1985): 397–402. Both of these writers opt for the gourd plant.

[24] The verb for "deliver," נצל, is a play on the word for "shade, " צל. There also is intentional ambiguity in the use of רָעָה, for while God's immediate purpose for the vine was to relieve Jonah's discomfort, his real purpose was to deliver Jonah from his sinful attitude.

[25] Kirk, *Life and Mission,* 217.

eveh. His happiness was induced by a plant. His emotion as expressed in 4:1, in fact, at Nineveh's deliverance was the exact opposite of that expressed here. Perhaps his reason for happiness was twofold. First, there was some relief from the horrible heat. But he also saw in the miraculous growth of this vine an indication of God's favor and thus a vindication of his own feelings of disappointment at Nineveh's repentance. This was not a game[26] or a trick[27] God was playing on Jonah; he was in the process of teaching him an important lesson. Jonah's supposed vindication would be as short-lived as the vine.

4:7 At times God chooses to move slowly, or so it seems to us. At other times, however, even by the reckoning of mere human beings God acts quickly. So it was in this instance. God moved quickly to end Jonah's happiness and any ill-conceived notions that might have contributed to that happiness. Step by step God's education of the prophet continued. Having prepared the vine (v. 6), as he had prepared the great fish, God then prepared a worm. Just as the vine was to make Jonah happy and the fish to rescue him, God used a lowly worm to drive home his intended message. The word for "worm" has been translated in a variety of ways, since the variety of crawling creature is uncertain. It may refer to the black caterpillar that abounds in the Nineveh region.[28]

The next clause, "which chewed the vine so that it withered," shows the devastating action of the worm. The destructive effect of worms on many types of vegetation is well known. The cutworm can easily destroy the stem of a plant and can do so almost immediately. Combining the effect of the worm with the torrid heat would cause a plant to wither quickly even without divine intervention. One irony of this segment is that although destruction is a recurring theme of the book, the only destruction that occurs in the Book of Jonah is that of this vine. So destruction came not upon Nineveh but upon something that had become very important to Jonah, something that had brought him great joy.[29]

4:8 Yet again God "prepared" an element of nature to be used in the education of his prophet. The word "prepared" (*manâ*) was not used flippantly. It showed the Lord's intention to demonstrate his control, his sovereignty over creation. This is the fourth time in the Book of Jonah the term appears. In this instance God provided or prepared a scorching east wind.

Losing precious shade in this harsh environment was one matter for Jonah. Experiencing this horrible wind was yet another. Most identify this wind as the "sirocco." When this wind is experienced in the Near East, the temperature rises dramatically, and the humidity drops quickly. It is a constant and extremely hot wind that contains fine particles of dust. It contains "constant

---

[26] Wolff, *Obadiah and Jonah,* 170.

[27] Allen, *Joel, Obadiah, Jonah and Micah,* 231.

[28] Glaze, "Jonah," BBC 7 (Nashville: Broadman, 1972), 186.

[29] Fretheim, *Message of Jonah,* 125.

hot air so full of positive ions that it affects the levels of serotonin and other brain neurotransmitters, causing exhaustion, depression, feelings of unreality, and occasionally, bizarre behavior."[30] The Septuagint translates it succinctly as a "scorcher."

The word "blazed" is the same Hebrew word translated "chewed" in v. 7. It is a general word (*nakâ*) meaning to "strike." Having been deliriously happy, Jonah was being struck down by a series of natural "calamities" until his misery was complete. The blazing sun beat down on Jonah's head, which was lacking any helpful shade. The verb translated "grew faint" (ʿ*alap*) is almost identical in form and meaning to the word Jonah used in 2:7 (ʿ*atap,* Heb 2:8) of his life "ebbing away." Jonah probably felt that God was finally answering his prayer in 4:3 by taking his life. So, since nothing has changed, he repeated the prayer. At his wits' end, Jonah was completely exhausted; the text says literally, "He asked his life to die."

The issue went even deeper than a lack of understanding about God's fairness. This verse shows Jonah's total frustration with his life. Having been asked by God to consider the rightness of his anger and then thinking for a brief time that perhaps his anger was vindicated, Jonah then was shown by the Lord that he was wrong. Not grasping the message of God's sovereignty and care, Jonah's depression deepened as he felt that his entire life had been wrong. Having failed as a prophet, now he had failed his God in his heart. He wished to die. This is not the picture of a mature disciple but one who is ready to give up. Kirk is right when he states, "He was now ready to say of his life, 'Ichabod, the glory is departed.' "[31]

(4) The Rebuke (4:9)

> **⁹But God said to Jonah, "Do you have a right to be angry about the vine?"** **"I do," he said. "I am angry enough to die."**

4:9 Again the text portrays God as the great teacher, trying to help Jonah recognize the divine character and his own inadequacy in understanding. In this text God attempted to show Jonah the absurdity of his attitude, yet in a tender fashion. Jonah's values were topsy-turvy, evidenced by his greater concern for personal physical comfort afforded by a vine than for the spiritual well-being of an entire city.[32] God's mercy toward Nineveh had made him angry, and then he was angered by God's withdrawing mercy from him. God attempted to deal with Jonah's inconsistency by asking him, "Do you have a right?" The question is identical to the one God asked in v. 4. Stuart is right in saying that this question is central to the whole book. "What right do we have

---

[30] Stuart, *Hosea-Jonah,* 505.
[31] Kirk, *Life and Mission,* 228.
[32] Kennedy, *Studies in Jonah*, 93.

to demand that God should favor us and not others? By reducing the question to the particular issue of the gourd, God focused it in a way that would cause Jonah to condemn himself by his own words. Jonah did just that."[33]

The next phrase is Jonah's reply to this word from God: "'I do,' he said; 'I am angry enough to die.'" The first time God asked for justification of Jonah's answer he received no reply. This time an answer came forth quickly. He turns God's question into an affirmation and adds a prepositional phrase that may be understood as hyperbole (as in the modern English idiom "I am so mad I could die"), although Sasson argues for a more literal meaning on the basis of Jesus' use of it in Matt 26:38 (// Mark 14:33).[34]

What if Jonah had paused for an instant? He might have recognized the "crossroads" of the moment. If he had answered with a negative, he would have had to admit the inconsistency of his logic and the inappropriateness of his anger; but he would have been on the road to recovery. The rashness of Jonah's reply was due in part to his suffering from heat exhaustion and possible dehydration as well as total frustration with his life. There was also a misconception that God had been more than fair with the pagan Ninevites and far less than fair in dealing with him. One finds here a pathetic picture. As Wolff explained, Jonah "neither wished to live under the governance of free grace (vv. 1–3), nor was he prepared to live under a government without grace (vv. 7–9)."[35]

(5) God's Mercy (4:10–11)

[10]But the LORD said, "You have been concerned about this vine, though you did not tend it or make it grow. It sprang up overnight and died overnight. [11]But Nineveh has more than a hundred and twenty thousand people who cannot tell their right hand from their left, and many cattle as well. Should I not be concerned about that great city?"

4:10 Whereas God's question in v. 9 seemed to contain the element of tenderness, the statement of the Lord in v. 10 conveys the idea of forcefulness. The reluctant pupil was then addressed in terms that commanded attention. Gaebelein states, "We may be sure, Jonah is at last ready to hear."[36] The wording in this verse obviously was chosen for emphasis. The emphatic "you" of v. 10 ("You have been concerned about this vine") is in contrast with the emphatic "I" of v. 11 ("Should I not be concerned about that great city?").

The word translated "concerned" (*ḥûs*) in vv. 10–11 also is significant. The translation "have compassion" would better express the emotional connotation of this word. While one normally does not have pity on a plant, the Lord was driving home Jonah's inappropriate expression of anger. The Lord continued

---

[33] Stuart, *Hosea-Jonah,* 506.

[34] Sasson, *Jonah,* 307. Also Wolff, *Obadiah and Jonah,* 172.

[35] Wolff, *Obadiah and Jonah,* 173.

[36] Gaebelein, *Servant and Dove,* 135.

his teaching lesson as he admonished Jonah for his inappropriate compassion for a plant for which he had done nothing. He had neither cultivated nor encouraged the growth of the plant, and yet he used it to express ultimate anger. Because of the withering of an inanimate plant whose life was measured by a single day, he wished to die. He simply had no right to make any claims regarding the plant. It had been a gift of God's grace. The Lord was trying forcefully to drive home the ultimate question, "Who are you [Jonah] to question me?" Jonah's anger expressed not only a lack of understanding but also a lack of trust.

4:11 Jonah's deep concern had been expressed on behalf of a relatively insignificant portion of God's creation, the vine, while God's deep concern was expressed on behalf of his highest creation, human beings. Jonah apparently had grown completely indifferent to the fate of God's creation beyond the bounds of Israel. At every point in this entire chapter, Jonah's attitude stands in complete contrast to God's relationship to Nineveh. God created and nurtured them and extended to them the hand of mercy.

Jonah did not answer correctly God's questions in vv. 4 and 9 and thereby showed his lack of understanding. Consequently, God drew the tremendous contrast between Jonah's anger over the death of a plant and his own delight in Nineveh's turn toward life. The first clause in the Hebrew text is literally, "Should I, on the other hand, not have compassion on the great city of Nineveh?" The NIV moves this phrase to the end of the verse in an apparent attempt to end the text with a question for the readers to answer. The rearrangement of the clause is unnecessary and perhaps unfortunate. Leaving it as it is found in the Hebrew text shows the connection better with v. 10.

God's question captures the very intention of the book. The issue is that of grace—grace and mercy. Just as Jonah's provision was the shade of the vine he did not deserve, the Ninevites' provision was a deliverance they did not deserve based upon a repentance they did not fully understand. God's wish for his creation is salvation, not destruction. He will work to see that the salvation is accomplished if there is willingness on the creation's part. Can a person ever rightly resent the grace of God shown to another? As G. V. Smith has said:

> God will (and does) act in justice against sin, but His great love for every person in the world causes Him to wait patiently, to give graciously, to forgive mercifully, and to accept compassionately even the most unworthy people in the world. To experience the grace of God and not be willing to tell others of His compassion is a tragedy all must avoid. Messengers of God can neither limit the grace of God nor control its distribution, but they can prevent God's grace from having an effect on their own lives.[37]

This message is driven home by the Lord as he describes Nineveh as having

---

[37] G. V. Smith, *The Prophets as Preachers: An Introduction to the Hebrew Prophets* (Nashville: Broadman & Holman, 1994), 97.

"more than 120,000 people who cannot tell their right hand from their left, and many cattle as well." This statement is a fascinating one and has been interpreted in various ways. Many writers have assumed it refers to the number of children or infants in the city of Nineveh.[38] According to even the most conservative estimates, such a number of children would suggest a total population in the city of well over 600,000 persons. This population estimate is not substantiated by archaeology if one assumes that the Nineveh in question refers only to the city proper, although if one holds to a district view of Nineveh, then the population estimate would be possible. Others have argued reasonably that the word for "people" (*ʾadam*) rules out the specification of children.[39] Thus the number 120,000 probably stands for the entire population.

The description, literally, "not able to distinguish between the left and the right," may refer to one or more characteristics. Perhaps it refers to their inability to distinguish between various forms of religion, especially monotheism, polytheism, and the worship of the constellations, which was a mark of the Assyrians.[40] Perhaps this phrase refers to the helplessness or pitifulness of the Ninevites.[41] Possibly the best understanding of this text is to recognize that the Lord was referring to an entire city of morally and ethically naive, though not morally innocent, individuals. The people of Nineveh had already shown sensitivity to their evil ways and so were not ignorant. In contrast to the prophet and the people of Israel, however, the people of Nineveh were in a kindergarten stage of religious knowledge. The Lord ended the statement with the phrase "and many cattle as well." Here he attempted to impart to Jonah that even cattle are superior to plants or vines.[42] His mercy is great for all his creation.

Some have remarked that the Book of Jonah ends abruptly or somehow in an incomplete manner. On the contrary, the book ends in a way that draws attention and, therefore, increases its teaching potential. While the book does not tell the final effect of God's teaching session on Jonah, the ending is not anticlimactic. It is true no words are wasted, but the message of the book is succinctly stated in v. 11. The book ends with a clear contrast between the ways of God and the ways of Jonah. Kennedy states it well, "It is the choice between gourds or souls."[43] The story is deliberately left open-ended for those who study its message to complete in their own lives. Ellul is right in saying, "The book of Jonah has no conclusion, and the final question of the book has no answer, except from the one who realizes the fullness of the mercy of God."[44]

---

[38] Keil and Delitzsch refer to the 120,000 as those in "mental infancy" (Keil and Delitzsch, "Jonah," COT, 10:416). Others who hold to this interpretation are Bewer, Fretheim, and Gaebelein.

[39] Wolff, *Obadiah and Jonah,* 175.

[40] Wiseman, "Jonah's Nineveh," 39.

[41] Stuart, *Hosea-Jonah,* 507.

[42] Wolff, *Obadiah and Jonah,* 175.

[43] J. H. Kennedy, *Studies in the Book of Jonah* (Nashville: Broadman, 1956), 97.

[44] Ellul, *Judgment of Jonah,* 103.

Selected Bibliography

Minor Prophets

Books and Commentaries

Boice, J. M. *The Minor Prophets: An Expositional Commentary.* 2 vols. Grand Rapids: Zondervan, 1983, 1986.

Bullock, C. H. *An Introduction to the Old Testament Prophetic Books.* Chicago: Moody, 1986.

Chisholm, R. B. Jr. *Interpreting the Minor Prophets.* Grand Rapids: Zondervan, 1990.

Craigie, P. C. *Twelve Prophets.* 2 vols. DSB. Philadelphia: Westminster, 1984–85.

Feinberg, C. L. *The Minor Prophets.* Chicago: Moody, 1980.

Hailey, H. *A Commentary on the Minor Prophets.* Grand Rapids: Baker, 1972.

Henderson, E. *The Twelve Minor Prophets.* Reprint. Grand Rapids: Baker, 1980 [1858].

Laetsch, T. *The Minor Prophets.* Grand Rapids: Baker, 1966.

Limburg, J. *Hosea-Micah.* INT. Atlanta: John Knox, 1988.

Smith, G. A. *The Book of the Twelve Prophets.* New York: Harper & Brothers, 1928 [1898].

Smith, G. V. *The Prophets as Preachers: An Introduction to the Hebrew Prophets.* Nashville: Broadman & Holman, 1994.

Stuart, D. *Hosea-Jonah.* WBC. Waco: Word, 1987.

Amos Bibliography

Books and Commentaries

Andersen, F. and D. Freedman. *Amos.* AB. New York: Doubleday, 1989.

Barstad, H. M. *The Religious Polemics of Amos.* VTSup 34. Leiden: Brill, 1984.

Barton, J. *Amos's Oracles against the Nations: A Study of Amos 1:3–2:5.* Cambridge: Cambridge University Press, 1980.

Cohen, Gary G. and H. Ronald Vandermey. *Hosea/Amos.* EBC. Chicago: Moody, 1981.

Coote, Robert B. *Amos among the Prophets: Composition and Theology.* Philadelphia: Fortress, 1981.

Cripps, R. *A Critical and Exegetical Commentary on the Book of Amos.* 2d ed. London: SPCK, 1955.

De Waard, J. and W. A. Smalley. *A Translator's Handbook on the Book of Amos.* New York: UBS, 1979.

Driver, S. R. *The Books of Joel and Amos.* The Cambridge Bible. Cambridge: Cambridge University Press, 1915.

Finley, T. J. *Joel, Amos, Obadiah.* WEC. Chicago: Moody, 1990.

Garland, D. D. *Amos.* Grand Rapids: Zondervan, 1966.

Gowan, D. E. "The Book of Amos: Introduction, Commentary, and Reflections." New Interpreter's Bible. Nashville: Abingdon, 1996.

Hammershaimb, E. *The Book of Amos: A Commentary.* Oxford: Blackwell, 1970.

Harper, W. R. *A Critical and Exegetical Commentary on Amos and Hosea.* ICC. Edinburgh: T & T Clark, 1905.

Hasel, G. F. *Understanding the Book of Amos: Basic Issues in Current Interpretations.* Grand Rapids: Baker, 1991.

Hayes, J. H. *Amos.* Nashville: Abingdon, 1988.

Hubbard, D. A. *Joel and Amos.* TOTC. Downers Grove: InterVarsity, 1989.

King, P. *Amos, Hosea, Micah—An Archaeological Commentary.* Philadelphia: Westminster, 1988.

Mays, J. L. *Amos*. OTL. Philadelphia: Westminster, 1969.

McComiskey, T. E. "Amos." EBC vol. 7. Grand Rapids: Zondervan, 1985.

Martin-Achard, R. and S. P. Re'emi. *Amos and Lamentations: God's People in Crisis*. ITC. Grand Rapids: Eerdmans, 1984.

Motyer, J. A. *The Message of Amos: The Day of the Lion*. Downers Grove: InterVarsity, 1974.

Mowvley, H. *The Books of Amos and Hosea*. London: Epworth, 1991.

Niehaus, J. "Amos." In *The Minor Prophets: An Exegetical and Expository Commentary*. Grand Rapids: Baker, 1992.

Paul, S. *Amos*. Her. Minneapolis: Fortress, 1991.

Polley, M. *Amos and the Davidic Empire*. New York: Oxford University Press, 1989.

Smith, G. *Amos: A Commentary*. Grand Rapids: Zondervan, 1989.

Smith, R. L. "Amos." BBC vol. 7. Nashville: Broadman, 1972.

Soggin, J. Alberto. *The Prophet Amos*. Translated by J. Bowden. London: SCM, 1987.

Watts, J. D. W. *Vision and Prophecy in Amos*. Leiden: Brill, 1958.

Weiser, A. *Die Profetie des Amos*. BZAW 53. Giessen: Töpelmann, 1929.

Wolff, H. *Joel and Amos*. Her. Philadelphia: Fortress, 1977.

Articles

Braun, M. A. "James' Use of Amos at the Jerusalem Council: Steps toward a Possible Solution of the Textual and Theological Problems." *JETS* 20 (1977): 113–21.

Brueggemann, W. "Amos 4:4–13 and Israel's Covenant Worship." *VT* 15 (1965): 1–15.

Burger, J. A. "Amos: A Historical-geographical View." *Journal of Semitics* 4 (1992): 130–50.

Chisholm, R. B., Jr. "'For Three Sins . . . Even for Four': The Numerical Sayings in Amos." *BSac* 147 (1990).

Clifford, R. J. "The Use of *HÔY* in the Prophets." *CBQ* 28 (1966): 458–64.

De Waard, J. "The Chiastic Structure of Amos V 1–17." *VT* 27 (1977): 170–77.

Gitay, Y. "A Study of Amos's Art of Speech: A Rhetorical Analysis of Amos 3:1–15." *CBQ* 42 (1980): 293.

Dempster, S. "The Lord Is His Name: A Study of the Distribution of the Names and Titles of God in the Book of Amos." *RB* 98 (1991): 170–89.

Dorsey, D. A. "Literary Architecture and Aural Structuring Techniques in Amos." *Bib* 73 (1992): 305–30.

Eslinger, Lyle. "The Education of Amos." *HAR* 11 (1987): 35–57.

Fensham, F. C. "A Possible Origin of the Concept of the Day of the Lord." *OTWSA* 7–8 (1966): 90–97.

———. "Common Trends in Curses of the Near Eastern Treaties and kudurru-Inscriptions Compared with Maledictions of Amos and Isaiah." *ZAW* 75 (1963): 155–75.

———. "Widow, Orphan and Poor in Ancient Near Eastern Legal and Wisdom Literature." *JNES* 21 (1962): 129–39.

Finley, T. J. "An Evangelical Response to the Preaching of Amos." *JETS* 28 (1985): 411–20.

———. "The *WAW*-Consecutive with 'Imperfect' in Biblical Hebrew: Theoretical Studies and Its Use in Amos." In *Tradition and Testament*. Edited by J. S. and P. D. Feinberg. Chicago: Moody, 1981, 241–64.

Gitay, Yehoshua. "A Study of Amos's Art of Speech: A Rhetorical Analysis of Amos 3:1–15." *CBQ* 42 (1980): 293–309.

Garrett, D. A. "The Structure of Amos as a Testimony to Its Integrity." *JETS* 27 (1984): 275–76.

Hauan, M. J. "The Background and Meaning of Amos 5:17b." *HTR* 79 (1986): 337–48.

Heicksen, M. "Tekoa: Historical and Cultural Profile." *JETS* 13 (1970): 81–89.

Hillers, D. R. "Amos 7:4 and Ancient Parallels." *CBQ* 26 (1964): 221–25.

Hoffman, Y. "The Day of the Lord as a Concept and a Term in the Prophetic Literature." *ZAW* 93 (1981): 37–50.

Howie, C. G. "Expressly for Our Time: The Theology of Amos." *Int* 13 (1959): 276.

Huey, F. B., Jr. "The Ethical Teaching of Amos: Its Content and Relevance." *SWJT* 9 (1966): 57–67.

Huffmon, H. B. "The Social Role of Amos' Message." In *The Quest for the Kingdom of God*. Edited by H. B. Huffmon et al.. Winona Lake: Eisenbrauns, 1983, 109–16.

Jackson, J. J. "Amos 5,13 Contextually Understood." *ZAW* 98 (1986): 434–35.

Jacobs, P. "'Cows of Bashan'—A Note on the Interpretation of Amos 4:1." *JBL* 104 (1985): 109–10.

Kaiser, W. C., Jr. "The Davidic Promise and the Inclusion of the Gentiles (Amos 9:9–15 and Acts 15:13–18): A Test Passage for Theological Systems." *JETS* 20 (1977): 97–111.

King, D. M. "The Use of Amos 9:11–12 in Acts 15:16–18." *Ashland Theological Journal* 21 (1989): 8.

Limburg, J. "Sevenfold Structures in the Book of Amos." *JBL* 106 (1987): 217–22.

Lust, J. "Remarks on the Redaction of Amos V 4–6, 14–15." *OTS* 21 (1981): 138–39.

McComiskey, Thomas E. "The Hymnic Elements of the Prophecy of Amos: A Study of Form-Critical Methodology." *JETS* 30 (1987): 139–58.

Paul, S. M. "Amos 1:3–2:3: A Concatenous Literary Pattern." *JBL* 90 (1971).

Richard, E. "The Creative Use of Amos by the Author of Acts." *NovT* 24 (1982): 48.

Richardson, H. N. "Amos's Four Visions of Judgment and Hope." *BibRev* 5 (1989): 19.

Schoville, K. N. "A Note on the Oracles of Amos against Gaza, Tyre, and Edom." In *Studies on Prophecy, Supplements to Vetus Testamentum*. Leiden: Brill, 1974.

Smith, G. V. "Critical Notes: Amos 5:13, the Deadly Silence of the Prosperous." *JBL* 107 (1988): 289–91.

———. "Continuity and Discontinuity in Amos' Use of Tradition." *JETS* 34 (1991): 33–42.

Steinmann, A. E. "The Order of Amos's Oracles against the Nations: 1:3–2:16." *JBL* 111 (1992): 683–89.

Tromp, N. J. "Amos V 1–17: Toward a Stylistic and Rhetorical Analysis." *OTS* 23 (1984): 56–84.

Tucker, G. "Prophetic Authority: A Form Critical Study of Amos 7:10–17." *Int* 27 (1973): 423–34.

van der Wal, A. "The Structure of Amos." *JSOT* 26 (1983): 107–13.

van Leeuwen, C. "The Prophecy of the *YÔM YHWH* in Amos 5:18–20." *OTS* 19 (1974): 113–34.

Wendland, E. R. "The 'Word of the Lord' and the Organization of Amos." In *Occasional Papers in Translation and Textlinguistics* 2 (1988): 1–51.

Williams, A. J. "A Further Suggestion about Amos IV 1–3." *VT* (1979): 206–12.

Williamson, H. G. M. "The Prophet and the Plumb-line: A Redaction-Critical Study of Amos vii." *OTS* 26 (1990): 121.

Wittenberg, G. "Amos 6:1–7." *Journal of Theology for South Africa* 58 (1987): 57–69.

Wolff, H. W. "The Irresistible Word (Amos)." *Currents in Theology and Mission* 10 (1983): 4–13.

Wolters, A. "Wordplay and Dialect in Amos 8:1–2." *JETS* 31 (1988): 407–10.

Zevit, Z. "A Misunderstanding at Bethel: Amos VII 12–17." *VT* 25 (1975): 787.

Obadiah Bibliography

Books and Commentaries

Allen, L. C. *The Books of Joel, Obadiah, Jonah, and Micah*. NICOT. Grand Rapids: Eerdmans, 1976.

Armerding, C. E. "Obadiah." EBC 7. Edited by F. E. Gaebelein. Grand Rapids: Zondervan, 1985.

Baker, D. W. *Obadiah: An Introduction and Commentary*. TOTC. Downers Grove: InterVarsity, 1988.

Barlett, J. R. *Edom and the Edomites*. JSOTSup 77. Sheffield, Eng.: Sheffield Academic Press, 1989.

Bewer, J. A. "Commentary on Obadiah and Joel." In *A Critical and Exegetical Commentary on Micah, Zephaniah, Nahum, Habakkuk, Obadiah, and Joel*. ICC. Edinburgh: T & T Clark, 1911.

Clark, D. J. and N. Mundhenk. *A Translator's Handbook on the Books of Obadiah and Micah*. London/N.Y./Stuttgart: UBS, 1982.

Coggins, R. J. *Israel among the Nations: A Commentary on the Books of Nahum and Obadiah.* ITC. Grand Rapids: Eerdmans, 1985.

Cresson, B. C. "Obadiah." BBC vol. 7. Nashville: Broadman, 1972.

Dicou, B. *Edom, Israel's Brother and Antagonist: The Role of Edom in Biblical Prophecy and Story.* JSOTSup 169. Sheffield: JSOT Press, 1994.

Finley, T. J. *Joel, Amos, Obadiah.* WEC. Chicago: Moody, 1990.

Glueck, N. *The Other Side of the Jordan.* Cambridge, Mass.: American Schools of Oriental Research, 1970.

Luria, B. Z. *The Book of Obadiah and the Prophecies Concerning Edom.* Publications of the Israeli Society for Biblical Research, 26. Jerusalem: Kiriath-Sefer, 1972.

Mason, R. *Micah, Nahum, Obadiah.* OTG. Sheffield: JSOT Press, 1991.

Miller, P. D., Jr. *Sin and Judgment in the Prophets.* Chico, Cal.: Scholars Press, 1982.

Pagán, S. "The Book of Obadiah: Introduction, Commentary, and Reflections." New Interpreter's Bible. Nashville: Abingdon, 1996.

Smith, B. K. "Obadiah." LBBC 13. Nashville: Broadman, 1982.

Thompson, J. A. *Obadiah.* IB. Nashville: Abingdon, 1956.

Watts, J. D. W. *Obadiah: A Critical Exegetical Commentary.* Winona Lake, Ind.: Alpha, 1981.

Wolff, H. W. *Obadiah and Jonah.* Translated by M. Kohl. Minneapolis: Augsburg, 1986.

Articles

Bartlett, J. R. "The Brotherhood of Edom." *JSOT* 2 (1977): 2–27.

————. "Edom and the Fall of Jerusalem, 587 B.C." *PEQ* 114 (1982): 22–23.

————. "From Edomites to Nabataeans: A Study in Continuity." *PEQ* 111 (1979): 53–66.

————. "The Land of Seir and the Brotherhood of Edom." *JTS* 20 (1969): 1–20.

————. "The Rise and Fall of the Kingdom of Edom." *PEQ* 104 (1972): 26–37.

Beit-Arieh, I. "New Light on the Edomites." *BAR* 14.2 [1988]: 41.

Clark, D. J. "Obadiah Reconsidered." *BT* 42 (1991): 326–36.

Dick, M. B. "A Syntactic Study of the Book of Obadiah." *Semitics* 9 (1984): 1–29.

Gordis, R. "Edom, Israel and Amos—An Unrecognized Source for Edomite History." In *Essays on the Occasion of the Seventieth Anniversary of the Dropsie University (1909–1979).* Edited by A. I. Katsh and L. Nemoy. Philadelphia: Dropsie, 1979, 109–32.

Lillie, J. R. "Obadiah—A Celebration of God's Kingdom." *Currents in Theology and Mission* 6 (1979): 18–22.

Lindsay, J. "Babylonian Kings and Edom, 605–550." *PEQ* 108 (1976): 23–39.

McCarter, P. "Obadiah 7 and the Fall of Edom." *BASOR* 221 (1976): 87–91.

Myers, J. M. "Edom and Judah in the 6th–5th Centuries B.C." In *Near Eastern Studies in Honor of W. F. Albright.* Edited by H. Goedicke. Baltimore: The Johns Hopkins Press, 1971, 377–92.

Robinson, R. "Levels of Naturalization in Obadiah." *JSOT* 40 (1988): 88–91.

Robinson, T. H. "The Structure of the Book of Obadiah." *JTS* 17 (1916): 402–8.

Wendland, E. "Obadiah's Vision of 'The Day of the Lord': On the Importance of Rhetoric in the Biblical Text and in Bible Translation." *JTT* 7.4 (1996): 54–86.

Woudstra, M. H. "Edom and Israel in Ezekiel." *Calvin Theological Journal* 3 (1968): 21–35.

Jonah Bibliography

Books and Commentaries

Aalders, G. C. *The Problem of the Book of Jonah.* London: Tyndale, 1948.

Almbladh, K. *Studies in the Book of Jonah.* Uppsala: University Press, 1986.

Alexander, T. D. *Jonah: An Introduction and Commentary.* TOTC. Downers Grove: InterVarsity, 1988.

Allen, L. C. *The Books of Joel, Obadiah, Jonah, and Micah.* NICOT. Grand Rapids: Eerdmans, 1976.

Baldwin, J. "Jonah." In *The Minor Prophets: An Exegetical and Expository Commentary.* Edited by T. E. McComiskey. Grand Rapids: Baker, 1993.

Bewer, J. A. "Commentary on Jonah." In *A Critical and Exegetical Commentary on Haggai, Zechariah, Malachi and Jonah.* ICC. Edinburgh: T & T Clark, 1912.

Bowers, R. H. *The Legend of Jonah.* The Hague: Martinus Nijhoff, 1971.

Brichto, H. C. *Toward a Grammar of Biblical Poetics: Tales of the Prophets.* New York: Oxford University Press, 1992.

Craig, K. M., Jr. *A Poetics of Jonah: Art in the Service of Ideology.* Columbia: University of South Carolina, 1993.

Ellison, H. L. "Jonah." EBC vol. 7. Grand Rapids: Zondervan, 1985.

Fairbairn, P. *Jonah: His Life, Character and Mission.* Grand Rapids: Kregel, 1964 [1849].

Fretheim, T. *The Message of Jonah: A Theological Commentary.* Minneapolis: Augsburg, 1977.

Gaebelein, F. E. *Four Minor Prophets: Obadiah, Jonah, Habakkuk, and Haggai.* Chicago: Moody, 1977.

―――. *The Servant and the Dove: Obadiah and Jonah.* New York: Our Hope, 1946.

Glaze, A. J., Jr. "Jonah." BBC vol. 7. Nashville: Broadman, 1972.

Good, E. M. *Irony in the Old Testament.* Reprint. Sheffield: Almond, 1981.

Gordis, R. *The Word and the Book: Studies in Biblical Language and Literature.* New York: Ktav, 1976.

Hasel, G. F. *Jonah: Messenger of the Eleventh Hour.* Mt. View, Cal.: Pacific, 1976.

Keil, C. F. and F. Delitzsch. "Jonah." COT. Reprint. Grand Rapids: Eerdmans, 1978.

Kendall, R. T. *Jonah: An Exposition.* Grand Rapids: Zondervan, 1978.

Kennedy, J. H. *Studies in the Book of Jonah.* Nashville: Broadman, 1956.

Knight, G. A. F. *Ruth and Jonah: The Gospel in the Old Testament.* London: SCM, 1966.

Knight, G. A. F. and F. W. Golka. *The Song of Songs and Jonah: Revelation of God.* ITC. Grand Rapids: Eerdmans, 1988.

Limburg, J. *Jonah: A Commentary.* OTL. Louisville: WJKP, 1993.

Magonet, J. *Form and Meaning: Studies in Literary Techniques in the Book of Jonah.* Bern/Frankfurt: Herbert Lang/Peter Lang, 1976.

Price, V. F. and E. A. Nida. *A Translator's Handbook on the Book of Jonah.* N.Y.: UBS, 1978.

Sasson, J. M. *Jonah.* AB. New York: Doubleday, 1990.

Stuart, D. *Hosea-Jonah.* WBC. Waco: Word, 1987.

Trible, P. "The Book of Jonah: Introduction, Commentary, and Reflections." New Interpreter's Bible. Nashville: Abingdon, 1996.

―――. *Rhetorical Criticism: Context, Method, and the Book of Jonah.* Minneapolis: Fortress, 1994.

Walton, J. *Jonah. Bible Study Commentary.* Grand Rapids: Zondervan, 1982.

Watts, J. D. W. *The Books of Joel, Obadiah, Jonah, Nahum, Habakkuk and Zephaniah.* CBC. Cambridge: Cambridge University Press, 1975.

Wolff, H. W. *Obadiah and Jonah.* Translated by M. Kohl. Minneapolis: Augsburg, 1986.

Articles

Alexander, T. D. "Jonah and Genre." *TynBul* 36 (1985): 35–59.

Barré, M. L. "Jonah 2:9 and the Structure of Jonah's Prayer." *Bib* 72 (1991): 237–48.

Blank, S. H. "'Doest thou well to be angry?' A Study in Self-pity." *HUCA* 26 (1955): 29–41.

Burrows, M. "The Literary Category of the Book of Jonah." In *Translating and Understanding the Old Testament.* Edited by H. T. Frank and W. L. Reed. Nashville: Abingdon, 1970, 80–107.

Childs, B. S. "The Canonical Shape of the Book of Jonah." In *Biblical and Near Eastern Studies.* Edited by G. A. Tuttle. Grand Rapids: Eerdmans, 1978, 122–28.

―――. "Jonah: A Study in Old Testament Hermeneutics." *SJT* 11 (1958): 53–61.

Christensen, D. L. "Narrative Poetics and the Interpretation of the Book of Jonah." In *Directions in Biblical Hebrew Poetry.* Edited by E. R. Follis. JSOTSup 40. Sheffield: Academic Press, 1987, 29–48.

―――. "The Song of Jonah: A Metrical Analysis." *JBL* 104 (1985): 217–31.

Clements, R. E. "The Purpose of the Book of Jonah." *VTS* 28 (1975): 16–28.

Craig, K. M., Jr. "Jonah and the Reading Process." *JSOT* 47 (1990): 103–14.

Crenshaw, J. L. "The Expression *mi yodea`* in the Hebrew Bible." *VT* 36 (1986): 274–88.

Cummings, C. "Jonah and the Ninevites." *TBT* 21 (1983): 369–75.

Day, J. "Problems in the Interpretation of the Book of Jonah." In *Quest of the Past: Studies on Is-raelite Religion, Literature and Prophetism.* Edited by A. S. Van der Woude. OTS 26. Leiden: E. J. Brill, 1990, 32–47.

Deeley, M. K. "The Shaping of Jonah." *TToday* 34 (1977): 305–10.

Dozeman, T. B. "Inner-Biblical Interpretation of Yahweh's Gracious and Compassionate Charac-ter." *JBL* 108 (1989): 207–23.

Dyck, E. "Jonah among the Prophets: A Study in Canonical Context." *JETS* 33 (1990): 63–73.

Ellul, J. *The Judgment of Jonah.* Grand Rapids: Eerdmans, 1971.

Eybers, J. H. "The Purpose of the Book of Jonah." *TE* 4 (1971): 211–22.

Halpern, B. and R. E. Friedman. "Composition and Paronomasia in the Book of Jonah." *HAR* 4 (1980): 79–92.

Hauser, A. J. "Jonah: In Pursuit of the Dove." *JBL* 104 (1985): 21–37.

Holbert, J. C. "Deliverance Belongs to Yahweh! Satire in the Book of Jonah." *JSOT* 21 (1981): 57–81.

Kidner, D. "The Distribution of Divine Names in Jonah." *TynBul* 21 (1970): 126–28.

Landes, G. M. "The Canonical Approach to Introducing the Old Testament: Prodigy and Prob-lems." *JSOT* 16 (1980): 32–39.

———. "The Kerygma of the Book of Jonah." *Int* 21 (1967): 3–31.

———. "The 'Three Days and Three Nights' Motif in Jonah 2:1." *JBL* 86 (1967): 446–50.

Lawrence, P. J. N. "Assyrian Nobles and the Book of Jonah." *TynBul* 37 (1986): 121–32.

Longacre, R. E. and S. J. J. Hwang. "A Textlinguistic Approach to the Biblical Hebrew Narrative of Jonah." In *Biblical Hebrew and Discourse Linguistics.* Edited by R. D. Bergen. Dallas: Summer Institute of Linguistics, 1994, 336–58.

Merrill, E. H. "The Sign of Jonah." *JETS* 23 (1980): 23–30.

Miles, J. A. "Laughing at the Bible: Jonah as Parody." *JQR* 65 (1975): 168–81.

Payne, D. P. "Jonah from the Perspective of Its Audience." *JSOT* 13 (1979): 3–12.

Peifer, C. "Sackcloth and Ashes: Jonah 3:6–8." *TBT* 21 (1983): 386–87.

Prout, E. "Beyond Jonah to God." *ResQ* 25 (1982): 139–42.

Roffey, J. W. "God's Truth, Jonah's Fish: Structure and Existence in the Book of Jonah." *AusBR* 36 (1988): 1–18.

Segert, S. "Syntax and Style in the Book of Jonah: Six Simple Approaches to Their Analysis." In *Prophecy: Essays Presented to Georg Fohrer.* Edited by J. A. Emerton. Berlin: Walter de Gruyter, 1980, 121–30.

Stek, J. H. "The Message of the Book of Jonah." *Calvin Theological Journal* 4 (1969): 23–50.

Stewart, R. A. "The Parable Form in the Old Testament and the Rabbinic Literature." *EvQ* 36 (1964): 133–47.

Walsh, J. T. "Jonah 2:3–10: A Rhetorical Critical Study." *Bib* 63 (1982): 219–29.

Walton, J. "The Object Lesson of Jonah 4:5–7 and the Purpose of the Book of Jonah." *Bulletin of Biblical Research* 2 (1992): 47–58.

West, M. "Irony in the Book of Jonah: Audience Identification with the Hero." *Perspectives* 11 (1984): 233–42.

Wilson, R. D. "The Authenticity of Jonah." *Princeton Theological Review* 16 (1918): 280–98.

Wilt, T. L. "Lexical Repetition in Jonah." *JTT* 35 (1992): 252–64.

Wiseman, D. J. "Jonah's Nineveh." *TynBul* 30 (1979): 29–51.

Wolff, H. W. "Jonah: The Reluctant Messenger." *Currents in Theology and Mission* 3 (1976): 8–19.

Zyl, A. H. van. "The Preaching of the Book of Jonah." *OTWSA* 14 (1971): 92–104.

Selected Subject Index

Abraham 71, 130
Achan 265
Achish of Gath 51
Adad-nirari III 25, 204
Ahab 24, 53, 57, 82, 209
altar, vision of 153–56
Amaziah 127, 135
Ammon 44, 52, 53, 56, 200
Ammon, oracle against 56–57
Ammon's sin 56
Amorites 65
Amos and Amaziah 134–42; day of the Lord in 32; end for Israel in 31–32; historical setting of 23–26; Israel's future restoration in 32–33; judgment upon sin in 32; justification for his ministry 71–75; language of 30; message of 31–35; rhetoric in the book of 30–32; sovereignty of the Lord in 31–32; the book 28–30; the man 26–28; years of ministry 23; wadi of the 123; visions of 126
Aram 44, 52; oracle against 46–50
Aramaic in the Bible 207
Argisti I 25
Armenia 86
Arpad 25
Ashdod 51, 52, 80
Ashimah 152
Ashkelon 51, 52, 152
Ashurnasirpal II 209
Asshur 208
Assur-dan III 205, 265
Assyria 26, 200
Assyrians 49
Augustine 278

Azariah 166

Baal Shamem 234
Babylon 200
Balaam 137
Barnabas 167
Beersheba 99, 100, 152
Ben-Hadad 48, 49
Beth Aven 99
Bethel 26, 61, 81, 87, 98, 99, 133; sanctuary, excavations of 157; worship at 82
Bozrah 55
burnt offerings 112

Cain 226
Calah 208, 257
Canaanite worship 91
Carmel 40
Carthage 278
communion with God 154
compassion 273, 275, 281
constellations and astrology 283
covenant 37, 39, 46, 51, 53, 59, 63, 65, 81, 93, 161, 170, 179
Cows of Bashan 84–86
Crete 161
Ctesias 257
Cush (Cushites) 160
Cyril of Jerusalem 218

Damascus 25, 44, 46, 47, 48, 49, 50, 53
Dan 26, 133, 152
David 51, 54
David's tent 166
day of deliverance for Jacob 198–99
day of restoration of Israel 199–202
day of the Lord 108–10, 151, 156, 195–203

Dead Sea   26, 57, 151
Debir   123
Deborah   23
Derketo   152
Diodorus Siculus   260
drought   90, 131, 150, 151
Dur-Sharrukin   208

earthquake   24, 37, 38, 91
Edom   43, 44, 45, 52, 53, 60, 167; completely ransacked 185–87; deceived by allies 186–87; destroyed forever 189–91; loots Judah's wealth 193–94; rejoices over Judah's destruction 192–93; oracle against 54–56; prophetic visions about 179; complete destruction 185–90; population decimated 188–89; sin of 55; wise men destroyed 188
Egypt   80, 108, 115
Egyptian bondage   242
Ekron   51, 52
Elijah   23, 82, 215, 274, 278
Elisha   23, 82, 204
Ephraim   100
Esarhaddon   228
Esau   54
evil   105
exodus from Egypt   65, 66, 93
Ezra and Nehemiah and Jewish nationalism   207

faith (as response to God)   196, 262
famine   90, 150, 151
Feast of Tabernacles   276
fellowship offerings   112
fire   199
fish, the   203, 215, 221, 239–42, 283; and the vine 277

Gath   51
Gath Hepher   204
Gaza   44, 50, 51, 52, 53
Gezer Calendar   128
Gilead   49, 56
Gilgal   26, 87, 99
God   and control over history 75; and his lordship over all creation 196; compassion of 127, 204; covenant love of 273; name of 277; what pleases 115; dwelling place 198; faithfulness 251; forgiveness 169; goodness 251; grace, Nineveh receives grace 274; graciousness 253; judgment 55; revelation to Jonah 226; sovereignty of 246, 249
golden calf   115
grain offerings   112

Hadadezer   24
Hamath   25
Hazael   24, 25, 48, 49
Hazor   38
Herodotus   266
Hezekiah   262
high places   133
Hiram king of Tyre   51, 53
Hittite treaties   135
holy war   81, 109
hope and restoration in the prophets   164
Hosea   23, 82, 134
Huldah   23
human rights   267
hymn fragment   93

idolatry   84, 115, 116, 253
Ir   260
Irhuleni   24
Isaac   133
Isaiah   23, 179
Ishtar   212
Israel   and the oracles against the nations 44; destruction of 159–61; downfall of 76–80; future restoration of 163–70; oracle against 60–70; false worship 113; rebellion at Kadesh 114; sin of 62; stubbornness, condemnation of 89–93; rejection of worship 110–15

Jacob   54; and Esau 190
James   167
Jehoahaz   25, 204
Jehoash   23, 25

Jehoram   25
Jehu   25
Jeroboam   23, 135, 139, 140, 148
Jeroboam I   37, 87
Jeroboam II   38, 80, 87, 204
Jerome   282
Jerome and Augustine, controversy between   278
Jerusalem   117; Council 167; profaned by the nations 197; fall of 181
Jesus and the people of Nineveh   261, 264
Jesus speaks of Jonah   218–19
Jezebel   53, 82
Joash   87
Jonah   and the prodigal son   250; and the storm at sea 229–32; obeys God 254; released by the fish 252; the historical 226; anger 279; displeasure at Nineveh's repentance 275–79; message to Nineveh 255; prayer of thanksgiving 241–53; shelter for 276, 277
Jonah, Book of   as allegory, the 212; as didactic fiction 213–16; as history 217–19; as Midrash 210–11; author of the 205; date of 206–9; genre and purpose of 210–19; miracles in the 214–16;
Joppa   226
Jordan   56
Jordan Valley   140
Joseph   119
Josephus   218
Jotham   166
Judah   52
Judah, oracle against   58–60
Judah's sin   59
Judith, Book of   269
justice   102, 106, 112, 113, 116, 213

Kaiwan   115
Karnaim   123
Kerioth   58
Khirbet el-Muqanna   52
King's Highway   56
Kir   50

leavened bread   88
lion   39, 72
locust swarm   128
locusts   91
locusts, vision of   127–29
Lord's authority over the nations   45
lots, casting of   232

Manasseh 100
marriages, mixed   207
Mediterranean coast   51
Mediterranean Sea   151
Menahem   262
Mesha   27, 37, 57
messengers of God (see also prophet)   47
Messiah and the Davidic Covenant   167
Micah   23
Micaiah   23
Minor Prophets   204
Moab   44, 52, 53, 56, 57–58
monotheism   283
Moses   93, 113, 242, 269, 274
Mount Esau   200, 202
Mount Hermon   86
Mount Sinai   71, 93
music and worship   112

Nabonidus   187
Nahum   180, 269
name of the Lord   122
Nathan   23
Nazirites   66
Nebat   87
Nebuchadnezzar   166, 191, 192, 194
Negev   200, 202
New Moon observance   145
Nile   147, 148
Nimrod   224
Nineveh   204; size of 257; conversion of 214

offerings   112, 114
Omri   57, 165; dynasty of 82
oracles against the nations   43–69
Orion   101
orphans   145

parable of the good Samaritan, the   210
Paul   167
peace offerings   88

Pekah   165
Persians   266
Peter   167
Pharaoh   242
Philadelphia   56
Philistia   44, 51, 52, 200; oracle against
      50–53
Phoenicia   44, 53–54, 228
plague   91
Pleiades   101
plumb line   131
polytheism   283, and the Assyrians 263
poor, the   121, 145, 146
prayers/psalms in the OT   245
prophetic intercession   127–30
prophets   66; classical 23
Pul (Tiglath-Pileser)   262

Queen of the South   218
Qumran fragment of Amos   48

Rabbah   56
Rehoboam   37
Rehoboth   257
Remman   86
Remnant   52
Resen   260
revelation of God   36, 129
Rezin   49
righteousness   100, 106, 112, 113, 116

Sabbath   145
sacrifices   88, 111, 114, 251
Samaria   81, 117, 121, 200; fall of 205;
      violence and oppression in 77–
      79
Samson   66
Samuel   23, 66
Sarah   71
Sardur III   25
Sargon II   209
Sea of Reeds   248
seeking the Lord   98, 106
Sennacherib   208, 224, 225
Shalmaneser   24, 25
Shalmaneser V   205
Shema, the   84
Sheol   245
shepherds   36

sin   87
sirocco wind, the   279
slavery   146
social injustice   144
Sodom and Gomorrah   91, 216, 277
solar eclipse   148, 149
Solomon   53
songs in the temple   143
Spain   228
storm, stilling of the   237–40
Tarshish   226
Tartessos   226
Tekoa   36, 140
Tell el-Kheleifeh   187
Teman   55
Ten Commandments   59
thank offering   88
theophany   39, 92, 158
Tiglath-Pileser III   204, 205, 225, 262
tithes   88
Transjordan   50
truth   102
Tyre   43, 44, 45, 52, 53, 54, 60
Tyrians   265

underworld in the ANE, journey to the
      241–42
United Kingdom   52
United States   52
Unleavened Bread or Passover   88, 111
Urartu   26
Uzziah   23, 24, 36, 38, 166

violence   118, 121

warfare   54
Weeks or Harvest   111
widows   145
wilderness   242
wilderness wanderings   66
wisdom and folly, worldly   188
word of God, famine of   150–52
word of the Lord   36
worship is condemned, Israel's   87–88
worship, apostate   39

Zarephath   202
Zion   73, 117, 197, 198

Person Index

Aalders, G. C.   212, 259

Ackerman, J. S.   221

Albright, W. F.   37

Alexander, T. D.   205, 207, 208, 209, 210, 215, 216, 217, 218, 222, 224, 227, 234, 240, 241, 247, 249

Allen, L. C.   172, 195, 206, 207, 208, 209, 213, 216, 219, 222, 228, 230, 231, 234, 235, 237,245, 248, 257, 258, 260, 261, 269, 273, 275, 277, 281, 283

Almbladh, K.   209, 233, 248, 249, 275

Alter, R.   44

Andersen, F. I. and Freedman, D. N.   26, 28, 29, 33, 43, 44, 55, 57, 59, 61, 63, 64, 66, 68, 71, 78, 79, 80, 82, 84, 93, 96, 98, 100, 101, 102, 105, 107, 109, 111, 113, 114, 115, 119, 122, 129, 130, 132, 133, 135, 136, 137, 139, 141, 143, 144, 146, 151, 152, 153, 154, 155, 157, 158, 161, 163, 169, 170

Armerding, C. E.   187, 195, 197

Baker, D. W.   195, 197, 200

Baldwin, J.   230, 231, 233, 255, 260

Banks, W. L.   261

Barre', M. L.   48

Barstad, H.   84, 119

Bartlett, J. R.   172, 174, 175, 187, 195

Bartley, James   242

Barton, J.   43, 45

Baumann, A.   143

Beit-Arieh, I.   200

Bergen, R. D.   220

Bewer, J. A.   200, 213, 214, 221, 231, 234, 258, 283

Blomberg, C.   213

Bowers, R. H.   218

Bowling, A.   53

Braun, M.   166

Breneman, M.   170

Brenner, A.   221

Brichto, H. C.   219, 222, 227, 229, 233, 277

Bright, J.   23, 37

Budde, K.   210

Burrows, M.   213

Buth, R.   182

Caird, G. B.   259

Calvin, John   272

Cate, R. L.   24, 26

Childs, B.   210

Chisholm, R. B., Jr.   44

Christensen, D. L.   221, 222

Clark, D. J.   191, 195, 197, 199

Clements, R. E.   207

Clendenen, E. R.   230

Clifford, R. J.   109

Clines, D. A.   221

Coggins, R. J.   174, 182, 189, 191, 192, 194, 197, 199, 200, 202

Cohen, H. R.   103

Cohen, S.   174

Cooper, A.   123, 276

Cooper, L. E., Sr.   179

Coote, R.   211

Craig, K. M., Jr.   219, 221
Craigie, P. C.   27
Crenshaw, J.   268
Cresson, B. C.   172, 181, 184, 194, 197, 199

Davies, P. R.   221
Davis, E. B.   240
De Waard, J.   96
De Waard, J. and W. A. Smalley   39
Dick, M. B.   181, 187, 199
Dicou, B.   174, 188, 190, 199, 200
Dockery, D. S.   230
Driver, S. R.   88
Dumbrell, W.   45

Edwards, D. R.   54
Eichrodt, W.   46
Eissfeldt, O.   207, 221
Ellison, H. L.   206, 225, 228, 231, 235, 236, 241, 258, 261, 267
Ellul, J.   260, 262, 268, 283
Emmerson, G. I.   213

Fairbairn, P.   261, 262, 263
Fanwar, W. M.   183
Finley, T. J.   35, 45, 51, 79, 80, 88, 91, 92, 94, 98, 101, 105, 113, 114, 115, 119, 128, 129, 131, 135, 139, 143, 147, 151, 155, 158, 165, 172, 180, 181, 186, 187, 188, 189, 196, 199, 202
Freedman, D. N.   119
Fretheim, T.   217, 225, 227, 246, 247, 248, 257, 259, 265, 269, 274, 279, 283
Friedman, R. E.   259
Gaebelein, F.   187, 225, 250, 253, 257, 261, 281, 283
Garrett, D. A.   97
Gitay, Y.   69, 71, 72, 73, 75, 76
Glaze, Jr., A. J.   223, 235, 238, 241, 243, 279
Glueck, N.   187
Goldingay, J.   216
Good, E. M.   259
Grayson, A. K.   205

Greidanus, S.   215

Halpern, B.   221, 262
Hammershaimb, E.   137
Harris, R. J.   131
Harrison, R. K.   204, 212, 221
Hartley, J. E.   101
Hasel, G.   28, 32, 163
Hass, Jr., J. W.   242
Hauan, M. J.   108
Hayes, J. H.   23, 24, 26, 37, 38, 43, 45, 47, 49, 50, 52, 54, 55, 59, 62, 63, 65, 70, 72, 74, 80, 86, 88, 90, 96, 98, 109, 115, 121, 135, 136, 143, 148, 160, 162, 163, 166
Herodotus   269
Hillers, D. R.   130
Hillis, D. W.   215
Hoffman, Y.   109
Holladay, W.   118, 129
Honeycutt, R.   54
Howie, C. G.   52
Hubbard, D. A.   33, 48, 51, 57, 63, 65, 67, 76, 127, 134, 150, 151, 152, 154, 155, 156, 158, 160, 161, 162, 163, 166, 169
Huey, F. B.   169
Hwang, S. J. J.   220

Isbell, C.   115

Jackson, J. J.   105
Jacobs, P.   84

Kaiser, Jr., W. C.   166, 167, 168
Katzenstein, H. J.   54
Keil and Delitzsch   204, 219, 242, 243, 247, 248, 251, 261, 280, 287
Kelley, J. N. D.   278
Kendall, R. T.   203, 241
Kennedy, J. H.   203, 224, 244, 258, 267, 265, 280, 283
Kidner, F. D.   277
King, D. M.   167
King, P.   119, 140
Kirk, T.   264, 265, 278, 280

Klein, G. L.   182
Knierim, R. P.   48
Knight, G. A. F.   211
Koch, K.   84

Landes, G. M.   206, 207, 213, 221, 222, 241, 242, 245
Lawrence, P. J. N.   205
Leeuwen, C. van   109
Levenson, J.   221
Licht, J.   217
Lillie, J.   172, 183, 193
Limburg, J.   30, 45, 47, 172, 175, 207, 209, 210, 214, 222, 228
Lindblom, J.   232
Lohfink, N.   226
Long, V. P.   210
Longacre, R. E.   220
Longman III, T.   210
Luckenbill, D. D.   204
Lust, J.   99, 249
Magonet, J.   206, 221, 225, 227, 243, 244, 248
Mathews, K. A.   232
Mays, J. L.   32, 35, 38, 43, 45, 47, 49, 54, 55, 58, 61, 65, 69, 102, 103, 104, 109, 115, 116, 121, 122, 127, 137, 143, 154, 162, 163, 169
McCarter, P. K.   187
McComiskey, T. E.   24, 63, 166, 167, 230, 255
McConville, J.   33
McGarvey, J. W.   218
McGee, J. V.   246
Merrill, E. H.   25, 71, 169, 246
Millard, A. R.   216
Miller, J. M.   23, 26, 37
Miller, Jr., P. D.   196
Mitchell, H. G.   214, 233
Mowvley, H.   64, 100
Muilenburg, J.   174
Muraoka, T.   240
Myers, J. M.   174

Neil, W.   212
Niehaus, J.   24, 54, 55, 58, 64, 80, 92,

105, 115, 119, 135, 139, 140, 145, 147, 148, 149, 151

Oesterly, W. O. E.   212
Ogden, G. S.   259
Overduin, J.   264, 264

Parunak, H.   130
Paul, S.   27, 29, 35, 38, 39, 44, 48, 49, 53, 56, 59, 62, 63, 64, 65, 67, 68, 70, 72, 73, 74, 75, 76, 78, 79, 80, 83, 84, 85, 86, 90, 92, 93, 99, 105, 109, 111, 112, 117, 118, 121, 122, 127, 129, 138, 151, 154, 155, 156, 158, 162, 163, 166, 169, 170
Petersen, D. L.   138
Pitard, W. T.   25, 49
Polhill, J. B.   167
Polley, M.   37, 39
Price and Nida   219, 233, 242, 244, 247, 251, 255, 267

Richard, E.   168
Richardson, H.   129, 130, 131, 132
Rimmer, H.   239, 240
Robinson, B. P.   278
Robinson, R.   179, 188
Rosenbaum, S. N.   26
Roux, G.   205

Sandmel, S.   221
Sasson J.   206, 207, 209, 210, 223, 224, 228, 229, 232, 233, 251, 256, 257, 267, 268, 281
Schoville, K. N.   43
Seybold, K.   197
Sloan, R. S.   230
Smith, B. K.   190
Smith, G.   28, 29, 35, 36, 65, 77, 80, 84, 92, 93, 94, 97, 100, 105, 107, 111, 113, 114, 119, 121, 122, 123, 130, 135, 136, 139, 143, 144, 147, 152, 154, 156, 158, 160, 163
Smith, J. M. P.   214
Smith, R.   47, 109, 121, 122

Soggin, J. A.   206
Stuart, D.   24, 33, 35, 38, 45, 49, 54,
         58, 70, 72, 77, 81, 96, 98, 102,
         105, 109, 114, 121, 129, 130,
         135, 137, 139, 140, 147, 154,
         160, 162, 163, 180, 192, 196,
         199, 202, 206, 209, 211, 212,
         214, 222, 230, 232, 238, 240,
         241, 244, 255, 257, 258, 260,
         261, 265, 266, 269, 272, 273,
         275, 280, 281, 283

Thiele, E. R.   23, 37
Thompson, J.   99, 173, 192
Trible, P.   210, 211, 212, 214, 217,
         218, 220, 221, 265, 267
Tromp, N. J.   96, 98
Tucker, G.   135

van Groningen, G.   167

Waard, J. de and W. A. Smalley   135
Walsh, J. T.   251, 252
Waltke, B. and O'Connor, M.   114,
         260
Walton, J.   208, 209, 215, 230, 233,
         245, 249, 257, 261, 263, 276,
         277
Watts, J. D. W.   27, 29, 127, 163, 173,
         197, 199
Weiser, A.   98

Weiss, M.   47
Wendland, E. R.   67, 84, 90, 96, 164
Wenham, G. J.   88
Williams, A. J.   84, 86
Williamson, H. G. M.   132
Wilson, A. J.   242, 254
Wilson, M. R.   141
Wiseman, D. J.   205, 208, 209, 216,
         257, 258, 266, 283
Wittenberg, G.   116, 118, 119
Wolff, H. W.   25, 28, 30, 32, 35, 45,
         48, 52, 54, 55, 58, 69, 74, 80,
         83, 85, 91, 92, 96, 97, 98, 102,
         103, 104, 109, 115, 118, 121,
         122, 127, 132, 135, 137, 138,
         140, 143, 144, 145, 148, 151,
         154, 162, 163, 172, 176, 179,
         180, 181, 190, 196, 197, 198,
         199, 200, 208, 209, 211, 213,
         221, 230, 243, 248, 249, 250,
         251, 260, 277, 279, 281, 283
Wolters, A.   142
Wright, C. H. H.   212
Wright, T. J.   27, 140

Yadin, Y.   24, 38
Yamauchi, E.   210
Young, E. J.   221

Zevit, Z.   138, 139

Scripture Index

Genesis
1–2 101
1:2. 131
1:3. 199
1:26–27 51
2:21. 230
3 255
3:15. 63
3:19 138
3:23 187
4:16. 226
6:7 161
6:11,13 216
7:4,23 161
8:1 249
8:21 111
8:22 143
9:2. 240
9:22 193
10:11. 226
10:11–12 . . . . 208, 257
12:1–3 161
12:1,4 229
12:3 . . . . 71, 207
12:8 87
12:15 57
14:22 152
15:12 230
18:5. 106
18:12. 85
18:22–23. 129
19 91
19:15 224
19:23–28 130
19:24 49
19:25. 216
19:30–38 . . . . 56, 57
20:7. 130
21:23. 152
22:2,3 227
22:4 244
22:16. 147
23:6 257
24:3,7 234
25:22–23. 54
26:23–25. 99

27:19 226
28:11–17 82
28:14 71
28:19 87
30:28 117
31:39 79
35:1–7 82
37:34 263
39:14 233
41:19 85
45:7 249
49:24 147
49:25 131
50:20 249
Exodus
1:15 233
3:18 242
12:12 108
15:7 199
19–24 66
19:3–6 70
19:10–19 92
19:17 93
20:8 250
21:7–11 63
21:22 64
21:30 104
22:10–13 79
22:11 152
22:26–27 64
23:6 63
23:8 104
23:14–17 111
24. 114
25:22 72
27:3 119
29:18 111
30:6,36 72
32 . . . . .114, 130
32:12 . . . . .161, 269
34:6 211
34:6–7 . . . . .129, 273
34:22–25 111
Leviticus
1:3–4 111
1:9 . . . . .111, 112

6:2,4 78
6:8–13 88
7:11–13 88
7:18 112
8–10 114
17:11 248
18:7–8 63
18:25 229
18:28 252
19:7 112
19:20–22 63
20:17–21 63
21:7 247
22:18–19 111
22:32 63
23:34 111
23:42–43 165
23:43 165
26:25 91
26:31 111
Numbers
4:14 119
5:21 152
7–9 114
10:33 244
11:1 130
11:1–3 49
11:15 274
11:22 240
13–14 114
13:28,31–33 65
14:18 273
15:2 114
15:40 250
16:35 130
20:12 . . . . 255, 261
22:1–6 137
22:20 224
23:19 269
31:10 49
Deuteronomy
2 160
2:7 115
4:24 92
4:36 92
6:4–5 . . . . 82, 84
6:13 152

7:6 161
7:25–26 49
8:3 150
9:3 130
10:11 224
10:14–26 145
11:24 94
12 82
12:3 49
12:5–11 64
12:23 248
12:31 111
14:2 161
14:28–29 88
15:7–11 145
15:9 225
16:19 104
16:22 111
17:6 77
21:10 102
22:19 64
24:12–13 64
24:15 225
24:17 64
24:19–21 145
25:4 48
28:22 91
28:29 . . . . 78, 148
28:30–44 103
28:38 128
28:49–59 91
28:52 121
28:62 98
29:22–24 92
31:17–18 151
32:9 131
32:10 194
32:13 94
32:14 84
32:21–22 49
32:22 131
32:35 193
33:29 94

Joshua
1:9 106
2:10 66
4:20–24 87
7:6–13 129
7:10 224
7:14–18 232
7:21 265
9:17 244
9:20 152
10:2 259
14:12 249
18:10 232

19:13 204
19:28 202
23:7 152

Judges
1:8 49
1:22 106
2:1 66
3:9,15 202
4:21 230
5:4 141
6:37 107
8:27 107
9:16 197
13:5,7 66
14:5 39
16:17 66
19:26 85

Ruth
2:5 154
3:13 152
4:1–12 102
4:7 62
4:17–22 57

1 Samuel
1:11 66
2:9 105
2:10 189
2:31 150
4:6 235
5:9,11 78
6:17 107
8:8 66
10:20–22 232
12:3 . . . . 78, 104
14:37 151
14:45 152
15:10 223
15:29 147
16:1–13 136
16:14–23 119
18:11 229
18:25 229
20:33 229
22:3–4 57
26:12 230
26:19 111
27:1–7 51
28:10 152
30:1 242

2 Samuel
1:12 97
1:19 . . . . 94, 186
5:11 51
7:6 66
7:8 140
7:10 147

8:13–14 54
14:1–24 37
14:11 250
14:13–14 229
15:31 188
16:1 143
18:13 192
18:33 147
23:1 119
23:26 37
24 242
24:15–17 154

1 Kings
1:19–30 152
1:50 82
2:23 92
2:28 82
4:33 240
5:12 53
6:11 223
7:50 119
8:37 91
9:13 53
10:16 86
10:27 140
11:15–16 . . . . 54, 189
11:29–39 136
11:37 140
12–13 . . . . 39, 64
12:16–17 37
12:26–30a 87
12:26–33 99
12:28 82
13:2,4,32 225
13:11–25 141
13:26 255
15:18,20 49
16:1 223
16:18 78
16:31 53
17–19 204
17:1 226
17:2 215
17:9 224
17:9–10 227
18:1–2 227
18:15 226
19:2 140
19:3–18 272
19:4 . . . . 216, 274
19:9–13 224
19:15–17 136
21:1 . . . . 83, 209
21:17,28 223
21:18 83
21:27 261

22:47 189
2 Kings
1:1 57
1:15. 227
2:17 242
3:4 . . . . 27, 37
3:5. 57
3:9,26 189
4:8. 138
6:24 49
8:7–15. 136
8:12 . . . . 49, 56
8:14–15. 49
8:20–22. 189
8:25–29. 25
9:1–28 136
9:21–10:14 25
10:9 136
10:28. 82
13:1–3. 204
13:2. 204
13:4,23 204
13:4–5. 25
13:5. 204
13:14–19 204
13:25 25
14:1–14. 25
14:7 183
14:21–25 25
14:24 204
14:25 123, 204, 205, 206, 211, 224
14:26–27 204
14:28 80
15–16 205
15:8–10 134
15:10 97
15:16 56
16:9 50
17:16 82
17:23 59
17:29–30 152
18:26–28 261
23:15–17 83
23:17 225
24:11–16 120
25:1–8 192
25:11–12 120
1 Chronicles
21:10–11. 227
21:26. 130
2 Chronicles
5:11–13 119
7:1. 130
7:13–14 128
11:2. 223

11:5–12 37
19:9–10 92
20:3 227
21:8–10 55
21:16–17 55
24:18 152
26:1–15 25
30:9 273
33:23 152
Ezra
1:1–11 33
1:2 234
5:12 234
8:21 227
9:3 149
Nehemiah
1:1 36
1:4,5. 234
8:14–17 165
9:17 273
9:27 202
13:15–22 145
13:18 92
Esther
8:3 231
9:24 231
Job
1:16 130
2:11 188
9:8 94
11:22 94
13:3 102
16:9 55
16:15 263
18:4 55
31:3 193
32:12 102
33:14–15 47
33:18 250
36:18 104
36:29 165
37:4 39
38. 225
38:10 249
38:41 267
42:6 268
Psalms
2:6 197
7:2 55
8:8 240
9:13 249
13:1 151
15:5 104
16:10 250
18:4 248
18:6 . . . . 244, 245

18:7 158
18:30 102
22:24 151
24:1–2 229
24:4 152
28:1 250
30:3 . . . . 245, 248
30:4 250
31:6 251
31:17 105
31:22 247
32:1 104
36:6 257
37:13,17,33 250
37:19 105
45:12 85
46:4 113
46:6 158
47:4 147
48:2 199
49:1 145
49:14 . . . . 245, 246
51:18 237
55:15 246
55:24 250
59:17 251
62:4 166
68:15–16 84
69:1 248
72:6 128
72:10 226
72:12–13 145
74:2 198
74:7 198
74:13–14 241
74:22–23 250
75:3 158
75:8 197
76:11 238
77:15 199
78:68 198
78:70–71 140
81:4–5 199
86:15 273
88:3 245
88:5,7. 252
89:35 . . . . 85, 147
91:13 94
94:11 94
102:2 151
103:4 250
103:8 273
104:21 39
104:26 241
105:16 225
105:18 248

111:4 273
112:4 273
115:3 237
116:8 273
116:17–18 238
118:5 244
120:1 244
122:7 78
125:1 199
133:3 199
135:6 237
137:5 147
137:7 55
139 155
139:5 228
139:7–12 156
139:8 245
143:7 252
144:2 251
145:8 273

Proverbs
1:12 246
6:16–19 47
7:23 248
8:32 70
10:5,19 104
14:35 104
15:3 229
16:18 183
16:33 232
17:23 . . . . 63, 104
19:8 248
21:1 237
23:2 248
27:20 246
30:1 36
30:15–16 47

Ecclesiastes
1:1 36
7:7 104
11:2 47

Isaiah
1:1 . . . . 35, 37
1:8 276
1:14 111
1:23 104
2:1 37
2:2–4 207
3:11 197
4:5 202
4:6 . . . . 165, 276
5:7,18–24 59
5:14 246
5:23 104
6:4 155
7:8 189

7:18 148
8:16–17 151
8:18 197
9:6–7 167
9:7–20 116
10:12 198
10:17 199
11:3 102
11:6–9 168
11:10 207
11:16 66
13:6 196
14:12–15 184
14:15,19 250
15:1 186
16:1 183
16:5 167
18:7 202
19:14 252
22:6 50
22:12 149
22:17 229
22:19 166
24:1–7 147
24:23 202
25:6–8 207
25:10 86
28:15 245
28:15–17 59
29:6 130
29:10 137
29:14 188
29:21 102
29:30 223
31:4 225
32:9–11 117
33:9 84
34:5 55
34:13 86
37:32 199
38:4 223
38:10 249
38:17 250
38:18 . . . . . 156, 245, 250
39:6 150
40:18–20 115
40:27 228
41:21–24 115
42:6 161
42:11 183
44:12–20 115
49:6 260
51:17,22 197
52:15 207
54:8 151
55:6 151

55:11 237
56:7 207
58:14 147
59:6 267
59:10 148
59:19 237
63:3 94
66:5 118
66:15–16 130

Jeremiah
1:1 36
1:11–12 . . . . 126, 143
1:1–3 35
2:2–3 115
2:2–8 115
2:6 66
2:13 137
2:37 111
3:18 199
4:9 148
4:27–28 147
6:11 137
6:12 142
6:26 149
7:22 66
7:32 150
8:9 188
8:14 105
9:23–24 . . . . 123, 188
10:1–16 115
10:9 22
10:10 137
11:4 66
11:14 134
11:20 94
11:21–23 141
12:16 152
13:4,6 224
13:16 148
15:8–9 148
15:11 105
15:19 . . . . 48, 226
17:5–8 123
17:17–18 118
18:1–10 . . . . 98, 129
18:7,8,11 216
18:7–8 257
18:7–11 269
18:18 151
20:1–6 141
20:16 92
21:12 78
22:8 256
22:18 109
22:26–28 229
23:5 167

23:7 66
23:9–40. 36
23:18,22 75
23:30–32. 59
25:9,18 198
25:17. 197
25:30 39
25:37. 105
26:2–3. 269
26:3 229
26:7–11. 136
26:8. 260
26:20–23. 138
28:16 161
31:19. 268
31:31 150
31:34. 147
33:9. 147
34:5 109
37:11–38:4 136
44:4 111
44:26 147
47:5. 186
48:9. 105
48:26 252
48:28 212
48:37 149
49:7 . . . . 55, 188
49:12 189
49:14 181
49:14–16. 181
49:20. 189
49:22. 189
49:26. 105
49:29. 225
50:19. 84
50:30. 105
51:2. 118
51:6,56 197
51:34,44 212
51:39. 230

Lamentations
1:15 . . . . 94, 227
2:9 151
2:10. 105
2:21. 97
3:37–39. 237
3:54. 247
5:18. 198
5:21. 48

Ezekiel
1:3. 36
5:6. 59
6:9. 250
7:23. 267
7:26 151

13. 59
15:5 102
17. 212
17:19 152
18:18 78
20:10 66
20:13,16,24 111
20:46 141
21:2 141
23:39 92
26–28. 53
26:16 265
26:20 250
30:3 196
31:4 131
31:14–16 250
32:18 250
34:23–24 167
35:5–6 55
36:2 94
37:16,19 100
37:16–28 199
38:18 148
38:21 227
39:6 130
39:18 84
39:23 151

Daniel
2:44 195
4:30 256
6:4 231
8:18 230
9:15 66
10:9 230

Hosea
1:1 36
1:2–9 164
1:5 148
2:2–13 164
2:15 66
4:1–13 59
4:6 . . . . .111, 186
4:15 . . . . 82, 99
5:8 99
6:2 47
6:6 115
6:11 116
7:11 . . . . .77, 212
8:5–6 84
8:6 115
8:11 65
9:3 77
10:1–2 65
10:5 99
10:8 94
11:1 115

11:11 212
12:1 267
13:16 56
14:4–7 168

Joel
1:1 36
1:4 . . . . 91, 128
1:8,13 149
1:15 196
2:1 197
2:1,10 147
2:5 199
2:10 148
2:13 273
2:13–14 . . . . 211, 216
2:14 268
2:32 198
3 196
3:14 196
3:16 39
3:17 197
3:19 55
4:18 148

Amos
1–6 128
1:1 26
1:1–2 30
1:2 . . . . 39, 72, 73
1:3,6,9 30
1:3–2:3 31
1:3–2:15 160
1:3–2:16 . . 30, 44, 45, 48, 69,
75
1:3–6:14 . . . . . 29, 43, 126
1:4 199
1:5 . . . . 50, 57, 86
1:6,9 . . . . 44, 86, 194
1:8 77
1:9 86
1:9–10 51
1:11–12 51
1:13–19 126
2:2,5 67
2:3 57
2:4–5 31
2:6 31
2:6–7 144
2:6–8 . . . . 26, 134
2:6–16 . . . . 31, 75
2:7 31
2:9–12 160
2:10 . . . . 43, 61, 66
2:12 151
2:13 30
2:13–15 160
2:13–16 31

2:16 .... 78, 144, 188
3:1 .... 97, 144
3:1–2 160
3:1–15 .... 30, 69, 96
3:2................. 81
3:2,12 164
3:3–6 72
3:3–8 .... 30, 72, 75
3:4–5,8 39
3:6 105
3:8................. 72
3:10........ 31, 81, 267
3:11 104
3:11–12......... 31, 97
3:12............... 81
3:13–15 120
3:14 ..... 26, 71, 81, 144
3:15 .... 31, 143
4:1 .... 26, 30, 31, 97, 144
4:1–13 ....30, 96
4:2 .... 30, 147, 150
4:2–3............. 97
4:4–5 .... 26, 31
4:6–8........... 150
4:6–11 ..89, 93, 94, 96, 164
4:6–12 30
4:6–13 132
4:7–8 101
4:9 128
4:10–19........... 134
4:12 .... 93, 104, 164
4:13 .. 30, 31, 96, 101, 106,
128, 157
4:18 57
5:1 .... 97, 103, 144
5:1–3............. 97
5:1–17 96
5:1–6:14 30
5:2................. 31
5:3–6 164
5:4............... 106
5:4,6 87
5:4–5 .... 26, 30
5:4–6 164
5:4–7.............. 31
5:6 .... 91, 106
5:7 .... 31, 96, 259
5:8–9 .. 30, 31, 93, 96, 101,
157
5:10 31
5:10–12............ 144
5:10–13....... 102, 134
5:11,16 104
5:11–13............. 26
5:12 63
5:14.......... 156, 157

5:14–15 . 96, 106, 107, 164
5:18 144
5:18–20 30, 31, 32, 69, 108,
192, 195
5:18–27 96
5:21–23 31
5:22–24 26
5:27 .... 86, 96
6:1–14 96
6:1–2 103
6:12 ....31, 96, 99
6:1–7 30
6:4 79
6:4–6 31
6:7 ....86, 104
6:7,14 31
6:8 ....30, 147
6:14 96
7:1,4,7 154
7:1–8:3 30
7:1–9 ....29, 30, 37
7:1–9:15 .... 43, 126
7:2,5............. 182
7:3 .... 143, 268
7:3,6 ....164, 269
7:7–9 136
7:8 31
7:9 ....94, 157
7:9,11........... 211
7:10 61
7:10–17.. 29, 30, 36, 134,
144, 159
7:12–13 ...... 28, 67, 151
7:14 ....27, 28
7:15 ...... 28, 31, 36
7:17 ....30, 104, 157
8:1–3. . 30, 37, 43, 61, 147
8:2 .... 31, 135
8:3,9,13 188
8:4–9:15 30
8:7 30
8:7–9 24
8:14 65
9:1–4 ......30, 31, 37, 43
9:2 245
9:3 186
9:4 156
9:5–6 ......30, 31, 93, 101
9:7 .... 50, 66
9:7–10 ......30, 159, 160
9:8 ....31, 32
9:8–9 120
9:8–10 164
9:11 276
9:11–15 .... 30, 31, 32
9:12 180

9:13 .... 141, 150
9:14 103
9:14–15 33
Jonah
1:1 .... 36, 215
1:1–2 .... 215, 257
1:1–3 219
1:2 .... 208, 270, 282
1:3 .... 249, 259
1:4–16 219
1:5 220
1:6 271
1:12 213
1:17 282
2:1–11 ...... 213, 219
2:2 221
2:3 221
2:4,7,9 221
2:5–8 222
2:7 274
2:9 271
2:10 241
3:1–2 215
3:1–4 219
3:2 208
3:3 208
3:5 220
3:5–10 219
3:6 208
3:7–8 208
3:9 220
3:10 129
4:1 282
4:1–11 219
4:2 .... 211, 268
4:6 239
4:7 239
4:10–11 213
4:11 208
Micah
1:1 .... 35, 36, 37
1:3–16 .... 116, 164
1:3–4 .... 94, 158
2:3 105
2:6,11 141
3:4 151
3:6 148
3:6–7 151
3:8–12 164
3:11 138
4:1–3 207
4:7 202
5:5 47
5:9 148
6:15 103
6:4 66

6:8. . . . . 73, 115
7:11 166
7:14 84
7:17 237
Nahum
1:1 179
1:3 273
1:4 84
1:5 158
2:7 212
Habakkuk
2:15–16 197
Zephaniah
1:1 36
1:2–3 161
1:7,14 196
1:11 . . . . 105, 186
1:13. 103
1:14–18. 69
2:11 237
3:11. 197
Haggai
1:1 36
2:4 106
2:17. 91
Zechariah
1:1 36
2:8 194
5:1–4 126
7:8. 223
9:9–10 165
11:4–17. 212
12:10. 149
14:5 . . . . 24, 38
14:13 78
Malachi
1:3–5 188

1:10 112
1:14 237
3:1 109
3:5 78
3:16 234
Matthew
4:4 150
8:12 149
11:25 237
12:40 . . . . . . .218, 242, 246
12:41 264
16:4 246
24:29–30 147
26:38 281
Mark
14:33 281
14:36 197
Luke
8:22–25 237
10:30–37 192
11:29–30 246
11:30–32 264
11:31 218
11:32 . . . . 218, 261
John
1:18 250
11:6,14 241
12:49–52 137
Acts
2:24 250
3:15 250
4:18–20 141
10:40 250
13:30 250
15:6–21 167
15:7–12 167
15:12–21 33

15:13–18 168
15:14 167
27:18–19 230
28:17–21 139
Romans
5:8 250
6:23 32
8:38–39 156
1 Corinthians
1:18–31 188
1:27 250
3:19 188
2 Corinthians
5:10 32
7:6 250
Galatians
6:16 170
Ephesians
1:5,9 237
2:4 250
4:26 275
5:19–20 245
Philippians
2:27 250
1 Thessalonians
5:6 230
Hebrews
2:8 284
12:22 199
James
1:17 269
3:13 188
Revelation
1:7 147
6:15–17 156
14:10 197
22:1–5 113